FEDERALISM
HEALTH
& POLICY

Also of interest from the Urban Institute Press:

Edited by John Holahan, Alan Weil, & Joshua M. Wiener

FEDERALISM
& HEALTH
POLICY

THE URBAN INSTITUTE PRESS
Washington, D.C.

THE URBAN INSTITUTE PRESS
2100 M Street, N.W.
Washington, D.C. 20037

Library of Congress Cataloging in Publication Data

Federalism and health policy / edited by John Holahan, Alan Weil, and Joshua M. Wiener.
     p. ; cm.
Includes bibliographical references and index.
  ISBN 0-87766-716-0 (alk. paper)
  1. Medicaid. 2. Poor—Medical care—United States—States. 3. Medical policy—United States.
  [DNLM: 1. Health Policy—United States. 2. Insurance, Health—economics—United States. 3. Medicaid—economics. WA 540 AA1 F293 2003] I. Holahan, John. II. Weil, Alan. III. Wiener, Joshua M.
  RA412.4.F43 2003
  362.1'086'9420973—dc21

                        2003011760

Printed in the United States of America

THE URBAN INSTITUTE is a nonprofit policy research and educational organization established in Washington, D.C., in 1968. Its staff investigates the social, economic, and governance problems confronting the nation and evaluates the public and private means to alleviate them. The Institute disseminates its research findings through publications, its web site, the media, seminars, and forums.

Through work that ranges from broad conceptual studies to administrative and technical assistance, Institute researchers contribute to the stock of knowledge available to guide decisionmaking in the public interest.

Conclusions or opinions expressed in Institute publications are those of the authors and do not necessarily reflect the views of officers or trustees of the Institute, advisory groups, or any organizations that provide financial support to the Institute.

Contents

Foreword

Today, Medicaid and the State Children's Health Insurance Program (SCHIP) finance health care for over 40 million of the nation's poorest and sickest residents—low-income pregnant women, children, and parents; those suffering from AIDS and other chronic and disabling conditions; and individuals in need of long-term care. Many of the proposals that seek to extend health insurance coverage for the uninsured in the future call for expanding these programs.

Critical though they are, Medicaid and SCHIP are currently under considerable stress and constitute a shaky base upon which to build a future system. States, which are required to pay a substantial portion of these programs' costs, face serious budget difficulties related to a weak economy, past tax cuts, and intense spending pressures. Rising health care costs and enrollment increases related to reductions in work-place coverage have made Medicaid and SCHIP major contributors to the spending pressures states face. This pressure will not lessen appreciably in the future because spending on these programs is projected to grow faster than state revenues, even after the economy rebounds.

This book provides a wide-ranging look at the way Medicaid and SCHIP operate today and the roles they might play in the future. It explores the extent of variation in program coverage and spending among states, the modest nature of the coverage initiatives undertaken by the states and the many uninsured that remain, and the important but limited innovations in managed and long-term care. It also examines the relationship between Medicaid and the state budget crisis and the distrust that has developed between the federal government and the states, which have employed various financial accounting games to increase their federal Medicaid payments.

One theme that runs throughout the book is that the current system is in need of significant reform, particularly if Medicaid and SCHIP are to play a significant role in future efforts to expand coverage for the uninsured. To have any chance of success, such reform proposals must reflect an understanding of the variation in private insurance coverage that now exists across states and the willingness to commit public resources to address coverage gaps. While reforms could take many shapes and forms, to achieve their objectives they, almost certainly, will require a much greater investment of federal dollars and higher national minimum standards of coverage.

Robert D. Reischauer
June 2003

Acknowledgments

This book would not have been possible without the financial support of the Robert Wood Johnson Foundation and other funders of the *Assessing the New Federalism* project, including The Annie E. Casey Foundation, the W. K. Kellogg Foundation, The John D. and Catherine T. MacArthur Foundation, and The Ford Foundation. The editors and authors are also extremely grateful for valuable comments received from Andreas Schneider, Leighton Ku, David Helms, Vicki Gates, and Michael Sparer. We also appreciate the insightful comments that Brian Bruen, Lisa Dubay, Genevieve Kenney, and Sharon Long provided on selected chapters.

1

Federalism and Health Policy

An Overview

John Holahan
Alan Weil
Joshua M. Wiener

The financing of health and long-term care for the low-income population in the United States is a joint federal and state responsibility. The states have major financial and administrative responsibilities, with the federal government providing substantial funding and oversight. The appropriate balance of these responsibilities has been a matter of considerable debate over the past 40 years. Some argue for a greater federal role, others for more devolution of responsibility to the states. In recent years, waivers have given states the flexibility to change many features of their Medicaid programs; moreover, the states have considerable flexibility in establishing State Children's Health Insurance Programs (SCHIP). More radical forms of devolution, such as block grants, have been proposed but not enacted.

This book examines the record. How well have states done in providing acute and long-term care services to low-income populations? How have they responded to financial incentives and various federal regulatory requirements? Have they used the flexibility available to them? How innovative have they been? Once some states developed new programs and methods of providing services, did others implement those changes?

The book begins by considering the theoretical arguments for federal or state primacy in financing and program design—for example, in determining eligibility, reimbursement rates, and quality standards. Studies show that some states have demonstrated a great willingness to support their low-income populations, whereas others have not. The result is considerable inequity across states: Coverage and spending are low in some states and high in others. The record also shows that several states have been innovative in expanding coverage, implementing Medicaid managed care, and designing long-term care systems. But the system supporting health care for low-income people is under considerable budget pressure, and questionable financial arrangements have affected the fiscal integrity of the Medicaid program. Finally, the book explores alternative models of federalism, meaning different allocations of responsibility between the states and the federal government, including SCHIP, Medicare, and health insurance regulation and patient protection laws.

This book has been produced as part of the *Assessing the New Federalism* (ANF) project at the Urban Institute. The project was designed to assess the devolution of health and income support programs to the states. Over the past seven years, Urban Institute staff have conducted two rounds of case studies to examine how states responded to new opportunities to expand coverage in the midst of a rapidly growing economy and, more recently, how they are responding to the budget pressures that have developed as the economy slowed. The ANF project is also conducting a quantitative evaluation of SCHIP and various state coverage expansions aimed at low-income adults.

This introductory chapter describes the current health care system for low-income Americans and all that it has achieved. It then summarizes the primary issues raised and conclusions reached in each of the other chapters. Throughout the book, unless otherwise noted, programmatic data refer to *federal fiscal years*, while survey and other data refer to *calendar years*.

The Health Care System for Low-Income Americans

Medicaid is the backbone of the financing system that provides health and long-term care to low-income Americans. It extends insurance coverage to more than 35 million people.[1] In recent years, SCHIP has expanded coverage to near-poor children and to some parents. The private insurance market also provides coverage to many low-income people; state governments affect private coverage through regulation of insurance markets, and the federal government exerts control through the Health Insurance Portability and Accountability Act (HIPAA). The operation of managed care plans is influenced by state patients' rights legislation, and Congress is currently debating a federal extension of patient protections.

Medicaid is an open-ended funding program in which the federal government matches state spending on health insurance. Matching rates range from 50 percent to 77 percent, depending on a state's per capita income, with poorer states receiving higher rates. The average federal match is 57 percent. Combined federal and state Medicaid expenditures in fiscal year (FY) 2002 were more than $256 billion, about equal to Medicare's $257 billion. Medicaid expenditures are expected to exceed Medicare's in FY 2003.[2]

Medicaid has improved access to health services for large numbers of low-income Americans. It covers low-income pregnant women, parents and children (and in some states, adults without children), elderly persons, and persons with disabilities. States must provide a wide range of acute care services, including hospital inpatient and outpatient care, physician services, and laboratory and X-ray services, and they have the option of covering prescription drugs, dental services, physical therapy, prosthetic devices, and other medical care services. The program also covers institutional and community-based long-term care, supports state systems for people with mental illness and developmental disabilities, and provides financial support for state and local public health systems. Studies have shown that people with Medicaid coverage have better access to care and use more services than people without insurance coverage, after controlling for differences in population characteristics (Dubay and Kenney 2001; Newacheck et al. 1998; Rosenbach 1989). The program has also reduced out-of-pocket spending on health care, relative to a comparable uninsured population (Davidoff et al. 2000).

By serving a large share of the neediest, most vulnerable populations, Medicaid plays a critical role in the American health care system. While coverage varies extensively by state, Medicaid, along with smaller, state-funded programs, covers about 35 percent of Americans with incomes below the federal poverty level (FPL, which is $18,400 for a family of four in 2003) and 25 percent of those with incomes of less than twice the FPL. About 51 percent of children and 24 percent of adults with incomes below the poverty level are covered.[3] Medicaid pays for more than one-third of all births in the United States and provides prenatal care for low-income pregnant women as well as preventive services for children.[4]

The Medicaid population is considerably less healthy than average—beneficiaries are far more likely than either the privately insured or the uninsured to report being in fair or poor health and to report having activity limitations and chronic conditions. This is particularly true of disabled beneficiaries, who also receive Supplemental Security Income, but it applies to nondisabled beneficiaries as well (Holahan 2001). These groups would have great difficulty obtaining conventional health insurance, and even if they could, premiums would be extremely high.

Medicaid covers people with a wide range of disabilities, including mental illness, developmental disabilities, physical disabilities, and HIV/AIDS. Increasingly, Medicaid is paying for long-term care in the community. It provides major support for institutional care of low-income elderly persons and disabled persons, paying for about one-half of all nursing home expenditures and contributing to the cost of care for two-thirds of all nursing home residents. It also pays Medicare premiums, deductibles, and coinsurance for 5.2 million elderly or disabled persons, as well as for a number of acute care services not covered by Medicare. In particular, Medicaid finances the purchase of prescription drugs for many of the nation's sickest individuals, spending about $16 billion in 2001 on prescription drugs for older people and persons with disabilities.[5]

Finally, Medicaid provides considerable financial support for safety net hospitals in urban and rural areas. These hospitals not only provide care to Medicaid populations but also serve large numbers of uninsured Americans. Medicaid supports these hospitals both through direct payments for services and through disproportionate share hospital (DSH) payments, which help them defray the costs of caring for the uninsured.

While Medicaid provides extraordinary benefits to the U.S. population, it is plagued by an array of problems that have made it difficult to use as a mechanism for expanding coverage and services. One such problem is the stigma attached to Medicaid in many states because of its link to welfare. Medicaid's negative image is also attributable to the program's cumbersome enrollment processes, low provider payment rates, variable quality of care in nursing homes and other settings, and its reputation as a budget buster. There are also such extensive variations in coverage and spending across states that some of Medicaid's positive and negative features are not found in all states.

Another problem with Medicaid has been some states' use of dubious financing arrangements, including DSH payments and, more recently, upper payment limits (UPLs), to bring in large amounts of federal dollars with little or no state contribution (Coughlin, Ku, and Kim 2000). These arrangements have undermined the core financing structure of the program and have created considerable tension between the federal government and the states. Finally, while the program brings in federal revenues to support many state functions, it is also a constant source of pressure on state budgets because of state matching requirements.

In 1996, Congress established SCHIP to extend health insurance coverage to near-poor children—those living in families with incomes too high to be eligible for Medicaid. States were allowed to expand eligibility to twice the FPL and, through the use of liberal definitions of income, to people with considerably higher incomes. States were granted substantial flexibility in program design, including the ability to establish enrollment caps, to offer more limited benefit packages than Medicaid, and to impose significantly higher premiums and cost-sharing arrangements than allowed under Medicaid. The federal government established budget allocations for states, and it matches state expenditures at a considerably higher rate than it does for Medicaid, up to the limit established by the allocation.

In its short life, SCHIP has been more popular than Medicaid. States have embraced it enthusiastically, but it is impossible to tell whether this is because the program focuses on children, has higher federal matching rates, features greater flexibility in design, or includes no entitlement to benefits. How the program will do over a longer period, as it grows to account for a more significant share of state spending, is hard to predict, especially if state fiscal conditions do not radically improve.

State and Federal Roles in Health Care: Rationales for Allocating Responsibilities

The federalism debate in the United States centers on how strong the central government should be, what functions logically belong at the national level, when state autonomy should reign, and what state responsibilities should be. In Chapter 2, Randall Bovbjerg, Joshua Wiener, and Michael Housman examine this debate, with a particular focus on health care financing.

The case for federal or state preeminence can be argued on the basis of political philosophy, political and economic competition, or pragmatism. The political argument for state dominance is that state government is closer to the people and therefore better able to determine what works than the federal government. Moreover, local autonomy is essential in a country as diverse as the United States. This is especially true in health care, where health care institutions, medical practice patterns, referral networks, and provider markets are local. Those who argue for a stronger federal role believe it is the responsibility of the national government to "promote the general welfare." As Americans, citizens in one state are concerned about the well-being of citizens in other states. National citizenship implies some level of cross-state consistency.

A second set of arguments is rooted in economic theories of competition. Those who favor a strong state role contend that interstate political competition will make states perform better: If individuals and businesses dislike one state's policies, they can move to another state. The threat of exit means that state policy will need to reflect the will of individuals and businesses. The alternative argument is that interstate competition will undercut programs that attempt to redistribute income. States with generous benefits will experience an influx of low-income users and the subsequent exodus of taxpayers unwilling to pay the higher taxes required to sustain benefits. As a result, benefits and taxes will spiral downward to less generous programs than the states would have offered otherwise.

Finally, the pragmatic approach considers whether states or the federal government would do a better job of administering programs. This perspective views states as laboratories of democracy. Policymakers in the various states design new approaches to meet their state's responsibilities. Innovations that are successful will be replicated in other states; those that are not will disappear. The pragmatic argument for a greater federal role is, first, that some benefits, such as healthy citizens, are national in scope. The nation as a whole is hurt to the extent that individual states underinvest in the health of their citizens. Second, solving some problems, particularly those involving redistribution of resources, requires the fiscal capacity of the federal government. The federal government can more efficiently tax because populations and businesses cannot easily cross national borders to escape tax burdens. Third, in times of recession or economic slowdown, the federal government can adopt countercyclical spending; states are limited in their fiscal responses because almost all of them must have balanced budgets.

U.S. health policy reflects a shared approach to federalism, particularly in regard to low-income populations. There is little agreement that either level of government would necessarily do better than the current arrangement. While many people believe that a smaller government is better, that competition can improve government performance, and that redistribution can lead to economic inefficiencies, they also recognize that federal action is needed to improve the welfare of the citizens most in need. Some degree of redistribution is necessary if a basic level of care is to be provided, if poor health is to be avoided, and if long-term gains in productivity are to be reached. Moreover, while it is generally agreed that truly local problems are best dealt with on the state or local level, it is also understood that a federal solution is probably needed for problems that affect other states, that prompt substantial concerns about the welfare of residents of other states, and that are very costly or require redistribution.

Most Americans are in the middle of the ideological spectrum, Bovbjerg, Wiener, and Housman argue, and most Americans are pragmatic—they want to do what works best. Therefore, it is important to understand how well current health care arrangements work. Is there a reasonable minimum standard of care? Has the system produced innovation? Do the states learn from one another? Are state revenues sufficient in good times and bad? Does interstate competition thwart redistribution efforts? With these issues in mind, the remaining chapters seek to provide evidence of how well the federal-state sharing of financial and administrative responsibilities has worked in providing care for low-income populations.

Federalism and the Financing of Health Care

After laying the groundwork with an exploration of federalism, the book moves to fiscal issues. Chapter 3 examines the reasons for the growth in Medicaid spending and assesses the pressure Medicaid places on state budgets. Chapter 4 provides data on variations in coverage and spending, resulting in part from the health care system's federal-state structure. Chapter 5 looks at how states have used provisions of Medicaid law to maximize federal funding.

Health Care within the Larger State Budget

Medicaid has been growing as a share of state spending for many years and is now one of the largest components of state budgets. Donald Boyd shows that, between 1990 and 2000, Medicaid spending per capita increased by 88 percent, adjusted for inflation, whereas total state spending net of inflation increased by 32 percent. By 2002, Medicaid spending accounted for 12 percent of state and local general fund expenditures—21 percent when federal funds are included.

There are many reasons why Medicaid spending has grown, including increased enrollment—particularly a gradual shift toward relatively larger numbers of aged and disabled people (whose care is more expensive), inflation in health care costs, growth in DSH payments to hospitals, and greater use of health services. Expenditures have also grown as a result of various state attempts to maximize federal Medicaid revenues, a practice discussed in depth in Chapter 5.

Between 1990 and 1995, Medicaid grew substantially faster than any other part of the state budget. Spending on elementary and secondary education, higher education, and corrections also grew, but less rapidly than state spending, on average. It is difficult to tell whether spending in these other areas would have grown more if the rate of Medicaid spending had grown more slowly.

Between 1995 and 2000, Medicaid spending slowed because of declining enrollment, the expansion of Medicaid managed care, federal controls on the use of DSH programs, and reduced inflation in medical care costs. During this period, states greatly increased the resources devoted to elementary and secondary schools, which were experiencing higher enrollment. In addition, many states were shifting spending on elementary and secondary education from localities to the state. Welfare rolls dropped, providing states with a fiscal windfall, because federal funding for welfare was no longer linked to enrollment. At the same time, sales and income tax revenues rose because of extraordinary growth in incomes, especially the capital gains related to new stock market wealth. Thus, states could expand spending on education and other areas, reduce taxes, and increase reserves or rainy day funds—all at the same time.

After 2000, the picture began to change dramatically. The economy slowed, and state revenue growth leveled off, then fell—precipitously in some cases. The terrorist attacks of September 11, 2001, the sharp decline in the stock market, and state tax cuts enacted in the late 1990s accentuated the revenue shortfalls. Elementary and secondary education enrollment slowed, but states were under increased pressure to improve education standards, reduce class sizes, and raise teacher salaries. While growth in K–12 enrollment slowed, enrollment in higher education increased, forcing state decisionmakers to consider increased revenues to support higher education.

Meanwhile, Medicaid spending began to accelerate again. It is expected to grow at a rate of approximately 8.5 percent per year over the next decade because of a combination of factors.[6] First, between rising health care costs and slower economic growth, employer coverage may decline and the number of uninsured increase. States will see increased Medicaid and SCHIP enrollment, even with no expansion of eligibility standards. Second, hospital costs and prescription drug expenditures are likely to continue increasing at fairly rapid rates. Third, Medicaid managed care is no longer providing the same savings as it did in the 1990s and will not provide states with the tools they need to constrain spending on acute care. Fourth, long-term care costs are also likely to rise because of the aging of the population, labor force shortages, and efforts to improve nursing home quality. Recent court decisions have required states to expand coverage of services in the community for disabled persons. And finally, the federal government is determined to curtail use of DSH and UPL programs, which have been an attractive source of revenue for states.

The bottom line is that states will face extraordinary budgetary pressures in the coming years. Increased spending on health care can only be accommodated if spending on services such as education is curtailed or if taxes are increased. States face difficult trade-offs, and the likelihood of significant retrenchment is real; furthermore, the prospects for expanding health care programs to serve the uninsured seem bleak.

Variations in Health Insurance Coverage and Medical Expenditures: How Much Is Too Much?

With states having considerable administrative and financial flexibility in their Medicaid programs, substantial variation in coverage should be expected, although observers can disagree about how much is acceptable. John Holahan examines these variations in Chapter 3, presenting data on health insurance coverage and expenditures across states. Average uninsurance rates of children from 1997 to 1999 ranged from 8 percent in Minnesota to 25 percent in Texas; for adults under age 65, the rates ranged from 11 percent in Minnesota to 27 percent in Texas. Uninsurance rates tend to mirror variations in employer-sponsored insurance; that is, states with high rates of employer-sponsored insurance have low uninsurance rates and vice versa. Accordingly, employer-sponsored insurance covers 76 percent of persons under age 65 in Wisconsin and 58 percent in

California. Public coverage affects uninsurance rates as well, particularly for low-income people. Again, coverage varies substantially among states: Massachusetts covered 35 percent of its low-income population between 1997 and 1999, while Colorado covered only 15 percent.

Spending per low-income person varies similarly. Medicaid spending on acute care services for the population under age 65 varies among states by roughly a factor of three—even more if only state spending is considered. State wealth is a major determinant of spending per low-income person. As state income rises, so does spending of state revenues on Medicaid and SCHIP. Although federal matching funds vary inversely with state income, they are not sufficient to reduce spending differentials greatly. Moreover, states that spend less on Medicaid and SCHIP do not increase other health spending to compensate. Finally, the chapter shows that low-income people in states with high uninsurance rates are less likely to have access to health care and more likely to be in fair or poor health.

Some states have very large gaps in employer-sponsored insurance coverage, while others have much smaller ones. The result is considerable differences in uninsurance rates, an outcome that is not wholly the fault of states. States with low rates of employer coverage have a very difficult time overcoming the fiscal problems they face because of their employment base. Nonetheless, some states make a greater effort than others to cover their low-income population. The chapter concludes that while some of the wide variations in Medicaid coverage are due to differences in ability to pay, much also depends on state willingness to expend resources on health care for their low-income populations.

State Strategies for Tapping Federal Revenues: Implications and Consequences of Medicaid Maximization

While growth in Medicaid spending has placed pressures on state budgets, the program's growth should not be surprising—nor has it always been unwelcome. Medicaid has responded to the desire to expand coverage of children and to the needs of a growing aged and disabled population. When the economy declines, more people will be eligible for coverage, even with no change in eligibility criteria. The program is also vulnerable to spending pressures facing the entire health system. Finally, Medicaid expansions are affected by federal incentives that encourage states to spend more by sharing the cost. States must spend their own money on the program, but more state spending brings in more federal dollars.

Thus, some of the growth in Medicaid spending is attributable to state efforts to maximize federal funding. As Teresa Coughlin and Stephen Zuckerman (Chapter 5) show, states have financial incentives to expand Medicaid eligibility and services to obtain additional federal matching funds. This has led to the shifting of state-funded programs and services (such as maternal and child health programs, mental health services, home care, and school-based services) into the Medicaid program. With Medicaid financing, these services are often improved and expanded, and the states realize some savings. Similarly, states have shifted populations previously covered through state-funded programs into the Medicaid program. Such Medicaid maximization strategies have been encouraged by federal policy.

DSH payments and UPL programs raise different issues. Under these arrangements, a state obtains money from providers, through donations or taxes, or from government agencies, through intergovernmental transfers. The state then uses these funds to make DSH or UPL payments to providers under Medicaid, thereby obtaining federal matching funds. State or locally generated funds are returned to the state or locality, along with some or all of the federal payments. Providers benefit to the extent that they retain some of the federal funds. These programs have generated a considerable amount of money for states and their providers. Between 1990 and 1992, DSH spending increased from $1.4 billion to $17.5 billion, but it fell to $14.4 billion in 2000. UPL programs, which began in the mid-1990s, increased from $313 million in 1995 to $1.4 billion in 1998 and $10 billion in 2000.

The programs pose several problems. First, while some of the payments are used as intended, to meet the needs of providers that serve substantial numbers of Medicaid and uninsured patients, some are primarily strategies for obtaining more federal funds for state government with no additional state spending. This causes Medicaid expenditures to be overstated. Second, when federal dollars are actually retained by providers, state and local subsidies are often lower. In this case, as in the previous one, there is little increase in health spending relative to the amount of the increase in Medicaid expenditures. Third, DSH and UPL payments are not distributed equitably. The amount of money coming into states through this mechanism depends on state creativity and the willingness to exploit these mechanisms. For example, DSH spending in 1998 varied from 23 percent of Medicaid spending in Louisiana, 20 percent in Missouri, and 19 percent in South Carolina to less than 1 percent in Arkansas, Nebraska, and Wisconsin.

In addition to the inequities and the overstatement of Medicaid expenditures, these mechanisms have led to considerable tension between the federal government and the states. The federal government has undertaken a series of legislative and regulatory efforts to curtail DSH and UPL spending, but these efforts have never attempted to redistribute DSH dollars in a more equitable way, such as equalizing expenditures per uninsured person or per low-income person. Rather, expenditures have been frozen or special deals have been worked out to leave many of the existing inequitable arrangements in place. DSH and UPL spending has also been highly politicized. Members of Congress have wanted to close the loopholes but at the same time have wanted to protect their home states.

States as the Laboratories of Democracy

In their capacity as laboratories of democracy, states have brought about change in many areas of the Medicaid program. Innovations have been made in data systems, reimbursement methodologies, development of preferred drug programs, and extension of drug coverage to older people. The majority of state initiatives have centered on three areas: expanded coverage, managed care, and design of long-term care systems. Chapters 6, 7, and 8 focus on innovation in those areas of Medicaid.

Leaders and Laggards in State Coverage Expansions

The states have several federal mechanisms at their disposal to extend insurance coverage of low-income populations. These include traditional Medicaid, Section 1115 research and demonstration programs, SCHIP, Section 1931 provisions in the 1996 welfare reform legislation,[7] and, more recently, Health Insurance Flexibility and Accountability (HIFA) waivers. John Holahan and Mary Beth Pohl (Chapter 6) analyze the states' use of these mechanisms to expand coverage. They divide states into four groups on the basis of whether they cover any adults without children and how extensively they cover parents and children. The first group includes all states that cover all nondisabled adults without children, at least up to the federal poverty level (these adults may have incomes that exceed the federal poverty level). The second group covers parents whose incomes may exceed the federal poverty level; some of these states have also extended coverage to adults without children, but with fairly restrictive caps on enrollment and services. The remaining two groups have not extended coverage of children and parents much beyond minimum standards. Eleven states met the criteria for the first group, 10 for the second.

States in the first group have generally been extremely creative in using different funding streams, both federal and state, to develop their programs. They have used combinations of Medicaid, SCHIP, and state funds; and they have used authorities permitted under Section 1931 and Section 1115 waivers of the Social Security Act. Some of the most generous programs—for example, those in Massachusetts, New Jersey, and Tennessee—have been scaled back in the 2002–03 budget squeeze. Thus, the data presented in Chapter 6 may represent a high water mark of coverage, innovation, and political will, all of which could decline over the next several years.

States in the first group are considered leaders. This means that only about one-quarter of the states have taken advantage of existing federal law or established their own programs to extend coverage in significant ways. Another 10 states have taken important steps to expand coverage. As of 2001, the states in the first group covered 30 percent of their low-income population in public programs; states in the other groups covered 23 percent. Uninsurance rates for the first group were also lower, at 25 percent versus 30 percent. The leading states are much more likely to be politically liberal, to have higher incomes and education levels, and to have larger urban populations.

In sum, the amount of success in extending coverage is fairly limited. Holahan and Pohl suggest that this is due to limits on state resources; different budget priorities (e.g., for education, transportation, or tax relief); ideological aversion to public program expansions; and the structure of federal programs, particularly Medicaid, which makes it hard to cover adults without children. Fundamentally, however, coverage expansion requires some amount of income redistribution, and there are clearly limits on states' willingness to do this.

Medicaid Managed Care: State Flexibility in Action

Robert Hurley and Stephen Zuckerman (Chapter 7) paint a more optimistic picture of the creative capacity of states when it came to implementing Medicaid managed care, perhaps because the issues involved were largely administrative, not matters of financing or income redistribution. Medicaid managed care has been widely implemented over the past 10 years, substantially changing how the program operates. It has endured and changed many times in response to state needs. It has faced a range of problems, including enrollment abuses, inadequate access to care, low payment rates, conflicting evidence of its effects on utilization and cost savings, and difficulty keeping commercial managed care plans in the program. Some of these problems have been overcome, at least in some states, while others persist.

Hurley and Zuckerman point to a number of important innovations states have made in managed care. California's two-plan model provides a way to contract with mainstream plans while protecting safety net providers. Florida maintained access to a wide range of providers and preserved beneficiaries' choice of providers by establishing a system of competing health maintenance organizations (HMOs) and primary care case managers. Texas, Virginia, and New York also have multiple models, often differing in rural and urban areas, demonstrating the ability of states to refine strategies and adapt them to local conditions.

Many states were faced with a major challenge in the late 1990s because of the exit of commercial plans, mostly due to low payment rates. New York responded by increasing payment rates and expanding its reliance on health plans sponsored by safety net providers. New Jersey, Maryland, and Washington contracted with fewer plans, primarily those that serve only the Medicaid population. Other states, such as Georgia and Vermont, went back to relying on primary care case management. State flexibility allowed this variety of responses.

States also gained administrative expertise. They learned from Tennessee's experience that rapid implementation of Medicaid managed care could result in contentious relationships between the state and providers, which could endure for many years, and in slow implementation. Florida's experience with health plan marketing abuses led states to enrollment brokers to help beneficiaries choose plans, one of Medicaid managed care's most important innovations. Colorado, Washington, and Maryland have been in the forefront of developing payment methodologies that protect plans from the financial risk of enrolling a large number of sick and disabled beneficiaries, and thereby encourage more appropriate care for these vulnerable populations. Massachusetts has added to its primary care case management program many of the desirable and effective features of more comprehensive delivery systems.

Not all states have been innovative. Many pay low rates, and relatively few have sophisticated risk-adjustment payment systems. Most have concentrated on populations that are relatively easy to serve and have avoided the elderly, disabled, and other populations with special needs. Hurley and Zuckerman cite Tennessee as an example of how overly ambitious enrollment goals, coupled with low payment rates and inadequate risk adjustment, can seriously undermine a Medicaid managed care program. However, they conclude that, as innovators, states compare quite favorably with private purchasers and Medicare when it comes to managed care.

Long-Term Care: Can the States Be the Engine of Reform?

Long-term care is a key area of state health policy and spending because people requiring such care rely heavily on publicly funded programs. Long-term care accounted for 27 percent of state and local spending for personal health services in 2000. As with acute care, spending on Medicaid long-term care ranged widely, from $709 per capita in New York to $147 per capita in California. Joshua Wiener and Jane Tilly (Chapter 8) analyze federal-state relations in long-term care, focusing on older people and adults with physical disabilities.

The primary argument for greater state responsibility for long-term care is the ability of states to tailor programs to local conditions and preferences, something that is critical to long-term care because the service is so personal. The main argument for a strong federal role is that the federal government already has primary responsibility for the older population's health care (through Medicare) and income support (through Social Security and Supplemental Security Income). Adding long-term care could result in better coordination across these programs.

Financing of long-term care is complex and fragmented. Although Medicaid funding dominates, financing from Medicare and programs funded by the Older Americans Act, the Federal Rehabilitation Act, and the states themselves all play a role. While the states have been demanding additional programmatic flexibility, federal funding of long-term care through Medicare and Medicaid has become increasingly dominant. This has been caused, in part, by states shifting costs to Medicare and by Medicaid's increasingly important role in funding home and community services.

For years, adults with disabilities have been given long-term care primarily in institutions, despite their strong preference for living in the community. For a variety of reasons, states have been increasing funding for home and community-based services, mostly through the use of the Medicaid home and community-based services waivers. Funding for these waivers and noninstitutional services varies across the states, resulting in very great disparities in access to care.

The states' claim to being long-term care innovators is strongest in the context of Medicaid waivers. The waivers allow states enormous flexibility in service design while providing them with a great deal of fiscal control. All states have at least one waiver for older people and adults with disabilities, although many of them are small. Some states have used waivers to enable individual beneficiaries to select and manage their caregivers and to provide care in nonmedical residential facilities, such as assisted living. A minority of states rely heavily on such innovative services.

Quality of care has been a perennial problem, particularly in nursing homes. The federal government has played the dominant role in ensuring quality, establishing standards, and determining the enforcement process, while states largely implement the federal rules. Despite the large federal role, nursing home quality has remained problematic. Although states have responsibility for ensuring the quality of home and community services, they have done relatively little, concentrating their energies on expanding services instead.

Wiener and Tilly conclude that all states have learned enough from each other to move toward a more balanced system of long-term care delivery, but some have made more progress than others. Most states offer a fairly modest set of home and community services, but there is tremendous variation across states, raising questions of equity. Neither federal dominance of nursing home quality assurance nor state dominance of noninstitutional quality assurance has guaranteed a high level of service.

New Models of Federalism

This section examines three models of health care in the United States. The most recent is SCHIP, an effort to combine increased federal financing with more state flexibility, described in Chapter 9. Medicare is included because, while it provides a national base of financing, it ultimately relies on states to fill in the cracks (Chapter 10). Finally, Chapter 11 examines federal and state roles in insurance regulation and patient protection.

The State Children's Health Insurance Program: A New Approach to Federalism

SCHIP, enacted as part of the Balanced Budget Act of 1997, enabled states to expand coverage for children. Alan Weil and Ian Hill examine the program and ask whether the model has promise for further expansions of health insurance coverage. States responded to the new opportunity enthusiastically, and most of them implemented the program rapidly. Enrollment grew slowly at first but reached 3.6 million by June 2002. States made major efforts to improve outreach and simplify enrollment procedures, and more than a dozen states have extended coverage to children with family incomes of more than twice the federal poverty level. Other states have extended coverage to parents of SCHIP enrollees, arguing that it will lead to greater participation among children.

States could impose premiums and cost sharing in amounts up to 5 percent of family income, but few did so. Analysis of benefit packages finds that non-Medicaid-based SCHIP programs have extended very broad benefits to children. In addition, a positive relationship has developed between states and the federal government, unlike the often contentious and adversarial relationship surrounding the Medicaid program.

The program does face challenges. The first is the formula for allocating federal funds to the states. The original intent was to base allocations on the number of low-income uninsured children in a state, as well as the number of all low-income children in the state, with a gradual shift toward the latter. States that had already expanded Medicaid coverage had fewer low-income uninsured children and were thus penalized for their earlier generosity.

Another potential limitation is that SCHIP is not an entitlement program, so states can cap enrollment. With the weakening economy, some states are planning to freeze enrollment and to lower eligibility limits and benefits. The inability of eligible families to enforce a right to services has not been a problem so far, but it could emerge.

There are several reasons for the apparent success of SCHIP. States are attracted to the program because of its high matching rates and the increased flexibility it gives them. The design allows governors and key legislators to do something for children, a politically popular group. The capped appropriation limits the exposure of the federal government, making Congress feel that the program is more controllable than an entitlement program would be. The capped federal appropriation also limits state incentives for manipulating the financing system, as has occurred with Medicaid DSH and UPL payments. States find the funding limits acceptable because they can cap enrollment or adjust benefits. However, once the population becomes used to the extended coverage, capping enrollment and reducing benefits may be more politically problematic, despite the authority states have to use such mechanisms.

It may be difficult to extend the SCHIP model to other populations, the authors contend. While federal matching rates are high, a state contribution is still required—and for a broad expansion beyond low-cost children, those expenditures could be quite high. Caps on federal spending translate into financial and political risks for states. In addition, groups such as low-income adults without children are not as popular politically as children and their parents. Economic conditions are not as positive as they were when SCHIP was launched, and they may not be for some time. Nonetheless, it is plausible that the higher federal matching payments and greater flexibility in program design, coupled with the pressures that the large low-income uninsured population places on health care institutions within the state, would make SCHIP an attractive model for coverage expansions.

Making Medicaid a National Program: Medicare as a Model

Extending federal funding to much of the Medicaid program through a Medicare-like administrative structure might be a way of improving on current arrangements while giving the states fiscal relief. Marilyn Moon examines the many ways in which this could be done. The federal government could provide an acute care benefit much like Medicare's, perhaps with prescription drugs and some preventive services, and with uniform eligibility criteria across the country. For example, coverage might be extended to all children and pregnant women with incomes as high as twice the poverty level and to all adults with incomes up to the poverty level. Medicaid benefits not included in the new federal program could continue to be provided by states with federal matching payments. Provider payment rates would be based on methods used by the Medicare program.

A federal structure would have the advantage of providing uniformity of core coverage and benefits. Unlike the considerable variation that exists in the current Medicaid and SCHIP arrangements, a federal program would treat all Americans the same no matter where they lived. The financing of the program would be more equitable because it would rely on more progressive federal personal and corporate income taxes, both of which have broad revenue bases. The federal government also has the advantage of being able to incur budget deficits, allowing the system to more easily maintain coverage and benefits during economic downturns.

The program would also benefit from having consistent rules and regulations across states; rules covering payment systems are an example. A federal program could improve coordination of services provided to elderly and disabled persons who are currently eligible for both Medicare and Medicaid. Finally, a central program would benefit from economies of scale in program evaluation, systems development, and refinement of administrative and payment structures.

The disadvantages of a federal model center on the fact that health care is delivered locally. The states differ in their reliance on hospital inpatient care, the importance of specialists as opposed to primary care physicians, and the extent to which managed care has penetrated the health care market. Medicaid allows states to adapt more readily to local conditions and permits more program innovation than a federal model would. Change is arguably harder in a federal program because national politics are more polarized and the implications of any significant change are so far-reaching. Medicare still lacks a drug benefit and protection against catastrophic illness, despite years of debate.

A final concern is that national minimum standards of coverage would probably be set below the level of the most generous states. In fact, states that have greatly expanded their coverage could maintain current standards only by using their own funds, and they might well choose to cut back. This could be avoided if the national program were structured in a way that created few losers among the states. But a policy that creates only winners will be very costly for the federal government, particularly if eligibility is expanded significantly in the new acute care program.

Alternative Models of Federalism: Health Insurance Regulation and Patient Protection Laws

Even as Medicaid policy has shifted toward more state control, regulation of health insurance has moved toward a stronger federal role. Randall Bovbjerg (Chapter 11) traces federal and state actions over time and shows that federal insurance regulations have increasingly preempted state roles, thereby increasing standardization of regulatory policy. In general, federal regulations have moved toward enforcing desired policy results on a national basis, typically through setting minimum national standards.

Prior to the 1970s, the federal government completely deferred to state authority to regulate health insurance. Then, a series of acts changed the federal-state balance. In 1973, the federal Health Maintenance Organization Act forced states to allow new forms of insurance and service delivery previously barred in some states. In 1974, the Employee Retirement Income Security Act (ERISA) wholly preempted state regulation of employee health benefit plans in favor of federal oversight. The Health Insurance Portability and Accountability Act of 1996 (HIPAA) created a new set of federal obligations, both for states and for private providers of insurance coverage, primarily designed to cover enrollees who left their jobs. More recently, proposed patient protection legislation has built upon the HIPAA model.

The HIPAA model changed federal-state relationships in two primary ways. First, it set national minimum standards for all health coverage affecting the general population, including HMOs and conventional insurance. Second, the new federal rules were designed to be implemented by the states, although they could choose not to do so. States that did not choose to implement HIPAA would get federal implementation instead, so the standards are effectively national. States could impose more stringent requirements and could choose among a variety of ways of ensuring insurance availability for individuals.

The evidence shows that state innovation often spread, consistent with the idea of states as laboratories of democracy. The federal government often followed the lead of pioneering states. For example, HIPAA adapted some state individual and small group insurance market reforms and applied them nationally.

The primary lesson Bovbjerg draws from health insurance regulation and patient protection laws is that, while federal policymakers have often adapted state methods for federal use, they have also overridden the states when they perceive a national interest. HIPAA and the patient protection bills are models of minimum standard setting by the federal government and of implementation by the states. Because the standards are minimums, states can go beyond them. Variation in regulations across states is reduced but not eliminated.

The Future of Federalism in Health Care

The final chapter reviews state performance under Medicaid and SCHIP and discusses where federalism in health care should go from here. Alan Weil, John Holahan, and Joshua Wiener conclude that the current federal-state partnership in health care has a decidedly mixed record. The current system has many strengths—it covers 35 million low-income Americans, supports the nation's long-term care system, provides an extensive range of acute and long-term care services to low-income disabled persons, and underpins, directly and indirectly, safety net hospitals in urban and rural areas. But the system also has numerous problems: the poor public image in many states, the substantial pressure on state budgets, the great differences in health coverage and benefits among states, the limited amount of state innovation, and the DSH and UPL arrangements that have allowed states to garner large amounts of federal dollars with little or no contributions of their own.

The current system provides a base, but it has proven a difficult base to build upon. Both the federal and state governments are reluctant to extend Medicaid to other uninsured populations and to aggressively change the balance of services in long-term care. Because of the large fiscal shortfalls they will face for the foreseeable future, states may not even be able to maintain their current levels of coverage and benefits. The innovations and the will to expand coverage that are analyzed in this book are probably as good as it gets, which leaves huge chunks of the population uninsured and without adequate services.

For these reasons, the present system of care for low-income people needs a stronger federal role—both in setting higher minimum standards for coverage and benefits and in providing financing. Two proposals along these lines are put forth.

The first proposal would redefine the base of Medicaid and SCHIP coverage while giving the states incentives to extend coverage further. For example, minimum eligibility standards would be set at twice the FPL for children and at the FPL for all adults, and the federal government would define a set of benefits for people who meet the standards. The current federal entitlement to coverage would remain in place. States could extend coverage beyond the federal base of eligibility as high up the income scale as they wish. They could impose copayments, premiums, limits on benefits, and enrollment caps on groups with higher incomes. Federal matching payments would be 15 percent higher than they are under Medicaid. The federal government would also take over all financial responsibility for Medicare-covered acute care services and prescription drugs for persons who are eligible for both Medicaid and Medicare (dual eligibles). A new and expanded Medicaid home and community-based services program would be adopted, with the 15 percent higher federal matching rate. There would be minimum standards for payments to providers, but the current DSH program would be eliminated and perhaps replaced with a program that would provide grants directly to designated providers.

The second proposal would be to shift responsibility for a substantial portion of the health care safety net to the federal government. For example, the federal government could assume full responsibility for covering the acute care costs of the same groups described above: children with family incomes up to twice the FPL and adults up to the FPL. The federal government would finance and operate this program uniformly across states, alongside the current Medicare program. There would be a federally defined, comprehensive package of benefits and a uniform national system of provider reimbursement. As above, the federal government would take over full responsibility for dual eligibles. States could continue to cover populations and provide benefits beyond the federally defined minimum, using the savings from the new federal program. Existing shared responsibility for long-term care would remain in place, but the new program for home and community-based services described above could be included as an option. The DSH program would be eliminated, as described above.

These basic goals could undoubtedly be achieved in other ways, but either of these approaches would provide fiscal relief to states, ensure a higher base of coverage, limit the extensive disparities that exist today, and eliminate at least some of the financial machinations that plague the current system. If the federal government wanted to expand coverage further, it could do so by increasing minimum coverage levels, through tax credits to individuals or through block grants or matching grants to states. Either option would be a major departure from the current system, and the cost to the federal government would be substantial. But if the current problems in financing health care for low-income people are to be successfully addressed, a greater fiscal and programmatic role by the federal government is essential.

NOTES

1. Authors' estimates of full-year equivalents based on the enrollment projections in the Congressional Budget Office (CBO) March 2002 baseline.

2. Authors' estimates of total Medicaid expenditures in 2002 based on the CBO March 2002 baseline estimate of federal expenditures.

3. Calculations from the 2002 Current Population Survey.

4. Urban Institute tabulations of the 1996 National Hospital Discharge Survey.

5. Authors' calculations from Centers for Medicare and Medicaid Services data.

6. CBO March 2003 baseline.

7. Section 1931 of the Social Security Act requires states to provide coverage to families that have income and resources that would have qualified them for Aid to Families with Dependent Children under the state's welfare plan, effective as of July 16, 1996, but also allowed them to use "less restrictive methodologies" for counting income and resources in determining eligibility.

REFERENCES

Coughlin, Teresa, Leighton Ku, and Johnny Kim. 2000. "Reforming the Medicaid Disproportionate Share Program in the 1990s." *Health Care Financing Review* 22(2): 137–57.

Davidoff, Amy, A. Bowen Garrett, Diane Makuc, and Matthew Schirner. 2000. "Children Eligible for Medicaid but Not Enrolled: Health Status, Access to Care and Implications for Medicaid Enrollment." *Inquiry* 37(2): 203–18.

Dubay, Lisa, and Genevieve M. Kenney. 2001. "Health Care Access and Use Among Low-Income Children: Who Fares Best?" *Health Affairs* 20(1): 112–21.

Holahan, John. 2001. "Health Status and the Cost of Expanding Health Insurance." *Health Affairs* 20(6): 279–86.

Newacheck, Paul W., Jeffrey J. Stoddard, Dana C. Hughes, and Michelle Pearl. 1998. "Health Insurance and Access to Primary Care for Children." *New England Journal of Medicine* 338(8): 513–19.

Rosenbach, Margo L. 1989. "The Impact of Medicaid on Physician Use by Low-Income Children." *American Journal of Public Health* 79(9): 1220–26.

2

State and Federal Roles in Health Care

Rationales for Allocating Responsibilities

Randall R. Bovbjerg
Joshua M. Wiener
Michael Housman

Federalism in the United States allocates powers and responsibilities between the states and the national government. Some responsibilities may be exclusively federal or state, yet in most areas, either or both may act. The federal and state governments have evolved during the nation's history, as Americans' needs and philosophies have changed. Governmental responsibilities in health care have grown over the last century, along with medicine's ability to improve the well-being of citizens, rising dramatically since the 1960s' enactments of Medicare and Medicaid. The federal government is largely responsible for Medicare, but federal and state responsibilities overlap in Medicaid. In the early 1990s, legislative changes—collectively termed *New Federalism*—expanded states' responsibilities in several areas, including health care.

What is federalism, and how has its practice changed over time? What difference does it make whether any particular responsibility is met by the states or the federal government—or some combination of the two? Various philosophical, political, and practical rationales have been given for relying more heavily on one level of government or the other. What are the ramifications of those rationales for health care, especially for low-income people?

This chapter outlines the theory and practice of federalism in the United States. It describes long-standing arguments in favor of greater state or federal responsibility as a backdrop to the recent devolution of power from the federal government to the states.

Federalism in the United States

Federalism is any national system of government with both a central authority and autonomous constituent jurisdictions. Without a central authority, there can be no overarching nation-state. Without autonomy, states would merely be administrative units of the nation. Both levels of government have broad and sometimes overlapping responsibilities for social well-being, which they can meet using similar toolboxes of public powers, including regulation, taxation, conferring of benefits, or contracting with private entities to achieve public goals.[1] Both exercise the full spectrum of public authority—they set policy, implement it, and fund it. States and the central government also have parallel institutions: executive, legislative, and judicial branches, along with assorted independent commissions and other public entities.

Constitutional federalism is an American innovation. Although fundamental to governance in the United States, the concept of federalism has resisted any single, lasting definition. (An academic exercise once identified some 267 different versions [Stewart 1984].) Ambiguity is built in because federalism embodies a national-state balance in sovereignty that can be struck in different ways at different times, by different actors, and for different activities. Further, although federalism universally entails autonomy for both levels of government within a united nation, observers and partisans differ in how they think authority should be allocated. Some thinkers, like Daniel Elazar, emphasize the sharing of functions between levels of government, while others, like Paul Peterson, stress the independence of each level of government and the sorting out of responsibilities for each (Elazar 1966; Peterson 1981).

Origins of Federalism

Federalism in the United States arose from the desire to reconcile two powerful, opposing forces: the need for more national authority and mistrust of a single sovereign. On one hand, the nation's founders recognized the need to strengthen the national government (Beer 1997). Under the Articles of Confederation (1777), the states printed money and maintained armed forces, and they oversaw not just public safety but also health, welfare, and morals. The weak national government could not forge agreements on national defense, finance, or commerce; enforce decisions once made; or even resolve disputes among states. It was also dependent on state contributions for revenue. A stronger central government was deemed to be essential "to promote the general welfare" (U.S. Constitution, Preamble).

On the other hand, the founders feared an overly strong central government. Their hostility arose both from a philosophical belief in the primacy of individual liberty and from bitter practical experience of abuses under a distant royal power. Therefore, they also supported continued state authority as a counterweight to enhanced national authority.

These tensions about public authority profoundly engaged the emotions and intellects of those attending the Constitutional Convention. Federalism was their solution. The new Constitution gave the central government stronger powers, including the right to levy taxes and regulate interstate commerce, and those powers were agreed to be supreme in any conflict with state authority. States explicitly surrendered certain sovereign powers, such as the ability to print money and regulate their borders, and agreed that they would give "full faith and credit" to other states' laws (U.S. Constitution, Article I, Section 10).

Concerns for the rights of individuals and states were safeguarded in multiple ways. The founders specified particular federal powers, thereby reassuring opponents that national government would not overstep its bounds. Moreover, the power of any one government would be curbed by having states and the central government share authority and responsibilities. The resulting political rivalry was expected to protect individual liberty (Dye 1990: 5). The vertical state-federal balance of power was complemented by the horizontal checks and balances resulting from independent legislative, executive, and judicial branches within the federal government (Madison 1787).

Some ambiguity in the allocation of powers remained, which helped achieve compromise at the time. This fluidity has allowed the federal system to evolve to meet succeeding generations' needs, as the built-in tensions among governments and between the public and private spheres periodically resurface (Peterson 1995: 10; Rivlin 1992: 83). The first changes were the adoption of the Bill of Rights two years after the

Constitution was ratified and the Eleventh Amendment four years later. These initial amendments constrained federal power by adding explicit protections for individual liberties and state autonomy. For almost 200 years thereafter, changes tended to increase federal authority and responsibilities.

Growth of Federal Responsibilities

Growth in federal powers began with considerable institution building— by Alexander Hamilton at Treasury, Benjamin Franklin in the Post Office, and John Marshall leading the Supreme Court, for example. Further growth resulted from judicial interpretation of constitutional provisions. The Civil War thoroughly established federal primacy over state governments. Thereafter, federal responsibilities and powers continued to grow to meet the sociopolitical demands of continental expansion, increased interstate and foreign commerce, and international conflict. Especially notable amendments limited the states' power to infringe civil rights guaranteed under the Constitution, confirmed the federal government's power to tax incomes, and ended state legislatures' election of U.S. senators.[2]

Federal spending remained small, however, until the Great Depression (Leuchtenburg 1995). President Franklin D. Roosevelt's New Deal of the 1930s greatly expanded domestic spending, especially on human services. Along with such federal programs as Social Security, the New Deal created a new "fiscal federalism" through welfare reform, which combined state administration with federal funding, federal minimum standards, and federal oversight (U.S. House of Representatives, Committee on Ways and Means 2000).

President Lyndon B. Johnson's Great Society programs of the 1960s applied New Deal principles to medical assistance. Medicare was created as a federal program of health insurance for people of retirement age and people with long-term disabilities. Like Social Security before it, Medicare was funded mainly by prospective beneficiaries' taxes and current beneficiaries' premiums. Administration was largely decentralized, but only to regional federal contractors. For the "deserving" poor, Medicaid expanded and made an entitlement the previously limited federal-state cooperation in financing medical services. It provided benefits for recipients of cash welfare payments, principally low-income mothers and children, and elderly and disabled persons. Like welfare, Medicaid combined minimum federal standards, joint federal-state funding, and state administration.

States could decide whether or not to participate in Medicaid, but participating states had to operate within the federal rules. Medicaid entitles states to federal funding for eligible beneficiaries and services and entitles beneficiaries to services meeting federal standards.

Most states were quick to accept the new federal support and began operating Medicaid programs.[3] The original Medicaid statute allowed states to set very generous eligibility limits, unrelated to welfare limits for some groups, but 1967 amendments tied federal matching to welfare ceilings.[4] The 1965 statute also called for states to increase the comprehensiveness and generosity of their programs over time, but this provision was first delayed, then repealed, to allow states to control the size of their programs.[5]

Intergovernmental relations and the size of government were profoundly changed by the expansions of the 1930s and 1960s. In 1930, federal revenues claimed less than 5 percent of the gross domestic product, state and local revenues about 10 percent. By 1993, just before the New Federalism initiatives, the federal share was 20 percent, state and local shares about 15 percent.[6] The expansions of Medicare and Medicaid in the 1960s were especially large. Between 1965 and 1970, the federal share of national health expenditures more than doubled, to almost 25 percent.[7] Many other new federal grant programs in the 1960s also sought to encourage grassroots achievement of federal goals, a concept that President Johnson termed "creative federalism" (Johnson 1964). These programs often bypassed states with direct grants to localities or nongovernmental organizations.

Early federalism maintained separate state and federal spheres that sometimes intersected. By the time Medicaid was enacted, the spheres were quite intermingled. The mid-20th century has been termed an era of "marble cake federalism," replacing the earlier "layer cake" separation of roles (Walker 2000). However, in this marbling, federal policy was usually on top. The high-water mark of centralization may have been the National Health Planning and Resources Development Act of 1974, which required states to adopt federally approved health planning laws or lose federal funds for public health. The U.S. Supreme Court upheld this expansion of federal power, which could even override a state's constitutional law (*North Carolina v. Califano* 1978). During Richard M. Nixon's presidency, federal power over states grew enormously, although less in health care than in environmental and other areas of regulation (Conlan 1988).

Recent Developments, Especially in Health Care

Somewhat paradoxically, President Nixon also promoted decentralization. He called for a "new federalism," meaning devolution of more federal responsibility to the states, which he portrayed as "closer to the people" and hence more responsive to their needs (Nixon 1970). At the same time, he proposed that states be given more federal funding and greater authority over funds. His administration created the first "block grant" in health care, combining numerous specialized, "categorical" public health grants into one general block of funds with reduced federal oversight. The Nixon administration also created general revenue sharing, which for over a decade gave states substantial federal funds with few strings attached.[8] Expanding the federal role in health care to guarantee health insurance for all citizens was rejected at this time, as it had been in the 1930s and 1960s.

President Ronald Reagan sought further decentralization, famously asserting in his first inaugural address that "government is not the solution" (Reagan 1981). He, too, called for a "new federalism." Like Nixon's, it would involve more devolution of responsibility, but it would also emphasize efficiency in state operations and, hence, cutting rather than expanding federal funding. For example, the Reagan administration proposed consolidating 25 separate health grant programs into two big general blocks with 25 percent less funding. It also proposed capping growth in federal Medicaid spending (Bovbjerg and Holahan 1982; Peterson, Bovbjerg, et al. 1986). Because much federal-state interaction was based on federal funding of state activities, maintaining budgetary control and taking political credit for benefits (or tax cuts) were becoming federalism issues as well.

States objected that President Reagan's funding cuts went beyond the bounds of any efficiencies they could achieve. Congress enacted narrower block grants and temporarily reduced federal matching rates for Medicaid, but it did not cap their rate of growth (Bovbjerg and Davis 1983). President Reagan proposed an even larger realignment in federalism, with states taking over all of welfare and food stamps (to make the programs "more responsive to genuine need" because of local operations) and the federal government assuming all of Medicaid (in line "with its existing responsibility for Medicare" [Reagan 1982]). Also opposed by states, this swap never came close to enactment. In the mid-1980s, the Democratic Congress agreed to stop regulating state health planning, but it expanded the states' obligation to cover children under Medicaid. In this era, states generally became more vocal about what they called "unfunded federal mandates" (Posner 1998).

The 1990s saw another clear rejection of mandatory national health insurance coverage, an early policy initiative of President Bill Clinton. Republicans won control of Congress in 1994 and launched a legislative agenda that some termed the New Federalism, others a "devolution revolution," building upon the Contract with America promised by House Republicans during the election campaign (Gingrich, Armey, and the House Republicans 1994). A strong effort was made to turn both welfare and Medicaid into block grants, and a chastened President Clinton declared that the era of big government was over (Clinton 1996). In 1996, despite Democratic opposition, Congress and the president agreed on welfare reform as a major devolution of responsibility to the states, with significant but limited federal funding. Congressional Republicans successfully legislated new procedures designed to discourage future unfunded federal mandates on states (Weil and Finegold 2002).

The Clinton administration and congressional Democrats fought successfully to keep Medicaid an open-ended entitlement program under federal guidance, although with somewhat greater state discretion in regard to eligibility. Other important federal laws enacted in 1996 and 1997 directed states to regulate aspects of health insurance (under threat of direct federal rules) and created new federal funding for states under the State Children's Health Insurance Program (SCHIP).[9] SCHIP changed the Medicaid model of coverage for children in low-income families. Its federal matching share was higher, although with a ceiling on total funds, and states were given much more control over program design and operations, including the ability to cap spending or enrollment. Under Medicaid, states also got new freedom to control nursing home payment rates and to require that beneficiaries be enrolled in managed care plans.

None of these initiatives radically realigned health policy, but all of them gave states more authority in setting policy and more flexibility in administering programs. Today, the allocation of responsibilities between state and federal governments differs widely across health care functions. At the federal end of the spectrum lies Medicare, which is clearly national in both financing and administration. Under Medicare, the states' main role is to pay premiums and coinsurance for certain low-income beneficiaries. The states do this via Medicaid, which also pays for a large portion of the services scantily covered by Medicare, especially long-term care and outpatient prescription drugs. At the state end of the spectrum lie such activities as licensure of medical organizations and personnel, over which the federal government claims little authority. Indeed, Medicare delegates implementation of its rules on provider qualifications to state licensing authorities.[10]

In between lie most other health care functions, including Medicaid and SCHIP, as well as traditional public health functions and regulatory activities, such as protection of persons enrolled in managed care organizations. The federal-state split can even vary within a single program, depending upon whether a particular activity is the creation of policy, its implementation, or its funding. Thus, federal law determines basic Medicaid rules, which can be quite detailed, but states decide whether to run a program at all, who will be covered, and most other administrative matters. Federal support of Medicaid is open-ended, ranging from 50 to 77 percent of spending on medical services (U.S. Department of Health and Human Services 2000). In SCHIP, federal funding is higher, but the federal role in program design and operations is smaller.

Among nations with a federal system of government, the United States ranks at the top in terms of decentralization, even taking into account its large size (Derbyshire and Derbyshire 1996; Elazar 1997; Lijphart 1999). Yet the call for even greater devolution has strong roots in U.S. politics and economic-political theory. Although total devolution of federal powers and responsibilities to the states is highly unlikely, it is important to understand how well states are performing under today's New Federalism.

Arguments for Various Models of Federalism

How can one measure the appropriateness of devolution? Advocates offer various reasons for preferring one level of government over the other, either in general or in specific areas. Their arguments fall into three main groups. The first is political philosophy, which rests mainly on fundamental values. The arguments for greater or lesser federal authority articulated at the founding of the nation were based on political philosophy, and they remain vital today. The second is the role of political and economic competition among the states. Arguments in this area have evolved along with the discipline of economics. The third is practical considerations about attributes or performance of government, based on observation. Such arguments appear to ebb and flow, depending on how governments are seen as performing relative to an era's problems, as well as on citizens' beliefs and expectations about government.

Political Philosophy and Federalism

Philosophical beliefs favoring greater state or national responsibility are older than the nation itself. The leading ones are described below.

PHILOSOPHICAL RATIONALES FAVORING STATE RESPONSIBILITY

Supporters of state primacy often assert that the government closest to the people is best-suited to govern. This assertion stems mainly from a philosophical perspective, not empirical observation. It prizes individual liberty and mistrusts governmental authority of any sort, especially a powerful central one. Advocates often state this position as a self-evident first principle or merely invoke the Tenth Amendment or states' rights to support their arguments.

Two other rationales for state superiority have a more empirical basis. First, a geographically smaller, more local government can know and represent its citizens' values better than a large one. Second, a smaller government knows the territory—that is, the possibly unique nature of its citizens' problems and the plausibility of any suggested solutions.

With respect to reflecting citizen values, Nixon argued that state government is "most responsive to the individual person," more than "the government in Washington can ever be" (Nixon 1971). Given a more intimate scale, citizens are more likely to participate in civic affairs, their representatives can more easily learn their views, and they can hold representatives more personally accountable.

With regard to knowing the territory, states are better able to understand their unique problems, craft policy responses, and implement them flexibly. After all, many factors that affect citizens' lives vary considerably from state to state, and it is the states, not the federal government, that exercise fundamental police power over health and welfare. Geographic diversity may have a particularly strong effect on health care services because health care institutions, medical practice patterns and referral networks, and market behavior are mainly local.[11] Specifically, the nature of provider networks, the proportion of the population receiving managed care, the size of the uninsured population, the availability of medical technology, and the extent to which practitioners and institutions provide charity care are all widely variable. Therefore, good governance requires, in this view, locally tailored policies and flexible administration, not inflexible, one-size-fits-all federal policy.

Thomas Jefferson was the leading proponent of the small-is-better ideal; his federalism would have built up from local wards to counties, states, and nation (Beam, Colan, and Walker 1983; DiZerega 1994). The final Constitution included only the existing states and the new national government, however; localities are not building blocks of state legitimacy but rather owe their existence and powers to state charter. A related viewpoint is that large nations need many governments. Big countries are apt to be more diverse than small ones and hence benefit more from autonomous local governments that reflect legitimate, important differences within the nation. The diversity of state preferences, as shown, for example, by differences in Medicaid eligibility, are quite large (see Chapter 6 of this volume). Sparer and Brown note that "America is an extraordinarily heterogeneous society, and Americans have long believed that public policy should, wherever possible, reflect disparate local needs and preferences" (Sparer and Brown 1996: 197). Catering to decentralized preferences may also reduce intergroup conflict at the national level. Indeed, studies have found that federalism and decentralization of power are more common in larger than in smaller countries.

The foregoing are arguments that states will govern better than the national government. Another aspect of this philosophy, however, is the expectation that states will do less—or at least that states are inherently less powerful than the national government, if only because people can leave one state for another, which is a point that blends into the competition rationale discussed below. A closely related belief is "that government is best which governs least."[12] Many people believe that any exercise of governmental power necessarily diminishes individual liberty, whether that power is exercised in the form of levying taxes or imposing rules (Nozick 1974). Proponents of such beliefs seem to prefer state government to federal government because state government is less threatening, and to prefer private action to any government. Others appear simply to object on principle to nearly any federal activity, while accepting larger state responsibility.

One consequence of state discretion, whether long-standing or recently devolved, is that policies are more divergent than they would be under a national regime. Medicaid eligibility, for example, varies greatly because past and recent devolutions have given the states discretion in determining who qualifies for benefits. Beyond fine-tuning programs to suit local needs or conditions, states also make major adjustments to Medicaid in response to their fiscal capacities at any given time and to the preferences of taxpayers and voters (Uccello and Gallagher 1997).

PHILOSOPHICAL RATIONALES FAVORING FEDERAL RESPONSIBILITY

Political philosophy can also favor stronger federal authority. Many people believe that certain matters are inherent in national citizenship, and they want to "promote the general welfare" of all Americans, irrespective of state of residence.[13] This belief results in political demands for national action or for states to meet minimum national standards, thus ensuring some degree of equity across the nation.

Two primary rationales support this philosophy. The first is the literal Constitutional primacy of national citizenship. The second is the figurative shrinking of the country through a national economy and improved communications and transportation. The Constitution confers citizenship on all Americans as a birthright, whereas state citizenship can be changed by moving residence. When the nation was first formed, most people still considered their state citizenship primary. Revolutionary battles were often fought under state flags, and until the question was settled by the Civil War, many believed that states could secede at will from the Union. State identification remains strong today but stirs much less fervor than it once did. City rescue workers at the World Trade Center hoisted the American flag in September 2001, not the banner of New York State or New York City (North Carolina Chapter of the National Emergency Number Association 2003).

A corollary of national citizenship is that certain rights and responsibilities should not vary too greatly across the states. People differ, however, in what rights they consider national and how much variation they consider acceptable. Many political attributes of national citizenship—such as basic civil rights and the ability to vote in presidential elections—were guaranteed by the Constitution and broadened through amendments. Other rights are arguably becoming components of a national sense of citizenship, including some degree of consistency in health care across states (Anton 1997). This sense is more universally felt in regard to older people, who are eligible for Medicare, than for poor people, at least for poor people who are able to work. Americans are not like Canadians, for whom universal health insurance coverage is a key aspect of their national citizenship, even though it is administered by the provinces. It is notable that the New Federalism of the 1990s gave states much more responsibility for cash welfare than for health care (Weil and Finegold 2002).

The second rationale for federal responsibility is that the country has become far less local since Thomas Jefferson's time. Partly as a result of federal structure, Americans live in an increasingly national, indeed global, economy. Expression of political views and political participation were once necessarily local, given natural limits on travel and communication. No longer. Social, cultural, and political differentiation by locale is on the decline: Americans nationwide have the same menu of TV shows (including political talk shows), listen to the same kinds of music, eat the same franchised food, and debate much the same public concerns.

Health care financing and delivery are also less local. Health insurers, hospitals and clinics, drug companies, medical suppliers—all have become regional and national rather than state or local. Medical education and standards of practice are more standardized. Although licensure is still state-specific, medical experts testifying in courts and legislatures may come from anywhere in the country, and increasing numbers of consumers are conducting Internet searches on their health care providers' credentials and comparing their providers' advice to advice posted on the World Wide Web. Finally, control of contagious diseases, bioterrorism monitoring, and numerous other public health functions are national in scope. Thus, there exist fewer local situations that truly require less-than-national governance.

Medicaid reflects a political and practical compromise between these two competing philosophies.[14] States enjoy wide discretion over eligibility, benefits, and provider payments, but national interests are maintained through federal minimum standards (Wiener 1996). SCHIP was enacted to increase coverage of children from low-income families and to reduce the cross-state disparities that remained even with open-ended Medicaid funding (Chapter 6, this volume). Concern for children may also reflect perceptions that children do not have independent adult rights and responsibilities, cannot choose for themselves, should not be held responsible for their own health insurance coverage, and deserve help to ensure that they develop into productive members of society.

Political-Economic Competition and Federalism

Given the multiplicity of state jurisdictions and the free movement of people and commerce, states inevitably compete with one another. Interstate competition provides rationales for both greater state and greater federal responsibility.

RATIONALES OF COMPETITION THAT FAVOR STATE RESPONSIBILITY

Another rationale for devolution is that interstate competition pressures states to improve their performance and thus attract and retain residents and businesses (Greve 2001a). This quasi-economic perspective complements the idea that multiple governments are needed to represent geographic diversity. Its theorists compare competitive state governments favorably with a monopolistic federal government. This type of thinking arose well after the Constitutional Convention, along with the rise of economic thinking generally.

Political scientist Thomas Dye observes, "Matching public policy to citizen preferences is the essence of responsive government" (Dye 1990: 14). Elections and political parties serve this goal, he notes, and competition among decentralized governments helps match varying citizen preferences with public policies. Dye elaborates:

> Competition in the private marketplace forces sellers to become sensitive to preferences of consumers. Competition among governments forces public officials to become sensitive to the preferences of citizens. Lessened competition in the marketplace results in higher prices, reduced output, and greater inefficiency in production. Lessened competition among governments results in higher taxes, poorer performance, and greater inefficiencies in the public sector. Competition in the marketplace promotes discoveries of new products. Competition among government promotes policy innovation (Dye 1990: 15).

Like economic competition, political competition is driven by informed choice among alternatives. People can choose not only how to vote, but also where to live, work, and run businesses—and thus also where to pay taxes and receive public services.[15] Thus, they can readily choose among the range of policies offered in such different states as New Hampshire and Massachusetts. The mobility of individuals and businesses increases as the size of governmental units decreases, because movement across nearby boundaries is culturally and economically much easier than longer-distance movement. Movement among states for political reasons intensifies the alignment of citizen preferences and state policies—that is, persons who leave one state for another are in greater agreement with the policies of the second state, whereas those who do not leave are in greater agreement with the policies of the first state. Furthermore, the first state may change its policies in response to actual or threatened movement, further increasing alignment.

Policymaking, administration, spending, and taxation all come into play in interstate competition (Cato Institute 2002). In comparing states, one might focus on the size of public programs' budgets (and hence taxes) relative to the perceived value of benefits. Medicaid is a prime example because it is a very large public program with benefits and costs that differ markedly by state. Other comparisons might focus on other values, such as regulation of private conduct, which adds little cost to state budgets but may matter a lot to voters, taxpayers, and the persons who would be regulated. An example is the regulation of hospital expansion through health planning. Competition might also improve efficiency in program administration, giving more value for money by managing better or more consistently with citizens' values. Thus, states might compete to simplify health care paperwork, increase program outreach to doctors or patients, improve management of medical care, or find good jobs with private health insurance for people who leave welfare.

For competition to be useful, citizens need information. Certain states have become generally known as low-tax, low-service states (or the reverse); others are known as heavy or light regulators of business. Some states have worked to change their image. Political "consumers" benefit, under this theory, by having their state provide them with a more optimal mix of costs and benefits. However, not all consumers have to be well informed, nor move or threaten to do so, in order to get results. The states are disciplined by marginal consumers; that is, less active consumers are thought to benefit from improvements states make in response to more demanding citizens at the political margins.

Federal intervention interferes with the cost-benefit comparisons, according to this theory (AEI 2002; Cato Institute 2002). Both unfunded federal mandates and federal subsidies lead to inappropriate state programs or spending. States need the freedom to choose among the full range of policy options and should face the full costs—and benefits—of their actions, theorists argue. Somewhat ironically, a solid national framework is needed to bring about this type of competition among states—a common language, currency, and freedom of movement. Similarly, economic competition presupposes that companies and consumers operate within a common rule of law and culture.

Costs of state health programs and the taxes that support them have a significant impact. For example, in 1999, New York spent just over $1,600 per person on health care (40 percent of all state expenditures), whereas Nevada spent about $460 per person (some 13 percent of all state expenditures).[16] The two states' income, sales, and payroll tax rates also diverged (Urban-Brookings Tax Policy Center 2002). Proponents of state competition suggest that residents of both states would be worse off if forced to shift toward a national norm.

RATIONALES OF COMPETITION THAT FAVOR FEDERAL RESPONSIBILITY
Arguments can also be made that interstate competition is harmful, not beneficial, and hence should be restricted through federal constraints. One argument is that competition can unleash a race to the bottom in benefits. Another is that competition undercuts states' ability to tax residents as much as they would like. A third argument is that competition undercuts legitimate, important redistributive programs such as health insurance coverage for the poor. Accordingly, the federal government should play some role in setting minimum standards.

The first argument for federal responsibility holds that competition promotes a race to the bottom in providing benefits rather than a race to the top in innovation and good administration, as competitive theorists imply. A common worry about the New Federalism legislation was that state control over welfare or Medicaid would lead to just such a destructive cycle of benefit cutting (Schram and Beer 2000; Weil and Finegold 2002).

Needy beneficiaries of public programs, it was feared, would move from less generous states to their more generous neighbors. As a result, states that wanted to improve their benefits would find they could not afford to do so, no matter how efficiently they ran their programs. Any more generous state programs might cause migration, and means-tested programs such as Medicaid were most likely to cause problems because their low-income beneficiaries make little or no net contribution to state revenues. Migration would prove especially burdensome under a block grant or cap on federal funding, because more generous states would have to pay the full marginal costs of any spending beyond the cap. To avoid becoming welfare magnets, it was feared that states would reduce program benefits below what they would otherwise have chosen. Once the high-benefit states cut back, they would become less attractive to beneficiaries, who would then migrate to the next highest states, which would continue the cycle by cutting their benefits as well. Or all the states might cut their benefits at once to preempt undesired migration.

Not only would such competition lead to the lowest common denominator in terms of benefits, it would also reduce the diversity across states extolled by competitive theorists. This argument for a federal role does not specify how low the race to the bottom might go, but presumably some states would always offer higher benefits because of cultural differences in voter-taxpayer altruism and differences in fiscal capacity unrelated to mobility.

The second argument in favor of federal responsibility is that interstate competition can cause a flight from the top, resulting in lower tax rates and revenues. Regardless of their own preferences, states cannot impose taxes that are much higher than neighboring states' because residential and commercial taxpayers will move. Those paying the highest taxes have the greatest incentive to leave—and they may also be the best able to afford to. Few people actually move from one state to another in a given year (only about 3 percent [Peterson 1995]), but shifts of high-income, marginal taxpayers have a disproportionate impact, and the threat of a cumulative imbalance is considerable. Advocates of a strong national role contend that competition among states to reduce taxes is likely to bene-fit marginal taxpayers more than typical residents and certainly more than low-income residents. Fear of losing high-income taxpayers is con-sistent with the observation that state taxation is less progressive than federal taxation—that is, state marginal income tax rates rise less steeply than federal rates. Finally, reductions in state benefits are likely to hurt low-income residents disproportionately.

Competition among states for citizens and businesses can therefore be profoundly different from competition among political candidates for votes, this argument holds. The economic theory of public choice finds that political competition tends to drive public policy toward the wishes of the median voter, much as common wisdom has long noted that elec-tions drive candidates' positions toward the middle of the electorate (Black 1958; Buchanan and Tullock 1962). That pressure exists because each voter's voice counts the same, and a broad spectrum of the popula-tion votes in general elections. In contrast, marginal citizens count more if states compete to avoid losing high-income taxpayers and to avoid attracting low-income beneficiaries. To what extent this sort of competi-tion actually occurs is an important policy issue.

Third, competition is most harmful to policies that redistribute income. In this view, redistribution is an important public function that promotes the general welfare and has philosophical support as well.[17] Redistribution in this country does not seek equality, simply a reduction in disparity; accordingly, redistribution often takes the form of a mini-mum floor of help for the disadvantaged (President's Commission for the Study of Ethical Problems in Medicine and Biomedical and Behavioral Research 1983). Medicaid, for example, creates larger net winners and losers than public programs that tax and serve everyone. So arguments in favor of competition are closely allied to arguments against income redistribution and progressive taxation of income or wealth. Wallace Oates, one of the earliest scholars of fiscal federalism, predicted "real trouble" for redistribution because states might reduce inequality, but they could do so mainly through "an outflow of the rich and an influx of the poor, with a consequent fall in the level of per capita income" (Oates 1972: 7).

Peterson draws sharp distinctions between the effects of competition on redistributive policies and the effects on "developmental" policies (Peterson 1995; Rivlin 1992). Like Oates, he argues that redistribution should occur at the federal level, but he says that states (and localities) should set developmental policies—investment in public infrastructure, education, and productivity enhancements. Both developmental and redistributive policies are sensitive to and disciplined by market conditions, he notes; however, areas whose developmental policies successfully create good jobs and attractive communities deserve to be rewarded through in-migration of workers and capital.

The 1996 devolution of welfare programs to the states was a decision that appears to contravene Peterson's theory of how functions should be allocated. However, proponents of welfare devolution suggested that it had developmental rationales: Ending "welfare dependency" was said to raise productivity and thus enhance both personal and community development. They successfully redefined welfare as a work program (development) rather than a cash assistance program (redistribution). States argued that they were in a better position than the federal government to administer job training and outplacement programs, which require local knowledge and operations and which must be tailored to the needs of individuals.

Practical Considerations and Federalism

Pragmatic arguments do not favor either level of government in principle. Instead, they recognize that responsibilities can differ with functions and circumstances. Moreover, initial allocations of authority may need to be changed when public attitudes about problems change or new information about the success of program operations comes to light. Finally, the same practical rationale may not apply equally to all parts of a program: Policymaking, implementation, funding, and evaluation may call for different strengths.

PRACTICAL RATIONALES FAVORING STATE RESPONSIBILITY

The classic practical argument in favor of autonomous states is that they serve as "laboratories of democracy." Justice Louis D. Brandeis explained his celebrated characterization: "It is one of the happy incidents of the federal system that a single courageous state may, if its citizens choose, serve as a laboratory; and try novel social and economic experiments without risk to the rest of the country" (*New State Ice Co. v. Liebmann* 1932). As David Osborne argues, this rationale has "little to do with ideology"—no one ever went to the barricades for laboratories of democracy—and "everything to do with trial-and-error, seat-of-the-pants pragmatism" (Osborne 1988: 3). Not only do laboratories allow experiments in the effectiveness and efficiency of policy innovation, but they also provide market testing of the innovation's popularity.

The laboratory metaphor requires autonomy for states to try different policies, and it offers clear support for not federalizing policies from the outset.[18] It also implies that there exist better and worse ways to run government, or at least some aspects of government. It suggests, further, that states should educate themselves about best practices—and perhaps even that there is one best practice in a given sphere and that federal intervention might impose the practice once experimental state results are complete.[19] This rationale is quite different from the states' rights philosophy, and some of today's most ardent advocates of states' rights federalism dislike the laboratory analogy. They prefer to emphasize individual liberty, state diversity, and independent state representation of local values for their own sake rather than any suggestion that states should learn from other states (Greve 2001b).

Recent federal policy in health care suggests some laboratory-like policymaking. Much state innovation in Medicaid occurs under research and demonstration waivers of federal rules—and with requirements that the results be studied.[20] Federal policy has also embraced some state-pioneered policies, like the now-abandoned national health planning scheme. The diagnosis-related group (DRG) method of hospital payment was tested in New Jersey under a federal waiver, then modified and implemented nationally for Medicare in 1983. Other states have opted to use aspects of DRGs for Medicaid hospital payment (Fetter, Brand, and Gamache 1991).

States may learn various things from one another—what policies achieve a shared goal, how to improve their administration of a benefit program, how to sue tobacco companies or defend welfare rights lawsuits, how to obtain more federal dollars under Medicaid rules, how to use mandatory managed care as a Medicaid reform, or which patient protection provisions to legislate. Yet, some policies may be too idiosyncratic to transfer to other states. There may also be considerable barriers to entry in the form of political reluctance in state B to overtly adopt policies from state A (Oliver and Paul-Shaheen 1997). Home-grown solutions are often preferred.

A second pragmatic argument for state control is that some activities work better when implemented from the bottom up rather than from the top down. K–12 education is a classic example (Peterson 1995; Rivlin 1992). Teaching faces very different challenges, depending on the region and populations served, as well as the workforce and resources available. States devolve responsibility for K–12 education to localities, which receive substantial state funding and some federal assistance.

Administration of health care programs can also call for officials to know the territory, though not always. To implement the Medicaid policy of mandatory beneficiary enrollment in managed care organizations, for example, state administrators needed detailed understanding of the organizations' structures, the service areas of their providers, their means of ensuring quality, their experience with low-income populations, and public perceptions of the organizations' performance.[21] Subsidizing employer-sponsored insurance premiums for families under SCHIP or Medicaid waivers is another example of a policy whose administration may take detailed, case-specific knowledge.

Implementation from the bottom up also takes into account local values and helps engender local enthusiasm for a program. Peterson argues that successful developmental programs typically require some initiative from the individuals directly involved. Federal mandates for such programs cannot succeed if local administration is indifferent or even hostile (Peterson 1995). Alice Rivlin argues that real progress in K–12 education depends on committed grassroots action (Rivlin 1992).

In this view, decentralized control promotes engagement and improves operations. States' control over SCHIP design and implementation may explain why they often take more pride in—and more political credit for—designing, administering, and even naming their SCHIPs than in running the much larger Medicaid program. Peterson and Rivlin might expect SCHIP to perform better than Medicaid, but SCHIP's largely federal funding could make states less careful about administering the programs. Lax state accountability was one of the arguments used to end Nixonian revenue sharing. Much depends upon how things play out in practice.

Whether the focus is local knowledge or local values, from-the-bottom-up pragmatism echoes the Jeffersonian philosophy that smaller is better. It differs from Jefferson's philosophy in that it allocates responsibility on a case-by-case basis, thus implying that some matters are not local and that implementation from the top down may sometimes be superior.

A third practical argument is that some problems are inherently local, and neither costs nor benefits spill over to neighbors. In such cases, each community should decide on its own what to do. This rationale is highly case-specific. Peterson explains that with localized decisions, playgrounds can be concentrated where young children are abundant, recreation centers for senior citizens can be clustered in adult communities, and parks can be maintained with varying degrees of formality, depending on local tastes (Peterson, Rabe, et al. 1986: 11). In each of those activities, people from outside the affected community have little interest in dictating policy or in paying for local decisions. Note, however, that these examples all suggest local rather than state decisionmaking, and localities are not formally part of the U.S. federal system.

Finally, a very common stereotype is often asserted in favor of state administration: The federal bureaucracy is not only distant from the grass roots, it is also bloated, inefficient, slow, and inflexible (Sperry 2000). The argument typically assumes that states are more efficient, though evidence is sparse. Having 50 state administrations can be quite cumbersome, particularly in situations where they must constantly reinvent the wheel or their standards must be harmonized to be effective. Indeed, for some activities, such as buying pharmaceuticals, states may actively seek to join in federal discounts or to join regional purchasing pools to achieve economies of scale and market share. Similarly, state insurance regulators pool expertise and some financial monitoring capabilities through the National Association of Insurance Commissioners.

PRACTICAL RATIONALES FAVORING FEDERAL RESPONSIBILITY

One practical argument for greater federal responsibility is that some problems or solutions are inherently national in scope. Their costs and benefits cross state boundaries or are common to all states. The framers of the Constitution recognized several national functions, including national defense, foreign and interstate commerce, printing of money, granting of patents, and postal services. Others have become national since then—notably immigration, monetary policy and economic management, securities regulation, and Social Security. In health care, oversight of pharmaceutical safety and effectiveness, biomedical research, and Medicare (with an assist from state Medicaid programs) are generally accepted as federal responsibilities.

Health care for low-income children, regardless of other family characteristics, appears to be an area of growing national agreement, partly on ethical grounds, partly pragmatic. A core argument for its being a national responsibility is that healthy children are more likely to develop into productive adults—and generating human and social capital is an interest that transcends state boundaries. Health insurance coverage of low-income adults is less generally agreed upon, and much greater state-to-state variation in their coverage is accepted.

A second practical argument holds that solving some problems requires the greater fiscal capacity of the federal government. Natural disasters may be highly localized, but their enormous costs can overwhelm local resources. Governors of all political persuasions show little hesitation in asking for federal disaster assistance. The federal government's deep pockets come partly from lack of governmental competition at the national level, progressive taxation, large-scale operations, and the ability to print and borrow money and hence continue spending even in deficit.[22]

A third, related argument for federal power is that many public programs, including welfare and Medicaid, seek to redistribute resources,[23] and the federal government is the "most competent agent of redistribution" (Peterson 1995: 27). The larger the jurisdiction, the more broadly it can pool resources and ameliorate the risk of illness or declines in income across its population. Thus, California has more capacity to redistribute income and other resources than the District of Columbia. Only federal action can pool resources across state lines, as states cannot be expected to lessen disparities among themselves by sending one another benefits checks (Rich and White 1996). Economic interdependence and redistributive federal policies have reduced cross-state differences in residents' well-being, but they remain "striking" (Dye 1990: 17). High-income states in 1999 had twice the per capita income of their low-income brethren, although the advantage lessened somewhat when adjusted for wealthier states' higher costs of living.

The federal government faces little danger of taxpayer or capital flight, and it can control the in-migration of beneficiaries. The federal ability to spend in deficit enables the national government—and only the national government—to adopt countercyclical spending to boost a recessionary economy and mitigate individual losses of jobs or health care (Oates 1972).[24] Such spending not only manages the economy but also redistributes resources from times of plenty to times of shortage. States, in contrast, see their fiscal capacity shrink during a downturn, even as needs increase.

Leaving redistribution to states can also be seen as creating unintended negative consequences, given interstate competition. Low-tax, low-benefit states can export some or all of their needy populations and prevent voter-taxpayers in more generous states from being able to afford the amount of redistribution they would prefer (Oates 1972: 8). Such unintended consequences may be much less direct than, say, exporting water or air pollution, but the argument for minimum national standards is similar.

A fourth argument for federal responsibility is that the national government can ameliorate substate problems created by disparities in states' spending. Federal monies can flow to individuals, local service providers, or local governments on a consistent basis across states. Health care examples include funding for community health clinics and extra Medicare payments to hospitals that serve a disproportionate share of low-income people. Federal payments can treat two local institutions the same, even if they are on opposite sides of a state border. When states have discretion in administering their own and federal funds, as they do under Medicaid, wide differences in funding of local needs naturally result.

Finally, in years past, it was often stereotypically asserted that federal administration was simply better than state administration. The federal government could attract the best and the brightest from a national pool of talent, offering them higher pay and more rewarding career paths. Federal legislative and executive staff seemed more numerous and more professional than their state counterparts. States were seen as less capable and more prone to corruption and scandal. Especially before the civil rights era, states' rights could serve as code for racial prejudice and official segregation, and state legislative districting underrepresented growing urban and suburban populations. Federal behavior, in contrast, was seen as more open to scrutiny and discipline by well-funded national interest groups and a competitive national press corps. This stereotype is largely discredited today, although state pay and professionalism vary greatly across states.[25] State innovations sometimes help shape federal policy.

Case-by-case pragmatic assessments have led thinkers like Peterson and Rivlin to favor a systematic sorting out of public responsibilities. The framers of the Constitution engaged in sorting out, based not only on principles but also on their experience with the English crown and post-colonial states. The process led them to assign the federal government authority over several cross-state functions.

Existing allocations between state and federal responsibility seem only roughly sorted. For example, public health functions such as monitoring and controlling contagious disease and bioterrorism seem logically federal. Yet, although federal involvement has grown over time through the Centers for Disease Control and Prevention, the principal responsibility remains with state and local governments. Immigration policy is national, and states do not patrol their own borders. Yet for uninsured immigrants' health care, federal rules have sought to reduce federal Medicaid funds for both legal and undocumented immigrants, leaving most burdens on states and localities (Ku and Coughlin 1997).

Conclusion

This chapter has reviewed the major philosophical, competitive, and practical arguments favoring greater state or federal responsibilities under U.S. federalism. Examined closely, the arguments and the history suggest that issues related to government allocations of authority are resolved along two axes: ideology and pragmatism.

Ideology and Pragmatism

One axis of attitudes about federalism is ideological. At each end of this axis lies a complex of strong political values and related beliefs about how the world does and should work and what creates human well-being.

At the right edge is systematic mistrust of government, especially the distant and too powerful federal government. This edge has four core beliefs. First, individual freedom is the key to a good life and good government. Second, free competition creates human happiness as well as economic productivity and efficiency. Third, government intervention is undesirable, especially in the form of redistributive programs, which tax productive citizens and reduce their freedom without providing direct benefits. Fourth, state loyalty transcends national citizenship (a belief that is much less influential today than in the past).[26]

The left edge of the ideological axis favors government action to improve citizens' welfare and tends to favor federal over state action because the federal government has greater powers. Core values are community, both national and local; equity among community members; and appreciation for government's ability to promote well-being and reduce inequalities. Advocates of these values often support the right of individuals to control their own health care but think that rights without resources are not meaningful; hence, they favor public action to enhance individual autonomy in seeking care.

At the extremes, advocates favor either state or federal responsibility almost regardless of the policy at issue. A large middle ground shares some of each extreme's ideological beliefs but is willing to compromise on most issues most of the time.

The other axis is pragmatic. Policy issues (problems and solutions) are arrayed along the axis from local matters at the bottom to national matters at the top. Location on the axis depends on the nature of the issue and the evidence gained from experience. People who analyze policy problems and solutions along this axis are not ideological about federalism: They are not predisposed to favor one level of government over another. Rather, they sort out responsibilities according to the nature of problems and their solutions. They may favor states as laboratories for experiments in public policy, deciding afterwards which approaches worked best and whether federal intervention should generalize the best practices. For most pragmatists, performance is what matters; they take the policy goals as givens and then ask which level of government could best achieve it.

Two questions must be answered before an issue or some aspect of it is deemed state or federal on practical grounds. First, what is the nature of the problem? If it is largely local—that is, if its costs are contained entirely within state borders and are not likely to move, if local knowledge and values matter a lot in determining whether there actually is a problem, and if other Americans have little interest in it—then arguments for relying on state action are strong (although states may choose to delegate responsibility to localities). If the problem's costs spill across state boundaries, if outsiders care greatly about the fate of local people affected, and if the problem is similar across geographic areas, then it is more likely to be considered federal.

Second, what is the nature of potential solutions? If crafting and implementing a solution requires detailed local knowledge, if successful administration requires enthusiastic local participation, if costs are manageable in relation to state resources, if benefits accrue mainly to the locality, and if benefits consist mainly of promoting local development, then the issue seems local. If the same program can work across geographic areas with equal effectiveness, if the solution consists of redistributing resources (especially countercyclically), if solutions are very expensive, if people across jurisdictions care about equality of operations or effects, then the issue is apt to be seen as federal.

Finally, a different kind of federalism pragmatist holds more absolute views—not about federalism but about some other value. Such pragmatists have no interest in sorting out responsibilities according to the nature of problems and solutions or in observing the practical performance of different states. They decide which level of government they favor based on what they expect that government to do (or not do) about a policy of great concern to them. Their decisions often vary with the prevailing political or economic climate.

This type of pragmatism can yield ironic juxtapositions of political stances. For example, some people supported waivers of federal Medicaid rules in the latter 1990s because states were using the waivers to expand beyond normal federal health insurance coverage; the same people oppose waivers now because states facing budget pressures can use waivers to cut back on eligibility and services. Liberals who want more federal regulation of managed care plans may also want increased state judicial authority so that managed care organizations can be sued more easily. Conservatives who want less federal regulation of managed care plans may want federal judicial authority because they believe the federal courts will be more sympathetic to managed care organizations. Some policymakers support more state control over Medicaid in the name of preserving the diversity of states' preferences, yet simultaneously favor a federal ban that prohibits any state from using Medicaid to fund abortions. Such observations do not detract from the importance of understanding the rationales of federalism. They merely recognize that other values are also important.

Almost by definition, categorizing an issue or a program as state or federal on the pragmatic axis mainly influences political decisionmakers in the middle ground of the ideological axis. Those at the extreme edges typically know in advance which level of government they want in charge. Contrariwise, when pragmatic analysis generates no consensus that an issue is state or federal—it could readily be either—the voices of those philosophically committed to one or the other level of government will probably be more influential.

The Central Importance of Pragmatism

The United States exists today because the pragmatic middle invented federalism to reconcile states' rights and a centralized government in a way that allowed contemporary compromise and evolution over time. In more than 200 years, ideologues favoring extreme nationalization or full decentralization have never prevailed.[27] Indeed, there has been no truly major sorting out of functions since the Constitution was ratified. Even the 1996 devolution revolution, designed to "end welfare as we know it," retained substantial federal funding obligations and limited states' authority to drop people from Medicaid rolls.

What has evolved instead of sorted-out federalism is philosophically untidy, often collaborative federalism, especially for low-income people. Shared health programs for the poor (such as Medicaid and SCHIP) dwarf purely federal efforts (such as grants for community health centers) and state-only programs (such as health insurance coverage for people who are ineligible for Medicaid).[28]

Budgetary outcomes suggest that mixed federalism has been a great success. The relative importance of federal and state initiatives has shifted over time, as have funding responsibilities and the extent of national minimum standards. Understanding the most recent shifts in shared federal-state responsibility is important. Improved knowledge about operations and their effects helps observers assess future changes, whether they take the form of further incremental adjustments or larger reallocations.

The Importance of Performance in Pragmatism

On examination, it is clear that the "distant" federal government can operate very locally when the national interest is clear—for example, delivering mail (including Social Security checks) to every household and investigating outbreaks of communicable diseases in local communities. States sometimes, though less frequently, operate nationally through interstate compacts to buy pharmaceuticals, regulate out-of-state insurers, or enforce one another's traffic tickets. Moreover, it is clear that Americans in the vast middle ground of political culture accept the need for health programs to operate under shared federal-state responsibility.

Equal access to health care is not a nationally shared value or an attribute of citizenship, but a minimum floor of assistance for some groups does appear to be. Federal money is critical to building that floor, and such funds inevitably come with at least a few strings attached. However, policymakers seem open to discussing just how many strings are vital to good performance.

For the mainstream of American pragmatists, therefore, the critical question is how well their governments perform under different arrangements. Actual examination of performance relative to policy objectives is a key input to Medicaid and other programs with national implications.

NOTES

1. Salamon (1989) cites particular sources that are directly on point; for considerable bibliographic material, see Ladenheim (1999, 2000).

2. U.S. Constitution, Amendments XIII–XVII. This broad-brush summary of political-constitutional development leaves detailed explanations to other scholars. See, for example, Tribe (2000). This chapter generally omits discussion of judicial developments.

3. Half the states began within Medicaid's first year. By the 1970s, all but Alaska and Arizona participated (Stevens and Stevens 1970). Arizona joined in 1982 when allowed to do so with a waiver to provide services through managed care at bid-upon prices (Arizona Health Care Cost Containment System 2001; Christianson, Hillman, and Smith 1983).

4. New York's implementation would have made 45 percent of the state's population eligible, almost exhausting the budget federal planners had anticipated for the entire nation (Stevens and Stevens 1970). The Social Security Amendments of 1967 barred federal assistance for eligibles with incomes greater than 133 1/3 percent of the state's cash welfare assistance (Public Law 90-248, Section 220).

5. Social Security Amendments of 1969, Public Law 91-56, Section 2; Social Security Act of 1972, Public Law 92-603, Section 320.

6. The percentages are of own-source revenues, not accounting for federal-state transfers, and include social insurance contributions (Shannon 1994).

7. By 2001, the federal share was almost one-third; the state share has remained just above 13 percent (Centers for Medicare and Medicaid Services 2001).

8. The State and Local Assistance Act of 1972 initially delivered about $4 billion per year in matching funds to states and municipalities. The program distributed some $83 billion before it ended under President Reagan in 1986 (Public Broadcasting Service 1997).

9. Federal SCHIP legislation was part of the Balanced Budget Act of 1997, Public Law 105-33, August 5. See Bruen and Ullman (1998); Centers for Medicare and Medicaid Services (2002); and Chapter 9 of this volume.

10. Commerce Clearing House, Medicare-Medicaid Guide ¶12,310, Certification of Provider or Supplier (undated, continuously updated online resource, accessible by subscription at http://health.cch.com/).

11. It has been argued that most institutions "belong" to their communities (Sparer and Brown 1996: 197).

12. The sentiment is often attributed to Thomas Jefferson or Thomas Paine, but the precise words begin Henry David Thoreau's tract "Civil Disobedience," arguing not for federalism but for principled resistance to any governmental authority believed to be contrary to individual beliefs.

13. Just as libertarian ideals often relate to "small is better" government, so communitarian beliefs emphasize the need for collective action at various levels of government. See the Communitarian Network's web site, http://www.gwu.edu/~ccps. (Accessed October 21, 2002.)

14. Two close observers of Medicaid titled Chapter 3 of their book "The Federal Role: An Aphilosophical Expansion" (Stevens and Stevens 1974).

15. In the terminology of a leading theorist, voters exercise their political "voice," while movers have influence through "exit" (or threat of exit) (Hirschman 1970).

16. See the Kaiser Family Foundation, "State Health Facts Online," http://www.statehealthfacts.kff.org. (Accessed October 21, 2002.)

17. Ethicist John Rawls propounded an influential philosophical principle for redistribution: A just society should treat its needy citizens as though all citizens had to decide on redistributive policies in ignorance of whether each of their lives would turn out to require them to contribute resources or to receive benefits. Deciding on social redistribution with knowledge of whether one will gain or lose is less just, in this view (Rawls 1971).

18. Two other potential readings of the labs metaphor have also been suggested— that of joint state study and of social science participation in studies of governance (Sparer and Brown 1996).

19. It seems no accident that Justice Brandeis used the laboratory analogy in a dissenting opinion in favor of governmental power to regulate private business. Nor can one ignore the fact that it was made in 1932, on the eve of the New Deal, in the midst of the Great Depression that had brought strong demands for national action. President Roosevelt later threatened to expand the size of the Supreme Court in order to appoint more justices friendly to public power, but he got his way through attrition instead (Leuchtenburg 1995).

20. See Chapter 8. Usually waivers result from state initiatives, but states sometimes respond to federal encouragement—quite a departure from the original Brandeis formulation.

21. Medicare may also move toward managed care organizations nationally but by offering local beneficiary choice.

22. States and even localities can to some extent borrow money in times of deficit, despite rules against running deficits. When they do, however, they must pay interest to outside investors, with an attendant loss of local welfare, as Oates observes; national debts are owed mainly to national citizen-investors (Oates 1972: 6).

23. This is textbook public finance; see, for example, Musgrave and Musgrave (1989).

24. Deficit spending to stimulate an economy in recession has won wide practical acceptance, at least since President Nixon, in discussing a stimulative budget,

proclaimed himself a Keynesian. See http://www.time.com/time/time100/scientist /profile/keynes03.html and http://www.house.gov/jec/fiscal/budget/surplus2/surplus2 .htm#endnot10. (Accessed October 21, 2002.)

25. See, however, Wishnie (2000).

26. According to the 2000 census, just under 60 percent of U.S. residents were born in their state of residence (U.S. Census/Factfinder QT-02. "Profile of Selected Social Characteristics: 2000," accessible from http://factfinder.census.gov). How much cross-boundary migration affects citizen identification cannot be known with certainty.

27. Compromise may prevail because "It is a truism that the American middle class is politically decisive and only occasionally ideological" (Bovbjerg 1988: 234; see also Shannon 1994 [arguing that the federal role remains large at this stage because of the moderation of a large middle class that benefits from many federal programs]).

28. There is also a major role in health care for a local safety net to serve as a provider of last resort. Free care for the poor from public and other hospitals is paid for mainly through transfers of federal and state funds (Hadley and Holahan 2003).

REFERENCES

American Enterprise Institute for Public Policy Research (AEI). 2002. "The Federalism Project." http://www.federalismproject.org. (Accessed October 21, 2002.)

Anton, Thomas. 1997. "New Federalism and Intergovernmental Fiscal Relationships: The Implications for Health Policy." *Journal of Health Politics, Policy, and Law* 22(3): 671–720.

Arizona Health Care Cost Containment System. 2001 "Beginnings and Future of AHCCCS." Chapter 1 in 2001 AHCCCS Overview. http://www.ahcccs.state.az.us /publications/overview/2001/chapter1/chap1_2001.asp. (Accessed October 21, 2002.)

Articles of Confederation. 1777. Agreed to by Congress November 15, 1777; fully ratified March 1, 1781. Text accessible online from The Avalon Project, Yale Law School. http://www.yale.edu/lawweb/avalon/artconf.htm. (Accessed October 21, 2002.)

Beam, David, R., Timothy J. Conlan, and David B. Walker. 1983. "Federalism: The Challenge of Conflicting Theories and Contemporary Practice." In *Political Science: State of the Discipline,* edited by Ada Finifter (247–79). Washington, D.C.: American Political Science Association.

Beer, Samuel. 1997. *To Make a Nation: The Rediscovery of American Federalism.* London: Belknap Press.

Black, Duncan. 1958. *Theory of Committees and Elections.* Cambridge, England: Cambridge University Press.

Bovbjerg, Randall R. 1988. "New Directions for Health Planning." In *Cost, Quality, and Equity in Health Care: New Roles for Health Planning in a Competitive Environment,* edited by Frank A. Sloan, James F. Blumstein, and James M. Perrin (206–34). San Francisco: Jossey-Bass.

Bovbjerg, Randall R., and Barbara A. Davis. 1983. "States' Responses to Federal Health Care 'Block Grants': The First Year." *Milbank Memorial Fund Quarterly* 61(4): 523–60.

Bovbjerg, Randall R., and John Holahan. 1982. *Medicaid in the Reagan Era: Federal Policy and State Choices.* Washington, D.C.: Urban Institute Press.

Bruen, Brian K., and Frank C. Ullman. 1998. "Children's Health Insurance Programs: Where States Are, Where They Are Headed." Washington, D.C.: The Urban Institute. *Assessing the New Federalism* Policy Brief A-20.

Buchanan, James M., and Gordon Tullock. 1962. *The Calculus of Consent: Logical Foundations of a Constitutional Democracy.* Ann Arbor: University of Michigan Press.

Cato Institute. 2002. "Constitutional Studies: Federalism." http://www.catoinstitute.com /ccs/federalism.html. (Accessed October 21, 2002.)

Centers for Medicare and Medicaid Services. 2001. "Health Accounts, Historical National Health Expenditures by Type of Service and Source of Funds: Calendar Years 1960–2001." http://cms.hhs.gov/statistics/nhe. (Accessed October 21, 2002.)

————. 2002. "State Children's Health Insurance Program." http://cms.hhs.gov/schip. (Accessed October 21, 2002.)

Christianson, Jon B., Diane G. Hillman, and Kenneth R. Smith. 1983. "The Arizona Experiment: Competitive Bidding for Indigent Medical Care." *Health Affairs* 2(3): 87–103.

Clinton, Bill. 1996. "State of the Union Address." January 23. http://www.washingtonpost.com/wp-srv/politics/special/states/docs/sou96.htm. (Accessed October 21, 2002.)

Conlan, Timothy. 1988. *New Federalism: Intergovernmental Reform from Nixon to Reagan.* Washington, D.C.: The Brookings Institution.

Derbyshire, J. Denis, and Ian Derbyshire. 1996. *Political Systems of the World.* New York: St. Martin's Press.

DiZerega, Gus. 1994. "Federalism, Self-Organization, and the Dissolution of the State." *Telos* 100: 57–86.

Dye, Thomas R. 1990. *American Federalism: Competition Among Governments.* Lexington, Mass.: Lexington Books.

Elazar, Daniel J. 1966. *American Federalism: A View from the States.* New York: Thomas Y. Crowell.

————. 1997. "Contrasting Unitary and Federal Systems." *International Political Science Review* 18(3): 237–51.

Fetter, Robert, David Brand, and Dianne Gamache. 1991. *DRGs: Their Design and Development.* Ann Arbor, Mich.: Health Administration Press.

Gingrich, Newt, Dick Armey, and the House Republicans. 1994. *Contract with America.* Edited by Ed Gillespie and Bob Schellhas. New York: Times Books.

Greve, Michael S. 2001a. "Conservatives Should Stop Getting Bogged Down in 'States' Rights.'" *Weekly Standard.* January 29. http://www.aei.org/ra/ragrev010129.htm. (Accessed October 21, 2002.)

Greve, Michael S. 2001b. "Laboratories of Democracy: Anatomy of a Metaphor." AEI Federalist Outlook. Washington, D.C.: American Enterprise Institute/The Federalism Project. May, No. 6. http://www.federalismproject.org/outlook/5-2001.html. (Accessed October 27, 2001.)

Hadley, Jack, and John Holahan. 2003. *Who Pays and How Much? The Cost of Caring for the Uninsured.* Menlo Park, Calif.: Henry J. Kaiser Family Foundation.

Hirschman, Albert O. 1970. *Exit, Voice, and Loyalty: Responses to Decline in Firms, Organizations, and States.* Cambridge, Mass.: Harvard University Press.

Johnson, Lyndon B. 1964. "Remarks at the University of Michigan" [The "Great Society" speech]. National Archives and Records Administration, The Lyndon B. Johnson Library and Museum. May 22. http://www.lbjlib.utexas.edu/johnson/archives.hom /speeches.hom/640522.htm. (Accessed November 5, 2001.)

Ku, Leighton, and Teresa A. Coughlin. 1997. "How the New Welfare Reform Law Affects Medicaid." Washington, D.C.: The Urban Institute. *Assessing the New Federalism* Policy Brief A-5.

Ladenheim, Kala. 1999, 2000. "U.S. Federalism Site." http://www.min.net/~kala/fed. (Prepared within George Washington University School of Business and Public Management; last modified October 12, 2000; accessed October 21, 2002.)

Leuchtenburg, William E. 1995. *The Supreme Court Reborn: The Constitutional Revolution in the Age of Roosevelt.* New York: Oxford University Press.

Lijphart, Arend. 1999. *Patterns of Democracy: Government Forms and Performance in Thirty-Six Countries.* New Haven, Conn.: Yale University Press.

Madison, James. 1787. "Federalist Paper #51." In *The Federalist Papers.* New York: Modern Library.

Musgrave, Richard A., and Peggy B. Musgrave. 1989. *Public Finance in Theory and Practice,* 5th ed. New York: McGraw-Hill.

New State Ice Co. v. Liebmann. 1932. 285 U.S. 262.

Nixon, Richard M. 1970. "Annual Message to the Congress on the State of the Union." January 22. The Richard Nixon Library & Birthplace Foundation, Public Papers of President Richard Nixon. http://www.nixonfoundation.org/Research_Center /1970_pdf_files/1970_0009.pdf. (Accessed November 5, 2001.)

————. 1971. "Annual Message to the Congress on the State of the Union." January 22. The Richard Nixon Library & Birthplace Foundation, Public Papers of President Richard Nixon. http://www.nixonfoundation.org/Research_Center/1971_pdf_files /1971_0026.pdf. (Accessed April 9, 2003.)

North Carolina Chapter of the National Emergency Number Association. 2003. Home web page. http://www.ncnena.org. (Accessed February 3, 2003.)

North Carolina v. Califano. 1978. 445 F. Supp. 532 (Eastern Dist. NC 1977), judgment affirmed, 435 U.S. 962.

Nozick, Robert. 1974. *Anarchy, State, and Utopia.* New York: Basic Books.

Oates, Wallace. 1972. *Fiscal Federalism.* New York: Harcourt Brace Jovanovich.

Oliver, Thomas R., and Pamela Paul-Shaheen. 1997. "Translating Ideas into Actions: Entrepreneurial Leadership in State Health Care Reforms." *Journal of Health Politics, Policy, and Law* 22(3): 721–88.

Osborne, David. 1988. *Laboratories of Democracy.* Boston: Harvard Business School Press.

Peterson, George E., Randall R. Bovbjerg, Barbara A. Davis, Walter G. Davis, Eugene C. Durman, and Theresa A. Gullo. 1986. *The Reagan Block Grants: What Have We Learned?* Washington, D.C.: Urban Institute Press.

Peterson, Paul. 1981. *City Limits.* Chicago: University of Chicago Press.

————. 1995. *The Price of Federalism.* Washington, D.C.: The Brookings Institution.

Peterson, Paul E., Barry G. Rabe, and Kenneth K. Wong. 1986. *When Federalism Works.* Washington, D.C.: The Brookings Institution.

Posner, Paul. 1998. *The Politics of Unfunded Mandates: Whither Federalism?* Washington, D.C.: Georgetown University Press.

President's Commission for the Study of Ethical Problems in Medicine and Biomedical and Behavioral Research. 1983. *Securing Access to Health Care, Volume One: Report, The Ethical Implications of Differences in the Availability of Health Services.* Washington, D.C.: U.S. Government Printing Office.

Public Broadcasting Service. 1997. "American Experience: The Presidents—Nixon, Domestic Policy." http://www.pbs.org/wgbh/amex/presidents/nf/featured/nixon /nixondp.html. (Accessed October 21, 2002.)

Rawls, John. 1971. *A Theory of Justice.* Cambridge, Mass.: Harvard University Press.

Reagan, Ronald. 1981. "First Inaugural Address." January 20. http://www.bartleby.com /124/pres61.html. (Accessed October 21, 2002.)

———. 1982. "First State of the Union Address." January 26. http://www.reagan2000 .com/1982FirstStateoftheUnion.asp. (Accessed October 21, 2002.)

Rich, Robert, and William White. 1996. "Health Care Policy and the American States: Issues of Federalism." In *Health Policy, Federalism, and the American States,* edited by Robert Rich and William White (3–38). Washington, D.C.: Urban Institute Press.

Rivlin, Alice. 1992. *Reviving the American Dream: The Economy, the States, and the Federal Government.* Washington, D.C.: The Brookings Institution.

Salamon, Lester M., ed. 1989. *Beyond Privatization: The Tools of Government Action.* Washington, D.C.: Urban Institute Press.

Schram, Sanford F., and Samuel H. Beer, eds. 2000. *Welfare Reform: A Race to the Bottom.* Baltimore: Johns Hopkins University Press.

Shannon, John. 1994. "Reflections on the Fourth Stage of Federalism." Washington, D.C.: The Urban Institute.

Sparer, Michael, and Lawrence Brown. 1996. "The Limits and Lessons of Laboratory Federalism." In *Health Policy, Federalism, and the American States,* edited by Robert Rich and William White (181–202). Washington, D.C.: Urban Institute Press.

Sperry, Peter B. 2000. "Federal Spending: Governing Less to Govern Best." In *Issues 2000: The Candidate's Briefing Book,* edited by Stuart M. Butler and Kim R. Holmes (1–32). Washington, D.C.: Heritage Foundation. http://www.heritage.org/issues /pdf/issues2000.pdf. (Accessed October 29, 2001.)

Stevens, Robert B., and Rosemary Stevens. 1974. *Welfare Medicine in America: A Case Study of Medicaid.* New York: Free Press.

Stevens, Rosemary, and Robert B. Stevens. 1970. "Medicaid: Anatomy of a Dilemma." *Journal of Law and Contemporary Problems* 35(2): 348–425.

Stewart, William. 1984. *Concepts of Federalism.* Lanham, Md.: Center for the Study of Federalism and University Press of America.

Tribe, Laurence H. 2000. *American Constitutional Law,* 3d ed. New York.: Foundation Press.

Uccello, Cori, and L. Jerome Gallagher. 1997. "General Assistance Programs: The State-Based Part of the Safety Net." Washington, D.C.: The Urban Institute. *Assessing the New Federalism* Policy Brief A-4.

Urban-Brookings Tax Policy Center. 2002. "Tax Facts, State." Washington, D.C.: The Urban Institute and Brookings Institution. http://www.taxpolicycenter.org /TaxFacts/state/sales_tax.cfm. (Accessed October 21, 2002.)

U.S. Department of Health and Human Services. 2000. "Federal Financial Participation in State Assistance Expenditures for October 1, 2000, through September 30, 2001." *Federal Register* 65(36): 8979–80.

U.S. House of Representatives. 2000. Committee on Ways and Means. *The 2000 Green Book: Background Material and Data on Programs within the Jurisdiction of the Committee on Ways and Means*, 17th ed., October 6. Accessible through http://aspe.hhs.gov/2000gb.

Walker, David B. 2000. *The Rebirth of Federalism*. 2d ed. New York: Seven Bridges Press.

Weil, Alan, and Kenneth Finegold, eds. 2002. *Welfare Reform: The Next Act*. Washington, D.C.: Urban Institute Press.

Wiener, Joshua M. 1996. "Medicaid and the 'New Federalism.'" Washington, D.C.: The Urban Institute. *Assessing the New Federalism* Policy and Research Report No. 28.

Wishnie, Michael J. 2000. "Laboratories of Bigotry? Devolution of the Immigration Power, Equal Protection, and Federalism." *NYU Law Review* 76(2): 493–569.

3

Health Care within the Larger State Budget

Donald J. Boyd

Federal and state governments fund many health programs jointly, creating potential conflicts between federal and state preferences and straining relations between the two levels of government. The federal government has used various federal matching requirements, especially in Medicaid and the State Children's Health Insurance Program (SCHIP), to encourage lower-income states to spend more on health care. It has also encouraged states to continue providing health insurance coverage during hard economic times by making federal support open-ended and making eligibility an entitlement.

Health care is only one of many state responsibilities, however, and states differ markedly in the priority they assign it. Health care competes for resources with other services and investments, as well as with the desire for lower taxes. Tax revolts in a number of states, including California, Colorado, Oregon, and Wisconsin, combined with long-standing resistance to taxes in others, such as Alabama and Texas, make it difficult for states to find money for health care for people who are uninsured or need long-term care.

Despite these difficulties, state governments spend more of their own funds on health care than on any other function except elementary and secondary education; when federal funding is included, states spend more on health care than on any other function, including education. In recent years, spending on health care has been growing more rapidly than states' overall budgets or their tax revenues.

The states experienced extraordinary fiscal windfalls during the 1990s, easing their ability to finance Medicaid and other health care programs. The fiscal boom of the late 1990s turned into a fiscal bust when manufacturing declined, the stock markets fell, and the economy slipped into a recession that was exacerbated by the attacks of September 11. As of this writing, the recession has been mild by some measures, but the fiscal crisis for the states has been quite severe and may have been worsened by uncertainties related to the war in Iraq. Estimated budget gaps of $70 billion to $85 billion for state fiscal year (SFY) 2004 are at least twice as large, as a percentage of revenue, as the budget gaps of the early 1990s, according to a recent analysis by the Center on Budget and Policy Priorities (Lav and Johnson 2003).

After the recession, will state finances boom again? How difficult will it be for states to fund Medicaid and other health care programs?

Health Care and Medicaid in the State Budget

By any measure, health care spending is a driving force in state budgets, and Medicaid is by far the biggest health care program. The importance of Medicaid in the budget varies from state to state and results from policy choices regarding spending and revenues.

Spending on Health Care

State governments spent $239 billion, or 27 percent of their total budgets, on health care services in SFY 1999, the latest year for which detailed data are available (table 3-1). This total includes direct expenditures to cover treatment of physical and mental health conditions, including substance abuse services, but not administrative costs. All expenditures made through state government budgets are included, whether financed by the states' own sources or by the federal government. Finally, the total includes the local share of Medicaid spending in the few states that require such spending but no other local government spending on health care.

Medicaid accounts for $174 billion or about three-quarters of total state government expenditures on health care. State employee health benefits run a distant second, at 8 percent, followed by community-based services

Table 3-1. *State Spending on Health Care, Fiscal Year 1999*

Category	Total State Spending on Health Care			Funding Source (%)		Federally Financed Spending on Health Care		State-Financed Spending on Health Care	
	Amount ($ billions)	Amount as % of Health Total	Amount as % of State Budget	Federal Grants	State Revenue	Amount ($ billions)	Share of Federal Financing (%)	Amount ($ billions)	Share of State Financing (%)
Medicaid	174.2	73.0	19.8	55.2	44.8	96.2	87.2	$78.0	60.9
State employees' health benefits	18.8	7.9	2.1	8.8	91.2	1.7	1.5	17.1	13.4
Community-based services	15.0	6.3	1.7	25.2	74.8	3.8	3.4	11.2	8.8
Public health–related expenditures	13.1	5.5	1.5	46.8	53.2	6.2	5.6	7.0	5.5
State facility–based services	7.5	3.1	0.9	7.7	92.3	0.6	0.5	6.9	5.4
Higher education	5.3	2.2	0.6	22.7	77.3	1.2	1.1	4.1	3.2
Corrections health expenditures	3.0	1.3	0.3	0.7	99.3	0.0	0.0	3.0	2.3
State Children's Health Insurance Program (SCHIP)	1.0	0.4	0.1	68.3	31.7	0.7	0.6	0.3	0.2
Insurance and access expansion	0.6	0.3	0.1	14.6	85.4	0.1	0.1	0.5	0.4
Health care total	238.5	100.0	27.1	46.3	53.7	$110.3	100.0	$128.2	100.0
State budget total	880.3								

Source: The Milbank Memorial Fund, the National Association of State Budget Officers, and the Reforming States Group (2001).

(such as alcohol and drug abuse treatment and community mental health services), and public health–related expenditures (such as child immunization and pharmaceutical assistance for the elderly).

SCHIP, created in 1997, was a very small component of state spending on health in SFY 1999, but it has been growing rapidly since then. Separate information on SCHIP spending shows that it quadrupled from $1 billion in SFY 1999 to $4.2 billion in SFY 2000, and states estimate that by SFY 2002, SCHIP spending had reached $4.7 billion (National Association of State Budget Officers [NASBO] 2002a, table A-2). Even after quadrupling, however, SCHIP accounts for less than 2 percent of state health expenditures.

According to the *1998–1999 State Health Care Expenditure Report* compiled by NASBO, the federal government financed 46 percent of state health expenditures, driven by a federal Medicaid match of 55 percent (table 3-1). (In other sources, discussed later, the reported federal share is closer to 57 percent, and, as Chapter 5 shows, the effective federal share is higher still.)[1] With its large size and relatively high federal matching rate, Medicaid accounted for 87 percent of all federally financed state health expenditures. Although states often proclaim Medicaid to be a state program, the federal government in fact pays the majority of the cost.

The second- and third-largest federal categories were public health–related services and community-based services. These top three categories accounted for 96 percent of federally financed state government spending on health. They also represent 96 percent of state-financed health spending.

The federal share of health spending varies significantly across categories. It is highest for SCHIP, with an average of 68 percent. SCHIP has been very popular among the states, in part because the large federal contribution has enabled them to address an issue that has great public support without using very much of their own money. Even after having quadrupled by SFY 2002, state-financed SCHIP spending amounted to only about 0.2 percent of all state-financed spending in state budgets.[2]

The federal share is lowest for corrections health expenditures, at less than 1 percent. Such spending is a relatively small element in state budgets (it was larger than SCHIP in SFY 1999 and is perhaps of comparable size now), but it is growing rapidly because of the aging inmate population and the relatively high incidence of diseases that require expensive treatments, such as AIDS and hepatitis. The next-smallest federal share, at about 8 percent, is for community services, such as alcohol and drug abuse treatment and community mental health services.

When all major elements and sources of health spending are aggregated, states spent more on health care than on any other function of state government, exceeding even the $197 billion spent on elementary and secondary education in SFY 1999 (NASBO 2001, table 7).

Spending on Medicaid

In SFY 2002, Medicaid, at $221 billion, accounted for 21 percent of total state spending and was the second-largest element of the average state budget, behind elementary and secondary education (table 3-2). (Data on most other individual components of state health expenditures are not available beyond SFY 1999.)

Interpretation of state Medicaid budget data is not straightforward and should be undertaken with caution. Because of the availability of federal matching funds, states have an incentive to shift existing program costs into Medicaid. In addition, as described in detail in Chapter 5, states have exploited a number of loopholes—most prominently through mechanisms known as disproportionate share hospital (DSH) payments and upper payment limit (UPL) arrangements—to draw down additional federal funds while spending little, if any, of their own money. Thus, Medicaid is a source of revenue as well as an area of spending.

The federal government financed 57 percent of Medicaid spending in SFY 2002, compared with only 19 percent of non-Medicaid programs (computed from table 3-3). States spent 12 percent of their own funds on Medicaid, putting it in third place in overall state spending, after elementary and secondary education and higher education. A substantial portion of higher education spending is financed by tuition payments, which these data generally treat as state-financed expenditures. If tuition-related funds are excluded, state-financed Medicaid appears to be considerably larger than state-financed higher education.[3]

Medicaid plays a larger role in some states' budgets than in others. State-financed Medicaid spending as a share of the total state-financed budget varies considerably, depending on policy choices about the overall generosity of Medicaid, the federal matching rate, success at maximizing federal reimbursement, and policy choices about other components of state spending. In SFY 2002, state-financed Medicaid spending ranged from almost 21 percent of total state-financed spending in Connecticut to just over 4 percent in Alaska (table 4-3).[4] State-financed Medicaid was less than 10 percent of total state-financed spending in 26 states. In states

Table 3-2. State Spending, Fiscal Year 2002

Category	Expenditures ($ billions)			Category as Percentage of All Categories			Federal Funds as Percentage of Total Funds
	State-Financed	Federally Financed	Total	State-Financed	Federal Financed	Total	
Elementary and secondary education	207.4	27.8	235.3	26	10	22	12
Medicaid	94.5	126.8	221.3	12	43	21	57
Higher education	106.1	14.7	120.9	14	5	11	12
Transportation	68.1	27.4	95.4	9	9	9	29
Corrections	38.8	0.9	39.6	5	0	4	2
Public assistance	12.6	10.8	23.4	2	4	2	46
Other	257.9	84.1	342.0	33	29	32	25
Total	785.4	292.5	1,077.9	100	100	100	27

Source: National Association of State Budget Officers (2002a).
Note: Amounts are estimates of 2002 actuals.

Table 3-3. *State-Financed Medicaid as Share of All State-Financed Spending, Fiscal Year 2002*

State	Percent	State	Percent
Connecticut	20.5	Massachusetts	9.8
Ohio	19.5	Virginia	9.7
Pennsylvania	19.3	Nebraska	9.6
Washington	19.1	California	9.6
New Hampshire	18.3	South Dakota	9.4
Tennessee	17.6	South Carolina	9.4
Rhode Island	16.8	Oregon	9.0
Missouri	15.7	Arizona	8.8
New Jersey	14.8	North Dakota	8.8
Illinois	14.0	Idaho	8.3
Georgia	13.5	Kansas	8.0
Florida	12.8	Kentucky	7.6
Texas	12.7	Wisconsin	7.6
Vermont	12.6	Oklahoma	7.4
New York	12.6	West Virginia	7.3
Michigan	12.0	Alabama	7.3
		Wyoming	7.0
U.S. average	12.0	Mississippi	6.9
		Montana	6.8
Indiana	11.8	Iowa	6.7
North Carolina	11.7	Arkansas	6.7
Louisiana	11.6	Delaware	6.3
Minnesota	11.5	New Mexico	5.8
Maine	11.5	Hawaii	5.0
Colorado	10.6	Utah	4.9
Maryland	10.3	Alaska	4.4
Nevada	10.1		

Source: National Association of State Budget Officers (2002a).

Note: Alaska data not available in *2001 State Expenditure Report,* and instead are from *2000 State Expenditure Report,* for fiscal year 2001.

where the Medicaid share of the budget is small, rapid growth in Medicaid spending may not dominate budget debates the way it does in states where the Medicaid share is more prominent. Many of the states with a smaller Medicaid share are in the West and the South, where there may not be as much political support for the program as in the Northeast and in heavily industrialized states.

Policy choices about Medicaid eligibility and benefits vary greatly across states, as do health care needs, poverty, and fiscal capacity. The result is very large differences in spending. The federal government has long attempted to reduce the impact of state fiscal disparities. The Medicaid matching rate is more generous to low-income states than to high-income states—it reimburses Mississippi for approximately 77 percent of Medicaid expenditures, for example, and reimburses Connecticut for only 50 percent.[5] As a result, a dollar of Medicaid services costs Mississippi only 23 cents, but it costs Connecticut 50 cents. Other things being equal, therefore, Mississippi has a greater incentive to finance Medicaid services than Connecticut does. The incentive does not fully offset other factors contributing to state decisions about Medicaid policies and spending, however, and high-income states spend far more in practice than low-income states. Most of the states with very low incomes, notably Arkansas, Mississippi, Montana, and New Mexico, also have very low Medicaid spending per poor person.[6]

State-financed Medicaid is even more skewed toward high-income states, so federal matching appears to have some redistributional impact. Nonetheless, it is clear that other factors are also at work, such as fiscal capacity, poverty and health care needs, political support for Medicaid, possibly efficiency and effectiveness in service delivery, and price differences across states.[7]

Although Medicaid spending and its budgetary importance varies, in most states it is large, growing quickly, and viewed with apprehension because its costs are hard to control. Holahan, Wiener, and Lutzky (2002) note that "pressures for state Medicaid expenditure increases include medical inflation facing the entire health system, increased costs for prescription drugs, demands for higher provider payment rates, expansion of community long-term care, and increased enrollment."

The Medicaid budget is difficult to cut for several reasons:

- Medicaid is an individual entitlement program, and services generally cannot be denied to beneficiaries unless states make explicit and difficult choices to limit eligibility or curtail covered services. While states generally appropriate expenditures under Medicaid as they do other expenditures, Medicaid's entitlement status gives it greater protection in the budget process. In nonentitlement programs, services may be capped by the size of the appropriation; if demand exceeds the amount of money available, services may be reduced pro rata, or people desiring services may be put on waiting lists. With a few exceptions, these approaches are not legally permissible under Medicaid.

- A related issue is that Medicaid spending is countercyclical. In recessions, when state revenue falls and states face fiscal difficulties, spending pressures grow. Holahan and Garrett estimate that an increase in the unemployment rate from 4.5 percent to 5.5 percent would cause the number of Medicaid beneficiaries to increase by 1.5 million, or almost 4 percent, causing Medicaid expenditures nationally to rise by approximately $2.7 billion, or more than 1 percent (Holahan and Garrett 2001).[8]

- The federal government establishes standards for some Medicaid eligibility groups and services, and states cannot make cuts that would violate those standards. For example, the Omnibus Budget Reconciliation Act of 1987 required that nursing homes accepting Medicaid beneficiaries provide round-the-clock licensed practical nurse care and have at least one registered nurse on duty at least eight hours a day, seven days a week.

- Judicial decisions limit state flexibility even further. The Supreme Court's *Olmstead* decision in June 1999, for example, concluded that inappropriate institutionalization of a person with a mental disability may be discrimination under the Americans with Disabilities Act.[9] In effect, the decision requires states to "provide community-based services for people with disabilities if treatment professionals determine that it is appropriate, the affected individuals do not object to such placement, and the state has the available resources to provide community-based services" (Fox Grage et al. 2002: 1).

- High federal matching rates mean that for states to save a dollar in state expenditures, they need to cut services by more than a dollar. For example, if Mississippi cuts Medicaid services by $1, the state will save 23 cents for itself and 77 cents for the federal government. Thus, Mississippi needs to cut Medicaid services by more than $4 to save $1 in state spending. Other states would need to cut services by amounts ranging from $2 to $4 to save $1. In all states, the large cuts that must be imposed to achieve significant state savings are a substantial disincentive for cutting Medicaid. On the other hand, given Medicaid's large size in most states, they still attempt some cuts in difficult fiscal times.

- Medicaid is a source of economic growth. The program and the institutions, activities, and care it supports can have a significant impact on individual communities, especially in low-income rural areas. If a state cuts its spending on Medicaid, it will lose matching funds from the federal government, revenue that the federal government will then use for other purposes and that may not be returned to the state. As a result, the economic benefits from the lost federal aid will be largely lost to a state that cuts Medicaid.[10]
- Powerful constituencies in the health care industry, in the long-term care industry, and among recipients and their advocates often favor continued spending on Medicaid.

Medicaid and the Fiscal Boom of the 1990s

The 1990s opened with a recession that was mild for the nation as a whole but quite severe in some parts of the country, particularly the Northeast and California. States raised taxes by $36 billion in SFY 1990 through 1994; they drew down total fund balances (consisting of year-end fund balances plus balances in budget stabilization funds) from almost 5 percent of expenditures in 1989 to 1 percent in 1991; and they cut spending significantly (National Governors Association and NASBO 2002).

This period of crisis was followed by an extraordinary boom in state finances. State tax revenues repeatedly came in well above projections, and elected officials were in a position that looks especially enviable now. States adopted policies that on their face seemed impossible to achieve in combination: cutting taxes year after year, increasing fund balances to a nearly 20-year high, and increasing spending significantly—all while keeping budgets balanced or in surplus.

Substantial Growth in Spending

State spending increases from SFY 1990 to 2000 were substantial and widespread (figure 3-1).[11] Three results are apparent:

Figure 3-1. *Changes in State Real Per Capita Spending, 1990–2000*

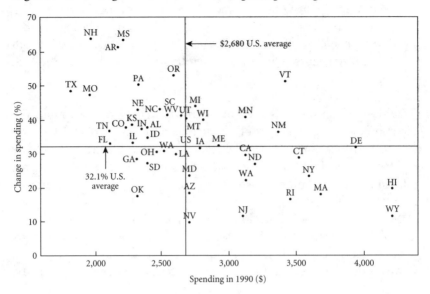

Sources: U.S. Census Bureau; U.S. Bureau of Economic Analysis.

a. Spending is "general expenditures," as defined by and obtained from the U.S. Census Bureau, and population data were obtained from the U.S. Census Bureau.

b. Alaska excluded as outlier.

- States as a whole increased spending significantly—by 32 percent, *after* adjusting for inflation and population growth. Put differently, state government spending per person increased by nearly one-third.
- Almost every state chose to increase spending, usually by a substantial amount: 38 states increased their spending by 25 percent or more. The only state that did not was Alaska (which is not included on the figure); however, Alaska's SFY 1990 real per capita spending, at $10,191, was more than twice that of the second-highest state, Hawaii, and thus it started from a very high level.[12] Several states experienced fiscal difficulty during some part of the boom, but they nonetheless managed to increase their real per capita spending for the decade as a whole.
- Most low-spending states increased spending far more rapidly than high-spending states (the state markers in the figure slope downward and to the right, although the pattern is loose). New Hampshire, which spent 26 percent less than the U.S. average in SFY 1990, led the

way, increasing real per capita spending by 64 percent. Mississippi and Arkansas, at 17 percent and 19 percent below the average in SFY 1990, respectively, also increased state government spending by more than 60 percent.[13] In contrast, states that began the decade with high spending generally increased spending less rapidly than the U.S. average.

While the pace of state government growth in the 1990s was rapid, the direction of change was part of a much longer trend of rising state and local government influence in the federal-state-local fiscal system. State and local governments have increased spending, even after adjusting for inflation and population growth, substantially and almost continuously throughout the post–World War II period (figure 3-2).[14]

Medicaid and K–12 education took turns dominating state finances in the 1990s. In the first half of the decade, Medicaid spending skyrocketed while education spending was subdued; in the second half, Medicaid growth slowed and education spending accelerated (table 3-4). For the

Figure 3-2. *State and Local Real Per Capita Spending, Fiscal Year 1950–2000*

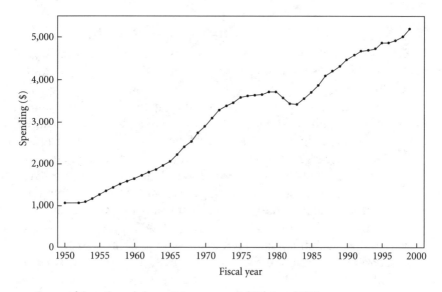

Source: Advisory Commission on Intergovernmental Relations (1994).

Table 3-4. *Growth in State Real Per Capita Spending in the 1990s*

Category	Change (%)		
	1990 to 1995	1995 to 2000	1990 to 2000
Total state spending	20.5	9.6	32.1
Elementary and secondary education	13.2	18.5	34.2
Medical vendor payments	77.6	5.9	88.1
Higher education	11.0	10.8	22.9
Transportation	9.6	9.3	19.8
Corrections	26.1	12.3	41.7
Cash assistance	9.3	(39.8)	(34.2)
All other	14.2	8.8	24.3

Source: Rockefeller Institute analysis of data from U.S. Census Bureau and U.S. Bureau of Economic Analysis.

decade as a whole, real per capita spending on "medical vendor payments" (a U.S. Census Bureau measure that is close in concept to Medicaid) and K–12 education combined accounted for 32 percent of state government spending. The two categories accounted for an even larger share of states' real per capita growth—53 percent.[15] Medical vendor payments grew by an astonishing 88 percent, even after removing the effects of population growth and general inflation (although, as discussed below, this greatly overstates the true impact of Medicaid on state budgets in this period). Real per capita spending on K–12 education grew "only" 34 percent.

Higher education real per capita spending grew 23 percent from SFY 1990 to 2000. Although this increase appears remarkable for a period in which enrollments grew by only about 6 percent, it was moderate relative to other spending categories. In fact, it continues a long-term trend of higher education consuming a shrinking share of state resources. All other spending categories grew in real per capita terms, except for cash assistance. State spending on cash assistance fell a dramatic 34 percent due to widespread and steep caseload declines in the last half of the decade and to benefits that did not keep pace with inflation. Most major components of the "all other" category, such as the judiciary and public health, grew rapidly. A significant exception was general interest expense, which declined with the fall in interest rates.

In the early years of the decade, states were hit with a double whammy of recession and rapidly escalating Medicaid costs. Between SFY 1990 and 1995, real per capita medical vendor payments grew by 78 percent (table 3-4), an average annual rate of 12 percent.[16] These payments consumed 42 percent of states' real per capita spending growth, despite accounting for only 11 percent of SFY 1990 spending.[17] Some of that growth is attributable to DSH payments, which are included in medical vendor payments. Information from the Centers for Medicare and Medicaid Services (CMS) indicates that nominal DSH payments increased more than tenfold between federal fiscal year (FFY) 1990 and 1995. Even without DSH payments, however, real per capita spending on Medicaid benefits increased by about 60 percent.[18]

What caused the sharp increase in real per capita Medicaid payments? The major factors, according to an analysis by Bruen and Holahan (1999), were as follows:

- Medicaid enrollment grew from 28.9 million to 41.7 million—a 44 percent increase during a period that saw a scant 6 percent growth in the overall population—reflecting expanded eligibility, the recession of 1990–91, and other factors. The 58 percent increase in enrollment of blind and disabled persons, who are more expensive to care for, was a major factor in the cost increases, whereas the 15 percent increase in enrollment of low-income children and adults, who are less expensive to care for, was not.[19]
- Inflation in the cost of medical care was 37 percent over the five-year period, compared with 13 percent general inflation for state and local governments.[20] Put differently, economywide increases in health care costs were a major factor behind increasing Medicaid costs.
- States became increasingly adept at shifting services from other programs into Medicaid.[21]

The dramatic rise in DSH payments resulted from efforts by states to maximize federal reimbursement. States recouped much of their increased DSH spending through "donations" from medical providers, taxes on those providers (which were then reimbursable through Medicaid), and intergovernmental transfers. In effect, this turned the DSH program into a form of revenue sharing for the states. How much did this reduce the true cost of spending to states? If states recovered the entire federal plus state DSH payments and used this revenue to, in effect, reduce the state share of Medicaid benefits, it would have reduced growth in state-financed real per capita benefits to 32 percent, for an average annual growth of less than 6 percent. While considerably less than the 12 percent annual growth cited above, 6 percent is still substantial. Thus, Medicaid posed real challenges to states that DSH may have ameliorated but could not have eliminated.

Real per capita spending on medical vendor payments slowed dramatically in the second half of the 1990s, growing by only 6 percent between SFY 1995 and 2000. Essentially all of that growth occurred in SFY 2000, with less than 1 percent growth between SFY 1995 and 1999.

The average annual growth in Medicaid expenditures between FFY 1995 and 1997 was the slowest in the history of the program, according to the Kaiser Commission on Medicaid and the Uninsured, using data from the CMS (Smith et al. 2002). The slowdown continued in FFY 1998. Medicaid enrollment declined during this time, primarily because the improving economy and federal and state welfare reform caused the number of enrolled children and parents to drop. Overall Medicaid expenditures grew at an average annual rate of almost 4 percent between FFY 1995 and 1998, reflecting annual average growth in medical services of 5 percent and declines in DSH payments of 8 percent. Spending for managed care, home care, and prescription drugs grew at double-digit rates, while most other spending categories grew at rates of 5 percent or less (Bruen and Holahan 2002).

Medicaid spending began to accelerate after FFY 1998, growing by 7 percent in FFY 1999 and almost 9 percent in FFY 2000. The increase reflected a rebound in enrollment of children and families, a surge in expenditures on prescription drugs, and accelerated spending on long-term care, driven by continued double-digit growth in home care expenditures (Bruen and Holahan 2002).

DSH payments declined by just over 1 percent annually from FFY 1998 to 2000. In this period, and perhaps earlier, states began to rely more heavily on UPL arrangements to maximize federal reimbursement. However, because UPL payments tend to be included in hospital and nursing home spending and are not separately identifiable, as DSH payments are, it is not easy to be precise about the magnitude or timing of the growing use of UPL arrangements (Bruen and Holahan 2002).

After 1995, elementary and secondary education reform gained a prominent place on the political agenda of many states. As a result, it took over Medicaid's role as the primary driver of state spending, accounting for 38 percent of state spending growth between SFY 1995 and 2000 and increasing by 19 percent in real per capita terms (table 3-4). Pupil enrollment grew moderately faster than overall population growth throughout the decade, slowing from almost 9 percent between SFY 1990 and 1995 to just over 6 percent between SFY 1995 and 2000 as the children of the baby boomers began to graduate from high school and move into the workforce or higher education (National Center for Education Statistics [NCES] 2002a: table 37).

Despite the slower rate of growth in K–12 enrollment, growth in spending accelerated. State and local real spending per pupil rose 14 percent in the 1990s, with almost all of that growth occurring in the last half of the decade (Boyd 2002; NCES 2002a: table 167). In addition to growth in enrollment and in real spending per pupil, many states also financed a larger share of elementary and secondary education spending, traditionally the responsibility of local government. States did this in an effort to ease pressures on property taxes and to reduce spending inequities across school districts, often in response to litigation or the threat of litigation.[22]

Revenues Outstrip Spending

The substantial spending increases of the 1990s would be remarkable by themselves, but the states also enacted sizable tax cuts for every SFY from 1995 through 2001. Overall, they reduced FY 2001 general fund revenues by at least $33 billion, or about 6 percent of what they otherwise would have been.[23] While the tax cuts were considerable, they were not as large as the spending increases that states adopted. Even while cutting taxes by 6 percent or more of 2001 revenue, states increased real general fund spending by 27 percent.[24]

How could states cut taxes while increasing spending and still maintain balanced budgets? One of the fiscal wonders of the second half of the 1990s was that, despite continued tax cutting, state income and sales tax revenues rose as a share of personal income throughout almost the entire period (figure 3-3).

State income taxes are generally progressive, although less so than the federal income tax, claiming a larger share of income as taxpayers' incomes rise. Most state income taxes are not indexed for inflation, so as inflation causes incomes to rise, taxpayers are pushed into higher tax brackets. In

Figure 3-3. *Major State Taxes as a Percentage of Personal Income*

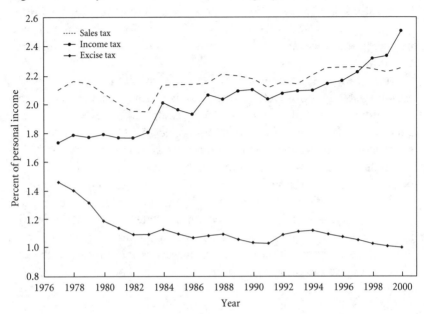

Sources: U.S. Census Bureau; U.S. Bureau of Economic Analysis.

addition, when real incomes rise, whether due to increased productivity or some other reason, taxpayers are again pushed into higher tax brackets. As a result, state income taxes tend to increase as a percentage of income over time unless a state adopts explicit policies to cut taxes.

Thus, it is not surprising that state income taxes rose as a share of income during the early 1990s—incomes were rising and states raised taxes at the end of the recession. What is surprising, though, is the extremely sharp rise in state income taxes as a share of income in the late 1990s, when states were cutting income taxes. Why this happened is discussed in the next section, but it was an important consequence of the particular kind of economic growth and financial market boom of the late 1990s, and it was a major contributor to states' good economic fortune.

Revenues from sales taxes rose considerably early in the 1990s as states raised sales taxes and consumer spending rebounded after the recession. In the latter half of the decade, the sales tax remained relatively constant as a share of personal income.[25] This relatively strong performance of the sales tax in the 1990s was unexpected. The long-term outlook for the sales tax was for slow growth as consumers shifted a larger share of their dollars from goods to services, which tend not to be taxed; many economists expect this trend in consumer spending to continue.[26]

Many kinds of services are difficult to include in sales tax bases, administratively, legally, and politically. It is relatively easy to decide how and where services to people and property should be taxed: If a barber cuts a person's hair in the barber's shop in New York, then New York can tax the service. If a gardener tends property in New Jersey, then New Jersey can collect tax on the landscaping service. It is much more difficult to determine where and how business services might be taxed. For example, should the sale of advertising be taxed in the state in which the business purchasing the advertising is located? In the state in which the advertising agency is located? In the state in which the advertising market is located? Or on some other basis? Similar issues arise in taxing the services of lawyers and many other professionals who operate in a multistate environment.

Another difficulty for states is collecting taxes from residents who buy goods and services via the Internet or mail order. States have little authority or practical ability to compel out-of-state sellers to collect and remit tax on such sales. As more commerce is conducted via the Internet, the revenue loss to states will grow, unless this issue is resolved in a fiscally benign manner by national legislation or interstate agreement.

Excise and selective sales taxes, such as those on gasoline and cigarettes, are often based on the quantity of the good sold and tend not to keep up with income growth; thus, they fall as a percentage of income unless states raise rates. These taxes continued their long-term decline in the 1990s, save for an increase early in the decade, when states raised them in response to the recession.[27]

Causes of the Boom in State Finances

State finances boomed in the latter half of the 1990s for many reasons. The main factors were stronger than expected economic growth, rapidly rising financial asset values, and benign spending pressures, topped off by a brand-new source of revenue: the legal settlement with tobacco companies.

Economy and Stock Markets

The national economy consistently grew faster than most economic fore-casters expected, in large part because workers' productivity grew rapidly. Productivity, which had grown at an annual average rate of 1.6 percent between 1991 and 1995, accelerated to 2.6 percent between 1995 and 2000 (Congressional Budget Office [CBO] 2002b: Chapter 2).

Not only was economic growth stronger than expected, but the nature of that growth was especially good for state finances. Taxable income con-sistently grew faster than broader measures of the economy, such as gross domestic product or personal income. That growth resulted in large part from the very rapid growth in realized capital gains, which was driven by strong economic growth, rising stock markets, widespread participation in the stock market, and lower tax rates on capital gains. According to data from the U.S. Department of the Treasury, capital gains increased from $152 billion in 1994 to $627 billion in 2000, an increase of more than 300 percent in six years.[28] Other income sources also grew faster than the economy, especially taxable retirement income such as distributions from 401(k) plans and IRAs (CBO 2002b: 50–51).

State income taxes benefited from the financial market boom in other ways as well. In particular, states reported to the Rockefeller Institute of Government in the late 1990s that withholding tax collections were grow-ing far faster than expected because many firms, especially high-tech firms, were compensating high-level employees with nonqualified stock options.[29] These options entitled employees to purchase company stock at fixed prices. As the stock market soared, the value of the options increased dramatically. When the options were exercised—that is, when the stock was purchased by employees—they generated taxable wages for the employees based on the difference between the purchase price and the selling price. Those taxable wages generated revenue for the states. Because the options seem to have been granted primarily to high-income employ-ees, much of the income was taxed at the highest rates.

There are relatively little data on the role that stock options played in driving up reported wages and state withholding tax collections, but it was significant. According to the U.S. Office of Management and Budget, federal individual income taxes on exercised stock options increased from $17 billion in 1997 to $42 billion in 2000—sizable amounts in either year and an extraordinary increase of 147 percent in just three years (U.S. Office of Management and Budget [OMB] 2002). The impact on states would generally have been less extreme because state income taxes are less progressive, but states with relatively progressive income taxes and relatively large numbers of high-income taxpayers, such as California and New York, would have benefited greatly.[30]

Not only did taxable income grow far more rapidly than the economy, but income growth was disproportionately concentrated among persons in the highest tax brackets. Governments with income taxes, including most states and the federal government, became even more reliant on the income and tax liability of a relatively small percentage of tax filers. Between 1995 and 2000, the number of federal tax returns showing incomes of $200,000 or more grew by 117 percent, while the total number of federal tax returns grew by only 10 percent. In addition, taxable income on these high-income returns increased by 161 percent, compared with 60 percent for taxable income on all returns.[31] Because states generally conform to federal income definitions, the share of total taxable income earned by high-income taxpayers would have increased similarly. As a result, states became far more reliant for their income tax revenues on a relatively small proportion of taxpayers,[32] thus increasing the volatility of state income taxes.

The enormous growth in the number of taxpayers and the amount of taxable income in the highest brackets meant that income tax liability grew far faster than forecasters might have expected in more nearly normal times. In the terminology of revenue forecasters, state income taxes had become highly elastic—that is, tax revenue was growing much faster than income. There is a flip side to this growth: If the forces responsible for the elasticity of state income taxes were to reverse, huge revenue shortfalls could result (Boyd 2000).[33]

State sales taxes also benefited from the nature of growth in the 1990s. Several long-term trends that are negative for sales tax revenue were masked in the 1990s by positive trends. From 1950 through 1993, the savings rate averaged almost 9 percent, after which it plummeted steadily and rapidly to a record low of 1 percent in 2000 before rising to almost 2 percent in 2001. When the savings rate falls, spending as a percentage of income rises, a situation that is good for state sales taxes. The drop in the savings rate was enough to boost consumption by the end of the decade to 8 percent higher than it otherwise would have been. Partly as a result, consumer spending on goods typically included in a state sales tax base grew faster than personal income in six of the eight years from 1993 through 2000.[34] The savings rate is unlikely to fall substantially further and may in fact rise, eliminating the extra boost that state sales taxes received in the late 1990s.

Figure 3-4, which plots consumption as a percentage of disposable income (the rate of consumption) and capital gains as a percentage of gross domestic product, shows just how atypical the late 1990s were.[35] Except for the anomalous capital gains spike in 1986 related to tax reform, no period in the last 45 years is similar to the extraordinary growth in gains that states saw in the late 1990s. Similarly, the rapid rise in the rate of consumption to successive new highs has no parallel in the previous 45 years.[36]

Benign Spending Pressures

State revenue was not the sole beneficiary of the roaring 1990s. As described earlier, the growth in Medicaid spending slowed dramatically in

Figure 3-4. *Trends in Capital Gains and Consumption*

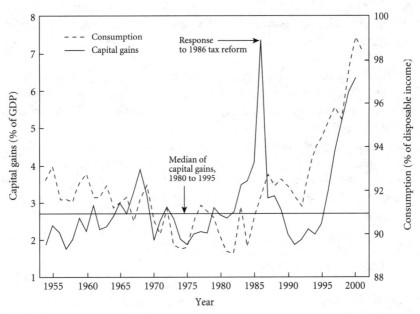

Source: Rockefeller Institute analysis of data from U.S. Department of the Treasury and U.S. Bureau of Economic Analysis.
Note: GDP = gross domestic product.

mid-decade, partly as a result of declining Medicaid enrollment and the spread of managed care (Smith 2002). The slowdown made it easier for states to finance rapid growth in education spending late in the decade.

States received a windfall when the federal government converted welfare funding from an entitlement to a block grant. The caseloads dropped rapidly because of the strong economy and state policy changes, but revenues from the federal government, which would have fallen along with caseloads under the prior welfare program, remained relatively fixed.

Tobacco Settlement

To top it off, in 1998, all but four states were party to a settlement with the five major tobacco companies that was designed to recoup the medical costs of treating tobacco-related illnesses. A large share of such costs were and are paid for by states under the Medicaid program. The federal government also shares in these medical care costs, but it ceded to the states the right to recoup them, with virtually no restrictions. The agreement will result in payments, over time, of $246 billion. Florida, Minnesota, Mississippi, and Texas had previously settled with the companies and agreed to receive $40 billion over 25 years. The initial annual payments averaged about 1 to 2 percent of tax revenue for states as a whole, a sizable amount.

States have begun receiving funds and implementing plans for spending the money. Although not required to, states often earmarked settlement funds for health-related programs or education programs, if not antitobacco programs (Fierro 2001). States can even use settlement funds to draw down additional federal funds for Medicaid. Earmarking does not guarantee an increase in the size of such health or education programs. If the programs were also supported by other state funds, states could reduce those other funds, effectively freeing up the tobacco settlement for other purposes.

The Current Fiscal Crisis

Despite the fiscal problems several analysts had predicted at the time, the typical state ran unanticipated surpluses in the late 1990s and had the wherewithal to cut taxes, raise spending, and increase reserve funds (Hovey 1998; Wallace 1995). As the 1990s came to a close, however, many of the extraordinary factors that caused the fiscal boom ended or began to reverse. National economic growth slowed and stock markets fell sharply. The S&P 500 Index, a fairly broad gauge of stock values, declined 10 percent between December 1999 and December 2000 and fell another 13 percent in 2001. The market experienced a third double-digit decline by the end of 2002. The negative economic trends were exacerbated by fallout from the terrorist attacks of September 11, 2001, and by uncertainty related to the war in Iraq.

Falling Tax Revenues

After years of heady growth, growth in state tax collections dropped sharply from 6 percent in SFY 2000 to less than 3 percent in SFY 2001, after adjusting for inflation and legislated changes (Jenny 2002a). Income tax growth was fairly strong, but the sales tax slowed and corporate tax collections declined. States that relied heavily on manufacturing industries were hardest hit, particularly the Great Lakes, southern, and Great Plains states, reflecting a so-called "stealth recession" in manufacturing that began before the national recession in April 2001.

Tax collections worsened significantly in SFY 2002, declining each quarter as the year progressed. In the October-December quarter, income tax payments related to capital gains and other nonwage income fell by 27 percent, withholding and sales tax growth was near zero, and corporate tax payments declined by 32 percent (Boyd and Jenny 2002; Jenny 2002b). The situation deteriorated markedly in the remainder of the fiscal year: The income tax declined by double-digit percentages in the January-March and April-June quarters, the corporate income tax fell for its sixth and seventh consecutive quarters, and sales tax growth hovered on either side of zero. Figure 3-5 shows the changes in tax revenue by quarter and the extremely sharp drop-off in the last year and a half.

Tax collection data suggest that capital gains and similar income declined far more in 2001 than state revenue forecasters expected. Many states budgeted on the assumption that capital gains would decline by 10 to 15 percent. According to recent data from the Investment Company Institute, capital gains distributions by mutual funds declined by 80 percent in 2001 (OMB 2002). The decline in overall capital gains probably was not as severe because only about half of capital gains are related to the stock market; the other half come from real estate and other assets that performed better than stocks (CBO 2002c). The California Legislative

Figure 3-5. *Change in Quarterly State Tax Revenue, Adjusted for Inflation and Legislation, 1995–2002*

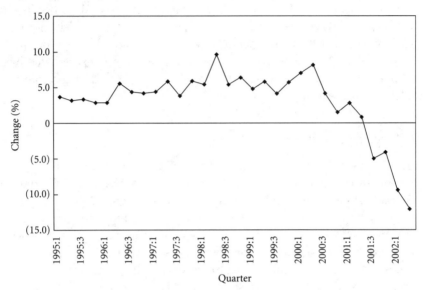

Change (%)

Quarter

Sources: Jenny (2002c), Table 1; second quarter of 2002 estimated by chapter author.

Analyst's Office (LAO) estimated that capital gains and nonqualified stock option income of Californians declined by an astounding 62 percent, from $200 billion in 2000 to $77 billion in 2001 (California Legislative Analyst's Office 2002). The Congressional Budget Office (CBO) noted that options income may have fallen by 50 percent in calendar year 2001 (CBO 2002c).

Accelerated Spending on Medicaid

Medicaid spending was tamed only temporarily in the late 1990s. As noted earlier, growth in spending accelerated in SFY 1999 and 2000, and the pace quickened thereafter. States reported that, in SFY 2001, total Medicaid spending grew by 10.9 percent, exceeding budgeted amounts in 31 states and requiring supplemental funding. States estimate that Medicaid spending grew 13 percent in SFY 2002 and that 36 states will spend more than originally budgeted.[37] According to a survey of state Medicaid officials, the recent growth surge has been driven by increases in the cost of prescription drugs (now approximating 20 percent annually), enrollment, and the cost of long-term care (Levit et al. 2002; Smith and Ellis 2002). Some of the acceleration may have resulted from greater use of UPL arrangements, but that cannot be determined from these data sources.

Budget Gaps and Actions to Close Them

The sharp revenue decline and increased spending pressures created large gaps in state budgets. In April 2002, 43 states reported $27 billion in total budget gaps, and the figure rose to $36 billion by June. Twelve states reported gaps exceeding 10 percent of their general fund budgets (National Conference of State Legislatures [NCSL] 2002). Most states that did not report budget gaps relied heavily on severance taxes on oil and minerals and were not hit as hard by sharp declines in income and sales taxes as other states.

While states did take some extremely difficult actions to close their budget gaps, many relied heavily on fund balances and rainy day funds, tobacco settlement funds, gimmicks to accelerate revenue or postpone spending, across-the-board cuts, and taxes on out-of-favor activities such as smoking. Key actions included the following:

- Drawing down fund balances from the near-record highs of the late 1990s. Aggregate balances declined from $32 billion to $18 billion between SFY 2001 and 2002 in 42 states that reported information to the National Conference of State Legislatures (NCSL). Fund balances will decline further in SFY 2003 (NCSL 2002: 1, 6).
- Tapping special funds. At least 23 states diverted capital funds, highway funds, and other funds ostensibly reserved for specific purposes to general operations (NCSL 2002: 7).
- Using tobacco settlement money to support general operations. At least 16 states took this route (NCSL 2002: 7).
- Cutting spending for SFY 2003. According to the NCSL, 26 states targeted spending, with 16 cutting higher education, 14 cutting corrections, 12 cutting Medicaid, and 11 each cutting K–12 education and local revenue sharing (NCSL 2002: 7).
- Containing Medicaid costs. According to the Kaiser Commission on Medicaid and the Uninsured, 45 states implemented measures designed to control Medicaid costs in SFY 2002, and at least 41 states were planning further actions in SFY 2003. The most popular measures for SFY 2002 were
  ○ Pharmacy-related controls or cuts, such as requiring prior authorization for certain products (32 states);

○ Cuts or freezes in provider payment rates (22 states);
○ Benefit reductions for optional services such as adult dental benefits and limits on vision and psychiatric counseling benefits (9 states); and
○ Eligibility cuts or limits, or delays in program expansions (8 states) (Smith et al. 2002).

- Raising taxes. At least 16 states raised taxes by 1 percent or more of tax revenues, for a total increase of $6.7 billion, or 1.2 percent of the budget. Hikes in cigarette taxes were most popular in frequency and magnitude, accounting for just over 40 percent of the tax increases. A handful of states (Kansas, Indiana, New Jersey, and Tennessee) enacted large, broad-based tax increases, but these were the exceptions rather than the rule (NCSL 2002: 8–10).

Many states closed SFY 2002 budget gaps primarily with one-time actions, spending deferrals, revenue accelerations, and cigarette taxes. Actions designed to bring revenue and spending into recurring balance were extremely rare.

Virtually every state faced a projected budget gap at the start of SFY 2003 and adopted a variety of policies to close gaps, including all three major approaches: spending cuts, use of reserve funds, and tax increases. Despite these efforts to enact balanced SFY 2003 budgets, at least 36 states reported that budget gaps reopened as the year progressed, due to revenue shortfalls and spending overruns. At this writing, nearly every state again faces a large budget gap for SFY 2004. According to the NCSL, at least 33 states faced gaps exceeding 5 percent of the state budget, and at least 18 faced gaps exceeding 10 percent (NCSL 2003).

Can the Boom Resume?

The next five years look much more difficult than the last: Revenue growth has slowed, spending pressures have picked up, and many actions states have taken to close budget gaps in SFY 2003 and 2004 have pushed part of the current fiscal problem into SFY 2005 and beyond.

Slower Revenue Growth

As the economic recovery progresses, stock market–related income could grow rapidly from the currently depressed lows, but it is important to keep this rapid growth in perspective. In California, the LAO projects that capital gains and options income will grow by 18 percent in each of the next two years. It would take an additional four years of growth at 20 percent annually—more than twice the growth in the broader economy—for capital gains and stock option income to exceed the 2000 peak.[38] Fortunately for other states, California relies more heavily on this type of income than they do, and its high-tech economy benefited more from growth in this income than theirs did. California represents an extreme case, but the same issues will arise in other states.

Rapid growth is not the only possible assumption. Capital gains could retrench further, returning to longer-term relations between gains and the economy (CBO 2002b).[39] Under this scenario, capital gains and similar income might experience a spurt of growth after the recession ends, followed by sluggish growth for several years. Moreover, the large buildup of capital losses may depress capital gains income for several years, even if the economy and stock market bounce back (CBO 2002b: 5–6). States vary widely in how much they rely on capital gains for tax revenue. Table 3-5 ranks states by a measure that takes into account the amount of capital gains realized by their taxpayers and the extent to which the state relies on the income tax.[40] States that rely heavily on capital gains taxes will probably face the greatest revenue difficulty if the stock market slump endures for a long period. Northeastern, western, and highly industrialized states tend to be most reliant on revenues from capital gains taxes. Southern states and states without income tax are least reliant.

All is not gloom for the income tax, however. It will probably benefit from a near-term burst in growth as the economy recovers. Over the long term, taxable retirement income will continue to grow more rapidly than the economy as a whole, because taxable pension and retirement plan distributions will increase as the population ages. Progressive income tax structures will cause income tax revenue generally to grow more quickly than the overall economy after financial markets stabilize.[41] When the recovery is fully under way, income tax revenue will grow faster than the economy as a whole but probably not at rates approaching those of the late 1990s.

The long-term outlook for the sales tax remains unattractive for three reasons. First, it is hard to imagine that people will consume an ever-increasing share of their income. If the savings rate simply stops falling and consumption stays at its current high level relative to income, states will lose the annual boost to consumption growth they benefited from

Table 3-5. *Importance of Capital Gains to Tax Revenues, 2000*

State	Income Tax as Percentage of General Revenue	Capital Gains as Percentage of Adjusted Gross Income[a]	Capital Gains Tax as Percentage of Income Tax
California	29.1	12.9	3.8
Colorado	28.1	11.3	3.2
Connecticut	24.9	12.4	3.1
Massachusetts	33.0	9.1	3.0
New York	27.4	10.8	3.0
Oregon	28.6	9.2	2.6
Idaho	23.0	9.4	2.2
Virginia	28.5	7.5	2.1
Maryland	25.7	8.1	2.1
Minnesota	26.5	7.8	2.1
Georgia	27.2	7.5	2.0
New Jersey	22.4	8.8	2.0
Maine	20.4	9.6	2.0
Illinois	19.7	9.6	1.9
Nebraska	20.8	9.0	1.9
Rhode Island	20.5	9.1	1.9
United States	19.7	9.3	1.8
North Carolina	26.0	6.6	1.7
Utah	21.6	7.3	1.6
Vermont	14.7	10.1	1.5
Missouri	21.5	6.9	1.5
Kansas	21.9	6.3	1.4
Montana	14.8	9.3	1.4
Hawaii	18.6	7.3	1.4
Arizona	15.6	8.5	1.3
Ohio	22.8	5.7	1.3
Pennsylvania	16.2	7.6	1.2
Delaware	16.9	7.1	1.2
Oklahoma	19.8	5.7	1.1
Michigan	18.2	6.1	1.1
Iowa	19.1	5.8	1.1
Kentucky	18.4	5.7	1.0
Indiana	19.9	5.2	1.0
Wisconsin	28.1	3.5	1.0
Alabama	14.7	5.8	0.9
South Carolina	18.5	3.9	0.7

Table 3-5. *Continued*

State	Income Tax as Percentage of General Revenue	Capital Gains as Percentage of Adjusted Gross Income[a]	Capital Gains Tax as Percentage of Income Tax
Louisiana	10.9	5.8	0.6
West Virginia	13.8	4.2	0.6
New Mexico	11.2	4.7	0.5
Mississippi	10.4	5.0	0.5
North Dakota	7.1	6.2	0.4
Arkansas	16.1	1.8	0.3
New Hampshire	1.7	11.9	0.2
Tennessee	1.1	6.7	0.1
Alaska	—	5.7	—
Florida	—	12.3	—
Nevada	—	13.8	—
South Dakota	—	8.8	—
Texas	—	8.5	—
Washington	—	10.8	—
Wyoming	—	17.7	—

Sources: Income tax as percent of general revenue obtained from U.S. Census Bureau. Capital gains as percent of adjusted gross income obtained from Internal Revenue Service, Statistics of Income branch.

a. Some figures have been adjusted for certain states to take into account the fact that they do not tax 100 percent of capital gains.

throughout the 1990s. If the savings rate rises and consumption rates fall to historic levels, states will lose even more revenue. Second, people have been shifting consumption from heavily taxed goods to lightly taxed services, and this shift is likely to continue. Finally, under current federal law, states often cannot require out-of-state sellers to collect and remit sales taxes on goods or services sold over the Internet, even though tax is legally due. As commerce over the Internet grows, states will lose increasing amounts of sales tax revenue.

Bruce and Fox (2001) estimate that the typical state sales tax base has narrowed by about a fifth over the last two decades, falling from just over 51 percent of personal income in 1979 to 42 percent in 2000. They project an additional erosion of 3 percent of total state and local tax revenue between 2001 and 2006, with the continuing shift to services consumption accounting for 1 percentage point and Internet sales accounting for 2 percentage points. The five states with the greatest anticipated revenue loss as a percentage of total tax revenue are Nevada, Texas, Florida, Tennessee, and South Dakota—all states that rely heavily on the sales tax because they have no income tax. Each faces erosion in its total tax base of 5 percentage points or more over five years, enough to place substantial strain on state and local budgets.

Selective sales and excise taxes will continue to be a weak third leg of state revenue structures. States are likely to raise rates in the current fiscal crisis—in fact, they have already done so, with more than 20 states raising cigarette taxes in the 2002 legislative session. After this short-term boost, however, such taxes will probably continue their long-term decline, because they are generally imposed on bases that do not keep up with economic growth.

Finally, the prospects for substantial and sustained increases in federal aid to states do not appear especially good. The federal budget benefited from many of the same forces as state budgets, and it is being buffeted now by the recession, the decline in financial markets, and accelerating spending. In budget projections released in August 2002, the CBO lowered its 10-year forecast by an additional $1.4 trillion, reducing revenue projections by $678 billion and increasing spending projections by $688 billion (much of it related to counterterrorism legislation. CBO's projected 10-year outlook worsened by an additional $385 billion in projections released in January 2003. In that document, CBO forecast deficits through FFY 2006, followed by several years of very small surpluses that are subject to uncertainty—and policy undoing—just as its earlier projections were. And the actual situation may be worse: CBO projections make some risky assumptions, among them that discretionary spending will grow more slowly than the economy and more slowly than recent experience, and that tax cuts scheduled to expire will not be extended (CBO 2002a, 2003). Finally, the January 2003 projections predate the war in Iraq and do not reflect the budgetary costs of either the war or its aftermath.

One ray of hope for states in this dour outlook is the potential spillover effect of prescription drug coverage under Medicare. If enacted, the program could result in the federal government's picking up 100 percent of the cost of prescription drugs for elderly Medicaid recipients. These costs are now shared between the federal government and the states.

Although the long-term outlook for sustained federal aid to the states is bleak, there may be some possibility of assistance in the short term. At this writing, a substantial fiscal stimulus package seems likely. Some policymakers have debated whether to include antirecession assistance to states in this package, as was done in response to the recession of the mid-1970s. One aid mechanism that has been discussed is an increase in the federal matching rate for Medicaid; if enacted, the increase could provide long-term fiscal relief to states as well.

A national economic forecast from Economy.com prepared in the summer of 2002 projected average growth in personal income of about 5 percent annually between 2002 and 2012 and growth in retail sales of about 4 percent annually.[42] While most states can expect their income taxes to grow a bit faster than personal income after the economy recovers from the current recession, sales taxes are likely to grow as slowly as retail sales, or perhaps even slower. As noted earlier, excise taxes are likely to be stable or decline unless states take action to raise tax rates. This suggests that unless states change their tax structures, tax revenue is unlikely to keep up with growth in the economy.

Increased Spending Pressures

States spent much of the good news of the 1990s on recurring programs, increasing the real per capita size of state government by about one-third. That increased spending is now sharply out of line with revenue structures in many states, particularly those most reliant on capital gains or susceptible to substantial erosion in their sales tax base. Furthermore, there are some signs of trouble ahead for state spending.

The three largest areas of spending in the typical state budget are elementary and secondary education, Medicaid, and higher education. Each will present states with special challenges in the next five years.

ELEMENTARY AND SECONDARY EDUCATION

Enrollment pressures will ease, but states will have their hands full with other issues affecting education spending. According to the "middle" projections of the National Center for Education Statistics (NCES), national K–12 public school enrollment will grow 0.1 percent annually between school years 2002 and 2007 and then decline at the same rate between school years 2007 and 2012. The net result is no projected growth between school years 2002 and 2012 (NCES 2002b: tables 1, 4).[43] This is welcome relief from the 11 percent growth between school years 1992 and 2002, when the large cohort of children of baby boomers was working its way through high school.

The NCES outlook for the nation as a whole may call for no growth, but the pattern varies markedly across the country. The western states of Alaska, Hawaii, Idaho, New Mexico, Utah, and Wyoming are projected to grow 10 percent or more between school years 2002 and 2012, and many southern and other western states are projected to grow between 3 and 10 percent.[44]

Although most states will not face enrollment pressures in the near term, they will face other pressures to increase spending on elementary and secondary education. Citizens value education highly, and they have demonstrated it by consistently supporting increases in resources. Table 3-6 shows just how dramatic those increases were over the last half-century: Rising enrollment rates, increases in the number of teachers per pupil, and rising inflation-adjusted pay resulted in a greater than fourfold increase in real spending per pupil. While the rate of increase slowed somewhat in the 1990s, it was still quite substantial. Moreover, states assumed an increasing share of elementary and secondary education financing over much of the last half-century, so the total impact of education spending increases on state governments has been quite dramatic.

Will the seemingly inexorable increases in real per pupil spending continue in the decade ahead? Although many economists have questioned whether there is any systematic relationship between spending and either educational opportunity or the results of education, elected officials, taxpayers, and courts appear to disagree. Therefore, states are highly likely to continue raising real per pupil spending.[45]

The federal government and many states have adopted policies that are likely to raise the costs of elementary and secondary education substantially, although estimates of those costs are not available. President George W. Bush proposed and ultimately signed the No Child Left Behind Act of 2001, which will greatly expand the federal role in education.[46] Among other things, the act requires states to

- Implement annual, standards-based assessments in reading and math for grades three through eight by the 2005–06 school year;
- Bring *all* students to the level of proficiency on state tests by 2013–14. Individual schools must make "adequate yearly progress" toward this goal. Students in schools that fail to make adequate progress three years in a row must be offered supplemental educational services, including private tutoring;

Table 3-6. *Resources Devoted to Elementary and Secondary Education, 1949–1999*

School Year	Enrollment (% of Population Age 5–17)	Pupil-Teacher Ratio, Public Schools	Average Salaries for Instructional Staff ($ 1998–99)	Spending per Enrolled Pupil ($ 2000–01)		State Share of Total School District Revenue (%)
				Amount	Average Annual Percent Change	
1949–50	83.1	—	20,913	1,708	—	39.8
1959–60	82.2	25.8	28,974	2,622	4.4	39.1
1969–70	87.0	22.3	39,407	4,075	4.5	39.9
1979–80	86.7	18.7	35,427	5,164	2.4	46.8
1989–90	90.2	17.2	42,294	7,135	3.3	47.1
1998–99	91.4	16.1	42,488	8,016	1.3	48.7

Source: National Center for Education Statistics (2002a), Tables 36, 65, and 167.

- Ensure that by 2005–06, all classes are taught by a "qualified teacher"—that is, a teacher who is licensed and demonstrably proficient in his or her subject matter;
- Issue annual report cards on school performance and on statewide test results; and
- Provide adequate funds to build, renovate, and repair the education infrastructure.

On their own initiative and in response to federal legislation, most states have adopted policies to further many of these goals. Policies adopted in recent years include high-stakes testing, higher graduation standards, prohibitions against social promotion, smaller class sizes, expanded student support services, enhanced professional development for teachers, and activities intended to help students and teachers achieve educational goals.[47] Many of the policies will increase costs by requiring more teachers, more highly skilled and highly paid teachers, more time in school for students and teachers, more extensive curricular material, additional building space, or some combination of these requirements. Efforts to make teacher certification requirements universal or more stringent may restrict the supply of teachers and drive up salaries. All of these actions are likely to increase the cost of K–12 education.

Many states are adopting policies to address an important demographic issue: looming teacher shortages, at least at current salaries, resulting from the impending retirement of the rapidly growing cohort of older teachers (Boe, Barkanic, and Leow 1999). In the 1999 through 2002 legislative sessions, at least 18 states adopted policies to address teacher recruitment and retention, often providing benefits to targeted teachers through scholarship programs, loans, salary increases, bonuses, tax credits, or relocation assistance (Education Commission of the States 2002b).

Taxpayers appear to support policies that would raise the costs of elementary and secondary education, and they appear willing to pay those costs. A 2002 Phi Delta Kappa/Gallup poll on attitudes toward public education found that 78 percent of U.S. adults would favor cutting other areas of government in order to maintain spending on education in difficult fiscal times; 58 percent favored increasing state taxes to produce enough funds to avoid education cuts (Rose and Gallup 2002: 41–57).

Courts have pushed many states toward higher spending. Most states have seen their system of financing schools challenged, usually in relation to state constitutional requirements that children receive a "thorough and efficient education" or a "sound basic education." Many early court cases challenged financing systems on the ground of inequality. Recent cases have been more successful with challenges on the ground of adequacy. The argument is that even if a financing system were acceptably unequal, certain school districts (often with disproportionate shares of poor, urban, or minority students) simply do not have enough funds to provide a constitutionally adequate education.

As a result of litigation, financing systems have been overturned in 18 states. In most of those cases, state policymakers had to increase school spending, often substantially. In addition, even some states whose financing systems were upheld increased spending as a preemptive response to the threat of litigation and shifted greater responsibility for financing schools from local government to the state. In the late 1990s, many states, including Arizona, Colorado, Kentucky, New Hampshire, New Jersey, Ohio, and Vermont, increased education funding in response to court orders or to the threat of litigation.

Finally, if states wish to continue the long-term trend toward greater state and less local financing of education, they will have to find additional funds for the task.

MEDICAID

The CBO and other forecasters project that national Medicaid spending will grow about 8 to 9 percent annually for the remainder of this decade, driven by health technology improvements, demographic changes, and a general absence of incentives to hold down costs in the health care sector.[48] According to the Center on Budget and Policy Priorities' analysis of CBO data, growth in cost per beneficiary is likely to account for a larger share of cost increases than growth in the number of beneficiaries, at least for the next several years (Ku and Broaddus 2003). The projected growth is sharply higher than growth in the mid-1990s, albeit much slower than in the first few years of the 1990s.

State Medicaid spending exceeded budgeted amounts again in SFY 2003. According to the Kaiser Commission on Medicaid and the Uninsured, states enacted appropriations for Medicaid as if the state share of this spending would grow by about 4 percent in SFY 2003. That rate was not plausible in light of the program's recent history of state-funded spending increasing by more than 10 percent in SFY 2001 and again in SFY 2002, and a predicted 6 percent growth in enrollment for SFY 2003 (Smith et al. 2002: 32). Therefore, it was not surprising that, late in SFY

2003, 32 states reported that Medicaid or health care spending programs were over budget (NCSL 2003: 2).

States should be concerned about Medicaid further in the future as well. Long-term care is an extremely expensive component of Medicaid, and expenditures in this category have been accelerating in recent years. It is well known that when the baby boomer cohort ages, Medicaid's long-term care costs are likely to surge.

For the nation as a whole, long-term care is not an immediate problem. Over the next 10 years, the population age 65 and older will grow by about 19 percent, according to a forecast by Economy.com. That rate is faster than the rate for the population as a whole, but not dramatically so. However, the older population is projected to grow by an additional 37 percent in the subsequent 10 years, exerting substantial pressure on Medicaid long-term care costs.

Some states, particularly those in the fast-growing West, will experience pressures from long-term care costs sooner. According to the Economy.com forecast, nine states are likely to face growth of more than 33 percent in their elderly population in the next 10 years, in order of fastest growing to slowest growing: Nevada, Arizona, Colorado, Utah, Oregon, Idaho, Georgia, Alaska, and Washington.

Herbert Stein, chairman of the Council of Economic Advisers under President Richard M. Nixon, once remarked about the federal budget deficit, "If something cannot go on forever, it will stop." He meant that federal policymakers would have to bring the deficit under control sooner or later to avoid calamity, and if they took action sooner it would be less painful than if they waited.[49] Undoubtedly, many governors and legislators feel the same way about Medicaid, as they contemplate the accelerating growth of the elderly population and the associated rise in long-term care and prescription drug costs. Their concern should not be with the Medicaid program per se but with the large and rapidly growing cost of providing health care to needy people. States can choose not to pay for much of that care—the federal government does not require states to pay for long-term care for the elderly or disabled—but most states choose to provide such care and to do so by obtaining federal funds through Medicaid.

HIGHER EDUCATION

The children of the baby boomers are leaving high school, increasing the pool of traditional college-age students. At the same time, rates of college attendance have been rising. The combination contributes to faster growth in enrollment in the decade ahead than in the last decade. The NCES projects that full-time-equivalent enrollment in degree-granting institutions of higher education will increase at an average annual rate of 1.4 percent for the 10 years from 2002 to 2012, up a little from the 1.0 percent rate for the 10 years ending in 2002 (NCES 2002b: table 22). There is some evidence, however, that these projections may be too low.[50]

Enrollment is likely to grow at substantially different rates around the country. Enrollment projections from NCES and population projections from Economy.com both suggest that the far western states and Florida will experience the fastest growth in enrollment and that the Rocky Mountain states are likely to experience the slowest growth (Economy.com 2002a; NCES 2002b).

The labor market is also likely to push higher education costs up. According to the U.S. Department of Labor, 43 percent of net new jobs in the 10-year period ending in 2008 will be in occupations that commonly require at least some higher education, even though those jobs constituted only 29 percent of the employment base at the time the projections were made (Braddock 1999).

As with elementary and secondary education, the real per student cost of higher education has been rising consistently and substantially for several decades, especially in the private sector. Several analysts have argued that these costs will continue to rise. Some argue that higher education, like many service industries, suffers from what economist William Baumol called "cost disease"—it is a highly labor-intensive industry in which it is difficult to increase productivity.[51] Without increased productivity, the relative price of education rises. Others argue, in what is sometimes called the revenue theory of college costs, that higher education institutions try to raise all the revenue they can and then spend it all in a continual quest to raise perceived quality, thereby hoping to attract better and perhaps more students. Costs are limited primarily by what the institutions can raise, and there is continual pressure to raise as much as possible (Breneman 2001; Johnstone 2001; Jones 2001).[52]

More Stringent Actions to Come

When states close budget gaps, they tend to follow relatively predictable patterns. They begin by taking the easiest, least controversial actions, such as drawing down reserve funds, accelerating revenue, delaying spending, or refinancing debt. States tend to hold off on large spending cuts and large tax increases until after they have been in crisis for several years. The early actions essentially create one-shot money that supports recurring spending, thus postponing but not obviating the difficult decisions about how much states can spend on an ongoing basis. Some early actions can have dire consequences, requiring repayment one or two years down the road.

As these bills come due, and as the fiscal crisis lengthens and deepens, states will take more stringent actions, either raising taxes or cutting spending—often so late in the economic cycle that recovery has already begun. In response to the two most recent recessions, states drew down reserves in the earliest years and finally raised taxes later (table 3-7). Preliminary information gathered by the Rockefeller Institute of Government suggests that this is happening again. States relied very heavily on reserve funds, gimmicks, and cigarette taxes to close their SFY 2002 and SFY 2003 budget gaps. In most states, the use of gimmicks and reserves will have the effect of making matters worse in later years.

Actions by the federal government can exacerbate state fiscal difficulties. The federal tax cut enacted in 2001 had the potential to reduce state revenue significantly because it repealed the estate tax and accelerated bonus depreciation, both of which would have passed through automat-

Table 3-7. *State Actions in Two Recent Recessions*

	Action as Percentage of Expenditures	
State Fiscal Year	*Fund Balance Change*	*Revenue Enactments*
1980–1982 Recession		
1981	(4.6)	0.3
1982	(1.5)	2.4
1983	(1.4)	2.3
1984	2.3	6.0
1985	1.4	0.5
1990–1991 Recession		
1990	0.6	0.3
1991	(1.4)	1.8
1992	(2.3)	3.7
1993	0.7	5.1
1994	2.4	1.0

Source: National Governors Association and National Association of State Budget Officers (1999, 2001, and 2002).

ically to many states' tax systems. Many states have since uncoupled from this legislation, muting or eliminating the revenue loss. President Bush's recent proposal to eliminate taxation of dividends under the personal income tax would pass through to most states that have an income tax, automatically reducing their revenue (unless the states enact legislation to the contrary). The Center on Budget and Policy Priorities has estimated that this proposal would reduce state tax revenue by more than $4 billion annually (Lav 2003).

Medicaid Spending Versus Other Priorities

The combination of slower growth in tax revenue, 9 percent anticipated annual growth in Medicaid, continued pressures on education budgets, and little prospect of relief from the federal budget suggests that states will have to make difficult choices in the remainder of this decade. One obvious and important question is whether Medicaid growth will crowd out other state spending. This question cannot be answered with any certainty, but it is useful to begin by looking at what happened in the last recession.

The period from SFY 1990 to 1995, which includes the 1990–91 recession, provides some insight. While the true cost of Medicaid to the states clearly did not grow as fast as the 78 percent real per capita growth in medical vendor payments might suggest, the impact on state budgets was substantial nonetheless. Yet other spending does not appear to have suffered in any material sense (although it may have been lower than it would otherwise have been). Even after adjusting for population growth and inflation, spending on K–12 education increased by 13 percent in this period, spending on higher education increased by 11 percent, and most other components of state spending also increased significantly.

Figure 3-6 shows the SFY 1990 to 1995 change in real per capita state government spending on functions other than medical vendor payments, plotted against the change in real per capita medical vendor payments. There is no obvious pattern. States with large increases in vendor payments do not appear to have smaller increases in other spending. In fact, a fair number of states with above-average increases in medical vendor payments also increased spending on other functions by more than the average.

This simple view does not take into account the many other forces affecting spending. Fossett and Wyckoff (1996) examined the question

Figure 3-6. *Change in Real Per Capita Spending, 1990–1995*

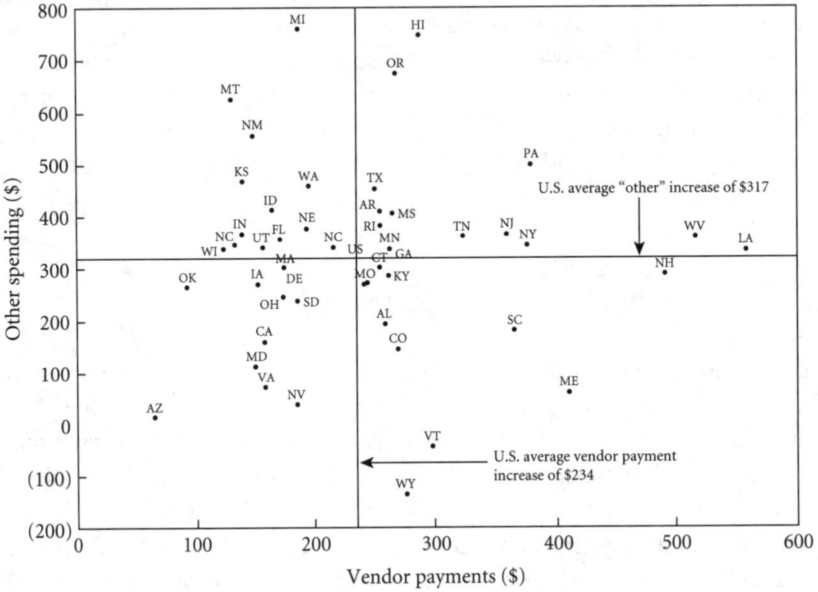

Source: U.S. Census Bureau; U.S. Bureau of Economic Analysis.

of whether the rapid growth in Medicaid between SFY 1980 and 1990 crowded out spending on K–12 education, taking into account key economic, demographic, and institutional factors influencing spending on these programs. Their results "imply that the growth of state educational aid has been reduced in the last few years by various factors, but state Medicaid spending is not one of them" (Fossett and Wyckoff 1996: 427).

Does this mean that rapid Medicaid growth did not strain state finances? No. It certainly did, but states and their residents apparently valued other activities of government enough to pay for them. Elementary and secondary education, higher education, and especially corrections all grew rapidly in this period. States appear to have been able and willing to support this spending with economic growth and with tax increases enacted after the 1990–91 recession, allowing state tax revenue to increase from 6.4 percent of state personal income in SFY 1991 to 6.8 percent in SFY 1995.[53] In the early 1990s, Medicaid actually provided some fiscal relief. The rapid expansion of DSH payments provided a growing source of revenue for states at a time when their tax revenue was depressed. But this time around, DSH and UPL are being scaled back, contributing to the crisis rather than easing it.

The earlier analysis suggests that Medicaid will strain state finances once again in the coming 5 to 10 years, maybe longer. If states choose to provide some of the most expensive care under Medicaid, the program is likely to grow substantially faster than tax revenues. Will states be willing to raise revenue once again to pay for Medicaid spending increases, or will they cut back in other areas, particularly education? Or will states simply cut Medicaid sharply?

There is considerable political support for lower taxes. Throughout the second half of the 1990s, states cut taxes repeatedly, especially income taxes; many politicians have pledged not to raise taxes; and several states have adopted new tax and spending limitations. At the same time, public support of spending on elementary and secondary education remains very strong, 50-year trends suggest that rising spending on elementary and secondary education is virtually inexorable, and states have recently enacted many policies that will increase costs of elementary and secondary education. Moreover, demographic trends and labor market requirements will push higher education costs up, and states raised taxes substantially after each of the last two recessions. Predicting which forces will dominate is risky business, but states appear headed for very difficult choices about their tax and spending priorities.

Challenges for the Future

The golden years of the 1990s have come to a crashing end, and states are struggling to cope with a major fiscal crisis, one that has been much worse than overall economic indicators would have suggested. Assuming that the economy improves, the fiscal position of the states should also improve, but a number of factors suggest great difficulties on both the revenue and spending sides.

Growth in income and sales tax revenues is likely to be modest because of the collapse of the stock market (which has sharply eroded capital gains taxes), slower income growth, the historically low personal savings rate (which makes rapid increases in consumption unlikely), and the growth of hard-to-tax Internet sales. To cope with existing fiscal problems, several states have already drawn upon future tobacco settlement revenues. At the same time, federally determined DSH allotments are scheduled to decline in FFY 2003, and the Bush administration has issued regulations limiting the use of UPL arrangements, making these Medicaid components less likely sources of revenue.

Finally, there is a very strong ideological bias in many states today against raising taxes to fund state government programs. Given the federal government's own budget problems and ideological bent, states are not likely to see any significant additional funds in the near term, outside, perhaps, of funds for homeland security and assistance as part of a federal stimulus package, although the latter appears increasingly unlikely. If the federal government enacts prescription drug coverage under Medicare, states could realize some fiscal savings, although not soon enough to help with the current crisis.

Pressure to increase spending is likely to grow, especially in regard to Medicaid. First, after declining for two years, the number of uninsured persons rose during 2001 and is likely to continue upward as employer-sponsored insurance erodes (Mills 2002). Some of the uninsured will end up on Medicaid rolls; others will show up in hospital emergency rooms, raising hospital costs.

Second, states have found that managed care is not likely to provide further large reductions in the growth of spending on acute care (Holahan et al. 2002). Hospital costs are rising, and states are limited in their ability to negotiate lower rates because Medicaid beneficiaries depend on safety net providers, who, in turn, depend on Medicaid revenues to support care for the uninsured. Prescription drug costs are skyrocketing, and states have limited options to control these expenditures.

Third, while the really big increase in the elderly population is some time off, widespread shortages in nursing home and home care staff, as well as concerns about quality of care, may affect access to and spending on long-term care. Staff shortages can force nursing homes to improve wages and benefits for existing workers, driving up costs, and to hire more workers to improve access. The Supreme Court's *Olmstead* decision may yet force higher spending on home care and community-based services.

Because Medicaid and health care more generally are a major part of the state budget, these pressures alone will strain state finances. But Medicaid is not the only area in which increases in spending are likely: K–12 education leads the list.

Given slow revenue growth, large increases in Medicaid spending, and considerable spending pressure in other areas of the budget, states are facing difficult choices. To balance their budgets, they will need to raise taxes, cut Medicaid, or reduce spending on other programs—and they are likely to do some of each. States are in a much more difficult position now than they were in the early 1990s, when they were willing to raise taxes and it was easier to exploit federal matching rate loopholes.

In the face of these pressures, states could have a difficult time maintaining current eligibility levels under Medicaid and SCHIP. The states have worked at cost savings for a long time, and few options remain that would not adversely affect low-income beneficiaries or the fragile system of cross-subsidization of the uninsured.

NOTES

1. The federal role in Medicaid is even larger than reported here as a result of states' having used disproportionate share hospital (DSH) payments and the upper payment limit (UPL) rule to increase federal payments for Medicaid without increasing the states' own expenditures. Note also that in other years and using other data sources, the federal matching rate is closer to 57 percent, as will be seen shortly with state budget data for 2002.

2. State-financed State Children's Health Insurance Program spending in fiscal year (FY) 2002 was $1.641 billion (National Association of State Budget Officers [NASBO] 2002b: table A-2) and total state-financed spending was $758.395 billion (NASBO 2002b: table A-1).

3. Higher education spending from state general funds and bond funds—excluding "other state funds," which typically include tuition-financed spending—were 14 percent smaller than state general-fund expenditures on Medicaid in 2002. The underlying data for this calculation were taken from NASBO (2002b: tables 12 and 28).

4. The state-financed budget share also can be affected by state-specific idiosyncrasies and year-to-year vagaries in reporting. National Association of State Budget Officers (NASBO) data, while extremely useful for many purposes, tend to be "noisy" because they are self-reported by states, with little means of verification and few consequences for misreporting; therefore, numbers can vary considerably from year to year and state to state for reasons that are not always apparent. For example, the FY 2000 data for New York reported in the *2000 State Expenditure Report* showed that Medicaid spending was 21.7 percent of the state-financed budget, but the data for the same year reported in the *2001 State Expenditure Report* showed Medicaid spending at 12.9 percent of the state-financed budget. This discrepancy resulted because NASBO's reported state-financed Medicaid spending by New York in FY 2000 fell from $10.9 billion in the expenditure report published in 2001 to $6.6 billion in the report published in 2002, even though FY 2000 data were described as actual results (not estimates) in both reports. Fortunately, discrepancies this large are unusual, and the reported spending shares for most states are highly similar across reports published in different years.

5. Based on the federal medical assistance percentage (FMAP) for FY 2000, as published in U.S. Department of Health and Human Services, Health Care Financing Administration (2000).

6. The poverty population used is the three-year average of official poverty esti-mates from the U.S. Bureau of the Census. Averaging smoothes out some of the sampling variability in state-level poverty estimates that results from the relatively small sample in the Current Population Survey, the primary official source of poverty data. Whether the poverty population is the right divisor to use to "standardize" Medicaid expenditures is an open question, but there really are not many practical alternatives.

7. These data are not adjusted for interstate price differentials, even though that would be preferable, because there are no readily available state-specific cost-of-living or health care price indexes.

8. Expenditures do not increase as rapidly as enrollment because a disproportion-ate share of the new enrollees would be children, who are relatively inexpensive to care for, and because the average new enrollee is expected to be healthier than otherwise sim-ilar existing enrollees.

9. *Olmstead, Commissioner, Georgia Department of Human Resources, et al. v. L. C.,* No 98-536.

10. See, for example, Doeksen and St. Clair (2002); Families USA (2003); Kilpatrick et al. (2002); and Moore School of Business (2002).

11. Most of the analysis in this section is based on detailed government finance data obtained from the U.S. Census Bureau. With regard to this analysis (1) references to total spending or total revenue are to the Census Bureau concepts of "general expenditures" and "general revenue"; (2) calculations of expenditures per capita or revenue as a per-centage of personal income follow the convention others often use of dividing spending or revenue for a given fiscal year by population or personal income for the calendar year in which the fiscal year began; and (3) calculations of real expenditures per capita use the state and local government chain-weighted price index prepared by the U.S. Bureau of Economic Analysis for the calendar year in which a state fiscal year began. At the time this chapter was written, the latest state fiscal year for which U.S. Census Bureau state government finance data were available was 2000.

12. Alaska's spending declined by 5.4 percent from 1990 to 2000. Alaska did not participate in the fiscal boom of the 1990s, because of declines in oil-related revenue.

13. Arkansas and Mississippi are now at the U.S. average for state spending but remain well below the U.S. average in terms of state-local spending combined. New Hamp-shire remains well below the U.S. average in state spending and state-local spending.

14. See Penner (1998) for a good discussion of these trends.

15. This category includes payments to hospitals, doctors, and other private med-ical vendors. It does not include payments by state governments to local government entities such as local hospitals.

16. Throughout this chapter, where average annual growth rates are discussed, the calculation takes compounding into account, yielding an annual average that is lower than the simple average when growth is positive.

17. Note that here and throughout the chapter, amounts are adjusted for inflation using the state and local government chain-weighted price index (unless data from another source that presented constant dollars are used). Thus, the adjustment here is for general inflation faced by state and local governments, rather than for health care inflation.

18. Based on data from Health Care Financing Administration (HCFA) Form 64. These data show that real per capita "total computable" spending on medical assistance

payments (including DSH) increased by 80 percent between federal fiscal years 1990 and 1995, which is remarkably consistent with the 78 percent increase in real per capita medical vendor payments (which also include DSH) between state fiscal years 1990 and 1995. As with the Census data on medical vendor payments, the analysis of HCFA data is based on combined federal-state spending, with adjustments for DSH.

19. Computed from table 2 in Bruen and Holahan (1999), and from population data from the U.S. Census Bureau.

20. Computed from annual average medical inflation rates given in the text of Bruen and Holahan (1999) and from data on the state and local government chain-weighted price index from the U.S. Bureau of Economic Analysis.

21. See table 1 in Bruen and Holahan (1999).

22. Kentucky, Massachusetts, Michigan, Oregon, Vermont, and several other states adopted policies that increased the state government's share of total spending on elementary and secondary education.

23. Tax reduction information from National Governors Association and NASBO (2002) table 7, and fiscal year general fund revenue data from table A-1. Note that this probably understates the aggregate size of state tax reductions. Most of the reductions were recurring and would have grown in size over time. In addition, some tax reductions were phased in over several years, and the publicly reported data do not fully capture multiyear tax reductions. For both reasons, "fully effective" tax cuts in FY 2001 were likely to be considerably larger than can be discerned from the publicly reported data.

24. Calculated from table 2 of National Governors Association and NASBO (2002).

25. "Personal income" is a broad-based measure of income earned by residents of a state or of the nation, and is reported by the U.S. Bureau of Economic Analysis.

26. For example, the June 2002 U.S. macroeconomic forecast from Economy.com, a major macroeconometric forecasting firm, projected that service consumption would rise from 56.2 percent of total consumption in 2002 to 57.9 percent of total consumption in 2006. See Economy.com (2002b: 41).

27. Nicholas Johnson and Daniel Tenny (2002) of the Center on Budget and Policy Priorities have pointed out that states' policy changes have tended to make state taxes more regressive, in part because states have been relatively unafraid to raise excise tax rates in recessions (and even in good times) and because they have focused their tax cutting on the income tax. Figure 3-3 shows that despite these policies, the net result of the strong economic forces at work may have been a more progressive state tax system, as states have become increasingly reliant on the income tax (and as the income tax has become more reliant on the incomes of high-income individuals), while states have become less reliant on excise taxes. More detailed empirical analysis would be needed to disentangle the impacts of policy and economic changes on the distribution of state taxes.

28. Based on data in capgain1-2001.pdf and in00cm54.xls, both of which are available on the Statistics of Income area of the Internal Revenue Service web site (http://www.irs.gov).

29. State revenue analysts in several states, including California, New York, and Ohio, reported this to Rockefeller Institute of Government staff in periodic informal telephone interviews conducted by Institute staff in the course of preparing the Institute's quarterly *State Revenue Report.* These interviews were conducted by Elizabeth I. Davis, Nicholas W. Jenny, and Donald J. Boyd.

30. See California Legislative Analyst's Office (2002); and Pataki (2002).

31. See Balkovic (2002) for the latest in a series of annual articles on this topic by the Internal Revenue Service. The data in this paragraph were obtained from spreadsheets entitled 95IN01AR.xls, 95IN02AR.xls, and 00in54cm.xls, provided by the Internal Revenue Service's Statistics of Income branch.

32. No comprehensive data are available on *state* income taxes paid by these high-income taxpayers, but those taxes would be very substantial.

33. Boyd (2000) provides examples of how state income tax growth could fall off far more sharply than economic growth, using the highly progressive California income tax and the nearly proportional Indiana income tax as examples.

34. Based on a "typical" sales tax base constructed from table 2.4 of the U.S. Bureau of Economic Analysis' consumption accounts, treating as nontaxable the following items: food purchased for off-premises consumption, housing consumption, medical care, personal business services (e.g., legal services), education and research, religious and welfare services, certain purchased transportation, and selected other items. Statutory sales tax bases may not have grown as fast as "taxable" consumption due to growing difficulties in imposing and collecting sales tax.

35. Both data series are plotted on the same graph not to posit a relationship between capital gains and the consumption rate, but simply to show that states fortuitously benefited from two major trends that occurred outside the bounds of postwar historical experience and at the same time. There could well be a relationship between capital gains and the consumption rate, such as a wealth effect that leads people to spend more when asset values and capital gains are high. But it would take more than simple graphical analysis to uncover such an effect.

36. There are some plausible reasons for why capital gains rose and the savings rate fell in the 1990s. Obviously, the stock market contributed to capital gains, but so did lower tax rates on gains—a benefit that will endure even if old market levels do not. Similarly, the lower savings rate could have reflected greater long-term confidence in the economy, greater stability in earnings, higher asset values, and other factors that might lead people to save less for an uncertain future—and some of those factors could endure as well.

37. See NASBO (2002a) for reported Medicaid spending; for budget shortfalls, see Smith et al. (2002).

38. $77 billion plus two years of growth at 18 percent and four more years of growth at 20 percent yields $222 billion, after compounding.

39. Note, though, that the Congressional Budget Office (CBO) remains agnostic about the prospects for future growth—see CBO (2002c: 5).

40. The measure does not take into account the income distribution in the state or the progressivity of the tax structure, both of which can affect significantly a state's reliance on capital gains; therefore, the measure is rather crude. In addition, because it does not take these factors into account, the product of the first two columns, which yields 1.8 percent for the nation as a whole, is not a measure of the percentage of state revenue that comes from capital gains. The percentage of state revenue derived from capital gains, while not easily measured, clearly would exceed this measure, in part because state income taxes generally are progressive.

41. See CBO (2002b: 50–51) for a discussion of retirement income.

42. Author's calculations based on the June 2002 macroeconomic forecast prepared by Economy.com.

43. This may be optimistic. The National Center for Education Statistics (NCES) projections are based on population projections from the U.S. Bureau of the Census that were prepared before the 2000 decennial census was available. These earlier projections were based on intercensal population estimates that in many cases underestimated population growth due to immigration, which is one of the most difficult components of population growth to predict. Although the Census Bureau has not yet updated its projections to reflect the decennial census, Economy.com has prepared projections based on the 2000 census. Under these projections, released in June 2002, the age 5 through 19 cohort is expected to grow by 1.9 percent between 2002 and 2012, compared with the NCES projection of no growth in elementary and secondary school enrollment.

44. NCES regional patterns of projected enrollment growth are broadly consistent with the Economy.com projections of age 5 through 19 population growth in note 43.

45. For a widely cited literature review arguing against evidence of a systematic relationship, see Hanushek (1996). For a counterargument, see Hedges and Greenwald (1996).

46. The description is drawn primarily from summaries of the No Child Left Behind (NCLB) Act on the NCLB section of the *Education Week* web site (http://www.edweek .org) and the NCLB section of the National Governors Association web site (http://www.nga.org). For a detailed analysis of the act, see Council of Chief State School Officers (2002).

47. See Education Commission of the States (2002a) for a listing of state policies that received serious consideration or were adopted in 2000 or 2001.

48. See Congressional Budget Office (2003: 80–83) for a discussion of the CBO Medicaid forecast.

49. Quoted from a mock presidential budget message by Herbert Stein, published in the *Wall Street Journal* on January 19, 1996, and available at http://www.aei.org.

50. The NCES projections are based on population projections from the U.S. Census Bureau that were prepared before the 2000 decennial census and do not incorporate subsequent information showing that the population had grown more quickly than previously believed. The census projections call for growth of 1.0 percent annually in the age 18 to 24 cohort. Coupled with NCES assumptions of very mildly rising enrollment rates and several assumptions of lesser importance, this yields the projected 1.4 percent annual growth in college enrollment. In contrast, Economy.com, a major econometric forecasting firm, has updated its projections to incorporate the 2000 census and projects that the age 20 to 24 cohort will increase by 1.4 percent annually over the same time period. If the Economy.com population projections were inserted into NCES college enrollment forecasts, it would raise enrollment growth by about 5 percentage points over the next 10 years (NCES 2002b: table B4). Growth rates of the Census Bureau's age 18 to 24 cohort are compared with Economy.com's age 20 to 24 cohort because data for cohorts that match precisely are not available.

51. The zero-productivity growth assumption may not be true, especially in the age of the Internet. It may well be that distance learning and other techniques will allow higher education to deliver high-quality education at lower costs than in the past.

52. See Ehrenberg (2000) for a discussion of many of these issues as they apply to selective private colleges.

53. Author's calculations using government finance data from the U.S. Census Bureau and personal income data from the U.S. Bureau of Economic Analysis.

REFERENCES

Advisory Commission on Intergovernmental Relations. 1994. *Significant Features of Fiscal Federalism*. Vol. 2. Washington, D.C.: Advisory Commission on Intergovernmental Relations.

Balkovic, Brian. 2002. "High Income Tax Returns for 1999." *Statistics of Income Bulletin*. Spring 2002.

Boe, E. E., G. Barkanic, and C. S. Leow. 1999. "Retention and Attrition of Teachers at the School Level: National Trends and Predictions." Data Analysis Report No. 1999-DAR1. Philadelphia: University of Pennsylvania.

Boyd, Donald J. 2000. *State Fiscal Issues and Risks at the Start of a New Century*. Albany, N.Y.: Rockefeller Institute of Government.

———. 2002. "Long Rise in Education Spending Slows as Economy Weakens." *State Fiscal News* 2(2): 1–3. Albany, N.Y.: Rockefeller Institute of Government.

Boyd, Donald J., and Nicholas W. Jenny. 2002. "States Will Raise Their Economic Forecasts But May Lower Their Revenue Forecasts." *State Fiscal News* 2(3): 1–3. Albany, N.Y.: Rockefeller Institute of Government.

Braddock, Douglas. 1999. "Occupational Employment Projections to 2008." *Monthly Labor Review* 122(11): 51–77.

Breneman, David W. 2001. "An Essay on College Costs." *NCES Statistical Analysis Report, Study of College Costs and Prices, 1988-89 to 1997-98, Volume 2* (13–20). Washington, D.C.: National Center for Education Statistics.

Bruce, Donald, and William F. Fox. 2001. *State and Local Sales Tax Revenue Losses from E-Commerce: Updated Estimates*. Knoxville: Center for Business and Economic Research, University of Tennessee.

Bruen, Brian, and John Holahan. 1999. *Slow Growth in Medicaid Spending Continues in 1997*. Washington, D.C.: The Kaiser Commission on Medicaid and the Uninsured.

———. 2002. *Acceleration of Medicaid Spending Reflects Mounting Pressures*. Washington, D.C.: The Kaiser Commission on Medicaid and the Uninsured.

California Legislative Analyst's Office. 2002. *2002–03 Budget Bill: Perspectives and Issues*. Sacramento: California Legislative Analyst's Office.

Congressional Budget Office (CBO). 2002a. *The Budget and Economic Outlook: An Update*. Washington, D.C.: Congressional Budget Office.

———. 2002b. *The Budget and Economic Outlook: Fiscal Years 2003–2012*. Washington, D.C.: Congressional Budget Office.

———. 2002c. "Where Did the Revenues Go?" Revenue and Tax Policy Brief. Washington, D.C.: Congressional Budget Office.

———. 2003. *The Budget and Economic Outlook: Fiscal Years 2004–2013*. Washington, D.C.: Congressional Budget Office.

Council of Chief State School Officers. 2002. "No Child Left Behind Act: A Description of State Responsibilities." July 2002 Draft. http://www.ccsso.org/pdfs/NCLB2002.pdf. (Accessed April 14, 2003.)

Doeksen, Gerald A., and Cheryl St. Clair. 2002. *The Economic Impact of the Medicaid Program on Alaska's Economy.* Oklahoma City: Oklahoma State University.

Economy.com. 2002a. *50-State Economic Forecast.* West Chester, Pa.: Economy.com

———. 2002b. *Precis: U.S. Macro* 7(3). West Chester, Pa.: Economy.com.

Education Commission of the States. 2002a. *2000–01 Selected State Policies.* Denver: Education Commission of the States.

———. 2002b. *State Incentive Policies for Recruiting and Retaining Effective New Teachers in Hard-to-Staff Schools.* Denver: Education Commission of the States.

Ehrenberg, Ronald G. 2000. *Tuition Rising: Why College Costs So Much.* Cambridge, Mass.: Harvard University Press.

Families USA. 2003. *Medicaid: Good Medicine for State Economies.* Families USA Publication No. 03-101. Washington, D.C.: Families USA.

Fierro, Michael. 2001. *2001 State Tobacco Settlement Spending Initiatives.* Washington, D.C.: National Governors Association.

Fossett, James W., and James H. Wyckoff. 1996. "Has Medicaid Growth Crowded Out State Educational Spending?" *Journal of Health Politics, Policy and Law* 21(3): 409–32.

Fox Grage, Wendy, Donna Folkemer, Tara Straw, and Allison Hansen. 2002. *The States' Response to the Olmstead Decision: A Work in Progress.* Denver: National Conference of State Legislatures.

Hanushek, Eric A. 1996. "School Resources and Student Performance." In *Does Money Matter?: The Effect of School Resources on Student Achievement and Adult Success,* edited by Gary Burtless (43–73). Washington, D.C.: Brookings Institution Press.

Hedges, Larry V., and Rob Greenwald. 1996. "Have Times Changed? The Relation between School Resources and Student Performance." In *Does Money Matter?: The Effect of School Resources on Student Achievement and Adult Success,* edited by Gary Burtless (74–92). Washington, D.C.: Brookings Institution Press.

Holahan, John, and Bowen Garrett. 2001. "Rising Unemployment and Medicaid." *Health Policy Online* No. 1. Washington, D.C.: The Urban Institute. http://www.urban.org /UploadedPDF/410306_HPOnline_1.pdf. (Accessed October 16, 2001.)

Holahan, John, Joshua M. Wiener, and Amy Westpfahl Lutzky. 2002. "Health Policy for Low-Income People: States' Responses to New Challenges." *Health Affairs Web Exclusive.* http://www.healthaffairs.org/2014Holahan2.pdf. (Accessed September 15, 2002.)

Hovey, Hal. 1998. *The Outlook for State and Local Finances: The Dangers of Structural Deficits for the Future of Public Education.* Washington, D.C.: National Education Association.

Jenny, Nicholas W. 2002a. "Fiscal 2001 Tax Revenue Growth: Weakness Appears." State Fiscal Brief No. 64. Albany, N.Y.: Rockefeller Institute of Government.

———. 2002b. "A Second Quarter of Decline in State Tax Revenue." *State Revenue Report* No. 47. Albany, N.Y.: Rockefeller Institute of Government.

———. 2002c. "Worst Quarter of State Tax Revenue Decline." *State Revenue Report* No. 48. Albany, N.Y.: Rockefeller Institute of Government.

Johnson, Nicholas, and Daniel Tenny. 2002. *The Rising Regressivity of State Taxes.* Washington, D.C.: Center on Budget and Policy Priorities.

Johnstone, D. Bruce. 2001. "Higher Education and Those 'Out of Control' Costs." *NCES Statistical Analysis Report, Study of College Costs and Prices, 1988-89 to 1997-98, Volume 2* (21–43). Washington, D.C.: National Center for Education Statistics.

Jones, Dennis P. 2001. "Cost Analysis and the Formulation of Public Policy." *NCES Statistical Analysis Report, Study of College Costs and Prices, 1988-89 to 1997-98, Volume 2* (45–55). Washington, D.C.: National Center for Education Statistics.

Kilpatrick, Kerry E., Joshua Olinick, Michael I. Luger, and Jun Koo. 2002. *The Economic Impact of Proposed Reductions in Medicaid Spending in North Carolina.* Chapel Hill: School of Public Health, University of North Carolina, Chapel Hill.

Ku, Leighton, and Matthew Broaddus. 2003. *Why Are States' Medicaid Expenditures Rising?* Washington, D.C.: Center on Budget and Policy Priorities.

Lav, Iris J. 2003. *Bush "Growth Plan" Would Worsen State Budget Crises.* Washington, D.C.: Center on Budget and Policy Priorities.

Lav, Iris J., and Nicholas Johnson. 2003. *State Budget Deficits for Fiscal Year 2004 Are Huge and Growing.* Washington, D.C.: Center on Budget and Policy Priorities.

Levit, Katharine, Cynthia Smith, Cathy Cowan, Helen Lazenby, and Anne Martin. 2002. "Inflation Spurs Health Spending in 2000." *Health Affairs* 21(1): 172–81.

Millbank Memorial Fund, National Association of State Budget Officers, and Reforming States Group. 2001. *1998–1999 State Health Care Expenditure Report.* New York: Millbank Memorial Fund; Washington, D.C.: National Association of State Budget Officers.

Mills, Robert J. 2002. "Health Insurance Coverage, 2001." Current Population Reports P60-220. Washington, D.C.: U.S. Census Bureau.

Moore School of Business. 2002. *Economic Impact of Medicaid on South Carolina.* Columbia: University of South Carolina.

National Association of State Budget Officers (NASBO). 2001. *2000 State Expenditure Report.* Washington, D.C.: National Association of State Budget Officers.

———. 2002a. *2001 State Expenditure Report.* Washington, D.C.: National Association of State Budget Officers.

———. 2002b. *2002 State Expenditure Report.* Washington, D.C.: National Association of State Budget Officers.

National Center for Education Statistics (NCES). 2002a. *Digest of Education Statistics, 2001.* Washington, D.C.: National Center for Education Statistics, U.S. Department of Education.

———. 2002b. *Projections of Education Statistics to 2012*, Publication 2002-030. Washington, D.C.: National Center for Education Statistics, U.S. Department of Education.

National Conference of State Legislatures (NCSL). 2002. "State Budget and Tax Actions 2002." *NCSL News.* August 28.

———. 2003. *State Budget Update: February 2003.* Washington, D.C.: National Conference of State Legislatures.

National Governors Association and National Association of State Budget Officers. 1999. *Fiscal Survey of States: December 1999.* Washington, D.C.: National Governors Association and National Association of State Budget Officers.

———. 2001. *Fiscal Survey of States: December 2001.* Washington, D.C.: National Governors Association and National Association of State Budget Officers.

———. 2002. *Fiscal Survey of States: May 2002.* Washington, D.C.: National Governors Association and National Association of State Budget Officers.

Pataki, George E. 2002. Governor of New York. *2002–03 New York State Executive Budget.* January 22. Albany.

Penner, Rudolph G. 1998. "A Brief History of State and Local Fiscal Policy." Washington, D.C.: The Urban Institute. *Assessing the New Federalism* Policy Brief A-27.

Rose, Lowell C., and Alec M. Gallup. 2002. "The 34th Annual Phi Delta Kappa/Gallup Poll of the Public's Attitude Toward the Public Schools." *Phi Delta Kappan* 84(1): 41–57.

Smith, Vernon K. 2002. "The Economic Downturn and Its Impact on Seniors: Stretching Limited Dollars in Medicaid, Health and Senior Services." Testimony for the Special Committee on Aging, United States Senate, March 14, 2002. http://www.statecoverage.net/pdf/smithtestimony.pdf. (Accessed April 14, 2003.)

Smith, Vernon K., and Eileen Ellis. 2002. *Medicaid Budgets under Stress: Survey Findings for State Fiscal Years 2000, 2001, 2002.* Washington, D.C.: Kaiser Commission on Medicaid and the Uninsured.

Smith, Vernon K., Eileen Ellis, Kathy Gifford, Rekha Ramesh, and Victoria Wachino. 2002. *Medicaid Spending Growth: Results from a 2002 Survey.* Washington, D.C.: Kaiser Commission on Medicaid and the Uninsured.

U.S. Department of Health and Human Services, Health Care Financing Administration. 2000. *A Profile of Medicaid Chartbook 2000.* Washington, D.C.: U.S. Department of Health and Human Services.

U.S. Office of Management and Budget (OMB). 2002. *Fiscal Year 2003 Mid-Session Review.* Washington, D.C.: United States Office of Management and Budget.

Wallace, Sally 1995. *The Effects of Economic and Demographic Changes on States and Local Budgets.* Washington, D.C.: The Finance Project.

4

Variation in Health Insurance Coverage and Medical Expenditures:
How Much Is Too Much?

John Holahan

Health insurance coverage of children and adults under age 65 in the United States varies considerably among states, both in the ways people are covered and in the extent to which they are covered. State spending on services for these groups also varies greatly. This chapter explores those variations in considerable detail, providing information on private and public health insurance coverage, rates of uninsurance, and expenditures on Medicaid and other programs that states and localities use to support health services.[1] All the analysis in this chapter relates to persons under age 65.

The fundamental questions are these: How much variation is acceptable in a system that is intended to cover low-income Americans but that leaves so many decisions about the extent of their coverage and the resources devoted to their care to the states? How well does this decentralized system provide Americans, particularly low-income Americans, with health insurance coverage and access to care, regardless of where they live?

The American health care system is a mix of private and public health insurance. Private insurance provided in whole or in part by employers is by far the most important source, covering 66 percent of the population under age 65. The likelihood that an employer will offer coverage depends on a number of factors, including employee wages, firm size, industry, and characteristics of the working population. Because these factors vary among states, employer-sponsored insurance also varies. About 7 percent of Americans buy coverage in the private insurance market, obtain it through Medicare because of disability, or receive it through federal programs for civilians associated with the military.

Many Americans who are not covered under private or federal programs are covered by state programs, primarily Medicaid and, more recently, the State Children's Health Insurance Program (SCHIP), both of which are funded by the federal government and the states together. A few states also fund insurance coverage for people who are not eligible for Medicaid or SCHIP, primarily adults without children and legal immigrants.[2]

Decisions on the extent of coverage offered by Medicaid and SCHIP are essentially a state responsibility, although more than half the costs of these public programs are borne by the federal government. Medicaid programs spent more than $256 billion for health care services in 2002. The federal government pays from 50 percent of the cost in 11 relatively high-income states to 77 percent in Mississippi, the state with the lowest per capita income. Overall, about $146 billion of total Medicaid spending comes from the federal government and $110 billion comes from the states.

Medicaid has traditionally provided coverage to low-income elderly and disabled persons, to parents (mostly women) and children receiving cash assistance, and to low-income children and pregnant women. Several of these groups must be covered as a condition of states' receiving Medicaid funds. Others, such as those who meet the categorical eligibility requirements for Medicaid but who have high medical expenses (i.e., the medically needy), may be covered at the option of the state. States may cover other groups, including higher-income parents with children and adults without children, through Section 1115 Medicaid research and demonstration waivers or at their own expense.

SCHIP, enacted in 1997, is less restrictive than Medicaid. Eligibility extends to children in families with incomes of more than twice the federal poverty level (FPL), and states have more flexibility in designing benefits, using premiums, and sharing costs. Federal matching rates for Medicaid and SCHIP vary inversely with state per capita income, but rates are 30 percent higher under SCHIP than under Medicaid. More recently, states have been allowed to use SCHIP funds to cover parents through demonstration waivers, and a limited number have done so.

States are free to extend coverage as far beyond the minimum federal standards as they choose. Under Medicaid (after welfare reform in 1996) and SCHIP, states can use income disregards to extend coverage to eligible groups virtually without limit. Considerable variation in health insurance coverage among the states may therefore be expected and perhaps intended. But there also seems to be a national interest in extending health insurance coverage and in addressing the problems of the uninsured. If there is a national interest, then wide state variations are problematic.

The national interest is evident from the fact that the United States enacted the Medicare program to cover all persons age 65 and over and persons with serious disabilities. Moreover, while the health reform debate of 1993–94 ultimately failed to expand coverage, it resulted in competing proposals from across the political spectrum; the issue was arguably not whether, but how, to do it. The large federal contribution to Medicaid and SCHIP, and the inverse variation in that funding with state per capita income, both recognize a need to extend insurance coverage to low-income groups, regardless of where they live. Finally, recent interest in extending subsidies to low-income persons through federal tax credits suggests that even people who oppose expanding government insurance programs in general accept the need to extend health insurance coverage.

While the nation has clearly expressed itself with regard to coverage of older persons and persons with serious disabilities, no consensus appears to exist with regard to covering low-income parents, much less adults without children. States are required to cover some parents— namely, those whose incomes would have qualified them for Aid to Families with Dependent Children (AFDC) in 1996—but any additional coverage of adults is completely at the states' discretion. Even where coverage of children is concerned, the consensus may be limited to the poor and near-poor (those with incomes between 100 and 200 percent of the FPL).

If there is no clear national interest, substantial variation in coverage is to be expected and may be acceptable. Coverage and spending are state responsibilities, and states are expected to make such choices consistent with their political preferences. Nonetheless, the current system may have produced variations that go beyond what most Americans would find acceptable. It is possible to believe both that coverage of low-income populations is a state responsibility and that state flexibility yields unacceptable variation in outcomes.

Assuming that some degree of national consensus exists, how well has this federal-state system met the health care needs of low-income Americans? How much do insurance coverage and the resources devoted to health care vary among states? How much of this variation is due to differences in employer-sponsored insurance? How well do states compensate for low levels of private coverage? How much variation in coverage is due to different state policies? Would variations in uninsurance rates remain great even if there were less variation in private coverage?

To answer these questions, the chapter first examines health insurance coverage in detail—who is covered, by whom, and how coverage varies among states. It then presents findings on state Medicaid spending—per capita, per low-income person, and particularly in relation to the population not covered by private or federal insurance. Variations in access to health care and in health status are explored, and conclusions are drawn from the findings.

The chapter draws on several sources. Data on insurance coverage come from the Current Population Survey (CPS), with three years of data merged to increase the size of the state samples. The CPS provides data on all 50 states, and this information is used in regression analyses and to provide results on selected variables in appendix 1. Information on variations in health status and access to care comes from the National Survey of America's Families. Many of the tables rely on data for the 13 states from the *Assessing the New Federalism* (ANF) project. Over the past several years, ANF has developed extensive information on health policy in these states. Comparisons of spending across states draw on Medicaid expenditure data from Health Care Financing Administration (HCFA) 2082 and HCFA 64 databases. Data for the 13 states are presented in the text; comparable data for all 50 states are provided in appendix 2. Data on "other state spending" come from the National Association of State Budget Officers and the American Hospital Association.

Health Insurance Coverage

Three measures are used here to analyze health insurance coverage: the insurance gap, the uninsurance rate, and the coverage ratio.

- The insurance gap is the proportion of a state's population under age 65 that is not covered by private (employer-sponsored or individually purchased) or federal (Medicare or the Civilian Health and Medical Program of the Uniformed Services [CHAMPUS]) health insurance. The insurance gap shows the size of the population that would be uninsured if not for state efforts (Spillman 2000).

- The uninsurance rate is the percentage of a state's population with no health insurance coverage from any source. It is equivalent to the insurance gap less the population covered by Medicaid, SCHIP, and state-financed health programs. The uninsurance rate depends both on the size of a state's insurance gap and on the state's efforts to reduce it.
- The coverage ratio is the percentage of the insurance gap covered by a state's health programs (Medicaid, SCHIP, and state-financed health programs)—that is, the ratio of the population with state coverage to the population that would have no coverage without the state. The coverage ratio is determined by public policy.

In short, the size of the insurance gap, together with the share of the gap closed by the state, determines the uninsurance rate.

Health Insurance Coverage in the 13-State Sample

The key features of state health insurance programs in the 13 ANF states vary considerably. In 1999, they were as follows (1999 data are used to be consistent with other available data; in most cases these programs remain intact):

Massachusetts—developed the MassHealth program with a Medicaid Section 1115 waiver and SCHIP funds. MassHealth covered children in families with incomes up to 200 percent of the FPL and the long-term unemployed with incomes up to 133 percent of the FPL. It included provisions for covering parents and adults without children between 133 and 200 percent of the FPL, either through their employers or through a special program for the uninsured. Massachusetts also covered the short-term unemployed who were receiving unemployment compensation and who had incomes up to 400 percent of the FPL.

Minnesota—provided coverage to children and pregnant women with incomes up to 275 percent of the FPL under its Section 1115 Medicaid research and demonstration waiver. Minnesota also had a state-subsidized health insurance program, MinnesotaCare, that provided coverage to children and parents with incomes below 275 percent of the FPL and to single adults with incomes below 175 percent of the FPL.

New York—had high AFDC income standards and extended Medicaid eligibility for pregnant women, infants, and children well beyond federally mandated levels. New York's SCHIP program, an extension of its state-subsidized Child Health Plus program, provided coverage for children with family incomes up to 230 percent of the FPL. The state also provided broad health insurance coverage to its general assistance or home relief population.

Washington—had generous Medicaid eligibility, covering all children under age 19 with family incomes less than 200 percent of the FPL. Individuals and families with incomes up to 200 percent of the FPL could buy into the state's Basic Health Plan on a subsidized basis. Those with higher incomes could join the plan by paying the full premium.

California—had broad eligibility for Medicaid, primarily because its AFDC income standards were well above the national average and the state had a program for the medically needy. The state extended coverage under SCHIP to children with family incomes up to 250 percent of the FPL. In 1999, California had not yet extended coverage to any adults under SCHIP.

Michigan—had relatively broad Medicaid eligibility, including a medically needy program. Children with family incomes up to 200 percent of the FPL were covered under SCHIP. The state had a small subsidized insurance program in Wayne County (Detroit) for the general assistance population.

New Jersey—had AFDC income standards above the national average and a program for the medically needy. The state expanded eligibility under SCHIP to children with family incomes up to 200 percent of the FPL. In 1999, the state had not yet adopted its current extensive coverage for parents and adults without children.

Wisconsin—extended Medicaid eligibility to children and parents with family incomes up to 185 percent of the FPL under its BadgerCare program. BadgerCare was funded under both Medicaid Section 1115 and a SCHIP waiver. BadgerCare does not cover adults without children.

Florida—extended coverage to 185 percent of the FPL for pregnant women and infants but otherwise provided little coverage beyond federally mandated levels. AFDC income standards were well below the national average. Florida covered children with family incomes up to 200 percent of the FPL under SCHIP, building upon its state-funded Healthy Kids program. Florida did not extend coverage to adults without children.

Mississippi and Alabama—had limited Medicaid coverage because of their low AFDC income standards and lack of a program for the medically needy. Both states covered children under SCHIP up to 200 percent of the FPL. Neither subsidized insurance coverage for adults without children.

Texas and Colorado—had limited Medicaid coverage because of their low AFDC income standards; Colorado had no medically needy program, and Texas had one with very low income thresholds. Colorado covered children under SCHIP up to 185 percent of the FPL, and Texas covered them up to the poverty level (it has subsequently increased coverage to twice the FPL). Neither state subsidized insurance coverage for adults without children.

Variations in Uninsurance Rates

Over the years 1997 through 1999, an average of 18 percent of Americans under age 65 were without insurance, although the rates varied greatly among states (table 4-1). The highest uninsurance rates—more than 20 percent—were in Texas, California, Florida, and Mississippi. The lowest rates—ranging from 10 to 15 percent—were in Minnesota, Wisconsin, Massachusetts, Michigan, and Washington.

More than 34 percent of all low-income persons in the United States lacked health insurance coverage (table 4-1). Again, the states with the highest rates of uninsurance were Texas and California, at about 45 percent and 40 percent, respectively, and the states with the lowest rates were Minnesota, Wisconsin, Massachusetts, Michigan, and Washington, ranging from 25 percent to 28 percent. The sample of 13 states had somewhat higher uninsurance rates than the United States as a whole.

For all children, the uninsurance rates averaged 15 percent, ranging from slightly more than 8 percent in Minnesota to 25 percent in Texas. The same four states (Texas, California, Florida, and Mississippi) had the highest uninsurance rates for all children, and the same five states (Minnesota, Wisconsin, Massachusetts, Michigan, and Washington) had the lowest rates. For children in low-income families, the national uninsurance rate was 26 percent. Texas had by far the highest uninsurance rate, at 38 percent, and Massachusetts had the lowest, at 15 percent.

Adults were much more likely to be uninsured than children, at 20 percent versus 15 percent. The highest uninsurance rates were again in Texas and California, both more than 25 percent, and the lowest rates were in Minnesota (11 percent) and Wisconsin (13 percent). The uninsurance rate for low-income adults nationally was 40 percent. Texas and

Table 4-1. *Variation in States' Uninsurance Rates*

State	Total (%) All Incomes	Total (%) Low Incomes	Children (%) All Incomes	Children (%) Low Incomes	Adults (%) All Incomes	Adults (%) Low Incomes
Texas	26.5	45.0	25.2	37.6	27.1	50.5
California	23.5	39.8	19.4	28.7	25.6	47.3
Florida	22.6	37.6	18.8	29.1	24.2	42.5
Mississippi	21.6	36.9	18.2	28.5	23.3	42.5
New York	19.4	33.4	14.0	21.6	21.9	41.0
Alabama	17.9	32.7	14.9	23.9	19.2	38.4
Colorado	17.2	37.4	14.4	30.2	18.4	41.6
New Jersey	17.2	36.7	13.3	25.4	18.8	43.0
Washington	14.5	28.4	10.3	15.4	16.4	35.8
Michigan	13.5	27.9	9.8	18.1	15.3	34.7
Massachusetts	12.6	23.9	8.7	15.0	14.2	29.4
Wisconsin	11.5	25.7	8.8	16.3	12.8	31.4
Minnesota	9.8	25.1	8.3	19.2	10.6	29.4
Remaining states (average)	16.0	31.4	13.5	23.7	17.2	36.4
Total U.S.	18.1	34.2	15.0	25.5	19.5	39.9

Source: The Urban Institute 2001. Tabulations of the March 1998–2000 Current Population Survey (CPS).

Note: Low income = < 200% of the federal poverty level. Data are given for population under age 65.

California had the highest rates, at roughly 50 percent, while Minnesota and Massachusetts had the lowest, at about 30 percent.

The Insurance Gap

Sixty-six percent of Americans are covered through employer-sponsored insurance, and 73 percent are covered through a combination of private insurance (employer-sponsored insurance and individual insurance) and federal insurance (Medicare and CHAMPUS). The remaining 27 percent constitute the insurance gap (table 4-2). Employer-sponsored insurance rates vary from 58 percent in California and 59 percent in Texas to 75 percent in Minnesota and 76 percent in Wisconsin. The combined private-

Table 4-2. *Employer-Sponsored and Federal Insurance Coverage and the Insurance Gap*

State	All Incomes (% of population)			Low Incomes (% of population)		
	Employer-Sponsored Insurance	Private and Federal Insurance	Insurance Gap	Employer-Sponsored Insurance	Private and Federal Insurance	Insurance Gap
California	57.6	65.1	34.9	27.2	34.5	65.5
Texas	59.2	65.4	34.6	29.9	36.5	63.5
Mississippi	59.9	68.4	31.6	32.1	41.3	58.7
New York	61.8	67.3	32.7	26.8	33.2	66.8
Florida	60.0	69.6	30.4	31.8	43.9	56.1
Alabama	65.9	73.4	26.6	34.4	44.7	55.3
Washington	66.8	76.1	23.9	30.3	42.3	57.7
Massachusetts	70.0	76.2	23.8	33.3	41.5	58.5
Colorado	69.8	78.6	21.4	34.2	48.1	51.9
Michigan	71.7	76.4	23.6	34.9	41.6	58.4
New Jersey	71.3	77.0	23.0	36.6	43.6	56.4
Minnesota	74.6	82.1	17.9	35.9	46.4	53.6
Wisconsin	75.9	82.4	17.6	40.6	52.7	47.3
Balance of total	68.5	76.1	23.9	36.8	47.0	53.0
Grand total	65.9	73.2	26.8	33.4	42.6	57.4

Source: The Urban Institute 2001. Tabulations of the March 1998–2000 CPS.

Note: Low income = < 200% of the federal poverty level. Data are given for population under age 65.

federal coverage rate averages roughly 7 percentage points above the employer-sponsored insurance rate. Accordingly, the insurance gaps are largest in California and Texas, at about 35 percent, and lowest in Minnesota and Wisconsin, at about 18 percent. These findings show that California and Texas begin with much larger uninsured populations than Minnesota and Wisconsin.

Nationwide, 33 percent of low-income persons under age 65 are covered by employer-sponsored insurance, and 43 percent are covered by combined private-federal insurance. Thus, the insurance gap for this group is 57 percent. Employer-sponsored insurance coverage ranges from a low of 27 percent in New York and California to a high of 41 percent in Wisconsin. These rates of coverage result in insurance gaps of almost 67 percent in New York and 66 percent in California to just over 47 percent in Wisconsin. Clearly, New York, California, and Texas begin with much larger gaps in coverage of the low-income population than Wisconsin, Colorado, and Minnesota.

Stated differently, the extent of employer-sponsored insurance coverage in a state largely determines the size of its uninsured population. Why is the variation in employer-sponsored insurance among states so great? Because certain factors affect the likelihood of an individual's having such coverage, and those factors vary among states (Cantor, Long, and Marquis 1995; Cunningham and Ginsburg 2001; Farber and Levy 1998; Hadley, Bovbjerg, and Rockmore 2002; Long and Marquis 1993; Trenholm and Kung 2000). First, workers in industries such as manufacturing and government are much more likely to have health insurance coverage than those in agriculture, construction, or retail trades. Second, workers in large firms are far more likely to have coverage than those in small firms. Third, unionized workers are far more likely to be covered than nonunion workers. Fourth, workers with higher earnings are more likely to have insurance than low-wage workers, who are typically less skilled and have less education. Firms may not offer health insurance to low-wage workers because the cost would be a very high share of their compensation. Moreover, workers with limited ability to command high pay may prefer cash to health insurance. Finally, holding all these factors constant, blacks, Hispanics, and noncitizens are much less likely to have employer-sponsored health insurance.

A recent study analyzed how these and other factors varied among states and attempted to explain why some states had high rates of employer-sponsored insurance and others had low rates (Shen and Zuckerman 2003). It found that while type of industry was important in explaining whether individuals had such insurance, it was not responsible for much of the variation among states. However, variables such as income, education, race-ethnicity, citizenship, firm size, and unionization all contributed to the likelihood of an individual's having employer-sponsored insurance and varied significantly among states. The study found that states with low rates of employer-sponsored insurance also have populations with fewer skills and less education. Because of these workforce characteristics, the states attract fewer high-paying jobs that require well-educated, skilled workers and offer insurance coverage; as a result, the states have high uninsurance rates.

State Coverage

Colorado covers 4 percent of its population under age 65 through Medicaid and other state insurance programs, while Mississippi, Michigan, Massachusetts, California, and New York cover at least 10 percent (table 4-3). Low-income populations are covered at a higher rate, ranging from just under 15 percent in Colorado and less than 20 percent in Texas, Florida, and New Jersey to more than 30 percent in Michigan, New York, and Massachusetts.

Generous coverage of the low-income population does not always translate into broad coverage of the overall population, however. Much depends on income distribution. Minnesota provides more generous cov-

Table 4-3. *Variation in Medicaid Coverage*

	Enrollment in Medicaid and State-Funded Health Programs (% of population)					
	Total		Children		Adults	
State	All Incomes	Low Incomes	All Incomes	Low Incomes	All Incomes	Low Incomes
Colorado	4.2	14.6	7.2	21.5	2.8	10.4
New Jersey	5.9	19.7	11.1	30.9	3.6	13.4
Wisconsin	6.1	21.7	10.2	31.2	4.1	15.7
Florida	7.7	18.5	15.7	30.4	4.5	11.7
Minnesota	8.1	28.5	13.5	37.6	5.3	21.7
Texas	8.1	18.4	15.5	28.3	4.4	11.3
Alabama	8.8	22.6	17.9	35.8	4.8	14.1
Washington	9.4	29.3	17.7	46.0	5.8	19.8
Mississippi	10.0	21.8	17.7	32.9	6.2	14.4
Michigan	10.1	30.5	17.7	43.9	6.3	21.2
Massachusetts	11.3	34.5	21.1	50.7	7.2	24.6
California	11.4	25.7	20.4	38.2	6.9	17.3
New York	13.3	33.4	23.6	47.5	8.6	24.3
Remaining states (average)	7.9	21.6	14.3	31.5	4.9	15.1
Total U.S.	8.8	23.3	16.0	34.3	5.4	16.0

Source: The Urban Institute 2001. Tabulations of the March 1998–2000 CPS.
Note: Low income = < 200% of the federal poverty level. Data are given for population under age 65.

erage to its low-income population than either Alabama or Mississippi does, but Minnesota also has a much smaller percentage of low-income residents than Alabama or Mississippi. Thus, even though Minnesota's coverage is more generous, it reaches less of the state's overall population. Alabama and Mississippi, with their less generous funding of a much larger low-income population, end up covering a larger share of their overall population than Minnesota does.

Children fare better than adults under state programs. California, New York, and Massachusetts cover more than 20 percent of all their children, while Colorado covers 7 percent. Washington, New York, and Massachusetts cover more than 45 percent of low-income children; Colorado and Texas, less than 30 percent. Coverage for the overall adult population ranges from 3 percent in Colorado to 7 percent in Massachusetts and almost 9 percent in New York. Less than 12 percent of low-income adults are covered in Colorado, Texas, and Florida, and more than 24 percent receive coverage in New York and Massachusetts.

Insurance Gaps and Coverage Ratios

The size of the insurance gap primarily reflects the rate of employer-sponsored insurance. The coverage rates—Medicaid or state program coverage divided by the gap—show the role of public policy. The uninsurance rate depends on both the size of the insurance gap and state efforts to reduce the size of the gap.

A state's insurance gap may also be affected by the generosity of its public programs. That is, if the state offers generous health insurance coverage, fewer employees may choose to be covered under their employers' plans, thereby increasing the size of the insurance gap. Such crowding out of private coverage has been well documented, though there is some dispute as to the extent of it (Dubay 1999). States that have extended coverage to persons well above the poverty level (such as Minnesota, Massachusetts, and Washington) may be pushing rates of employer-sponsored insurance downward, and thus their (exogenous) insurance gaps may actually be greater than reported here (tables 4-4 and 4-5). States such as Texas or Mississippi are less likely to crowd out employer-sponsored insurance because eligibility for state coverage does not extend far enough up the income ladder to affect the working population very much.

Given this caveat, the insurance gap follows the pattern described above, ranging from 35 percent in California and Texas to 18 percent in

Table 4-4. *Insurance Gaps, Coverage Ratios, and Uninsurance Rates, All Incomes*

State	Total			Children			Adults		
	Insurance Gap (% of population)	Coverage Ratio (%)	Uninsurance Rate (% of population)	Insurance Gap (% of population)	Coverage Ratio (%)	Uninsurance Rate (% of population)	Insurance Gap (% of population)	Coverage Ratio (%)	Uninsurance Rate (% of population)
California	34.9	32.6	23.5	39.8	51.3	19.4	32.5	21.3	25.6
Texas	34.6	23.4	26.5	40.7	38.0	25.2	31.5	13.9	27.1
New York	32.7	40.7	19.4	37.6	62.7	14.0	30.5	28.2	21.9
Mississippi	31.6	31.7	21.6	35.9	49.2	18.2	29.5	20.9	23.3
Florida	30.4	25.5	22.6	34.5	45.5	18.8	28.7	15.7	24.2
Alabama	26.6	32.9	17.9	32.8	54.7	14.9	24.0	20.1	19.2
Massachusetts	23.8	47.2	12.6	29.8	70.7	8.7	21.4	33.7	14.2
Washington	23.9	39.5	14.5	28.0	63.4	10.2	22.1	26.1	16.4
Michigan	23.6	42.9	13.5	27.5	64.4	9.8	21.6	29.0	15.3
New Jersey	23.0	25.5	17.2	24.4	45.5	13.3	22.4	16.3	18.8
Colorado	21.4	19.6	17.2	21.6	33.5	14.4	21.2	13.3	18.4
Minnesota	17.9	45.1	9.8	21.8	61.8	8.3	15.8	33.3	10.6
Wisconsin	17.6	34.4	11.5	19.0	53.7	8.8	16.9	24.4	12.8
Remaining states (average)	23.9	33.0	16.0	27.7	51.5	13.5	22.1	22.3	17.2
Total U.S.	26.8	32.7	18.1	31.0	51.6	15.0	24.9	21.8	19.5

Source: The Urban Institute 2001. Tabulations of the March 1998–2000 CPS.
Note: Data are given for population under age 65.

Table 4-5. *Insurance Gaps, Coverage Ratios, and Uninsurance Rates, Low Incomes*

State	Total			Children			Adults		
	Insurance Gap (% of population)	Coverage Ratio (%)	Uninsurance Rate (% of population)	Insurance Gap (% of population)	Coverage Ratio (%)	Uninsurance Rate (% of population)	Insurance Gap (% of population)	Coverage Ratio (%)	Uninsurance Rate (% of population)
New York	66.8	50.0	33.4	69.1	68.7	21.6	65.3	37.2	41.0
California	65.5	39.2	39.8	67.0	57.1	28.7	64.6	26.8	47.3
Texas	63.5	29.0	45.0	65.9	42.9	37.6	61.7	18.2	50.5
Mississippi	58.7	37.1	36.9	61.4	53.6	28.5	56.9	25.3	42.5
Massachusetts	58.5	59.1	23.9	65.7	77.1	15.0	54.0	45.6	29.4
Michigan	58.4	52.3	27.9	62.0	70.8	18.1	55.9	37.9	34.7
Washington	57.7	50.8	28.4	61.5	74.9	15.4	55.6	35.5	35.8
Florida	56.1	32.9	37.6	59.5	51.1	29.1	54.1	21.5	42.5
New Jersey	56.4	34.9	36.7	56.3	54.9	25.4	56.4	23.7	43.0
Alabama	55.3	40.9	32.7	59.7	60.0	23.9	52.5	26.9	38.4
Minnesota	53.6	53.2	25.1	56.8	66.1	19.2	51.2	42.4	29.4
Colorado	51.9	28.1	37.4	51.7	41.6	30.2	52.0	20.0	41.6
Wisconsin	47.3	45.8	25.7	47.6	65.7	16.3	47.2	33.3	31.4
Remaining states (average)	53.0	40.8	31.4	55.2	57.1	23.7	51.5	29.3	36.4
Total U.S.	57.4	40.5	34.2	59.8	57.4	25.5	55.9	28.6	39.9

Source: The Urban Institute 2001. Tabulations of the March 1998–2000 CPS.

Note: Low Income = < 200% of the federal poverty level. Data are given for population under age 65.

Minnesota and Wisconsin (table 4-4). A comparison of the insurance gap and the uninsurance rate (table 4-4) shows clearly that the size of the gap positively affects the size of the uninsurance rate: California and Texas have the largest gaps and the highest uninsurance rates, whereas Minnesota and Wisconsin have the smallest gaps and the lowest uninsurance rates.

But not all the variation in uninsurance rates is explained by the insurance gap. The four states with the highest coverage ratios (New York, Massachusetts, Michigan, and Minnesota) have significantly reduced the size of their uninsured populations; that is, they have substantially reduced their uninsurance rates by providing generous public coverage. The impact of public policy can be seen simply by comparing states that have similar insurance gaps. For example, gaps in Texas and New York are similar in magnitude, but New York has a coverage ratio of almost 41 percent, while Texas has a coverage ratio of just over 23 percent. The result is an uninsurance rate of 19 percent in New York and 27 percent in Texas. Similarly, Colorado and Minnesota have gaps of 21 percent and 18 percent respectively, but Minnesota's coverage ratio is more than twice Colorado's. As a result, the uninsurance rate in Colorado is 17 percent versus 10 percent in Minnesota.

The size of the insurance gap affects the uninsurance rates of children similarly (table 4-4). Texas and California have the largest gaps and the highest uninsurance rates; Minnesota and Wisconsin have the smallest gaps and the lowest uninsurance rates. The coverage ratio reveals the differences in states' efforts to extend coverage to uninsured children. New York, Washington, Michigan, and Minnesota cover more than 60 percent of the children in the gap through Medicaid and other state programs, and Massachusetts covers more than 70 percent. The result is that the uninsurance rates for children in these states are lower than one would expect, given the size of the insurance gaps. Comparisons of states with similar gaps are again instructive. California has a gap of 40 percent and New York a gap of 38 percent, yet New York covers 63 percent of children in the gap and California covers 51 percent. Accordingly, New York has a substantially lower uninsurance rate. The situation for adults is much the same.

The picture changes somewhat when looking at the low-income population (table 4-5). Here again there is a rough correspondence between the size of the insurance gap and the uninsurance rate, but the role of public programs is much more significant. Comparing New York and California again, one finds that the insurance gaps are similar, but New York has a much higher coverage ratio. As a result, the uninsurance rate in New York is much lower than in California. Minnesota and Colorado have similar size gaps, but Minnesota has a much higher coverage ratio for its low-income population. The result is that the uninsurance rate in Minnesota is 25 percent versus 37 percent in Colorado. The rest of table 4-5 shows the effect of state programs on children and on adults separately. In both cases, the size of the gap, state coverage ratios, and the uninsurance rate correspond roughly.

In summary, the size of the insurance gap is clearly important in explaining the uninsurance rate of the population at all income levels. State programs play a greater role in determining whether low-income people will be covered, because this population is less likely to work in firms that offer employer-sponsored coverage. State programs are particularly important for children, but state efforts to cover low-income adults also affect state uninsurance rates.

To test the relative importance of the size of a state's insurance gap and the effectiveness of state policies in closing it, data from all 50 states have been used to estimate two simple regression models in which the uninsurance rate is the dependent variable. The log of the insurance gap is the independent variable in the first model, and the log of the ratio of Medicaid and state coverage to population is the independent variable in the second. (Including both in the same regression results in very high standard errors and unreliable results.) The two models were estimated separately for the entire state population under age 65, by income, and for children and adults separately.

The results demonstrate clearly that, for the overall population, the size of the insurance gap is more important than Medicaid/state coverage in explaining the uninsurance rate (table 4-6). In the regressions for the total population, children, and adults, the insurance gap is clearly positive and highly significant. This single variable explains a large part of the variation in the uninsurance rate across states: The first row of table 4-6 shows that a 1 percent increase in the gap would result in a 1.06 percent increase in the uninsurance rate for the total population and similar increases for both children and adults. At the same time, these results show that Medicaid/state coverage is not statistically significant in any of these regressions and contributes nothing to explaining the uninsurance rate.

For the low-income population, however, the results are different. The insurance gap is less important. The coefficients are smaller in magnitude, and thus increases in the insurance gap among low-income popu-

Table 4-6. *Relative Importance of Insurance Gaps and Coverage Ratios*

Population	Coefficient	T-Statistic	R^2
All incomes total			
Insurance gap	1.06	11.63	0.74
Coverage ratio	0.06	0.56	0.01
Children			
Insurance gap	0.96	6.43	0.46
Coverage ratio	0.02	0.31	0.00
Adults			
Insurance gap	1.08	15.44	0.83
Coverage ratio	0.02	0.04	0.00
Low-income total			
Insurance gap	0.84	3.72	0.22
Coverage ratio	−0.37	−4.15	0.26
Children			
Insurance gap	0.59	1.72	0.06
Coverage ratio	−0.70	−5.13	0.35
Adults			
Insurance gap	0.95	5.27	0.37
Coverage ratio	−0.27	−3.97	0.25

Source: The Urban Institute 2001. Tabulations of the March 1998–2000 CPS with dollar figures from Health Care Financing Administration (HCFA) 2082 and National Association of State Budget Officers (NASBO) data.

Note: Regressions are estimated using logs of the dependent and independent variables so that results can be interpreted as percentage differences.

lations result in a smaller increase in the uninsurance rate. The insurance gap is statistically significant for the overall and adult low-income populations but not for children. The reduced importance of the insurance gap in the low-income population is not surprising, because many low-income people are not in the labor force and therefore would not be affected by the provision of employer-sponsored insurance.

In contrast, the Medicaid/state coverage variable is negative and significant (at the 0.05 level) for all three low-income groups. For the overall population, a 1 percent increase in the coverage ratio results in a 0.37 percent reduction in the uninsurance rate. For children, a 1 percent increase in Medicaid/state coverage results in a 0.70 percent reduction in the uninsured rate. And for adults, a 1 percent increase in coverage results in a 0.27 percent reduction. Because Medicaid and state health insurance coverage is directed at the low-income population, it is not surprising that it has a greater effect on this group than on the total population.

Thus it is clear that the size of the insurance gap is the key determinant of uninsurance rates for the population as a whole. But for the low-income population, both the insurance gap and the coverage rate are important. The bigger the gap, the higher the uninsurance rate; but the greater the extent of public coverage, the lower the uninsurance rate.

Spending on Health Care

Expenditures are another important indicator of states' relative contributions to the health of their low-income residents. Expenditures reflect not only the extent of coverage, but also the generosity of benefits, levels of provider payments, and so on.

Medicaid Spending on Acute Care

Per capita Medicaid spending on acute care for the total population, low-income persons, and persons in the insurance gap is shown in table 4-7. Per capita spending reflects not only the generosity of benefits but also the share of the population covered. Colorado and Wisconsin spend the least on the overall population, at $196 and $218, respectively, while Massachusetts and New York spend the most, at $431 and $688, respectively. Medicaid spending per low-income person is slightly different. The states with the lowest spending are Texas ($599) and Mississippi ($706), while Massachusetts ($1,478) and New York ($1,841) remain the highest. It is noteworthy that the highest state spending per low-income person is roughly three times the lowest state spending. Medicaid spending on people in the insurance gap is similar—Texas and California spend the least, and Massachusetts and New York spend the most. The difference between highest and lowest spending is roughly threefold.

These figures reflect total Medicaid spending, not federal funds and state funds separately. Federal Medicaid spending matches each state's expenditures in inverse proportion to state income—that is, states with the lowest incomes have the highest federal matching rates. The intent is to even out spending. But the intent is far from reality, as table 4-7 clearly shows: When state funding of Medicaid is considered separately, even greater variations appear. On a per capita basis, the states with the lowest

Table 4-7. *Medicaid Spending on Acute Care Per Person in the Insurance Gap, 1998*

State	Federal and State Funds ($)			State Funds ($)		
	Per Person	Per Low-Income Person	Per Person in the Insurance Gap	Per Person	Per Low-Income Person	Per Person in the Insurance Gap
Colorado	196	747	917	94	359	440
Wisconsin	218	849	1,239	90	350	510
Minnesota	234	941	1,309	112	450	626
Texas	249	599	721	94	226	272
Alabama	269	718	1,011	83	220	310
New Jersey	274	997	1,190	137	498	595
Florida	288	761	949	128	338	421
California	308	748	883	150	365	430
Washington	312	1,107	1,302	149	530	623
Mississippi	314	706	994	72	162	228
Michigan	334	1,103	1,417	155	512	658
Massachusetts	431	1,478	1,808	215	739	904
New York	688	1,841	2,101	344	920	1,050
Remaining states (average)	301	897	1,257	115	342	479
Total U.S.	322	924	1,200	138	396	513

Source: The Urban Institute 2001. Tabulations of the March 1998–2000 CPS with acute care Medicaid spending for children, adults, and the nonelderly disabled from 1998 HCFA 2082 data.

Note: Low income = < 200% of the federal poverty level. Data are given for population under age 65.

expenditures are Mississippi and Alabama (at $72 and $83, respectively), and the two highest are, again, Massachusetts and New York (at $215 and $344). The difference between the highest and lowest state expenditures is at least threefold, even when New York is excluded. The contrast is even starker for the low-income population, with at least a fourfold difference between the lowest-spending states (Mississippi, Alabama, and Texas, at about $200 per capita) and the highest-spending states (Massachusetts at $739 per capita and New York at $920). The discrepancy results in part from differences in health insurance coverage per low-income person, but the variations in spending are greater than the variations in coverage.

A similar picture emerges when one looks at people in the insurance gap. Mississippi and Texas cover fewer individuals in the insurance gap than do states such as Massachusetts and New York. Thus, the differences in spending are large: Mississippi spends $228 and Texas $272, but Massachusetts spends $904 and New York $1,050. Again, differences in spending per person in the gap are greater than differences in coverage.

Variations among states in Medicaid and SCHIP spending tend to mirror variations in residents' per capita incomes. States with higher per capita incomes have not only a greater ability to pay for services but, typically, fewer low-income people to serve. To test the relationship between spending and income, data for 50 states are again used to estimate two simple regressions. The first is the log of combined federal-state Medicaid and SCHIP spending per capita against the log of state income per capita; the second is the log of just state spending per capita against the log of state income per capita. We then repeated these regressions using the log of spending per low-income person. The results (table 4-8) show that a 1 percent increase in income per capita is not related to combined federal-state spending per capita, but it is associated with a 1.03 percent increase in state spending per capita. Thus, federal matching funds, which are greater in low-income states, do offset the effects of higher state spending in high-income states. The bottom line is that federal-state spending per capita does not vary systematically with income.

Spending per low-income person is somewhat different. A 1 percent increase in state per capita income is associated with a 1.09 percent increase in combined federal-state spending per low-income person. Thus, as state income increases, so does Medicaid spending per low-

Table 4-8. *Change in Medicaid and State Children's Health Insurance Program (SCHIP) Spending with Increasing Per Capita Income*

Spending	Coefficient	T-Statistic
Per capita		
Federal and state	0.00	−0.01
State	1.03	3.04
Per low-income person		
Federal and state	1.09	4.00
State	2.13	6.60

Source: The Urban Institute 2001. Expenditures from HCFA 2082 and NASBO data. Population estimates from tabulations of the March 1998–2000 CPS.

Note: Data are given for population under age 65.

income person, both state spending and federal matching funds. Further-more, a 1 percent increase in state per capita income is associated with a 2.13 percent increase in state spending per low-income person. In fact, state Medicaid and SCHIP spending expands so much when state incomes increase that the higher federal matching rates for low-income states are not sufficient to offset them.

State Spending on Other Health Programs

Some states that spend less on Medicaid do so, it has been argued, because of their aversion to federal entitlement programs, but they make up for it by spending more on public hospitals and clinics and other pro-grams that provide services directly to low-income persons. Data from several sources were used to test this hypothesis.[3]

The results show that combined federal-state spending on other health programs for low-income persons tends to track spending on Medicaid and SCHIP (table 4-9). Expenditures on other programs are lowest in Alabama and Mississippi, where spending on Medicaid and SCHIP are also close to the bottom. Similarly, New York and Massachusetts spend the most for other programs, just as they do for Medicaid and SCHIP. The pic-ture is the same when looking at funding from state sources only: States with the lowest spending on other programs (Mississippi, Alabama, and Colorado) are among the states with the lowest funding of Medicaid and SCHIP. Once more, New York and Massachusetts are among the states spending the most of their own funds on both Medicaid and SCHIP and on other programs.

To test whether there is an inverse relationship between spending on other programs and spending on Medicaid and SCHIP, data from all 50 states were used in a regression analysis. The results show that the higher the spending on Medicaid and SCHIP, the higher the spending on other health programs (table 4-10). This finding is true regardless of whether we look at spending per capita or per low-income person or whether we look at state expenditures from their own resources or fed-eral and state spending.

Long-Term Care

The discussion has focused on Medicaid spending for acute care, but Medicaid also pays for a substantial amount of long-term care for aged, disabled, and blind persons. Not all elderly and disabled enrollees use

Table 4-9. *Spending on Medicaid and SCHIP, and on Other State Programs for Low-Income Persons*

| | Federal and State Funds ($) | | State Funds ($) | |
| | Medicaid and SCHIP | Other State Programs | Medicaid and SCHIP | Other State Programs |
State				
Texas	606	502	228	367
Mississippi	715	319	163	216
Alabama	738	297	225	238
California	756	390	368	257
Colorado	761	448	364	214
Florida	777	448	343	321
Wisconsin	852	600	350	313
Minnesota	941	628	450	570
New Jersey	1,012	654	504	578
Michigan	1,111	468	515	314
Washington	1,107	544	530	431
Massachusetts	1,513	1,220	751	1,008
New York	1,902	752	942	576
Remaining states	910	539	361	396
Total U.S.	940	531	405	389

Source: The Urban Institute 2001. Expenditures from HCFA 2082, NASBO, and American Hospital Association (AHA) data, with denominators from the March 1998–2000 CPS.

Note: Low income = < 200% of the federal poverty level. Data are given for population under age 65.

long-term care services, but these enrollees are as good an estimate of the eligible population as is available. Most long-term care spending is for nursing home care, although the most rapidly growing component is home and community-based services.

Medicaid expenditures for long-term care services per aged, blind, and disabled enrollee vary from almost $12,000 in New York and Minnesota to more than $3,000 in Alabama and $2,000 in Mississippi (table 4-11). The federal government pays more for such services in low-income states than in high-income states, thus the discrepancies are even greater if one looks simply at state funding. Variations in state-funded care range from about $6,000 in New York and Minnesota to less than $1,000 in Alabama and less than $600 in Mississippi. Clearly, the availability of long-term services also varies enormously among states.

Table 4-10. *Spending on Other State Programs Relative to Spending on Medicaid and SCHIP*

Spending	Coefficient	T-Statistic
Federal and state		
All incomes	0.18	1.85
Low income	0.27	2.71
State		
All incomes	0.34	2.04
Low income	0.52	3.37

Source: The Urban Institute 2001. Expenditures from HCFA 2082 and NASBO data. Estimates of the low-income population from tabulations of the March 1998–2000 CPS.

Note: Low income = < 200% of the federal poverty level. Data are given for population under age 65.

Table 4-11. *Expenditures on Long-Term Care for Aged, Blind, and Disabled Medicaid Enrollees, FY 1998*

State	Expenditure per Enrollee ($)	
	Federal and State	State
New York	11,968	5,984
Minnesota	11,682	5,591
Massachusetts	8,051	4,026
Wisconsin	7,648	3,148
New Jersey	7,504	3,752
Washington	6,300	3,014
Colorado	5,909	2,838
Michigan	5,554	2,578
Texas	4,468	1,685
Florida	3,285	1,457
California	3,208	1,565
Alabama	3,167	971
Mississippi	2,408	552
Remaining states (average)	5,285	2,151
Total U.S.	5,639	2,484

Source: Urban Institute estimates, 2002. Based on data from the Centers for Medicare and Medicaid Services (CMS).

Note: Long-term care includes nursing facilities, intermediate care facilities for the mentally retarded, home and community-based care for the functionally disabled elderly, home and community-based waiver services, home care, personal care services, targeted case management, and hospice services. The denominator is the number of aged, blind, and disabled enrollees who participated in Medicaid for any length of time during the fiscal year 1998. The number of people actually using these services cannot be accurately counted using publicly available data sources.

Variations in Access to Care and Health Status

Not surprisingly, then, the percentage of low-income children and adults with no usual source of health care (a measure of access) and the percentage in fair or poor health (a measure of health) also vary greatly across the 13 states in the sample (table 4-12). Low-income children are most likely to lack a usual source of care in California, Mississippi, and Texas, and least likely to lack a usual source of care in Massachusetts, Wisconsin, and Minnesota. Among low-income adults, those in Texas and California are most likely to lack a usual source of care, and those in Massachusetts, Michigan, Minnesota, and Wisconsin are least likely. The results tend to track variations in uninsurance rates.

Similarly, low-income children are more likely to be reported in fair or poor health in California, Mississippi, New Jersey, and Texas. With the

Table 4-12. *Variations in Access to Care and Health Status, Low-Income Children and Adults*

State	No Usual Source of Care (%)		In Fair or Poor Health(%)	
	Children	Adults	Children	Adults
Texas	14.4	27.5	11.7	27.0
California	13.7	26.8	11.0	26.6
Mississippi	11.0	15.2	12.9	28.8
New Jersey	9.1	20.4	11.0	27.3
Florida	9.1	22.6	7.6	26.8
Alabama	9.0	17.3	8.1	27.9
Colorado	9.0	19.7	9.3	16.1
Washington	8.1	22.0	8.0	20.3
New York	7.8	16.5	9.7	27.4
Michigan	7.7	14.8	7.9	23.5
Wisconsin	6.4	16.0	6.0	15.9
Minnesota	3.8	12.0	4.9	12.8
Massachusetts	3.6	14.6	7.0	21.3
Remaining states (average)	6.9	16.6	5.7	21.8
Total U.S.	8.9	19.5	7.9	23.8

Source: Urban Institute tabulations of the National Survey of America's Families 1999.

Note: Low income = < 200% of the federal poverty level. Data are given for population under age 65.

exception of New Jersey, all of these states have high uninsurance rates. At the other extreme are Minnesota and Wisconsin, with the lowest percentages of children in fair or poor health. Low-income adults in Alabama, Florida, Mississippi, New Jersey, and Texas are most likely to be in fair or poor health, while those in Minnesota, Wisconsin, and Colorado are least likely.

These results do not necessarily imply causal relationships among insurance coverage, access to care, and health status, although these relationships have been established convincingly elsewhere (Hadley 2002). But the data do clearly suggest that low rates of health insurance coverage and high uninsurance rates are not the result of readily accessible health care and good health among a state's low-income residents. On the contrary: With few exceptions, the states with high uninsurance rates among low-income residents tend to be the same states with significant problems in access to care and higher percentages of the population in fair or poor health.

Summary and Conclusions

Uninsurance rates vary widely among the states—by a factor of roughly two for low-income populations and about three for the population under age 65 as a whole. States with higher uninsurance rates tend also to have larger low-income populations. These variations hold true for both children and adults.

The extent of employer-sponsored insurance coverage—a key determinant of uninsurance rates for all persons, regardless of income—also varies substantially. Employer-sponsored insurance is largely determined by population characteristics such as race and ethnicity, education, and citizenship and by employment factors such as firm size and unionization. Depending primarily on the availability of employer-sponsored insurance, states face insurance gaps of different dimensions, with some states having a very large gap to fill and others having a relatively small gap. A state's efforts to close the insurance gap through Medicaid, SCHIP, and other programs are a reflection of public policy. For people with low incomes, both the extent of employer-sponsored coverage and the generosity of state coverage affect uninsurance rates.

Spending on Medicaid and other programs varies by roughly a factor of three in the 13 states in the sample. State spending from their own resources varies even more. State-funded Medicaid and SCHIP spending per low-income person increases sharply with state per capita income—so sharply, in fact, that federal matching contributions, which vary inversely with state income, are not sufficient to reduce spending differentials. The result is that Medicaid spending (federal and state combined) increases in proportion to increases in state income. Finally, the states with low rates of public coverage and high uninsurance rates are also the states whose low-income residents are more likely to have problems with access to health care and to be in fair or poor health.

One can only conclude from this evidence that the existing federal-state financing structure has left the United States with serious inequities in regard to health care. The redistribution of resources built into the Medicaid matching formula, which varies federal contributions inversely with state financial capacity, has simply not resulted in anything close to equity in health insurance coverage or in the resources expended on low-income populations.

States are not wholly to blame for this outcome. Some of the problems they face result from their employment base: Low rates of employer-sponsored insurance coverage raise the fiscal stakes for states and have proven very difficult to overcome. But there are also major differences in states' efforts, some of which result from differences in the ability to pay, but most of which result from differences in the willingness to devote resources to health care for low-income populations. This is a matter of political philosophy and political will, and is perhaps to be expected in a system that has devolved primary responsibility for health care decision-making to the states.

Whether the variation in outcomes is acceptable is another matter. Unfortunately, the resulting differences in lack of coverage affect both access to care and health—and ultimately affect work, productivity, and contributions to national well-being. In this sense, decisions states make with respect to their own citizens ultimately affect the citizens of other states.

The results suggest that states need to be given incentives to go further in providing health care for their low-income residents. Possibly with higher matching rates and greater flexibility in program design, as in SCHIP, states may be induced to expand coverage, expend more resources, and improve outcomes. With strong enough incentives, even the most reluctant states may be unable to ignore the availability of federal funds.

But it is also likely that stronger incentives would not be sufficient. If they are not, achieving a reasonable degree of equity in coverage and access may require shifting much more of the responsibility for financing low-income Americans' health care to the federal government.

Appendix 1. *Population Uninsured, Employer-Sponsored Insurance (ESI), or in the Insurance Gap, by State*

State	Total (%)			Low Income (%)		
	Uninsured	ESI Rate	Insurance Gap	Uninsured	ESI Rate	Insurance Gap
Minnesota	9.8	74.6	17.9	25.1	35.9	53.6
Rhode Island	10.6	73.0	19.7	23.7	33.6	53.8
Hawaii	11.1	71.1	20.6	21.2	42.6	45.2
Iowa	11.3	73.2	16.8	23.3	42.5	40.4
Wisconsin	11.5	75.9	17.6	25.7	40.6	47.3
Pennsylvania	11.6	72.9	20.4	23.1	41.1	48.2
Nebraska	11.6	68.8	18.8	24.4	37.6	45.5
Vermont	11.8	66.7	25.0	17.9	32.5	54.9
Missouri	12.1	71.4	20.4	24.4	37.8	49.6
New Hampshire	12.4	74.7	19.1	26.9	38.6	51.9
Ohio	12.5	74.1	20.3	25.3	41.9	49.1
Massachusetts	12.6	70.0	23.8	23.9	33.3	58.5
Connecticut	13.2	74.9	19.0	32.6	35.6	53.7
Kansas	13.3	68.7	19.3	28.4	38.9	46.8
Michigan	13.5	71.7	23.6	27.9	34.9	58.4
Indiana	13.7	74.9	18.5	31.4	43.3	46.1
Tennessee	14.1	62.1	30.3	22.2	33.6	58.6
Washington	14.5	66.8	23.9	28.4	30.3	57.7
South Dakota	14.6	65.2	20.3	28.2	40.3	42.5
Maine	14.9	69.5	22.4	30.0	38.4	51.8
Delaware	15.0	71.3	24.1	31.6	36.8	56.7
Utah	15.1	73.0	19.4	26.9	50.0	39.1
Virginia	15.4	69.7	20.5	34.2	36.1	50.8
Illinois	15.4	71.5	22.9	33.1	36.0	56.1
Oregon	15.8	67.4	25.3	31.6	36.1	54.9
Maryland	15.8	74.1	19.3	40.1	34.1	53.4
North Dakota	16.2	62.5	22.6	29.8	33.1	47.2

(*continued*)

Appendix 1. *Continued*

	Total (%)			Low Income (%)		
State	Uninsured	ESI Rate	Insurance Gap	Uninsured	ESI Rate	Insurance Gap
Kentucky	16.5	66.1	25.9	32.5	31.7	57.3
New Jersey	17.2	71.3	23.0	36.7	36.6	56.4
Colorado	17.2	69.8	21.4	37.4	34.2	51.9
North Carolina	17.4	66.8	24.8	33.2	36.7	52.8
Alabama	17.9	65.9	26.6	32.7	34.4	55.3
Wyoming	18.2	65.2	24.4	31.9	38.2	47.5
South Carolina	18.8	66.3	25.8	35.9	36.8	53.1
Georgia	18.9	63.8	28.7	33.8	34.0	57.6
New York	19.4	61.8	32.7	33.4	26.8	66.8
Alaska	19.6	60.3	26.5	38.5	27.5	58.1
Idaho	20.4	64.4	26.5	37.0	38.8	50.9
West Virginia	20.7	61.0	33.8	32.8	32.0	61.1
Oklahoma	20.8	63.1	27.1	36.0	35.0	51.0
Mississippi	21.6	59.9	31.6	36.9	32.1	58.7
Montana	21.8	58.8	30.2	35.5	31.4	54.7
Nevada	22.2	67.3	26.1	41.8	39.6	52.6
Arkansas	22.4	59.2	31.8	35.6	34.6	55.4
Florida	22.6	60.0	30.4	37.6	31.8	56.1
Louisiana	23.0	59.9	33.3	36.5	32.2	59.0
California	23.5	57.6	34.9	39.8	27.2	65.5
New Mexico	26.2	55.3	37.9	40.0	30.0	62.7
Arizona	26.4	57.6	34.0	44.6	31.4	61.2
Texas	26.5	59.2	34.6	45.0	29.9	63.5
U.S. total	18.1	65.9	32.0	34.2	33.4	63.5

Source: The Urban Institute 2001. Tabulations of the March 1998–2000 CPS.

Note: Low income = < 200% of the federal poverty level. Data are given for population under age 65.

Appendix 2. *Per Capita Spending and Enrollment, by State*

State	Total Nonelderly			Low-Income Nonelderly		
	Federal and State Medicaid Spending ($)	State Medicaid Spending ($)	Total Enrollment (%)	Federal and State Medicaid Spending ($)	State Medicaid Spending ($)	Total Enrollment (%)
Virginia	174.48	84.64	5.1	632.69	314.87	17.0
Nevada	177.49	88.74	3.9	533.23	269.88	11.0
Kansas	179.10	72.16	6.0	588.12	236.89	18.6
Wyoming	187.77	69.44	6.1	538.43	205.31	16.1
Indiana	191.62	73.95	4.7	714.92	277.66	15.4
Colorado	195.79	94.04	4.2	761.32	370.63	14.7
Oklahoma	201.60	59.45	6.3	540.34	164.29	15.3
Idaho	213.23	64.84	6.1	560.49	170.94	13.9
North Dakota	214.59	63.46	6.4	600.80	179.28	17.1
Wisconsin	217.77	89.63	6.1	851.87	357.82	22.1
Utah	224.16	61.47	4.3	690.57	189.97	12.2
Nebraska	231.85	90.03	7.2	736.41	288.46	21.3
Minnesota	233.96	111.97	8.1	940.97	452.85	28.4
Texas	249.25	94.02	8.1	605.68	231.12	18.7
New Hampshire	249.99	124.99	6.7	1,022.05	517.88	25.2
Missouri	253.17	99.55	8.3	849.85	339.17	25.6
Montana	257.89	75.92	8.4	622.40	185.12	19.3
Ohio	260.36	108.98	7.8	848.82	362.32	24.4

(continued)

Appendix 2. Continued

State	Total Nonelderly			Low-Income Nonelderly		
	Federal and State Medicaid Spending ($)	State Medicaid Spending ($)	Total Enrollment (%)	Federal and State Medicaid Spending ($)	State Medicaid Spending ($)	Total Enrollment (%)
Iowa	264.52	95.89	5.5	916.98	334.24	17.1
South Dakota	266.71	86.01	5.7	814.56	266.53	14.3
Alabama	269.38	82.65	8.8	738.44	229.84	23.0
New Jersey	273.94	136.97	5.9	1,012.14	512.00	19.8
Georgia	281.04	110.06	9.8	747.04	296.38	24.1
Connecticut	285.25	142.62	5.8	1,179.16	609.30	21.9
Florida	288.17	127.80	7.7	777.37	350.47	18.7
South Carolina	290.26	86.41	7.0	851.60	254.97	17.6
California	308.12	150.27	11.4	756.28	371.59	25.9
Washington	311.56	149.08	9.4	1,107.32	538.82	29.1
Arkansas	311.68	84.65	9.4	702.20	195.58	20.0
Pennsylvania	311.92	145.39	8.8	992.20	465.71	24.8
Mississippi	314.31	72.01	10.0	715.32	166.41	21.9
Oregon	315.82	121.72	9.5	908.87	352.78	23.3
Arizona	325.99	113.02	7.6	752.19	264.76	16.9
Maryland	328.66	164.33	3.5	1,411.32	714.12	13.1

Louisiana	332.66	99.70	10.4	773.28	236.28	22.9
Michigan	334.35	155.20	10.1	1,111.22	519.80	30.7
North Carolina	339.68	125.37	7.4	994.38	373.98	20.0
Illinois	343.46	171.73	7.5	1,131.91	575.14	23.3
Delaware	350.06	175.03	9.0	1,084.48	557.05	25.5
Hawaii	355.44	177.72	9.6	976.40	493.35	24.2
Vermont	366.82	138.73	13.1	1,209.78	465.38	37.5
Alaska	416.23	167.32	6.9	1,493.84	604.33	19.6
Kentucky	417.55	123.72	9.4	1,212.20	368.50	25.1
New Mexico	427.40	117.06	11.7	875.68	245.11	23.1
Massachusetts	430.95	215.47	11.3	1,513.34	766.11	35.0
Maine	448.17	152.20	7.4	1,499.36	519.50	22.2
West Virginia	451.92	118.99	13.2	1,024.82	276.30	28.8
Tennessee	486.69	178.32	16.2	1,271.94	470.52	36.5
Rhode Island	557.63	261.14	9.1	1,975.28	940.62	30.5
New York	687.74	343.87	13.3	1,902.26	954.67	33.8
Grand total	321.97	137.80	8.8	940.06	412.35	23.5

Source: The Urban Institute 2001. Expenditures from HCFA 2082 and NASBO data. Estimates of the low-income population from tabulations of the March 1998–2000 CPS.

Note: Low income = < 200% of the federal poverty level. Data are given for population under age 65.

NOTES

1. In this chapter, low-income refers to incomes less than 200 percent of the federal poverty level.

2. For a more thorough summary of these state programs, see Holahan and Pohl (2002).

3. The National Association of State Budget Officers (NASBO) collects data on many types of state health care spending. NASBO data on state expenditures for higher education, insurance and access expansion initiatives, public health–related initiatives, state facility–based services, and community-based services were included because all of these expenditures can contribute to care for the poor. Higher education includes state university–based teaching hospitals, which usually provide significant amounts of care to the uninsured. State insurance and access expansions include state coverage initiatives as well as funding for high-risk pools and other insurance subsidies. Public health–related initiatives include local health clinics; the Ryan White AIDS program; nonfederal Indian health care; pharmaceutical assistance for the elderly; childhood immunization programs; women, infants, and children (WIC) programs; AIDS testing; and breast and cervical cancer screening. State facilities offering services include state hospitals, state-operated long-term care facilities, and a variety of other facilities. Community-based services include rehabilitation services, alcohol and drug abuse treatment, mental health community services, and vocational rehabilitation services.

Some spending on local hospitals is financed with local revenues. American Hospital Association data are used to estimate local government contributions. Unfortunately, not all hospitals report such data; however, data from the hospitals that do report reveal that local government revenues amount to only 1 percent of hospital revenues. Thus, the underreporting could not have a significant effect on the results described below. State spending on Medicaid is estimated using the same data shown in table 4-7, together with federal data on State Children's Health Insurance Program expenditures in 1999.

REFERENCES

Cantor, Joel C., Stephen H. Long, and M. Susan Marquis. 1995. "Private Employment-Based Health Insurance in Ten States." *Health Affairs* 14(2): 199–211.

Cunningham, Peter J., and Paul B. Ginsburg. 2001. "What Accounts for Differences in Uninsurance Rates Across Communities?" *Inquiry* 38(1): 6–21.

Dubay, Lisa. 1999. "Expansions in Public Health Insurance and Crowd-Out: What the Evidence Says." Incremental Health Reform Project. Washington, D.C.: The Henry J. Kaiser Family Foundation.

Farber, Henry S., and Helen Levy. 1998. *Recent Trends in Employer-Sponsored Health Insurance Coverage: Are Bad Jobs Getting Worse?* NBER Working Paper 6709. Cambridge, Mass.: National Bureau of Economic Research.

Hadley, Jack. 2002. "Sicker and Poorer: The Consequences of Being Uninsured." Washington, D.C.: The Henry J. Kaiser Family Foundation. http://www.kff.org/content /2002/20020510/4004.pdf. (Accessed April 23, 2003.)

Hadley, Jack, Randall Bovbjerg, and Marc Rockmore. 2002. *Factors Associated with Variations Across States and Communities in Low-Income Workers' Insurance Coverage.* Washington, D.C.: The Urban Institute. Unpublished paper.

Holahan, John, and Mary Beth Pohl. 2002. *States as Innovators in Coverage.* Washington, D.C.: The Urban Institute. *Assessing the New Federalism* Discussion Paper 02-08.

Long, Stephen H., and M. Susan Marquis. 1993. "Gaps in Employer Coverage: Lack of Supply or Lack of Demand?" *Health Affairs* Supplement 1993: 282–93.

Shen, Yu-Chu, and Stephen Zuckerman. 2003. "Why Is There State Variation in Employer-Sponsored Insurance?" Urban Institute Working Paper. Washington, D.C.: The Urban Institute.

Spillman, Brenda C. 2000. "Adults without Health Insurance: Do State Policies Matter?" *Health Affairs* 19(4): 178–87.

Trenholm, Christopher, and Susanna Kung. 2000. *Disparities in State Health Insurance Coverage: A Matter of Policy or Fortune?* Washington, D.C.: AcademyHealth.

5

States' Strategies for Tapping Federal Revenues

Implications and Consequences of Medicaid Maximization

Teresa A. Coughlin
Stephen Zuckerman

M edicaid's financing rules require that states spend their own funds in order to receive federal matching funds, but there are no limits on program spending. This open-ended commitment of federal resources invites states to be generous in designing their programs. At the same time, because states share in the costs, it encourages them to use Medicaid funds judiciously. State cost-sharing is also a way to assure federal policymakers and taxpayers alike that Medicaid spending is worthwhile.

States have considerable discretion about the specific groups of people and services they cover. In addition, states determine to a large extent how they raise their share of program costs and how much they pay providers of health services. While decisions about eligibility and the benefit package have tended be fairly uncontroversial, how states raise their share of Medicaid costs and the amount they pay providers has created conflict between federal and state governments, especially over the past decade.

Much of the controversy centers on states' figuring out ways, all of them legal, to claim as many federal Medicaid dollars as possible. The practice of implementing Medicaid policies designed to expand federal financing is commonly referred to as Medicaid maximization. Some forms of maximization were intended and actively encouraged. Others were not, and these have sometimes made maximization a contentious issue. The unintended maximization strategies have brought about several changes in the structure and character of Medicaid—notably, increasing federal spending in the absence of a real state match, creating inequities in the distribution of Medicaid funds among states, and distorting program spending.

This chapter provides a brief background on Medicaid financing and program design, then discusses some of the maximization strategies states have used and how the strategies have affected the Medicaid program. It concludes with a consideration of some policy issues related to Medicaid maximization, and options for addressing state actions and their impact on the structure of the program.

Medicaid Design and Financing

The Medicaid statute sets out basic guidelines about which populations and services states are required to cover. The guidelines also impose some limitations on how providers are paid and how services are delivered to beneficiaries. Beyond these basics, however, the law gives states considerable latitude in the design of their Medicaid programs. States may cover a wide range of additional populations, such as the medically needy, the working disabled, and low-income working parents, and they may offer up to 34 optional services. Both how and how much Medicaid providers are paid is also left almost entirely to the discretion of each state.

States thus face a range of important decisions. First is the decision to participate in Medicaid. Although all states have a Medicaid program, they are not required to do so. Once a state elects to participate, several decisions must be made about the design of its program: Which populations will be covered? What services will be included in the benefit package? Should service limitations be imposed? How should care be delivered— managed care or fee-for-service? At what level should provider reimbursement be set?

Owing to the federal promise to pay for a share of all Medicaid costs, states have an incentive to assess opportunities for Medicaid maximization when designing their programs. Indeed, a primary goal of the federal Medicaid match is to lower states' costs of providing coverage to low-income residents, thereby encouraging states to undertake initiatives they would not have attempted otherwise or to extend services beyond what they would have offered on their own. The federal match basically discounts the price of health care programs for a state's low-income population. The match also makes it less attractive for states to cut Medicaid during economic downturns, when need is great and state revenues are low.

The federal share of Medicaid spending is determined by a formula—the Federal Medical Assistance Percentage—that gives poorer states (based on per capita income) a higher matching rate than wealthier states. A state's matching rate cannot be less than 50 percent or more than 83 percent. In 2002, 11 states received the minimum 50 percent, while Mississippi had the highest match, 77 percent. Of the roughly $256 billion spent on Medicaid that year, about 57 percent ($146 billion) came from the federal government; the remainder came from states and localities.[1]

When Medicaid was enacted, states realized quickly that the federal funding available through Medicaid would allow them to finance health care for the poor with less of their own money. By 1971, five years after Medicaid was implemented, costs totaled $6.5 billion, more than twice the initial projections. Analysts attributed the unanticipated growth to an underestimate of the extent to which states would cover optional eligibility groups and services (Klemm 2000). Medicaid is now one of the largest expenditure items in all states' budgets and is one of the fastest growing components of the federal budget.

Clearly, the structure of the federal match gives states an incentive to maximize federal funds for Medicaid. If a state is going to provide a service to its low-income population funded with state or local dollars, it is to the state's benefit to include that service in its Medicaid package. Similarly, the state might cover people through Medicaid, as opposed to local or state health programs, and pay providers more generously. Broad Medicaid eligibility rules and generous provider payment rates can offset state or local health expenditures for the uninsured and help cover providers' uncompensated care costs (i.e., their charity care and bad debts).

Recognizing the potential pressures to expand Medicaid—which can cause program costs to spiral upward—the federal government retained the right to review and approve states' Medicaid plans and changes to those plans. Further, if a state wants a major exception to Medicaid eligibility, payment, or service coverage rules, the federal government can require the state to seek a research and demonstration, freedom-of-choice, or home and community-based service waiver, all of which are subject to review by the Centers for Medicare and Medicaid Services (CMS).

Not all states are inclined to maximize Medicaid to the same degree. Economic resources and underlying population differences that affect health care needs (such as the number of uninsured residents) play important roles in determining how a state designs its Medicaid program and the extent to which it maximizes Medicaid. A state's political culture and the sophistication and expertise of state Medicaid officials and legislators regarding the many nuances of the Medicaid program are also very important factors.

How States Have Maximized Medicaid

Over the years, maximization strategies have come in various forms, but they generally fall into two broad categories: program expansions and revenue expansions. Program expansions involve Medicaid eligibility and services and operate on the basic principle that a state is free to increase spending on more or better services. Thus, a state may choose to maximize federal support by operating a more generous Medicaid program. States can expand their programs by electing various options allowed under Medicaid or by seeking waivers.

The second group of Medicaid maximization strategies is revenue expansions. These expansions have been much more controversial than program expansions, because they have the effect of increasing federal spending with limited or no state contributions. In some instances, the increased funds are not used to cover or improve health care services or to expand coverage to new populations.

Program Expansions

SHIFTING STATE-FUNDED HEALTH SERVICES INTO MEDICAID
A common practice among states has been to reconfigure state-funded services so that they are in keeping with Medicaid standards and regulations. States then shift the services into Medicaid, where federal dollars will help pay for them. If states maintain their level of spending, shifting a program into Medicaid makes more funds available, thus enabling more health care needs to be met. If states reduce their own spending they free up resources to use on other priorities.

Shifting of services into Medicaid really took hold in the mid- to late-1980s. Medicaid is now an important source of revenue for many public health programs, particularly maternal and child health services and home health care (Coughlin et al. 1999). States also pursued Medicaid maximization in mental health care. Beginning in the mid-1980s, states increasingly moved patients out of state psychiatric hospitals, where adults age 22 to 64 are generally ineligible for Medicaid, into the community, where they are eligible for Medicaid (Manderscheid et al. 2000). Likewise, some states—for example, Wisconsin, California, and Washington—have gradually shifted state-funded home care services into Medicaid. More recently, through a Section 1115 waiver called Pharmacy Plus, some states—for example, Illinois, Maryland, and South Carolina—have moved state-funded pharmacy assistance programs for low-income elderly persons into Medicaid.

EXPANDING POPULATIONS SERVED UNDER MEDICAID

Over the past decade, several states have increased the flow of federal dollars by expanding Medicaid eligibility to populations that were either uninsured or covered by state-funded programs. The vehicle many states used was Medicaid's Section 1115 demonstration waiver authority.[2] Although 1115 waivers had been available for many years, they had not been used widely prior to the early 1990s, in part because federal policymakers feared that program costs might increase under waivers and in part because states viewed the federal review process as too burdensome and lengthy. Soon after President Bill Clinton took office in 1993, his administration made it easier for some states to meet the budget neutrality provisions required by Section 1115 waivers (Holahan et al. 1995)[3] and made a commitment to streamline the waiver process. States embraced the new flexibility: Between 1993 and 1995 alone, 13 states received Section 1115 waivers. Before 1993, Arizona was the only state with such a waiver.

While each of the Section 1115 programs implemented in the mid- and late-1990s is unique, a common feature of many, especially the early ones, was expansion of coverage (Holahan et al. 1995).[4] The Oregon Medicaid demonstration expanded Medicaid eligibility to all adults with incomes under the federal poverty level. Tennessee's TennCare waiver also expanded eligibility: When first established, TennCare was open to all uninsured persons, regardless of employment status or income.

Using a somewhat different approach, several states now receive federal Medicaid matching dollars through Section 1115 waivers for health insurance programs that originally were funded exclusively with state dollars. One such waiver is Minnesota's Prepaid Medical Assistance Program demonstration, under which the state receives Medicaid funds to help finance its subsidized health insurance program, MinnesotaCare.

Likewise, New York gets federal matching funds under its Partnership Plan waiver for its general assistance population, which was previously covered under the state and local Home Relief program.

If Medicaid waivers must be budget-neutral, how can they be a mechanism for increasing federal funds to states? The answer is that budget projections in waiver applications are complex and may include alternative revenue sources such as disproportionate share hospital (DSH) and hypothetical coverage and benefits expansions. For example, if a state has the option of bringing a new population into the program without a waiver, the cost of serving that population may be included in the baseline cost calculation against which budget neutrality is measured, even if the state would not actually have chosen to cover that population if no waiver were granted. Similarly, under current waiver guidelines, states may include unspent State Children's Health Insurance Program (SCHIP) allocations that might have been returned to the federal treasury or allocated to other states if the state did not receive a waiver. While budget-neutrality requirements are a major constraint on how states' waiver programs are designed, they do not prevent states from adopting waivers that have the overall effect of increasing federal funds flows to states.

Revenue Expansions

Medicaid Funding of General Safety Net Programs

Some states have used the Section 1115 authority to secure new federal funds for their general health care programs (Coughlin and Liska 1998). California and New York are among the states that have used this maximization strategy. In 1995 and in 2000, Los Angeles County received Section 1115 waivers that provided additional federal dollars to the county health care system, on the condition that the system be restructured to include an emphasis on ambulatory care (Long and Zuckerman 1998; Zuckerman and Lutzky 2001). The initial purpose of the waiver was to stabilize a system that was experiencing serious fiscal difficulty and was considering closing its largest public hospital and privatizing others. Despite the promise of restructuring, the waiver was viewed by many as a bailout of the county health system and was reported as such in the media (American Health Line 1995). Over the seven-year waiver period, Los Angeles received more than $1 billion in federal Medicaid money. The state match required to receive these federal payments was financed with intergovernmental transfers (IGTs) from Los Angeles County; thus the county was helped without any additional expenditure on the part of the state of California.

Similarly, New York, as part of its Partnership Plan 1115 waiver, was granted additional federal funds to help safety net hospitals make the transition to a more competitive marketplace. The five-year waiver enabled New York hospitals to get $1.25 billion in federal funds. The funds were used for a wide range of things, including worker retraining and management information systems. New York was able to secure the federal funds through the budget neutrality provisions in the Section 1115 waiver authority. That is, as long as a state can show that expenditures under the waiver are no more than they would have been without the waiver, then the state—with federal approval—can get Medicaid matching funds.

FINANCING AND PAYMENT POLICIES

Without doubt, the most controversial Medicaid revenue expansion strategy has been to combine financing policies and payment policies. Often, this type of maximization is done without spending from a state's general revenues. It is important to note that, in order for maximization to work, the financing and payment policies must work in tandem.

Financing policies aimed at maximizing Medicaid began with provider donations and taxes, which were widely used by states beginning in the mid-1980s. Provider taxes and donations were initially approved by the Health Care Financing Administration (HCFA, now called the Centers for Medicare and Medicaid Services, or CMS). To give states greater flexibility in raising Medicaid funds, HCFA issued a rule in 1985 allowing states to use donations from private medical care providers as part of their state share.

West Virginia was the first state to use provider donations for this purpose. In 1986, West Virginia did not have enough money to pay hospitals for Medicaid services and thus could not draw federal matching dollars. Hospitals helped out by donating money to the state. The state then paid the hospitals for their Medicaid services with the donated funds, thereby earning a federal Medicaid match. Thus, West Virginia was able to receive the federal match without having to spend any state dollars. Although the federal dollars may not have fully covered hospitals' costs in treating Medicaid patients, the donation program allowed hospitals to receive at least partial payment.

Also in the mid-1980s, some states adopted provider tax programs, which operated along the same lines as the donation programs. States would collect tax revenue from providers, often hospitals, and use the funds as the state's share of Medicaid payments, especially Medicaid DSH payments. Typically, these payments were issued to the providers that had been taxed. Thus, at the end of the transaction, the hospital was fully reimbursed for its tax contribution. Florida established the first provider tax program in 1984.

Donation and provider tax programs became common in the early 1990s. In 1990, just six states had such programs; by 1992, 39 states had them (Ku and Coughlin 1995). While the bulk of the provider tax and donation programs involved hospitals, intermediate care facilities for the mentally retarded (ICF/MRs), nursing homes, and physicians were sometimes involved. To deal with the rapidly rising number of programs, Congress enacted legislation in 1991 that essentially banned states' use of provider donations and limited provider taxes to "real" assessments, with no guaranteed payback of the tax contributions. Many states had trouble enacting provider taxes that complied with the new law.[5]

Because of these difficulties, many states turned to IGTs as a way to raise their share of Medicaid funding. As the name implies, IGTs are exchanges of funds among or between different levels of government. They are a common feature in state finance—for example, a state transfer of money to a county to support primary education constitutes an IGT. Beginning in the early 1990s, many states began to use IGTs as a way to leverage federal Medicaid dollars, and IGT programs became a variation on provider tax and donation programs. Although IGTs are a legally acceptable means of raising a state's share of Medicaid funding,[6] their current use is not in keeping with the spirit of how Medicaid was to be financed.

To understand how states benefit from financing policies involving IGTs (or tax and donation programs), a typical transaction is outlined in figure 5-1. The transaction begins with the state's receiving $10 million—in the form of an IGT, provider tax, or donation—from a provider. The state would then make a $12 million Medicaid payment back to the provider. Assuming that the state has a 50 percent federal matching rate, the state would get $6 million in federal Medicaid funds. At the end of the transaction, the provider would have netted $2 million ($12 million minus $10 million) in Medicaid payments, all from federal funds. The federal government would have paid $6 million in Medicaid payments, $2 million of which went to the provider and $4 million of which went to the state, where the money could be used for various purposes, whether health

Figure 5-1. *How Medicaid Maximization Can Work*

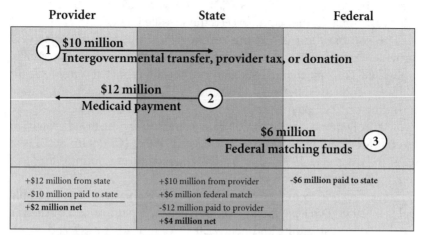

Source: The Urban Institute 2002.
Notes: DSH = disproportionate share hospital; UPL = upper payment limit.

or general state expenditures. Neither the state nor the locality expended any funds—only the federal government did. This situation is contrary to a basic tenet of Medicaid: that the federal government and the states or localities share the financial burden.

Such financing policies have enormous advantages for the states. Each dollar of revenue raised from IGT, provider tax, or donations could generate one to three federal dollars, depending upon the Medicaid matching rate. Moreover, depending upon the specifics of the program, the federal dollars could be generated without using any of the state's own money.

Because federal Medicaid matching payments are based on state expenditures, not revenues, the states had to spend the money generated through provider taxes, donations, and IGTs. Many states did so through Medicaid DSH payments and, more recently, upper payment limit (UPL) payments.

In an effort to maintain low-income persons' access to health care, Congress mandated in the Omnibus Budget Reconciliation Act (OBRA) of 1981 that states consider the special payment needs of hospitals that serve a disproportionately high share of Medicaid and uninsured patients. These special payments came to be known as DSH payments.[7] Although DSH payments were mandated in the early 1980s, states were slow to adopt them. To encourage such payments, Congress passed as part of OBRA 1986 a provision allowing states to pay more to hospitals that cared for a large number of low-income patients. With DSH payments, Medicaid reimbursement to such hospitals could be higher than those paid by Medicare—that is, they could exceed the so-called UPL.[8]

The combination of raising revenues without state expense (via provider taxes, donations, and IGTs) and allowing states to make virtually unlimited DSH payments fueled an extraordinary increase in Medicaid DSH expenditures. Between 1990 and 1992, reported federal and state spending on DSH payments grew from $1.4 billion to $17.5 billion. The growth in DSH expenditures was a major reason for the rapid growth in overall Medicaid expenditures in the early 1990s (Coughlin and Liska 1997; Holahan et al. 1993). By 1996, DSH expenditures accounted for $1 of every $11 spent on Medicaid.

States vary widely in their use of the DSH maximization strategy (table 5-1). In 1998, DSH payments accounted for 22 percent of Louisiana's total Medicaid spending and nearly 20 percent of Missouri's and South Carolina's. In contrast, DSH payments accounted for less than 1 percent of Medicaid spending in Arkansas, Nebraska, and Wisconsin.

It is important to understand that some of the gross DSH payments do not represent real additional dollars to help cover hospitals' uncompensated care costs, because provider taxes or IGTs may have been used for the state share of the DSH payments. Although some of the IGTs may represent local funds that are retained by providers and ultimately used to fund health care services, potentially only the federal share of gross DSH payments represents new funds to providers. However, some states retain most of the federal share of DSH payments, so their hospitals actually receive little, if any, additional Medicaid revenue under the DSH program. Furthermore, state and local subsidies of public hospitals may be reduced in anticipation of the federal funds; these cutbacks may offset any new revenue received under the DSH program. A 1997 survey revealed that only about 40 percent of total DSH expenditures in that year went to help hospitals cover the cost of caring for Medicaid and uninsured individuals (Coughlin, Ku, and Kim 2000). Thus, the bulk of DSH spending in 1997 was not going to cover safety net hospitals' uncompensated care costs, as was the original intent behind the special payments. Not surprisingly, DSH payments have been a highly contentious issue between the states and the federal government; on three separate occasions, Congress has enacted legislation to curtail such spending.[9]

States have also used UPL programs to draw down extra federal matching dollars (Coughlin et al. 2000; U.S. General Accounting Office

Table 5-1. *Federal and State Medicaid Disproportionate Share Hospital (DSH) Expenditures, by State, 1998*

State	DSH Expenditures ($ millions)	DSH as a Share of Total Medicaid Spending (%)
United States	14,997.6	8.5
Alabama	393.7	16.6
Alaska	15.4	3.9
Arizona	123.4	6.2
Arkansas	1.7	0.1
California	2,450.7	12.5
Colorado	174.8	10.3
Connecticut	370.1	12.7
Delaware	8.0	1.8
District of Columbia	32.9	3.6
Florida	370.5	5.6
Georgia	409.6	11.0
Hawaii	N/A	0.0
Idaho	2.2	0.5
Illinois	269.6	3.8
Indiana	194.7	7.3
Iowa	19.8	1.4
Kansas	45.0	3.9
Kentucky	194.7	7.3
Louisiana	738.3	22.6
Maine	122.4	10.9
Maryland	136.0	4.9
Massachusetts	497.3	8.8
Michigan	319.3	5.1
Minnesota	56.3	1.8
Mississippi	183.9	10.7
Missouri	666.1	19.6
Montana	0.2	0.1
Nebraska	5.9	0.7
Nevada	73.6	13.6
New Hampshire	128.4	16.6
New Jersey	1,020.4	17.8
New Mexico	9.4	0.9

(continued)

Table 5-1. *Continued*

State	DSH Expenditures ($ millions)	DSH as a Share of Total Medicaid Spending (%)
New York	1,860.4	6.6
North Carolina	354.1	7.5
North Dakota	1.2	0.3
Ohio	657.0	9.6
Oklahoma	22.7	1.6
Oregon	27.0	1.5
Pennsylvania	546.3	6.2
Rhode Island	56.0	5.6
South Carolina	445.7	18.9
South Dakota	1.1	0.3
Tennessee	N/A	0.0
Texas	1,438.9	13.9
Utah	4.1	0.6
Vermont	22.3	5.2
Virginia	160.7	6.5
Washington	332.8	9.3
West Virginia	21.9	1.6
Wisconsin	11.2	0.4
Wyoming	0.1	0.1

Source: Spending data are from the Health Care Financing Administration (HCFA)-64 and represent both federal and state spending. Enrollee data from the HCFA-2082. Both enrollee and spending data are for federal fiscal year 1998.

Note: N/A = not applicable. Hawaii and Tennessee fold DSH payments into their Medicaid managed care capitation payments.

[GAO] 2000, 2001; Ku 2000). While these programs date back to the early 1990s, state use of them increased dramatically in the late 1990s. UPL programs are essentially a variant of the DSH program: A state makes an additional Medicaid payment (i.e., a payment over and above regular Medicaid reimbursement) to a targeted group of providers (such as nursing homes or hospitals) that are typically owned by a county or local government. (States generally use county- and locally owned providers in UPL programs because they can make IGTs to fund the state's share.) The enhanced payments are well in excess of the actual cost of medical services provided to Medicaid beneficiaries. The state claims federal Medicaid funds for the enhanced payments and then requires the providers to give back much or all of the enhanced payment to the state in the form of IGTs. Thus, the state receives federal matching dollars without putting up any real state funds.

Although Medicaid law grants states broad discretion in setting provider reimbursement levels, it does impose upper limits—namely, Medicaid payments (except DSH payments) can be no greater than the amount Medicare would have paid for the same service. However, the UPL is not determined by the Medicare payment for a single procedure or even the payment for all services a provider renders to Medicaid beneficiaries. Rather, the UPL is based on the *aggregate* amount that can be paid to an entire class of providers if every provider in that class were paid the Medicare rate for all services they provided to Medicaid beneficiaries.

Until 2001, UPL rules differentiated between two classes of providers: state-owned and non-state-owned.[10] The latter class included both local publicly owned facilities and private providers. A state could thus determine its UPL for, say, nursing homes by calculating, on a statewide basis, the difference between its total Medicaid payments to all county-owned and private nursing homes and what Medicare would have paid. To use the UPL maximization strategy, the state would then pay the entire difference, in supplemental Medicaid payments, to the publicly owned nursing homes. States were allowed to pay the full UPL difference to just the public nursing homes because the public and private nursing homes were in the same provider class. Given that Medicaid payment levels have historically been considerably lower than Medicare levels, the potential for gaining additional federal dollars through UPL arrangements was enormous.

An example of how a UPL program works is shown in figure 5-2. On June 14, 2000, Pennsylvania paid $697.1 million in supplemental payments to 23 county nursing homes. With its 54 percent federal matching rate for Medicaid, the state received $393.3 million in federal funds. On the same day, the nursing homes returned $695.6 million (of the $697.1 million in supplemental payments) to the state. At the end of the transaction, the nursing homes had a small net gain ($1.5 million), whereas the state of Pennsylvania had a $391.8 million gain. Furthermore, while the federal government had paid $393.3 million in Medicaid nursing home reimbursement, no new Medicaid services appear to have been provided with

Figure 5-2. *Flow of Upper Payment Limit Funds in Pennsylvania, June 2000*

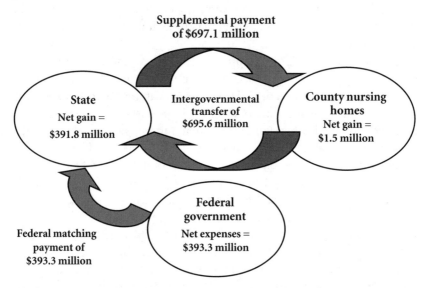

Source: The Urban Institute, based on data from Mangano (2000); adapted from Ku (2000).

the funds (Mangano 2001). Other states' UPL programs operate similarly (Coughlin, Bruen, and King 2003).

A recent survey of state UPL programs revealed that, in 2000, more than 80 percent of the gains available through UPL accrued to the states (Coughlin et al. 2003). States reported that those gains went to finance health care services: A few states put gains into a dedicated health spending account, but most put them into the Medicaid general fund. Once in the Medicaid fund, UPL gains were generally recycled to finance the state share of other Medicaid payments, thereby enabling the state to earn another federal match—or a match-on-match payment. A report by the Inspector General of the Department of Health and Human Services (HHS) also reported such match-on-match payments (Mangano 2001).

Although some states have had UPL programs for many years, the number of programs has grown dramatically in recent years (GAO 2000, 2001; Ku 2000). One study showed that in 1995, states spent $313 million on UPL programs; in 1998, they spent $1.4 billion (Coughlin et al. 2000). In 2000—when most state economies were strong—28 states had at least one UPL program, and an estimated $10 billion (in combined federal and state funds) was spent on Medicaid UPL programs nation-wide (Mangano 2001). Federal legislation has been passed to phase UPLs out beginning in 2001.

Implications of Maximization Strategies

The matching rate mechanism encourages states to spend more on health care for low-income populations through Medicaid than they would have spent on their own. However, the implications of Medicaid maximization strategies go beyond merely elevating spending. They can alter provider and health plan payments, increase state variation in Medicaid eligibility and benefit packages, and disrupt the intended balance between federal and state payments. However, the federal government allowed for some program variation in Medicaid; therefore, the fact that differences exist across states is not directly an implication of Medicaid maximization.

States' maximization strategies in the areas of service coverage and eligibility have made Medicaid bigger and more costly. They have also made Medicaid a source of funding for many health care services that had been or could have been financed just with state and local dollars. Washington's Basic Health Plan, New York's Home Relief Program, California's In-Home Support Services, Tennessee's TennCare, and Vermont's Pharmacy Assistance Program are all examples of programs that states run but whose funding is partly or fully dependent on federal Medicaid dollars. However, the state share of the costs of adding beneficiaries or services is generally paid for from state general funds. In this way, federal policymakers know that the states are putting real dollars into Medicaid. These funds represent real opportunity costs for the states—state spending on Medicaid program expansions come at the expense of state spending on other objectives, including tax cuts. This situation is in stark contrast to Medicaid revenue programs, where states often view the federal Medicaid match as a funding source that can be used to offset rising health care costs, to offset the costs of nonhealth programs, or to obviate the need to raise taxes.

Provider and Health Plan Payments

Provider payments made through DSH and UPL programs are viewed as a central component of Medicaid maximization. The development of these programs, particularly the DSH program, has caused dramatic differences in state Medicaid payments. For example, although DSH payments are intended to offset uncompensated costs that hospitals incur in treating Medicaid and uninsured patients, data on DSH spending (table 5-2) show that payments go well beyond state variation in uninsurance rates. In 1998, 14 states reported less than $50 in federal

Table 5-2. *Federal Medicaid Disproportionate Share Hospital (DSH) Expenditures, by State, 1998*

State	Federal Share of Medicaid DSH Payments ($ millions)	Federal DSH Spending ($)	
		Per Medicaid Enrollee	Per Uninsured Person
United States	8,470.45	209.76	195.05
Alabama	272.9	434.45	408.49
Alaska	9.2	104.52	79.25
Arizona	80.6	124.16	71.93
Arkansas	1.2	2.83	2.42
California	1,255.5	202.78	176.26
Colorado	72.3	208.34	114.20
Connecticut	185.1	459.74	489.34
Delaware	4.0	38.04	39.85
District of Columbia	23.0	165.80	275.33
Florida	206.2	101.04	74.75
Georgia	249.2	203.67	189.50
Hawaii	N/A	N/A	N/A
Idaho	1.5	12.62	6.53
Illinois	134.8	75.55	79.82
Indiana	119.5	195.92	167.15
Iowa	12.6	39.38	45.20
Kansas	26.9	108.99	90.46
Kentucky	137.0	209.62	242.02
Louisiana	517.0	714.23	593.76
Maine	80.9	412.86	491.31
Maryland	68.0	112.65	96.59
Massachusetts	248.6	260.77	367.44
Michigan	171.1	126.30	142.85
Minnesota	29.3	52.64	69.12
Mississippi	141.8	269.18	272.18

Table 5-2. *Continued*

State	Federal Share of Medicaid DSH Payments ($ millions)	Federal DSH Spending ($)	
		Per Medicaid Enrollee	Per Uninsured Person
Missouri	404.2	523.11	708.39
Montana	0.2	1.66	0.89
Nebraska	3.6	17.23	21.16
Nevada	36.8	281.49	100.72
New Hampshire	64.2	652.89	473.83
New Jersey	510.2	594.71	409.40
New Mexico	6.8	20.12	16.24
New York	930.2	265.76	297.02
North Carolina	223.4	185.91	196.76
North Dakota	0.8	13.55	9.66
Ohio	382.0	272.40	308.61
Oklahoma	16.0	34.86	27.28
Oregon	16.6	30.93	35.15
Pennsylvania	291.7	169.58	245.23
Rhode Island	29.8	200.06	342.08
South Carolina	313.0	476.94	492.08
South Dakota	0.7	8.76	8.13
Tennessee	N/A	N/A	N/A
Texas	896.1	334.31	186.96
Utah	3.0	15.10	10.24
Vermont	13.8	105.15	221.01
Virginia	82.7	119.98	89.71
Washington	173.6	189.64	230.63
West Virginia	16.1	43.21	53.65
Wisconsin	6.6	12.22	12.27
Wyoming	0.1	1.51	0.98

Sources: Medicaid expenditures and enrollment are Urban Institute estimates (2002) based on data from the Centers for Medicare and Medicaid Services (CMS), Center for Medicaid and State Operations, Financial Management Reports. Uninsured data are Urban Institute tabulations of a three-year merge of the March 1998, 1999, and 2000 Current Population Surveys.

Note: N/A = not applicable. Hawaii and Tennessee fold DSH payments into their Medicaid managed care rates.

DSH payments per uninsured person, while 8 states received payments in excess of $400 per uninsured person. In short, Medicaid DSH payments are not equitably distributed; rather, they reflect primarily the creativity of state policymakers and a state's willingness to engage in this form of Medicaid maximization.

Program Financing

To the extent that states used IGTs in conjunction with DSH and UPL programs to maximize federal funds, they altered the intended balance of Medicaid dollars between the federal government and the states, as well as the distribution of federal matching dollars across the states. The change in effective federal matching rates brought about by UPL programs in selected states has been explored recently by the Inspector General of both HHS (Mangano 2001) and the U.S. General Accounting Office (GAO 2000). The GAO concluded that the use of UPL programs in some states "inappropriately increases federal Medicaid payment . . . and violates the integrity of Medicaid's federal/state partnership" (GAO 2000). For example, a UPL program run through county nursing homes in Michigan raised the federal share of Medicaid program expenditures from 56 percent (the statutory rate) to 68 percent. A UPL program in Pennsylvania raised that state's effective matching rate from the official 54 percent to 65 percent (Mangano 2001).

Although it is not possible to pinpoint the impact of DSH and UPL programs in *all* states with the available data, it is possible to estimate the effective matching rate for 23 states that were included in the Inspectors General's report and that responded to a 1998 Urban Institute survey on the Medicaid DSH program (Coughlin et al. 2000). Table 5-3 shows the Medicaid expenditures reported by the states when claiming federal matching funds, as well as adjusted Medicaid expenditures—that is, the states' reported figures lowered to reflect the fact that some of the money was raised through IGTs and, thus, does not represent real health care spending. (The details of this estimation are discussed in the appendix.) Table 5-3 also presents the federal matching rates (federal medical assistance percentage, or FMAP), calculated from the reported expenditure data, and the effective federal matches, calculated from the adjusted data. Finally, the table shows the difference between the calculated and the effective federal matching rates. Based on these data, it appears that, on average, the 23 states used federal DSH and UPL payments to increase

Table 5-3. *Federal and State Medicaid Expenditures and Alternative Federal Medical Assistance Percentages, FY 2000*

State	Reported Medicaid Expenditures[a] ($ millions)			Adjusted Medicaid Expenditures[b] ($ millions)			Federal Medical Assistance Percentage		
	Total	Federal	State	Total	Federal	State	Calculated	Effective	Difference
Alabama	2,696.40	1,877.42	818.95	2,557.41	1,877.42	679.99	0.6963	0.7341	0.0378
Alaska	481.28	322.80	158.48	473.28	322.80	150.48	0.6707	0.6821	0.0113
Arkansas	1,579.67	1,154.83	424.84	1,564.47	1,154.83	409.64	0.7311	0.7382	0.0071
California	21,150.59	11,002.86	10,147.73	19,510.42	11,002.86	8,507.56	0.5202	0.5639	0.0437
Georgia	4,321.25	2,592.50	1,728.75	3,890.23	2,592.50	1,297.73	0.5999	0.6664	0.0665
Illinois	7,487.65	3,754.29	3,733.36	6,751.34	3,754.29	2,997.06	0.5014	0.5561	0.0547
Indiana	3,469.95	2,145.16	1,324.80	3,191.60	2,145.16	1,046.45	0.6182	0.6721	0.0539
Iowa	1,637.95	1,034.27	603.68	1,563.35	1,034.27	529.08	0.6314	0.6616	0.0301
Kansas	1,410.78	847.75	563.04	1,358.98	847.75	511.24	0.6009	0.6238	0.0229
Louisiana	3,443.27	2,422.68	1,020.59	3,241.27	2,422.68	818.59	0.7036	0.7474	0.0438
Minnesota	3,322.27	1,717.37	1,604.90	3,317.77	1,717.37	1,600.40	0.5169	0.5176	0.0007
Missouri	3,939.47	2,386.12	1,553.35	3,708.72	2,386.12	1,322.60	0.6057	0.6434	0.0377
Montana	450.23	335.36	114.87	449.93	335.36	114.57	0.7449	0.7454	0.0005
New Jersey	6,069.85	3,038.46	3,031.38	5,344.99	3,038.46	2,306.53	0.5006	0.5685	0.0679
New York	30,186.29	15,124.34	15,061.96	28,611.21	15,124.34	13,486.87	0.5010	0.5286	0.0276
North Carolina	5,464.86	3,421.05	2,043.81	5,209.90	3,421.05	1,788.85	0.6260	0.6566	0.0306
North Dakota	428.66	304.22	124.43	417.76	304.22	113.53	0.7097	0.7282	0.0185
Oregon	2,110.84	1,275.18	835.65	2,076.64	1,275.18	801.45	0.6041	0.6141	0.0099

(*continued*)

Table 5-3. Continued

State	Reported Medicaid Expenditures^a ($ millions)			Adjusted Medicaid Expenditures^b ($ millions)			Federal Medical Assistance Percentage (FMAP)		
	Total	Federal	State	Total	Federal	State	Calculated	Effective	Difference
South Carolina	2,664.61	1,869.21	795.40	2,533.37	1,869.21	664.17	0.7015	0.7378	0.0363
South Dakota	395.67	281.16	114.50	386.37	281.16	105.20	0.7106	0.7277	0.0171
Tennessee	4,941.57	3,122.66	1,818.91	4,799.17	3,122.66	1,676.51	0.6319	0.6507	0.0188
Washington	3,962.52	2,062.75	1,899.78	3,750.51	2,062.75	1,687.77	0.5206	0.5500	0.0294
Wisconsin	3,266.90	1,923.43	1,343.47	3,193.30	1,923.43	1,269.87	0.5889	0.6023	0.0136
Total^c	114,882.50	64,015.88	50,866.63	107,902.00	64,015.88	43,886.12	0.5625	0.5933	0.0307

Source: Urban Institute estimates, 2002.

a. Expenditures reported by states when claiming federal matching funds.

b. Reported Medicaid expenditures reduced by estimated amounts of intergovernmental transfers (IGTs) and provider taxes. See appendix for details of estimates.

c. For FMAP columns, numbers represent the average FMAP across sample states, not a total FMAP.

their federal matching rates by 3 percentage points in 2000, from 56 percent to 59 percent, relative to what they would have received in the absence of DSH and UPL.

To understand the financial impact of this seemingly small change in the federal matching rate, it is necessary to recall how the matching rate affects federal spending. At a 56 percent matching rate, the federal government spends $1.27 for each dollar the state spends. If the effective matching rate is shifted to 59 percent through the use of IGTs, the federal government will be required to spend $1.43 for each dollar of state spending financed out of general revenues. Therefore, across the 23 states, federal spending per dollar of state general revenue spending was increased by about 13 percent, on average, as a result of IGT financing. In New Jersey, where the matching rate is estimated to have increased from 50 percent to 57 percent, federal spending per dollar of state general revenue increased by almost 33 percent. Note that the spending increase was not typically linked to an increase in the number of low-income people covered or in the number or quality of services provided under Medicaid.

In addition to altering the effective matching rate, UPL and DSH programs financed through IGTs also obscure actual program spending. The Inspector General's report showed that spending through these programs in 28 states totaled $10.3 billion in 2000, with $5.8 billion coming from the federal government and $4.5 billion from the states (Mangano 2001). However, if the states' $4.5 billion was paid with IGTs that were ultimately returned to the local governments to use as they pleased, then it is wrong to view these UPL payments as having increased aggregate Medicaid spending by $10.3 billion. In reality, Medicaid expenditures increased only by the amount of the federal outlay, or $5.8 billion. The same 28 states spent $11.3 billion on Medicaid DSH payments in 2000, but only $6.3 billion of this amount was derived from federal funds, with the remaining $5 billion coming from state funds. However, the vast majority of the states' share of DSH payments was financed by IGTs or analogous mechanisms. Thus, the 28 states' DSH and UPL programs recorded a total of $21.6 billion in Medicaid spending in 2000, but actual spending may have been as little as the $12.1 billion federal share.

Moreover, there is no reason to believe that all of this $12.1 billion in federal spending was used to pay for Medicaid-covered or health-related services. As noted earlier, some states have used these dollars as the state share of other Medicaid spending—recycling the match—or have directed them to nonhealth areas of their budgets (HHS 2001; Ku 2000; Rein 2001).

State Health Care Policy

While difficult to assess fully, maximization has also affected state health care policy and general budget making. The influx of federal dollars and the growing reliance on Medicaid to fund health care programs or even general budget items may enable states to delay tough decisions such as raising taxes or cutting back on programs. A recent response to a budget crisis in the state of Washington, a revamped supplemental nursing home payment system in Wisconsin, and an ongoing supplemental hospital payment program in California are all examples of how the ability to think creatively and draw in federal dollars can influence state health care policy.

During Washington's 2001–03 biennial budget debate, the legislature was facing serious financing problems as a result of growing costs in a number of health care programs (Holahan and Pohl 2002a). Although significant Medicaid cutbacks were considered, the state realized it could legally alter the way it set UPLs for nursing homes and generate $450 million in additional federal Medicaid dollars. The state took this route and made only limited cuts in health care spending.

Similarly, in preparing its 2001–03 biennial budget, Wisconsin replaced a supplemental payment program that was designed to cover the unreimbursed costs of county and municipal nursing homes with a program that applies the Medicare UPL to all nursing homes (Bruen and Wiener 2002). The state estimated that the change would generate approximately $604 million in federal dollars and that the money could be used to fund the state share of future Medicaid payments. However, federal rule changes may limit the state's ability to continue this approach. Although other strategies—such as raising taxes or making Medicaid cuts—were available, the UPL maximization approach was described as being the only politically feasible option that could generate enough funds to finance the reimbursement increase.

In an even bigger effort to draw federal dollars, California's Medicaid program has used supplemental payments as part of a response to hospital complaints that the state's selective hospital contracting program was not adequately compensating providers (California Medical Assistance Commission 2001). Rather than adopt a major across-the-board change in the rates paid to all contract hospitals, California developed a more targeted approach that cost the state nothing from its general fund revenues. The state agreed to a supplemental payment program that paid extra amounts to contract hospitals that operated emergency rooms and qualified for Medicaid DSH payments. The state share of these supplemental payments was funded entirely with IGTs from county and University of California hospitals. The program grew from less than $100 million in federal payments in state fiscal year (FY) 1993 to more than $650 million in state FY 2001.

Conflicts between States and the Federal Government

Perhaps the most visible consequence of maximization is the heightened tension between states and the federal government over the Medicaid program. In the past decade, that tension has brought about several pieces of federal legislation and regulation aimed at curbing maximization, especially the DSH and UPL strategies. As mentioned earlier, federal policymakers began to intervene in 1991, when Congress passed the Medicaid Voluntary Contribution and Provider-Specific Tax Amendments. The act was passed after the first Bush administration and the National Governors Association negotiated reforms to the DSH program. In addition to greatly restricting the use of provider donations and taxes, the law severely limited growth in federal DSH spending by imposing expenditure caps on the states. However, the law did not attempt to cut the DSH program, nor did it address any of the underlying inequities in federal DSH spending across states. Instead, it more or less froze the program in 1992.

Federal concerns about the DSH program persisted. In particular, policymakers wanted to regulate how payments were made to individual hospitals. Many states' DSH payments exceeded the uncompensated care costs that hospitals incurred in serving the Medicaid and uninsured populations. To eliminate this practice, Congress included a provision in OBRA 1993 limiting DSH payments to any single hospital to no more than 100 percent of the hospital's actual unreimbursed costs. This limit has become known as the hospital-specific cap.

Controversy about the DSH program resurfaced again during the 1997 federal budget debate. This time, Congress enacted substantial cutbacks in federal DSH spending as part of the Balanced Budget Act (BBA). Indeed, of the $17 billion in gross Medicaid reductions mandated by the act between 1998 and 2002, about $10 billion, or 60 percent, were attributable to cuts in federal DSH payments (Schneider, Chan, and Elkin 1997).[11]

The BBA contained no formula for distributing federal DSH payments to the states. Instead, in what has been described as "a classic compromise" between the House and Senate versions of the bill, it set state-specific allotments on the basis of past state DSH spending patterns—and sometimes in response to a state's political influence (Schneider et al. 1997). The final legislation gave states the higher of the DSH amounts allowed under the Senate bill and those allowed under the House bill. In addition, no state's federal DSH funding could be reduced in any given year by more than 3.5 percent of the state's total 1995 federal Medicaid payments. This limit helped several states, including Alabama, Connecticut, and Kansas. In addition, the act made a special exception for California: The state's hospital-specific cap was increased from 100 percent to 175 percent of actual expenses incurred in 1998 and 1999. In subsequent legislation, California's exception was made permanent. Thus, while Congress as a whole was interested in cutting federal DSH expenditures, individual representatives sought to protect their states.

The federal government has turned its attention more recently to controlling UPL programs. In the Medicare, Medicaid, and SCHIP Benefits Improvement and Protection Act (BIPA) of 2000, Congress directed the Secretary of Health and Human Services to issue regulations that would limit federal Medicaid spending on UPLs. The final rule, issued in January 2001, created aggregate UPLs for three types of inpatient services (hospital, nursing facility, and ICF/MR) and three classes of providers (state-owned facilities, local publicly owned facilities, and private providers). As noted earlier, grouping local publicly owned facilities and private facilities in one class had enabled states to make excess payments to publicly owned providers under the UPL program, leveraging the federal Medicaid match in the process.

The January 2001 rule made an important change: It created two levels of UPLs. For state facilities and private facilities (nursing homes or hospitals) and for local publicly owned nursing homes, the UPL is set at 100 percent of the amount that Medicare would have paid for the service. However, in recognition of the "higher costs of . . . services in public hospitals," the UPL limit was set at 150 percent for local publicly owned hospitals (*Federal Register* 2001). In other words, a state could pay local public hospitals up to 50 percent more than Medicare would have paid for the collective services the hospitals provided to Medicaid patients. In sum, the federal government took important steps in controlling UPL programs with the 2001 rule, but it weakened the rule by making the 150 percent payment exception for local public hospitals.

This payment exception, which was issued in the last days of the Clinton administration, stirred considerable controversy among the incoming appointees of the second Bush administration (Combs and Gilroy 2001; *Washington Health Beat* 2001). In 2002, in an effort to "restore fiscal integrity to the Medicaid program and to reduce the opportunity for abusive funding practices," a new rule was issued to remove the 150 percent payment exception for local public hospitals (*Federal Register* 2002). The administration was concerned that more federal dollars were going to states ostensibly to pay for hospital care, but with no assurances that the dollars stayed at the hospitals.[12]

The repeal of the 2001 regulation sparked strong reaction among state and local officials (Pear 2002). States claim that the new rule will create significant financial hardship and aggravate their budget problems. States also claim that their efforts to provide services to Medicaid beneficiaries and to the uninsured will be adversely affected (Ku 2001; Pear 2002).

In BIPA 2000, congressional policymakers also backtracked on some of their efforts to reduce DSH spending. As a way to offset state revenue losses caused by the closing of the UPL loophole, Congress postponed the DSH cuts for 2001 and 2002 set out in the 1997 BBA.[13] BIPA also included provisions that allowed states to increase DSH payments to public hospitals. Modeled after the California exemption, the provisions allow all states, beginning in 2002, to pay public hospitals 175 percent of uncompensated care costs rather than the 100 percent stipulated by OBRA 1993. This payment exemption is for two years; California's exemption remains indefinite.

The federal-state tug-of-war over Medicaid UPL and DSH programs probably will be a continuing area of conflict. Furthermore, the battle lines have become somewhat blurred: Congress enacted DSH spending cuts and then postponed them, and it passed provisions to limit UPL spending but now appears to be backing away from them. Over time, through various pieces of legislation and rules, the federal government has helped to legitimize the states' Medicaid revenue strategies. Moreover, the back-and-forth between the two levels of government reflects an important political reality of the Medicaid program—namely, Congress wants to be fiscally responsible and close financial loopholes, but individual members of Congress want to protect their states' governors and providers from reductions in federal dollars.

The Future of Medicaid Financing

The structure of Medicaid financing, with its often vague federal rules and considerable state flexibility, all but guarantees that states will have the opportunity to maximize federal matching funds.[14] However, in considering changes that might alter financing incentives, it is important to recognize that the current system has both strengths and weaknesses, depending on one's perspective.

As intended, the federal match encourages states to spend more than they might have otherwise. At the same time, however, the match provides incentives for state and local officials to find financial loopholes. With more than $200 billion spent each year on Medicaid, the financial stakes are high, and the states have found and used loopholes very effectively. In addition to driving up program costs, this gaming of Medicaid creates tension between federal and state policymakers. However, once states and health care providers have become accustomed to the additional federal dollars, it is very difficult for Congress to eliminate the loopholes.

The effective changes in Medicaid financing brought about by states' efforts to maximize revenues have created other problems. As discussed earlier, creative financing arrangements have fundamentally changed how Medicaid is financed. To varying degrees, the bulk of states now draw down some federal matching dollars with little or no state contribution. As a result, the matching formula has been skewed, and overall Medicaid spending has been distorted.

These problems raise fundamental questions about the future of the program. To the extent that federal policymakers view Medicaid maximization as a problem, are there ways to prevent states from engaging in these strategies? Or is the federal-state financing partnership inherently flawed? Are there ways to ensure that states and localities are financial partners in Medicaid to the degree that program rules require? More broadly, does it make sense to maintain the current structure of Medicaid financing, or would another approach, such as federalizing the program or using a block grant, be better? Although current financing methods have both negative and positive attributes, some changes are needed to address the conflicts that have surfaced in recent years, especially with respect to UPL programs, which involve large payments to a range of providers.

The creative financing arrangements also raise questions about whether and how the financial integrity of Medicaid can be restored. In the past, the federal government has sought to limit abuses through various laws or regulations. For example, when states started using DSH payments to draw down extra federal funds, Congress, on several occasions, passed legislation to bring the payments under control. While they curtailed the growth of DSH expenditures, those provisions did not attempt to reshape the DSH program into one that provided subsidies for uncompensated care on a rational basis. Instead, the measures left the program largely intact, with many states continuing to draw federal matching dollars with little or no contribution. Further, over the last couple of years, federal policymakers seem to have been pulling back from earlier efforts to reform the DSH program. In short, the DSH program has become part of the Medicaid financial landscape and is politically too entrenched to undo. A similar situation appears to be taking shape in the debate over UPL financing.

If federal policymakers are interested in regaining greater control over Medicaid financing, several alternatives are available. One is to work within the current program design but to reduce the amount of state discretion. Among other things, a formula could be devised to distribute DSH funds more equitably, the DSH payment allowance for public hospitals could be reset at 100 percent of uncompensated care costs, and—most important—the federal government could identify specific revenue sources that it would and would not match. For example, the federal government might decide not to match state expenditures financed via ITGs, a measure that would help ensure that states truly pay their share of program costs but that might impede a few legitimate uses of IGTs.

Another alternative is for the federal government to assume greater financial responsibility for Medicaid. This would entail reducing the states' contributions and increasing the federal match. In return for increased funding, the federal government would have to be given more control over Medicaid. With broader authority, the federal government could, for example, define more uniformly who should be covered, what types of services should be included in the benefits structure, and how providers should be paid. It could also eliminate or overhaul the Medicaid DSH program.

However, if federal policymakers conclude that DSH and UPL programs financed with IGTs cannot be eliminated, or if states further compromise the design of Medicaid financing, then solutions completely outside the current system may be necessary. For example, Medicaid could be federalized and financed just with federal dollars, like Medicare. It may be that the loopholes available under the current federal-state arrangement can only be closed by eliminating the financing partnership entirely. Another reason for the more radical approach is that tension between federal and state policymakers over program financing has escalated under both Democratic and Republican administrations, and it will be very difficult, if not impossible, to restore trust between them. A federalized Medicaid program would also reduce interstate variation in eligibility rules and service coverage and would promote greater equity for all low-income individuals. For people in some states, this might lead to a less generous program, while for people in other states, eligibility and service coverage could be expanded.

A completely different approach would be to convert Medicaid from a matching grant design to a block grant to states. If state funds are not matched, there is no opportunity for states to play financial games with DSH, IGTs, and the like. Aside from the substantive implications of such an approach, the federal government might find that this shift does not resolve all of its concerns regarding fiscal integrity. All block grant proposals for Medicaid have required states to maintain their financial effort, so federal dollars do not just replace state dollars. Monitoring maintenance of effort is not simple, and states have demonstrated substantial creativity in defining spending as fitting within federal requirements. States that have relied heavily upon creative financing techniques may find it difficult to maintain their current effort. Similarly, in order to protect Medicaid recipients, block grant proposals have always required states to continue providing a defined set of services to a defined population (albeit not the entire group currently eligible for Medicaid). The federal government would need to oversee compliance with these requirements. Thus, block grants solve some fiscal integrity problems, but do not eliminate possible tension between levels of government regarding financial responsibility.

Whether Medicaid's federal-state partnership is overhauled will be determined by how seriously policymakers view the problems created by current financing schemes. To date, most changes have not fundamentally altered states' incentives or ability to draw down some share of federal Medicaid dollars without spending their own general revenues. With spending on Medicaid now approaching $250 billion, it is likely that the matter of what to do about Medicaid financing will remain at the center of the nation's health policy debates.

NOTES

1. As shown later, the 57 percent figure probably underestimates the actual share of federal Medicaid spending.

2. Section 1115 of the Social Security Act authorizes waivers of specified provisions of Medicaid law allowing states to test a range of policy ideas, including how the program is financed, how services are delivered, and what populations are served under the waiver.

3. One of the requirements of Section 1115 waivers is that they be budget-neutral: That is, over the life of the waiver, the costs to the federal government cannot exceed what the costs would have been otherwise.

4. See Holahan and Pohl (2002b) for details.

5. There were certainly exceptions; several states (such as Connecticut and New York) continued to use provider taxes to fund DSH and other parts of their Medicaid programs.

6. Indeed, several states have long used IGTs from local governments to help pay the state's share of Medicaid. New York, for example, requires counties to pay 20 percent of the nonfederal share of Medicaid long-term care expenses and 50 percent of the non-federal share of all other Medicaid services.

7. The rationale behind the special payments was that hospitals that render a large volume of care to low-income persons often lose money as a result of low Medicaid reimbursement rates. They also lose money because they generally care for high volumes of indigent patients, who cannot pay for care. In addition, hospitals with large caseloads of low-income patients frequently have small caseloads of privately insured patients and thus are less able to shift the cost of uncompensated care to the privately insured patients.

8. As a way to limit federal Medicaid expenditures, HCFA established over the years a set of upper limits on the total amount it would agree to pay states for certain services. The payment limits are based on service payments allowed under the Medicare program. The payment limit is not the price to be paid for each service provided, but rather a ceiling on total Medicaid expenses above which the federal government will not match. UPLs are set for different classes of service (such as nursing home care, inpatient hospital services, and ICF/MRs).

9. More recent work suggests that the share of DSH expenditures retained by providers had increased by 2000 (Coughlin et al. 2003).

10. In January 2001, a UPL regulation separated local publicly owned facilities from private providers, so the UPL is now determined across a narrower range of providers.

11. The BBA contained several other important DSH provisions, including one requiring that DSH payments made on behalf of Medicaid beneficiaries enrolled in managed care be paid directly to hospitals rather than to managed care plans. The BBA also contained some DSH spending limits that were scheduled to take effect in 2002.

12. However, recent survey work indicates that, distinct from nursing home UPLs, hospital UPLs often represented additional revenue to hospitals (Coughlin et al. 2003).

13. In 2003, however, the BBA's cuts in DSH payments are scheduled to go into effect.

14. Other federal assistance programs—such as social services block grants and federal manpower programs—have experienced similar issues with states successfully leveraging federal funds or finding a loophole that allowed them to use federal dollars for unintended purposes (Anton 1997).

REFERENCES

American Health Line. 1995. "Statelines—California: L.A. County Receives Bailout from Washington." http://www.nationaljournal.com, September 22.

Anton, T. J. 1997. "New Federalism and Intergovernmental Fiscal Relationships: The Implications for Health Policy." *Journal of Health Politics, Policy, and Law* 22(3): 691–720.

Bruen, Brian K., and Joshua M. Wiener. 2002. *Recent Changes in Health Policy for Low-Income People in Wisconsin.* Washington, D.C.: The Urban Institute. *Assessing the New Federalism* State Update No. 25.

California Medical Assistance Commission (CMAC). 2001. *Annual Report to the Legislature.* Sacramento: California Medical Assistance Commission.

Centers for Medicare and Medicaid Services (CMS). 2000. *Financial Management Report, FY 2000.* The Center for Medicaid and State Operations. http://www.hcfa.gov /Medicaid/ofs-64.html. (Accessed April 10, 2002.)

Combs, Jennifer V., and Thomas Gilroy. 2001. "CMS Still Working on UPL Rule Eliminating Leeway for Public Hospitals, Official Says." *Health Care Policy Report* 9(37): 1423–25.

Coughlin, Teresa A., and David Liska. 1997. "The Medicaid Disproportionate Share Hospital Payment Program: Background and Issues." Washington, D.C.: The Urban Institute. *Assessing the New Federalism* Policy Brief A-14.

———. 1998. "Changing State and Federal Payment Policies for Medicaid Disproportionate-Share Hospitals." *Health Affairs* 17(3): 118–36.

Coughlin, Teresa A., Brian K. Bruen, and Jennifer King. 2003. *State Use of Medicaid UPL and DSH Financing Mechanisms.* Washington, D.C.: The Kaiser Commission on the Future of Medicaid and the Uninsured.

Coughlin, Teresa A., Leighton Ku, and Johnny Kim. 2000. "Reforming the Medicaid Disproportionate Share Program in the 1990s." *Health Care Financing Review* 22(2): 137–57.

Coughlin, Teresa A., Stephen Zuckerman, Susan Wallin, and John Holahan. 1999. "A Conflict of Strategies: Medicaid Managed Care and Medicaid Maximization." *Health Services Research* 34(1): 281–93.

Federal Register. 2001. 66(9): 3147–770 (January 12).

———. 2002. 67(13): 2602–11 (January 18).

GAO. See U.S. General Accounting Office.

HHS. See U.S. Department of Health and Human Services

Holahan, John, and Mary Beth Pohl. 2002a. *Recent Changes in Health Policy for Low-Income People in Washington.* Washington, D.C.: The Urban Institute. *Assessing the New Federalism* State Update No. 24.

———. 2002b. *States as Innovators in Low-Income Health Coverage.* Washington, D.C.: The Urban Institute. *Assessing the New Federalism* Discussion Paper 02-08.

Holahan, John, Teresa A. Coughlin, Leighton Ku, and Shruti Rajan. 1995. "Insuring the Poor through Medicaid 1115 Waivers." *Health Affairs* 14(1): 200–17.

Holahan, John, Dianne Rowland, Judy Feder, and David Heslam. 1993. "Explaining the Recent Growth in Medicaid Spending." *Health Affairs* 12(3): 178–93.

Klemm, John. 2000. "Medicaid Spending: A Brief History." *Health Care Financing Review* 22(1): 105–12.

Ku, Leighton. 2000. *Limiting Abuses of Medicaid Financing: HCFA's Plan to Regulate the Medicaid Upper Payment Limit.* Washington, D.C.: Center on Budget and Policy Priorities.

———. 2001. *Administration's Regulation to Reduce Medicaid "Upper Payment Limit" Would Further Worsen State Budget Crises.* Washington, D.C.: Center on Budget and Policy Priorities.

Ku, Leighton, and Teresa A. Coughlin. 1995. "Medicaid Disproportionate Share and Other Special Financing Programs." *Health Care Financing Review* 16(3): 27–54.

Long, Sharon K., and Stephen Zuckerman. 1998. "Urban Health Care in Transition: Challenges Facing Los Angeles County." *Health Care Financing Review* 20(1): 45–58.

Manderscheid, Ronald W., Joanne E. Atay, María del R. Hernández-Cartagena, Pamela Y. Edmond, Alisa Male, Albert C. E. Parker, and Hongwei Zhang. 2000. "Highlights of Organized Mental Health Services in 1998 and Major National and State Trends." In *Mental Health, United States, 2000,* edited by R. W. Manderscheid and M. J. Henderson (135–71). HHS Pub. No. (SMA) 01-3537. Washington, D.C.: Superintendent of Documents, U.S. Government Printing Office.

Mangano, Michael F. 2000. "Medicaid Upper Payment Limit Requirements to Increase Federal Funds to States." Testimony before U.S. Senate Committee on Finance. September 6.

———. 2001. "Review of Medicaid Enhanced Payments to Local Public Providers and the Use of Intergovernmental Transfers." Memo from principal deputy directory of U.S. HHS OIG to Thomas Scully, September 11. Washington, D.C.: Department of Health and Human Services.

Pear, Robert. 2002. "Budget Would Cut Medicaid Payments." *New York Times,* February 2, p. A14.

Rein, Lisa. 2001. "Virginia Tries Medicaid Maneuver: Federal Funds for Nursing Homes Would Help Cover Tax Shortfall." *Washington Post,* November 3, p. B1.

Schneider, Andy, Stephen Chan, and Sam Elkin. 1997. *Overview of Medicaid DSH Provisions in the Balanced Budget Act of 1997, P.L. 105-33.* Washington, D.C.: Center on Budget and Policy Priorities.

U.S. Department of Health and Human Services. Office of Inspector General. 2001. *Review of Medicaid Enhanced Payments to Local Providers and the Use of Intergovernmental Transfers.* Washington, D.C.: U.S. Department of Health and Human Services.

U.S. General Accounting Office. 2000. *Medicaid: State Financing Schemes Again Drive Up Federal payments.* GAO/T-HEHS-00-193. Washington, D.C.: U.S. General Accounting Office.

———. 2001. *Medicaid: HCFA Reversed Its Position and Approved Additional State Financing Schemes.* GAO-02-147. Washington, D.C.: U.S. General Accounting Office.

Washington Health Beat. 2001. "A Fast-Paced Session With Straight-Talking Tom," editor John Reichard, October 15.

Zuckerman, Stephen, and Amy Lutzky. 2001. "The Medicaid Demonstration Project for Los Angeles County, 1995–2000: Progress, But Room For Improvement." Final Evaluation Report to Centers for Medicare and Medicaid Services. Washington, D.C.: The Urban Institute. http://urban.org/pdfs/mdp_la_FINAL.pdf. (Accessed April 25, 2003.)

Appendix—Estimating the Effective Matching Rate

To assess the potential impact of the DSH and UPL financing practices on the federal match (federal medical assistance percentage, or FMAP), the FMAP was computed under two alternative sets of assumptions. The first set assumed that all of the state Medicaid spending reported on Medicaid Financial Management Reports represents a real expenditure of general funds. The second set accounted for states' use of IGTs and providers taxes to finance their DSH and UPL programs and reestimated the FMAP using state expenditures net of these funds. Netting out IGTs and provider taxes assumes that these financing sources do not represent a real state outlay.

The first FMAP calculation is based on Medicaid Financial Management Reports from the Centers for Medicare and Medicaid Services (CMS).[1] These reports are annual summaries of data from quarterly expenditure reports (Form CMS-64) submitted by states to show the distribution of Medicaid spending for the quarter being reported and corrections for previous quarters and fiscal years. From these reports, total federal and state Medicaid expenditures for medical services and DSH programs were obtained for federal fiscal year (FFY) 2000. These data were used in calculating the FMAP for each state, according to the following formula:

$$Calculated\ FMAP = \frac{Total\ Federal\ Expenditures}{\begin{array}{c} Total\ Federal\ Expenditures \\ + \\ Total\ State\ Expenditures \end{array}}.$$

The calculated FMAP for each state, based on the federal and state expenditures reported in CMS data, are shown in table 5-3. The calculated matching rate often differs from the official matching rate for each state printed in the *Federal Register*. Reasons for the discrepancies are most likely higher matching rates for certain services (such as family planning) and adjustments for amounts reported in prior fiscal years, when the state may have had a different rate. The FMAP calculated here is more accurate than the published rate, because it accounts fully for actual state and federal spending and adjustments to Medicaid spending.

The calculated FMAP assumes that all state Medicaid expenditures represent actual outlays by state governments. However, expenditures financed with IGTs and provider taxes generally do not represent real state outlays, so the second matching rate calculation—the effective FMAP—employs an alternative formula:

$$Effective\ FMAP = \frac{Total\ Federal\ Expenditures}{\begin{array}{c}Total\ Federal\ Expenditures \\ + \\ Adjusted\ State\ Expenditures\end{array}},$$

where adjusted state expenditures are the reported amount of state expenditures minus state Medicaid DSH and UPL expenditures funded with IGTs and provider taxes. The effective FMAP is also shown in table 5-3.

The first step in calculating the adjusted state expenditures is to subtract the state share of DSH expenditures funded by IGTs and provider taxes. Because data from the federal management reports provide only total state Medicaid DSH expenditures, the calculation uses DSH revenue data for state fiscal year 1997 (collected and reported by Urban Institute researchers) as the source of the state share of DSH expenditures in each state funded by IGTs and provider taxes (Coughlin, Ku, and Kim 2000). Implicit in this calculation is that states' funding of DSH has not fundamentally shifted between 1997 and 2000.

The second step in calculating adjusted state expenditures is to subtract the entire state share of Medicaid UPL payments from state spending. A report on UPL programs released by the Inspector General of the Department of Health and Human Services in September 2001 shows that 28 states made or planned to make at least $10.3 billion in Medicaid enhanced payments in FFY 2000, including $5.8 billion in federal funds (U.S. HHS Office of Inspector General 2001). The Inspector General's data on total and federal enhanced payments for the states are used to calculate the state share, which was then subtracted from total state Medicaid expenditures.

Ideally, one would use an adjustment for UPL that counted state Medicaid enhanced payments financed with outlays from state general funds as actual expenditures, particularly if the state did not recoup its general fund expenditures (e.g., by requiring hospitals to return DSH funds or some portion of the UPL payment to the state).[2] However, we were not able to identify an analysis of enhanced payment programs that provided sufficient data for this task. As a result, the calculation may overestimate the amount of state funding for enhanced payments that comes from nonstate sources; this overestimation, in turn, results in a higher estimate of effective FMAP for states that fund enhanced payments with state general funds and do not recoup those funds later in the process.

Table 5-3 shows the results of this analysis for 23 states that were included in both the Urban Institute's DSH survey and the Inspector

General's data. Although not shown, the first adjustment reduced state Medicaid DSH expenditures for FFY 2000 in these 23 states from $4.5 billion to $1.0 billion. The second adjustment lowered reported state expenditures in these states by another $3.5 billion. In total, the adjustments lowered state Medicaid expenditures in the 23 states from $50.9 billion to $43.9 billion, a 13.8 percent reduction. The effective matching rate in the 23 states changed from 56 percent before the adjustment to 59 percent after the adjustment.

APPENDIX NOTES

1. Formerly the Health Care Financing Administration (HCFA).

2. The Inspector General's study cited earlier in this appendix found that states sometimes use UPL payments in place of DSH payments to certain hospitals, or require hospitals receiving both UPL and DSH payments to return some of the DSH payments to the state through IGTs.

6

Leaders and Laggards in State Coverage Expansions

John Holahan
Mary Beth Pohl

The majority of Americans under age 65 are covered by health insurance obtained through their own or a family member's employer. Others are insured through programs funded entirely by the federal government, such as military health programs or, for some people, Medicare. A small share buys private coverage in the individual insurance market. The remainder must rely on combined federal-state programs such as Medicaid and the State Children's Health Insurance Program (SCHIP) or on state-financed programs—or remain uninsured. The number of uninsured residents in a state depends primarily on how many people are not covered by private or federal insurance and secondarily on how far the state is willing to go in developing Medicaid and other publicly financed programs to cover them.

This chapter examines the extent to which states have led the way in expanding publicly funded health coverage to low-income Americans. Have the states functioned as laboratories, with successful innovations in some states being replicated in other states? Or have some states extended coverage while the majority have done little beyond the minimum required to obtain federal matching funds under Medicaid and SCHIP? Can the existing federal-state partnership be relied upon to solve the problem of the uninsured, particularly those with low incomes?

After a brief discussion of the mechanisms available to states to expand their health insurance coverage, this chapter divides states into four groups on the basis of how innovative they have been in using those mechanisms. The results show that only a minority of states have seriously attempted to expand coverage beyond what is essentially required by Medicaid and SCHIP. Those states have shown considerable political will in employing diverse sources of funds. In contrast, the majority of states have done relatively little to expand coverage beyond minimum federal requirements, even in periods of economic prosperity.

Next, the programs developed by the leading states are described. Although current economic pressures have caused some states to scale back their coverage expansions through program caps and reductions of benefits, the focus here is on how far states have been willing to go to cover their low-income populations. The final section of the chapter highlights the differences between states that have chosen to expand coverage substantially and those that have not.

State Expansion Mechanisms

States have at their disposal several mechanisms for expanding health coverage: traditional Medicaid, Medicaid Section 1115 research and demonstration waivers, SCHIP coverage for children (and, recently, parents), and exclusively state-funded programs.[1] Legislation enacted in the past several years has created new opportunities for states to receive federal matching funds. Section 1931 of the Social Security Act considerably increased a state's ability to extend Medicaid coverage to parents and children in low-income, working families. The SCHIP legislation of 1997 provides a generous federal match for states that expand coverage of children and, to some extent, parents (primarily with waivers). States are also using interesting combinations of Section 1115, Section 1931, and SCHIP funding authorities to craft new coverage designs for children and adults.

Traditional Medicaid

Medicaid uses combined federal and state funds to provide health insurance coverage to low-income elderly and disabled persons, parents (mostly women) and children receiving cash assistance, low-income pregnant women and children, and medically needy populations who do not meet Medicaid eligibility requirements but who have unusually high medical expenses.

Medicaid is an entitlement program. Once eligibility policies have been set, both the federal government and the states have an obligation to pay for all eligible persons. The federal government matches at least 50 percent of a state's Medicaid costs.[2] To receive the matching funds, a state must adhere to federally mandated rules and requirements regarding minimum benefits, family composition, and eligibility. Within those limitations, states have a great deal of flexibility.

Applicants must meet certain eligibility requirements and pass a means test before receiving benefits. Historically, Medicaid linked eligibility to receipt of cash assistance through Aid to Families with Dependent Children (AFDC), for parents and children, or Supplemental Security Income, for the disabled and elderly. Today, applicants are covered if they fit into one of four categories (pregnant women, parents and children, the elderly, and persons with disabilities) and if their income and assets drop below certain levels specified by the state for their particular category. Those income levels are often very low—for example, they are approximately 22 percent of the federal poverty level (FPL) for recipients of cash assistance in Louisiana (i.e., $3,983 for a family of four in 2001) (Maloy et al. 2002).

In addition to the traditional eligibility categories, states are now required to cover, or may opt to cover, many other groups. Beginning in the late-1980s, a series of federal legislative initiatives created a broad income-related eligibility category for pregnant women, infants, and children with family incomes significantly higher than the traditional AFDC levels. Coverage was federally mandated for pregnant women, infants, and children up to age 6 with family incomes up to 133 percent of the FPL. States were also required to phase in coverage of older children who were born after 1983 and whose family incomes were below the poverty level. In 1988, section 1902(r)(2) of the Social Security Act enabled states to expand Medicaid coverage to pregnant women, infants, and children with higher incomes by disregarding certain amounts of income or assets. Other optional categories target small populations, such as the recent extension of eligibility to women diagnosed with breast or cervical cancer. For both required and optional groups, the state receives federal matching funds.

States may also develop medically needy programs to cover people with slightly higher incomes and people with unusually large health care expenses. Under medically needy programs, states may elect to cover any categorically eligible person who has an income or asset that is up to one-third higher than the AFDC limit in place as of July 16, 1996 (U.S. House of Representatives 1998: 955–56). Many people, particularly those with chronic health problems or long-term care needs, may also qualify as medically needy through the spend-down process, in which their medical expenses are deducted from their income and assets in computing eligibility.

Transitional Medical Assistance (TMA) was established in 1988 to prevent families that become ineligible for welfare because of an increase in earnings from immediately losing Medicaid. If a family loses its Medicaid eligibility because of higher wages, TMA will provide coverage for 6 months without regard to income and for 12 months with an income test. TMA has been relatively underutilized because of the requirement that families must have been on welfare, the program's time limitations, and the burdensome reporting requirements for both states and recipients (Ellwood and Lewis 1998).

MEDICAID SECTION 1931: FAMILY COVERAGE

The Personal Responsibility and Work Opportunity Reconciliation Act of 1996 reformed the welfare system, replacing AFDC with Temporary Assistance for Needy Families (TANF). The act also created a category of children and parents who did not have to be receiving cash assistance in order to be eligible for Medicaid. This action allowed states to expand Medicaid coverage to higher-income families without having to expand their cash assistance programs, making coverage more economically feasible and giving states an incentive to include more families. The category covers only families (children and parents), however, so a large number of uninsured adults are still ineligible for Medicaid. Created by federal law under Section 1931 of the Social Security Act, the new category has mandatory minimum rules as well as more liberal eligibility rules.

The key provision of Section 1931 is that states must provide health insurance coverage to families whose income and resources would have qualified them for AFDC under the state's welfare plan as of July 16, 1996.[3,4] As long as a state's rules for determining countable income do not cause anyone who would otherwise be eligible to lose coverage, the state may disregard earnings or assets of families without limit and without any need for a waiver. This option is similar to the flexibility granted states under section 1902(r)(2) to expand coverage to children and pregnant women (Guyer and Mann 1998).

As of August 7, 1998, the Department of Health and Human Services eliminated the mandatory 100-hour rule: That rule extended Medicaid eligibility to two-parent families only if the primary wage earner was incapacitated or worked less than 100 hours per month. Elimination of the rule gave states the option of expanding coverage to low-income adults in two-parent families, regardless of the employment status of the parents. While some states had Section 1115 waivers from the 100-hour rule, all states now have the option of treating eligible one- and two-parent families equally (Guyer and Mann 1998).[5]

MEDICAID SECTION 1115 WAIVERS

Medicaid expansions are also possible through research and demonstration waivers authorized under Section 1115 of the Social Security Act. The waivers are designed to enable states to test innovative policy initiatives. Federal rules require that 1115 waivers meet budget neutrality requirements, undergo a formal evaluation, and last no more than five years without being renewed. For a demonstration to be budget neutral, it must not cost more than Medicaid would have cost over the same period (Centers for Medicare and Medicaid Services 2003a).

Section 1115 waivers have been used often to institute mandatory managed care under Medicaid; the waivers set aside specific benefit requirements and freedom-of-choice rules otherwise available under Medicaid. Moving beneficiaries from fee-for-service to managed care has created savings for the states and made it possible for them to expand coverage and still meet the waiver's requirement for budget neutrality. In addition, Section 1115 waivers are the only means states have of obtaining federal Medicaid funds to cover low-income adults who are not disabled and who do not have children.

In August 2001, the Bush administration introduced a new Section 1115 waiver authority, the Health Insurance Flexibility and Accountability Demonstration Initiative (HIFA), which permits states to scale back benefits for optional eligibility groups and use the savings, as well as other funding (such as any unspent SCHIP allotment), to extend coverage. It is too soon to judge the impact of this initiative.

State Options under the State Children's Health Insurance Program

Established in August 1997 as Title XXI of the Social Security Act, SCHIP extended health insurance coverage to children in low-income families that did not qualify for Medicaid. The Balanced Budget Act of 1997 allocated almost $40 billion to SCHIP over 10 years; the allocation took the form of matching grants to states based on their share of the nation's low-income children and low-income uninsured children (Kenney, Ullman, and Weil 2000). SCHIP allows a state to design its own stand-alone program, to cover children through Medicaid, or to create a program that combines both types of coverage. The federal matching rate for children enrolled in SCHIP is 30 percent higher than the matching rate for Medicaid.

SCHIP targets children with family incomes above state Medicaid eligibility cutoffs and below 200 percent of the FPL. However, states are not required to expand coverage up to 200 percent of the FPL, and they may extend SCHIP coverage to children in families with higher incomes through the use of income and resource disregards. SCHIP funds cannot be used to provide coverage for children who are already covered through private insurance or Medicaid, even if their coverage is insufficient or constitutes a financial burden for their families (U.S. General Accounting Office (GAO) 1999).

Until recently, the Centers for Medicare and Medicaid Services (CMS) (formerly the Health Care Financing Administration) restricted SCHIP funds to children. To provide family coverage under SCHIP, a state had to demonstrate that the costs of covering parents and children were no greater than the costs if only the children were covered, making parental SCHIP coverage a viable option for only a few states. CMS was also unwilling to approve Section 1115 waivers for SCHIP parental coverage because the agency felt that states should develop successful traditional SCHIPs before attempting any type of demonstration project (GAO 1999).

In August 2000, with SCHIPs entering their second and third years, CMS began accepting applications for waivers (CMS 2000). Thus far, the agency has approved waivers allowing Arizona, California, Minnesota, New Jersey, New Mexico, Rhode Island, and Wisconsin to receive the SCHIP matching rate for parents of children enrolled in the program. The two latter states have not implemented the expanded coverage. Many other states have opted to submit a HIFA waiver instead (CMS 2003d).

State-Funded Initiatives

States have always had the option of creating entirely state-funded programs to cover uninsured adults. Such programs give the states complete freedom and flexibility of design. They can cover adults with or without children, no minimum benefits are required, and they may cap enrollment at any point in order to stay within their budget. The most prominent state-funded program has been Washington's Basic Health Plan. Many other states have general assistance programs to provide services, including limited health insurance coverage, to adults with very low incomes, including those not traditionally eligible for Medicaid or cash assistance. However, these programs are generally small and help only the very poor. New York's Home Relief program was an exception, and the state has now incorporated the program into its Section 1115 demonstration.

States as Innovators

Some states have been considerably more innovative than others in using these mechanisms to expand their coverage of low-income persons. The states can be divided into four groups on the basis of the coverage they provide, from those with the most expansive coverage to those with the least. The typology is based, first, on whether the state extends coverage to adults without children and, second, on the extent of coverage to parents and children.

- Group I: States (11) that cover adults without children and with incomes up to at least the FPL.
- Group II: States (10) that cover parents with incomes up to at least the FPL.
- Group III: States (17) that cover children whose family incomes are at or above 200 percent of the FPL through SCHIP and that have eliminated the 100-hour rule, thereby covering two-parent working families.
- Group IV: States (12) that do not cover children with incomes as high as 200 percent of the FPL or that have not eliminated the 100-hour rule for parents.

Table 6-1 shows which group each state has been placed into, as well as each state's Medicaid eligibility standards for children, parents, and adults without children. Because of budget pressures, several states that had expanded coverage have recently tightened eligibility standards or capped enrollment. The higher eligibility levels are given in table 6-1, along with notations when retrenchment has occurred.

Table 6-1. *State Groups with Current Eligibility Levels for Children, Parents, and Adults without Children*

| State | Eligibility (% of FPL)[a] | | | Coverage Expansion Mechanism | 100-hour rule eliminated? | Notes |
	Children	Parents[b]	Adults without Children			
Group I						
Arizona	200	200	100	1115/HIFA	Yes	HIFA parent expansion (100–200% FPL) began October 1, 2002.
Delaware	200	100	100	1115	Yes	
Hawaii	200	200	100	1115	Yes	
Massachusetts[c]	200	200	133	1115	Yes	Other coverage of short-term unemployed up to 400% FPL (Medical Security Plan). Will lower eligibility of adults without children to 100% FPL in April 2003 because of budgetary problems.
Minnesota[c]	275[d]	275	175	SCHIP 1115	Yes	
New Jersey	350	200	100	SCHIP 1115	Yes	For budgetary reasons, reduced coverage of parents to AFDC levels in June 2002 and other adults to general assistance levels in Sept. 2001. Grandfathered existing enrollees.
New York[c]	250	150	100	1115	Yes	

Oregon	185	100	100	1115/SF HIFA	Yes	Expansion for adults to 110% FPL to be implemented in July 2003 if funding permits. Option to expand to 185% in subsequent years if funding is available.
Tennessee	200	100	100	1115	No	1115 waiver implemented in July 2002 scaled back eligibility to 200% FPL for children, 100% FPL for adults. Eligibility originally at 400% FPL, but enrollment for new adults closed since 1995.
Vermont[c]	300	185	150	1115	Yes	Submitted 1115/HIFA waiver to receive match for state-funded populations.
Washington[c]	250	200	200	SF	Yes	
Group II						
California[c]	250	100	—	1931	Yes	State's budget crisis delayed SCHIP 1115/HIFA expansion to parents up to 200% FPL.
Connecticut[c]	300	150	—	1931	Yes	At 185% FPL when legislation passed, but scaled back to 150% FPL prior to implementation.
Maine	200	150	100	1931/1115 HIFA	Yes	Waiver expanded Medicaid to adults without children up to 100% FPL in Oct. 2002, but enrollment limited by availability of DSH funds.

(continued)

Table 6-1. *Continued*

	Eligibility (% of FPL)[a]					
State	Children	Parents[b]	Adults without Children	Coverage Expansion Mechanism	100-hour rule eliminated?	Notes
Missouri	300	100, 125	—	1115	Yes	Custodial parents up to 100% FPL, non-custodial parents actively paying child support up to 125% FPL. Lowered eligibility of parents to 77% FPL and eliminated eligibility for noncustodial parents in July 2002 for budgetary reasons.
New Mexico	235	60	—	1115 HIFA	Yes	Received a HIFA waiver to extend coverage in premium assistance program to parents and other adults to 200% FPL. Scheduled to be implemented in July 2003.
Ohio	200	100	—	1931	Yes	
Pennsylvania[c]	235	200	200	—	Yes	July 2002, began state-funded program to cover adults up to 200% FPL. Enrollment limited by available funds.
Rhode Island[c]	250	185	—	SCHIP 1115	Yes	
Utah	200	150	150	1115	Yes	Comprehensive care only to TANF families; other adults eligible only for primary care services.

	185	185	—	SCHIP 1115		
Wisconsin[c]	185	185	—		No	No 100-hour rule elimination for Medicaid, but two-parent working families are eligible through BadgerCare; recipient remains eligible to 200% FPL.
Group III						
Alabama	200	31	—	—	Yes	
Alaska	200	82	—	—	Yes	Recipient remains eligible to 124% FPL.
Arkansas	200	22	—	—	Yes	No 100-hour rule elimination for Medicaid; recipient remains eligible to 54% FPL.
Florida	200	33	—	—	Yes	Recipient remains eligible to 68% FPL.
Georgia	235	64	—	—	Yes	
Indiana	200	32	—	—	Yes	Eligibility threshold at 100% FPL for TANF families.
Iowa[c]	200	90	—	—	Yes	
Kansas[c]	200	42	—	—	Yes	Recipient remains eligible to 65% FPL.
Maryland	300	44	—	—	Yes	
Michigan[c]	200	66	—	—	Yes	
Mississippi	200	39	—	—	Yes	Recipient remains eligible to 57% FPL.
Nevada	200	59	—	—	Yes	Allows 134% FPL for the first 3 months of coverage, then eligibility drops to 59% FPL.
New Hampshire[c]	300	64	—	—	No	No 100-hour rule elimination; recipient remains eligible to 102% FPL.
North Carolina	200	64	—	—	Yes	
South Dakota	200	68	—	—	Yes	

(continued)

Table 6-1. Continued

State	Eligibility (% of FPL)[a]			Coverage Expansion Mechanism	100-hour rule eliminated?	Notes
	Children	Parents[b]	Adults without Children			
Texas	200	34	—	—	Yes	Allows 45% FPL for the first 4 months of coverage, then eligibility drops to 34% FPL.
Virginia	200	32	—	—	Yes	Recipient remains eligible to 47% FPL.
Group IV						
Colorado	185	43	—	—	Yes	
Idaho	150	35	—	—	Yes	
Illinois	185[d]	49	—	1115 HIFA	Yes	HIFA waiver implemented in October 2002 extended coverage of parents to 49% FPL, giving the state the option to expand to 185% FPL in subsequent years, depending on funding.
Kentucky	200	52	—	—	No	100-hour rule applied to applicants only; recipient remains eligible to 77% FPL.

Louisiana	200	22	—	No	
Montana[c]	150	71	—	Yes	
Nebraska	185	45	—	No	
North Dakota	140	89	—	No	Allows 151% FPL for the first 6 months of coverage, then eligibility drops to 89% FPL.
Oklahoma	185	50	—	No	
South Carolina	150[d]	56	—	Yes	
West Virginia	200	46	—	No	
Wyoming	133	67	—	Yes	

a. FPL = federal poverty level, $15,020 for family of three and $18,100 for a family of four in 2002.
b. FPLs for parent coverage estimated by the dollar amount for a family of three (Maloy et al. 2002).
c. State has a medically needy program with eligibility at 60% FPL or higher.
d. State offers coverage at a higher level for infants: Minnesota, 280% FPL; Illinois, 200% FPL; South Carolina, 185% FPL.

States in group I are the real leaders, those that have gone considerably beyond required minimums. By covering at least some adults without children, these states are clear innovators for three reasons. First, to extend coverage to adults without children, states must either obtain a Section 1115 waiver that will allow them to use federal matching funds or they must use solely their own funds. Second, coverage of adults who have no children living with them is not as politically popular as coverage of children and their parents. Third, the population of uninsured adults without children is generally larger, older, and less healthy—and hence more costly on a per person basis—than the population of uninsured parents.[6] Group I includes several large states, including Massachusetts, New Jersey, and New York.

Group II includes states that have significant expansions of coverage to parents. California, Connecticut, Maine, Missouri, Ohio, Rhode Island, and Wisconsin have extended coverage for parents to 100 percent of the FPL or higher. More recently, New Mexico, Maine, Pennsylvania, and Utah have extended coverage to adults without children as well, although with fairly tight caps on enrollment or limitations on benefits (thereby differentiating them from states in group I). Group III states have reached the target coverage levels established in SCHIP, 200 percent of FPL, and cover two-parent families with incomes below AFDC/TANF levels. This group of states is mostly in the south and west and includes several large states, including Florida, Georgia, Michigan, North Carolina, and Texas. Group IV states have not increased coverage of children to the SCHIP target level and have not gone beyond minimum levels for adults. These states are again mostly in the south and west; most are small states, except for Illinois.

Leading State Innovators

The states in group I have devised complex, ingenious ways of extending their coverage of low-income residents. The states, listed in descending order of population size, and their innovations are described below:

New York. New York provides extensive coverage of its low-income population, including adults without children, through a comprehensive Medicaid and SCHIP program (table 6-2). Coverage of children was expanded to 250 percent of the FPL under SCHIP, which built upon an older, state-funded initiative, Child Health Plus, begun in

Table 6-2. *New York (Family Income as a Percentage of FPL)*

Program	Children				Parents	Adults without Children
	Infants	Age 0–5	Age 6–16	Age 17 and 18		
Traditional Medicaid	185%	133%	100%	AFDC, ~51%	TANF	—
SCHIP-Medicaid	—	—	—	100%	—	—
SCHIP-Separate	250%	250%	250%	250%	—	—
1931 Authority	—	—	—	—	150%	—
1115 waiver	—	—	—	—	—	100%
Premiums	<160%: none; 160–222%: $9/child/month ($27 family max); 223–250%: $15/child/ month ($45 family max)[a]				None	None
Cost sharing	None				None	None

a. CMS, *New York's State Fact Sheet*, http://www.hcfa.gov/init/chpfsny.htm. (Accessed October 29, 2001.)

1991. SCHIP was implemented in April 1998; by December 1999, it had already enrolled 425,522 children,[7] making it by far the largest SCHIP program in the United States.

For many years, the state's Home Relief program provided health benefits to very low-income adults without children. Beginning in 1997, the state received federal Medicaid matching funds for that population through a Section 1115 waiver. In December 1999, New York legislators approved the Health Care Reform Act of 2000, which created Family Health Plus, a program that expanded eligibility to parents with incomes up to 150 percent of the FPL and other adults with incomes up to the FPL. A Section 1115 waiver amendment for Family Health Plus was approved by CMS in June 2001 (CMS 2002a). The benefit package under Family Health Plus is nearly identical to the Child Health Plus package.

New York also developed a program, Healthy New York, that aims to make health insurance more affordable for small businesses with low-income employees and for low- to moderate-income working people without employer-sponsored insurance. Rather than providing direct subsidies, Healthy New York attempts to reduce the cost of private insurance by shifting some of the risk of high-cost cases to the state. The state is establishing stop-loss funds for certain small firms with many low-wage workers and for low-income uninsured individuals, from which health plans will be reimbursed for 90 percent of claims that fall between $30,000 and $100,000 (Coughlin and Lutzky 2002).

New Jersey. Spurred by the new federal SCHIP funds offered in 1997, New Jersey significantly increased coverage of children, parents, and adults without children (table 6-3) (Ullman and Bovbjerg 2002). Prior to SCHIP, New Jersey's Medicaid program covered AFDC-eligible children age 6 to 14 and their parents (with family incomes of approximately 41 percent of the FPL) and other poor children age 6 to 14 with family incomes up to the FPL (Maloy et al. 2002). Although New Jersey chose to develop its New Jersey KidCare SCHIP outside of Medicaid, the state first increased its Medicaid thresholds to 133 percent of the FPL for children of all ages so that all children in a family would receive the same coverage. SCHIP cov-

Table 6-3. *New Jersey (Family Income as a Percentage of FPL)*

Program	Children				Parents	Adults without Children	Pregnant Women
	Infants	*Age 1–6*	*Age 6–17*	*Age 17 and 18*			
Traditional Medicaid	185%	133%	100%	~41%	TANF, ~41%	—	185%
SCHIP-Medicaid	—	—	133%	133%	—	—	—
SCHIP-Separate	350%	350%	350%	350%	—	—	—
SCHIP-1115 waiver	—	—	—	—	200%	—	200%
State-funded	—	—	—	—	—	100%	—
Premiums	<150%: none; 150%+: sliding scale based on family income				Yes	None	None
Cost sharing	$5–$35				$5–$35	None	None

Notes: Cost sharing was scheduled to increase above $35 at the end of 2002. Emergency Department visits are the most expensive copay. There is also some cost sharing for outpatient prescription drugs.

erage is offered to uninsured children with family incomes up to 350 percent of the FPL, the nation's highest cutoff (Ross and Cox 2000).

In January 2001, New Jersey received a Section 1115 waiver to use SCHIP funding for coverage of parents, one of the first states to do so (CMS 2003d). The expansion, now called New Jersey FamilyCare, attempted to create a seamless health insurance system for families by providing care through a single program, although funding sources and benefits could vary with the enrollee. In anticipation of the waiver, the state used its Section 1931 authority in September 2000 to cover parents with incomes up to 133 percent of the FPL. The SCHIP waiver then gave the state higher matching rates for any parent with a child insured under SCHIP. Benefits for parents earning more than 133 percent of the FPL are based upon private insurance benchmarks, and cost-sharing is based on family income. Contributions to the insurance premiums are required of families with incomes greater than 150 percent of the FPL, and the contributions rise with income. Because of budget problems, new enrollment of parents above the AFDC eligibility level was suspended effective June 15, 2002 (Legal Services of New Jersey 2002).

New Jersey has gone beyond most other states in allowing adults without children to qualify for coverage under FamilyCare, which receives no federal match. Adults with incomes less than 50 percent of the FPL are eligible for Medicaid-like benefits, and those with incomes between 50 percent and 100 percent of the FPL receive a somewhat less comprehensive package. Just months after implementation, FamilyCare surpassed enrollment expectations (Ullman and Bovbjerg 2002). However, on September 1, 2001, the state ceased accepting new applications from adults without children and reduced the benefit package for those already enrolled.

Massachusetts. Massachusetts has developed a broad, comprehensive health insurance program funded through a Medicaid Section 1115 waiver and SCHIP (table 6-4). It combines a public program expansion and employer and employee subsidies. Known as MassHealth, the program has several components with different funding sources, but it is largely seamless to the beneficiary. The first and largest component is MassHealth Standard, which includes traditional Medicaid, as well as a Medicaid expansion covering pregnant women and infants with family incomes up to 200 percent of the FPL, children age 1 to 18 up to 150 percent of the FPL, and parents and disabled adults up to 133 percent of the FPL. All beneficiaries except pregnant women and disabled people are enrolled in managed care plans under Medicaid. The second component is MassHealth Common-

Table 6-4. *Massachusetts (Family Income as a Percentage of FPL)*

Program	Children			Parents	Adults without Children	Pregnant Women
	Infants	Age 1–16	Age 17 and 18			
MassHealth Standard	200%	200%	200%	133%	133%[c]	200%
MassHealth Family Assistance[a]	—	—	—	200%[d]	200%[d]	—
MassHealth Basic/Buy-in[b]	—	—	—	—	133% (planned reduction to 100%)	—

Type of coverage	MassHealth Standard: Medicaid managed care; MassHealth Family Assistance: state-approved employer-sponsored insurance; MassHealth Basic: reduced benefit package, adult day and foster care, hospice, nursing facility, and nonemergency transportation services are not covered.
Premiums	Medicaid: none; SCHIP: $10 per month for each child, family maximum of $30 per month; MassHealth Family Assistance: any cost not paid by employer or state; MassHealth Basic: none.
Cost sharing	Medicaid and SCHIP: none; MassHealth Family Assistance: any cost not paid by employer or state; MassHealth Basic: none.

Notes: The state receives both Medicaid and SCHIP matching funds for MassHealth Standard. The state receives federal Medicaid matching funds for MassHealth Family Assistance and MassHealth Basic enrollees.

a. Adults without children must work for a qualified employer. To be qualified, an employer must (1) have 50 or fewer employees, (2) contribute at least half the cost of the health insurance premium for benchmark coverage, (3) purchase health insurance from an approved billing and enrollment intermediary, (4) participate in the Insurance Partnership, a financial incentive program to encourage small businesses to offer health insurance to their employees. Self-employed individuals can also meet the requirements to become qualified employers. MassHealth Family Assistance is also available to children in families with incomes less than 200 percent of the FPL who do not meet SCHIP requirements or whose family has access to state-approved employer-sponsored insurance.

b. MassHealth Basic is available only to chronically unemployed individuals.

c. If disabled.

d. Parents and adults without children not eligible for MassHealth Family Assistance are eligible for the state program for the uninsured.

Health, which covers a small number of high-expense disabled children and adults who are not eligible for MassHealth Standard.

The third component, Family Assistance, is the second largest component of MassHealth, but it has less than 10 percent as many enrollees as MassHealth Standard. Most assistance takes the form of health insurance coverage for children in families with incomes of 150 to 200 percent of the FPL, which is above the ceiling for the MassHealth Standard component. Families in this income range that do not have access to employer-sponsored insurance are covered directly by the state; the small share that do have access to private insurance have almost all of their premiums paid by the state. In either case, most families make a small monthly contribution to the premium.

The newer, smaller, more innovative aspects of Family Assistance give low-income parents and other adults access to private insurance through qualified small employers (who have fewer than 50 full-time employees). Qualifying employers can receive up to $1,000 a year for each qualifying low-income enrollee by offering comprehensive health insurance and by paying half the cost of the premium. Qualified low-income enrollees (with incomes up to 200 percent of the FPL) have their share of the premium paid by the state, except for a small monthly contribution that is larger for adults than for children.

MassHealth Basic is the fourth component of the MassHealth program. It provides a fairly comprehensive set of medical services to chronically unemployed, uninsured persons with incomes less than 133 percent of the FPL. MassHealth Buy-In, the fifth component, provides premium assistance to the chronically unemployed with incomes less than 133 percent of the FPL who have health insurance for which they pay a premium. The state plans to reduce the income standards for MassHealth Basic and Buy-In to the FPL between February and April 2003, changes that will affect an estimated 50,000 adults (Kulp 2002).

Under a recent expansion of its Section 1115 waiver, Massachusetts extended MassHealth eligibility to cover persons under age 65 who are infected with HIV, but who do not have AIDS and who have incomes up to 200 percent of the FPL. The state also runs a Children's Medical Security Plan that provides limited coverage for basic services to otherwise uninsured children under age 19 (this program temporarily suspended enrollment in November 2002 but began accepting new applicants in January 2003). A state Medical Security Plan covers adults with family incomes up to 400 percent of the FPL who are eligible for unemployment compensation; the plan provides managed care coverage or contributes to continuation of employer-sponsored insurance under the Consolidated Omnibus Budget Reconciliation Act of 1985 (COBRA), with cost sharing and annual limits.

Finally, Massachusetts funds two large managed care programs, run by the state's two biggest safety net hospital systems, for the otherwise uninsured. It also funds a large pool that pays for uncompensated care (charity care and bad debts) at all hospitals and community health centers.

Washington. In 1993, the state of Washington passed health care reform legislation intended to create universal coverage through four initiatives: expanded Medicaid eligibility for children with family incomes up to 200 percent of the FPL and for pregnant women with incomes up to 185 percent, a state-subsidized health insurance program (the Basic Health Plan, BHP), an employer mandate, and insurance market reforms. The employer mandate and market reforms were repealed in 1995, but the state's basic commitment to providing affordable health insurance to low-income individuals and families has not changed, as evidenced by the coverage network created by Medicaid, the BHP, and a multitude of smaller programs designed to fill in the gaps left by these programs (table 6-5) (Nichols et al. 1997).

The BHP allows all adults and children to buy health insurance through the state, with a benefit package comparable to most employer-sponsored insurance plans. The intention was to offer individuals coverage both directly and through employers. Subsidized coverage was to be available for adults and families with incomes less than 200 percent of the FPL. Those with incomes greater than 200 percent were to be allowed to join by paying the full premium. Today, the subsidized portion of BHP is strong, with about 130,000 enrollees, but employer-purchased BHP and the unsubsidized program have not fared as well.

State officials had hoped that, by giving small businesses the opportunity to buy affordable insurance with the BHP, many would offer coverage to their employees. However, the availability of heavily subsidized insurance that individuals could buy directly gave employers little incentive to participate. Washington was relying on employer contributions to reduce the cost of the program; when they failed to do so, the state exhausted the program's appropriated funds and capped enroll-

Table 6-5. *Washington (Family Income as a Percentage of FPL)*

Program	Children	Parents	Adults without Children	Pregnant Women
Traditional Medicaid (Healthy Options or BHP+)	200%	TANF	—	185%
SCHIP-Separate	250%	—	—	—
State-funded	—	200%	200%	200%
Premiums	None	Sliding scale premiums.		None
Cost sharing	None	Copayments for prescription drugs and many outpatient and inpatient services.		None

ment at approximately 133,000 people in 1996. Budget shortfalls projected in the 2001–03 biennium will reduce enrollment further, to 125,000 (Holahan and Pohl 2002). The governor's 2003–05 budget proposes to end BHP coverage for all adults without children (about 60,000 people), thus cutting the program in half (Washington State Health Care Authority 2003).

The unsubsidized, or full premium, part of BHP has essentially collapsed. Because of adverse selection, premiums rose sharply and enrollment dropped dramatically. Adverse selection also struck the individual insurance market, where the state had mandated guaranteed issue and controlled premium levels. As insurers pulled out of the individual market, many high-risk individuals attempted to join BHP, further exacerbating its cost problems. After capping the number of people receiving unsubsidized coverage in 2002, Washington finally decided to eliminate such coverage altogether in 2003 (Washington State Health Care Authority 2002).

Children with family incomes up to 200 percent of the FPL are eligible for Medicaid. The state creates seamless coverage for families in BHP by allowing children to be enrolled in the same health plan as their parents;

however, children receive a Medicaid benefit package and do not have to pay BHP premiums or share costs. If families are not enrolled in BHP, their children are enrolled directly in Medicaid. The state was reluctant to initiate a SCHIP, believing that it had been penalized by not receiving the enhanced SCHIP match for its early expansions of coverage to children. After pressure from advocates and the federal government, Washington began a very small SCHIP that now provides insurance for children with family incomes between 200 and 250 percent of the FPL.[8]

Tennessee. In 1994, Tennessee embarked on a broad expansion of Medicaid designed to increase coverage by about 50 percent with little new money. In response to projected annual losses of a half billion dollars and potential losses of federal disproportionate share hospital (DSH) funding, Tennessee developed a Section 1115 waiver to move all Medicaid recipients into managed care and expand Medicaid to include the uninsured and the "medically uninsurable," a high-risk group that meets the state's medical underwriting standards. Starting in January 1994, all people without access to insurance, including those not usually eligible for Medicaid, were permitted to enroll in the TennCare plan by paying an income-related premium. By pooling all state, federal, and local funds dedicated to providing care to low-income populations and requiring cost sharing for those with incomes above the FPL, Tennessee expanded coverage to more than 400,000 previously uninsured people. With expenses higher than anticipated, enrollment was frozen in 1995 at 1.3 million beneficiaries and was left open only to persons eligible for Medicaid and those who were medically uninsurable.

By 2000, TennCare faced impending collapse. The state temporarily froze entry of the medically uninsurable because of high costs and the suspicion that insurance companies were rejecting the chronically ill because they knew that TennCare would cover them. TennCare also faced deteriorating relations with managed care plans and health care providers because of the state's low per capita payment rates, and many of the largest plans threatened to withdraw from TennCare. The fundamental problem was that there was never enough new money to finance a roughly 50 percent increase in coverage while paying rates that plans and providers would find acceptable, particularly given the likelihood of considerable adverse selection into the program (Conover and Davies 2000).

With program costs continuing to increase and the state facing recession, the governor developed a modified Section 1115 waiver that was approved by CMS in May 2002 and implemented in July. The waiver restructured and constricted TennCare to decrease enrollment and reduce costs. Today, TennCare's three parts—TennCare Medicaid, TennCare Standard, and TennCare Assist—target separate populations and have different benefit packages and cost sharing (table 6-6).

Residents who were eligible for Medicaid in 1993 (pre-TennCare) and uninsured women with breast and cervical cancer are eligible for TennCare Medicaid. TennCare Standard covers three groups. First, residents who are deemed medically uninsurable and who were previously enrolled in TennCare are eligible regardless of income; new medically uninsurable applicants must not have incomes that exceed the FPL. Second, children with family incomes less than 200 percent of the FPL and adults with incomes less than the FPL and with no access to group insurance are eligible. The waiver specifically reserves the General Assembly's right to revise this income ceiling downward or to increase coverage in this category to everyone with an income up to 200 percent of the FPL. The modified TennCare waiver also grandfathers two groups into TennCare Standard—persons who are eligible for Medicare and who receive

Table 6-6. *Tennessee (Family Income as a Percentage of FPL)*

Program	Infants	Children Age 1–6	Age 1–15	Age 15–19	Pregnant Women	Parents	Adults without Children	Medically Uninsurable[a]
TennCare Medicaid	185%	133%	100%	TANF	185%	TANF	—	—
TennCare-Standard	Children: <200% and without access to group insurance.							<100%
	Adults: <100% and without access to group insurance.							
TennCare-Assist	PROPOSED: <250% and with access to group insurance.							—
Premiums	Medicaid eligible: none;							
	Non-Medicaid beneficiaries: sliding scale based on income and family.							
Cost sharing	All beneficiaries: no costsharing for preventive services;							
	Medicaid eligible: $1–$3 pharmacy copays;							
	Non-Medicaid beneficiaries: $25 emergency room,[b] $5–$25 pharmacy copays.							

a. Determined "medically uninsurable" by state underwriting standards.
b. Waived if the patient is admitted.

prescription drugs through TennCare and children with family incomes less than 200 percent of the FPL, regardless of whether group insurance is available.

No other TennCare members were grandfathered into the modified program; disenrollment of those not meeting the new criteria began in mid-2002 amid much criticism. In December 2002, the Federal District Court ordered Tennessee to reinstate the eligibility of all people disenrolled from TennCare because of the new waiver. The U.S. Sixth Court of Appeals granted a stay of the district court order awaiting conclusion of the appeal; it is expected that at least 150,000 people will be dropped from the program.

The state also plans to initiate TennCare Assist, an insurance assistance program for persons with family incomes less than 200 percent of FPL, in July 2003. The program would be available to those with access to group insurance and would help them pay health insurance premiums (TennCare 2002).

Minnesota. Minnesota boasts one of the nation's most expansive publicly funded health insurance programs (table 6-7). As part of its

Table 6-7. *Minnesota (Family Income as a Percentage of FPL)*

	Children				Adults without	Pregnant
Program	<Age 2	Age 2–5	Age 6–17	Parents	Children	Women
Traditional Medicaid[a]	275%	133%	100%	~70%	—	275%
MinnesotaCare with federal Medicaid match	—	275%	275%	70–100%, 200–275%	—	—
MinnesotaCare without federal Medicaid match	—	—	—	—	175%	—
SCHIP	280%	—	—	100–200%	—	—
Premiums	Traditional Medicaid: none; MinnesotaCare: scaled to income					

a. Most groups eligible for Medicaid may opt to enroll in MinnesotaCare.

1992 comprehensive health care reform initiatives, Minnesota created a state-funded health insurance program, MinnesotaCare, which targets low-income residents. MinnesotaCare supplements the state's Medicaid program, which began moving enrollees into managed care through a Section 1115 waiver as early as 1985 (Kendall and Long 2002). Originally, MinnesotaCare provided a basic benefit package of primary care services only to parents and children with incomes less than 185 percent of the FPL; it funded the package through cigarette taxes, health care provider taxes, and enrollee premiums (Minnesota Department of Human Services 2003a). Today, between Medicaid and MinnesotaCare, parents and children with incomes up to 275 percent of the FPL are eligible and other adults are eligible up to 175 percent. The benefit package was extended to include inpatient coverage, and the program was converted from fee-for-service to managed care. Monthly premiums are based on family size and income (Minnesota Department of Human Services 2003b).

Under a Section 1115 waiver, funding for MinnesotaCare was changed to include Medicaid matching funds for children in 1992 and parents in 1999. Some children and parents are eligible for both Medicaid and MinnesotaCare, and they may join either. The state receives the federal Medicaid match regardless of which program the beneficiary chooses. The groups eligible for either Medicaid or MinnesotaCare are pregnant women and infants up to age two with family incomes up to 275 percent of the FPL, children age two to five with family incomes up to 133 percent of the FPL, children age 6 to 13 with family incomes up to the FPL, and children age 14 to 20 with incomes up to AFDC/TANF levels (approximately 58 percent of the FPL). Children with family incomes greater than these thresholds but less than 275 percent of the FPL must enroll in MinnesotaCare. Parents must pay premiums for children enrolled in MinnesotaCare, but they receive the Medicaid benefit package and the state receives federal matching funds (Kendall and Long 2002).

Because of its vast coverage expansions prior to the enactment of SCHIP, Minnesota was stymied by the program's requirement that SCHIP funds be used only to expand coverage beyond current eligibility levels, not to subsidize existing programs. Therefore, Minnesota's SCHIP coverage is limited to infants below the age of two with family incomes between 275 and 280 percent of the FPL. While this did little to provide a real increase in coverage, it did prevent other states from receiving Minnesota's SCHIP allotment (Minnesota Department of Human Services 2003b). In June 2001, CMS approved a SCHIP Section 1115 demonstration waiver, and the state now receives the enhanced SCHIP match for parents with incomes between 100 and 200 percent of the FPL (CMS 2003b).

Oregon. In 1994, Oregon adopted the Oregon Health Plan, a major set of reforms developed under a Section 1115 waiver that expanded Medicaid to cover all adults with incomes under the FPL through mandatory managed care (table 6-8). Oregon's plan is most notable for limiting the number of health services it covers in order to expand the number of residents it covers. To do this, the state developed a list of the diagnoses and treatment groups it would cover, as funds permitted. Oregon's SCHIP, beginning in 1998, expanded Medicaid to cover children from birth to age six with family incomes between 133 and 170 percent of the FPL and to cover children from age 6 to 18 with incomes between 100 and 170 percent of the FPL (CMS 2002b).

Oregon created the Family Health Insurance Assistance Program, which helps low-income families buy insurance through their employers, as a supplement to the Oregon Health Plan and SCHIP. Enacted in August 1997, the fully state-funded program originally offered assistance to families with incomes up to 200 percent of the FPL, but state officials quickly

Table 6-8. *Oregon (Family Income as a Percentage of FPL)*

Program	Children Age 0–6	Children Age 6–18	Parents	Adults without Children
Traditional Medicaid	133%	100%	TANF, ~78%	—
Medicaid Waiver	—	—	100%	100%
SCHIP-Separate	170%	170%	—	—
FHIAP	—	—	170%	170%
Premiums	None		Traditional Medicaid and pregnant women: none; Other Medicaid: $6–$125 sliding scale based on income; FHIAP: 5–30% of the employee's share of the premium cost.	
Cost sharing	None		None	

Note: FHIAP = Family Health Insurance Assistance Program.

reduced eligibility to 170 percent and capped enrollment at 7,000 because of unexpectedly high costs (Sparer 1999). In October 2002, Oregon received a HIFA waiver that allowed it to cap enrollment and reduce the benefits of those covered under its existing Section 1115 waiver. The new waiver allows the state to expand coverage to persons with incomes up to 110 percent of the FPL if funding is available and ultimately to those with incomes up to 185 percent of the FPL, again contingent on funding.

Other States. Other states in group I have expanded coverage to all low-income adults:

- *Arizona*—Under a HIFA waiver, the state has used Title XXI funds to cover parents with incomes between 100 percent and 200 percent of the FPL and other adults with incomes less than the FPL. The state receives the higher SCHIP matching rate for these populations; once SCHIP funds are exhausted, adults without children will be funded with Medicaid funds. Arizona has a separate SCHIP that covers children with family incomes up to 200 percent of the FPL.
- *Hawaii*—One of the pioneers in coverage expansion, Hawaii has instituted mandatory employer-sponsored health insurance, a public health care purchasing pool for Medicaid beneficiaries and general assistance recipients, and a state-subsidized insurance program for children and all adults. The state had extended public coverage to everyone with an income up to 300 percent of the FPL, but it now covers children up to 200 percent of the FPL (under SCHIP) and adults up to the FPL.
- *Delaware*—Delaware established its Diamond Health plan in 1996 under a Section 1115 waiver. The plan extended coverage to low-income adults with incomes up to the FPL. The state's Healthy Children program covers children who are not eligible for Medicaid and who have family incomes up to 200 percent of the FPL.
- *Vermont*—Using Medicaid and SCHIP funds, including a Section 1115 waiver, the state has created a comprehensive program for low-income children and adults. Children are covered up to 300 percent of the FPL, parents and caretaker relatives are covered up to 185 percent of the FPL, and adults without children are covered up to 150 percent of the FPL.

The states in group II are a mix of those that have expanded coverage of parents substantially and those that have extended limited coverage to adults without children. All of them offer fairly extensive coverage of children; only Wisconsin does not cover children with family incomes up to at least 200 percent of the FPL. California, Connecticut, Missouri, New Mexico, Pennsylvania, and Rhode Island cover children well above the SCHIP target level of 200 percent of the FPL. Using Section 1931, California and Ohio have extended coverage of parents to include those with incomes up to the FPL, and Connecticut and Maine provide coverage up to 150 percent of the FPL. Wisconsin and Rhode Island used Section 1115 SCHIP waivers to extend coverage to parents with incomes up to 185 percent of the FPL.

Recently, more states have used HIFA waivers (sometimes in conjunction with other sources of funds) to expand coverage of adults. Maine received a HIFA waiver in September 2002 to use unspent DSH funds to cover adults without children and with incomes up to the FPL; enrollment is limited by the availability of the DSH funds. Utah received a Section 1115 waiver to extend coverage to all adults with incomes up to 150 percent of the FPL; however, Utah provides only primary care and preventive services to these populations, and thus arguably does not offer what most people would consider insurance coverage. Pennsylvania established a program with state funds to cover all adults with incomes up to 200 percent of the FPL, but enrollment is subject to the availability of funds and hence is severely limited. New Mexico received a HIFA waiver to extend coverage to all adults with incomes up to 200 percent of the FPL. The state plans to establish a limited commercial benefit package: Individuals must have their employers contribute $75 per month or pay both the employer and individual contributions themselves.

Discussion

After the states are divided into four groups on the basis of how widely they expanded their health insurance coverage, the question arises as to whether the groups differ in other important respects as well. This section examines differences in income, education, urbanization, political preferences, and federal matching rates under Medicaid (table 6-9).

The more innovative group I states have a higher average per capita income than states in the other groups. In fact, per capita income declines along with eligibility expansions across the four groups. Conversely, the percentage of the population with low incomes (less than twice the FPL) increases across the four groups. Average income per low-income person

Table 6-9. *Demographics of State Groups*

Characteristic	State Group I	II	III	IV
Income per capita	$24,062	$22,800	$22,326	$20,306
Percent with income below 200% FPL	27%	27%	29%	32%
Income per low-income person[a]	$87,411	$83,300	$79,275	$63,910
Percent college-educated	28%	25%	25%	22%
Percent urban	79%	77%	68%	57%
Percent Gore/Nader vote	57%	52%	46%	41%
Average federal matching rate[b]	0.552	0.597	0.599	0.659

Source: The Urban Institute, tabulations of the March 2001 and 2002 CPS and 2002 FMAP.
a. Low income = < 200% of the federal poverty level.
b. Federal medical assistance percentage (FMAP).

(total income divided by the number less than 200 percent of the FPL) moves steadily downward across the groups, from $87,411 in group I to $63,910 in group IV. Consistent with their higher incomes, states in group I have the lowest federal matching rate, at 55 percent, and states in group IV have the highest, at almost 70 percent.

The percentage of the population with a college education is highest in group I and lowest in group IV. Similarly, states in groups I and II have much larger urban populations than states in group III, which in turn are more urban than states in group IV. States in groups I and II are politically more liberal, as indicated by the percentage of voters who supported Al Gore or Ralph Nader in the November 2000 election. In sum, states in group I have higher incomes, have higher education levels, are more urban, are politically more liberal, and have lower federal matching rates. It seems clear that the higher matching rates available to states in groups III and IV are not sufficient to offset their lower incomes or their more conservative political philosophy.

Table 6-10 summarizes the impact of each group's coverage expansions on the overall population and on various low-income populations. It does so first by determining the size of the insurance gap (Spillman 2000). The insurance gap is the percentage of a state's population not covered by private or federal insurance. The people in this gap would be uninsured without Medicaid or state insurance (e.g., Medicare or CHAMPUS). Next, the table expresses the population covered by Medicaid and state insurance relative to the population. The table then calculates the

Table 6-10. *Coverage Characteristics by State Group*

Coverage	State Group			
	I	II	III	IV
Total population (%)				
Insurance gap	23.2	23.1	23.1	24.9
Medicaid and state coverage relative to population	10.1	9.4	7.7	8.6
Medicaid and state coverage relative to gap	43.3	41.3	33.1	34.4
Uninsurance rate	13.1	13.7	15.4	16.3
Low-income population (%)				
Insurance gap	54.8	54.6	50.3	52.8
Medicaid and state coverage relative to population	29.9	29.0	22.0	23.2
Medicaid and state coverage relative to gap	54.7	53.3	43.6	44.1
Uninsurance rate	24.9	25.6	28.3	29.6
Low-income children (%)				
Insurance gap	57.3	56.7	52.1	55.9
Medicaid and state coverage relative to population	41.6	41.5	33.2	36.3
Medicaid and state coverage relative to gap	72.7	73.2	63.5	64.6
Uninsurance rate	15.7	15.2	18.9	19.6
Low-income adults (%)				
Insurance gap	53.2	53.1	49.0	50.8
Medicaid and state coverage relative to population	22.5	20.4	14.0	14.5
Medicaid and state coverage relative to gap	42.3	38.8	28.6	28.7
Uninsurance rate	30.7	32.7	35.0	36.3

Source: The Urban Institute, tabulations of the March 2001 and 2002 CPS and 2002 FMAP.
Note: Low income = < 200% of the federal poverty level.

population covered by Medicaid and state insurance relative to the insurance gap. Finally, the table gives the uninsurance rate: the percentage of the population with no insurance of any kind. The smaller a state's insurance gap and the greater the state's coverage of the people in the gap, the lower its uninsurance rate will be. (For a detailed discussion of these concepts, see Chapter 4.)

Surprisingly, there is not a great deal of difference in the insurance gaps across the four groups of states (table 6-10). There is essentially no difference for the total population, because these figures are driven by higher income groups, most of which have employer-sponsored coverage in all states. For the low-income population, the insurance gaps are actually higher in groups I and II, because private and federal coverage rates are lower.[9] The ratios of Medicaid and state coverage to the population and to the insurance gap show that states in groups I and II cover a higher share of their populations and a higher share of those in the gap. This is true of the total low-income population, low-income children, and low-income adults. For example, group I states cover 30 percent of their total low-income population and 55 percent of those in the gap, while group IV states cover 23 percent of their low-income population and 44 percent of those in the gap. Similarly, group I states cover 23 percent of all low-income adults and 42 percent of those in the gap, while group IV states cover 14 percent of low-income adults and 29 percent of those in the gap.

The larger insurance gaps in group I and II's low-income populations may reflect, in part, a substitution of public coverage for private coverage. That is, employers may be less likely to offer private coverage when the state makes generous public coverage available. To test this possibility, table 6-11 presents the same data with the population divided into three income groups. The first group has incomes of less than twice the FPL, and the second has incomes between two and three times the FPL. People in these two income groups are the most affected by coverage initiatives. The third group, those with incomes of three times the FPL or greater, is largely unaffected by differences in Medicaid policy.

The third income group has virtually identical private-federal coverage rates across state groups, which is not surprising because high-income people tend to have employer-sponsored insurance everywhere. But table 6-11 also shows that while group I and II states have more extensive public coverage and lower uninsurance rates than other states, they also have lower rates of private-federal coverage and hence a larger insurance gap. Although there is no way of knowing what the private-

Table 6-11. *Coverage Characteristics by Income and State Group*

| | Income and State Groups | | | | | |
| | <200% FPL | | 200–300% FPL | | 300%+ FPL | |
Coverage	I–II	III–IV	I–II	III–IV	I–II	III–IV
Total population (%)						
Private and federal	45.4	48.9	79.1	80.0	91.8	91.1
Medicaid and state	29.4	22.4	5.8	3.8	1.3	1.0
Uninsurance rate	25.2	28.7	15.1	16.2	6.9	7.9
Children (%)						
Private and federal	43.0	46.3	82.3	82.7	93.7	93.3
Medicaid and state	41.5	34.5	8.9	6.8	2.5	1.8
Uninsurance rate	15.5	19.2	8.8	10.5	3.8	4.9
Adults (%)						
Private and federal	47.0	50.6	77.5	78.7	91.2	90.4
Medicaid and state	21.5	14.1	4.2	2.2	0.9	0.7
Uninsurance rate	31.5	35.3	18.3	19.1	7.9	8.8

Source: The Urban Institute 2002. Tabulations of the March 2001 and 2002 CPS and 2002 FMAP.

Note: FPL = federal poverty level.

federal coverage rates would have been in the absence of the states' initiatives, the data are consistent with the possibility that some public coverage may be displacing private coverage.

Conclusions

The states that have developed innovative ways to expand coverage deserve considerable credit. They have no doubt overcome serious political and budgetary obstacles to achieve what they have. The broader picture that emerges is not encouraging, however. If the key question is whether current federal-state partnerships can be relied upon to expand coverage to the nation's low-income uninsured, the answer is probably no.

Only about 11 states have taken advantage of existing federal law, or established their own programs, to extend coverage in significant ways. Even in the group I states, uninsurance rates average 13 percent for the total population. About one-quarter of the total low-income population and almost one-third of low-income adults in these states lack health insurance. The initiatives undertaken by group I states extend coverage to an additional 7 to 8 percent of low-income people, but they may also displace some private coverage. People who leave private coverage for public are no doubt better off: They have very low incomes and end up paying less, receiving better coverage, or both, with public coverage. So while the innovative states have clearly made progress, much remains to be done. At least 29 states have done little beyond what is required by law. Uninsurance rates in these states average about 16 percent, with about 30 percent of the low-income population uninsured and 35 percent of low-income adults uninsured.

Clearly, the federal-state partnership is not working for low-income Americans in most states. The reasons are complex. In several states, low per capita income and limited wealth constrain the resources that are available. In many states, health care for the low-income population is a lower priority than such budget items as education and transportation. Other states may believe that coverage should be expanded in the private market, that providing services directly through public hospitals and clinics is sufficient for the uninsured, and that expanded public coverage will crowd out private coverage. Finally, the structure of federal programs, particularly Medicaid, makes it hard to cover adults without children. Research and demonstration waivers, which are subject to budget neutrality limits under Medicaid, are needed in order to obtain federal matching funds. In addition, some states allege that the benefit package and cost-sharing requirements of Medicaid cause the program to be a prohibitively expensive way to extend coverage.

Possibly, the current system could be transformed to achieve broader coverage. Enabling states to cover low-income adults under Medicaid would help. Allowing states more flexibility in establishing benefit packages and cost sharing might encourage them to extend coverage further. However, it seems unlikely that the new HIFA initiative, which allows states to reduce coverage of optional services and use the savings to expand coverage, is likely to make much difference. There is simply too little money in optional services.

Higher federal matching rates, as proposed by the National Governors Association (NGA) and by Holahan, Nichols, and Blumberg (2001), are essential if a combined federal-state system is to work. The NGA proposal would boost matching rates for optional populations and allow the states more flexibility in program design. It does not require states to expand coverage, but it gives them powerful incentives to do so. Holahan, Nichols, and Blumberg propose to provide states with higher matching rates for all existing Medicaid spending *if* the states extend coverage to everyone with incomes less than 250 percent of the FPL, as well as to all persons with above average health care costs. Either proposal would allow states to expand coverage substantially with little new state spending.

The states' response to SCHIP makes one optimistic that they may react positively to higher matching rates and more control over program design. If coverage could be expanded to more low-income adults under similar terms, states might also respond favorably. But the problems with DSH payments and upper payment limit programs—initiatives in which states have leveraged considerable federal money with relatively little in the way of state matching funds—give one caution about extending the current system. These arrangements have introduced new inequities in federal-state financing arrangements and have greatly increased tensions between the federal government and the states. It may well be that serious consideration needs to be given to simply making insurance coverage for low-income Americans a federal responsibility.

NOTES

1. This chapter builds on work by Krebs-Carter and Holahan (2000).

2. States' matching rates (Federal Medical Assistance Percentage, or FMAP) range from 50 to 77 percent and are based on average per capita income in the state.

3. Section 1931 does give states flexibility to use lower income standards as long as they do not go below the standards in place on May 1, 1988.

4. States' eligibility policies and standards must be consistent throughout the state and must treat applicants and current recipients equally, with the exception of earned income disregards, which may be applied differently to applicants and recipients.

5. States may link their Section 1931 income and resource standards to the consumer price index (CPI), increasing the standards as the CPI increases and ensuring that inflation does not lead to a gradual reduction of eligibility over time. Under this provision, states may also restrict coverage by reducing income standards to those in effect as of May 1, 1988. In addition, states may continue to use the income, resource, and family composition rules established under an AFDC waiver to determine Medicaid eligibility, even if the waiver is no longer being used under TANF or has expired.

6. Authors' tabulations from the March 2001 Current Population Survey.

7. New York's SCHIP enrollment has remained fairly constant for several years. By December 2001, California's growing enrollment matched New York's (Smith and Rousseau 2002).

8. Based on a site visit conducted October 11, 2000, as part of the Urban Institute's SCHIP evaluation *Assessing the New Federalism* project.

9. Chapter 4 shows that employer-sponsored insurance is negatively related to coverage rates of low-income populations. When states are grouped by the extent of their

coverage expansions, that relationship seems to disappear. This is a function of the diverse characteristics of the innovative states and the displacement effect discussed in Chapter 4.

REFERENCES

Centers for Medicare and Medicaid Services (CMS). 2000. "Letter from Timothy M. Westmoreland to State Health Officials, July 31, 2000." http://cms.hhs.gov/schip/ch73100.asp. (Accessed April 29, 2003.)

————. 2002a. "New York Statewide Health Reform Demonstration Fact Sheet." http://cms.hhs.gov/medicaid/1115/nyfact.asp. (Accessed April 29, 2003.)

————. 2002b. "Oregon Title XXI State Program Fact Sheet." http://cms.hhs.gov/schip/chpfsor.asp. (Accessed April 29, 2003.)

————. 2003a. "1115 Waiver Research and Demonstration Projects." http://cms.hhs.gov/medicaid/1115/default.asp. (Accessed April 28, 2003.)

————. 2003b. "HHS Approves Minnesota Plan to Insure Parents in SCHIP, Medicaid." http://cms.hhs.gov/schip/061301mn.asp. (Accessed August 9, 2001.)

————. 2003c. "Minnesota Health Reform Demonstrations." http://cms.hhs.gov/medicaid/waivers/mnwaiver.asp. (Accessed April 29, 2003.)

————. 2003d. "State Children's Health Insurance Program (SCHIP) Approved Section 1115 Demonstration Proposals." http://cms.hhs.gov/schip/1115waiv.pdf. (Accessed April 29, 2003.)

Conover, Christopher, and Hester Davies. 2000. *The Role of TennCare in Health Policy for Low-Income People in Tennessee.* Washington, D.C.: The Urban Institute. *Assessing the New Federalism* Occasional Paper No. 3.

Coughlin, Teresa, and Amy Westpfahl Lutzky. 2002. *Recent Changes in Health Policy in New York.* Washington, D.C.: The Urban Institute. *Assessing the New Federalism* State Update No. 22.

Ellwood, Marilyn, and Kimball Lewis. 1998. *On and Off Medicaid: Enrollment Patterns for California and Florida in 1995.* Washington, D.C.: The Urban Institute. *Assessing the New Federalism* Occasional Paper No. 27.

Guyer, Jocelyn, and Cindy Mann. 1998. *Taking the Next Step: States Can Now Take Advantage of Federal Medicaid Matching Funds to Expand Health Coverage to Low-Income Working Parents.* Washington, D.C.: Center on Budget and Policy Priorities.

Holahan, John, and Mary Beth Pohl. 2002. *Recent Changes in Health Policy in Washington.* Washington, D.C.: The Urban Institute. *Assessing the New Federalism* State Update No. 24.

Holahan, John, Len Nichols, and Linda Blumberg. 2001. "Expanding Health Insurance Coverage: A New Federal/State Approach." In *Covering America: Real Remedies for the Uninsured,* vol. 1 (103–18). Washington, D.C.: Economic and Social Research Institute.

Kendall, Stephanie, and Sharon Long. 2002. *Recent Changes in Health Policy in Minnesota.* Washington, D.C.: The Urban Institute. *Assessing the New Federalism* State Update No. 19.

Kenney, Genevieve, Frank Ullman, and Alan Weil. 2000. "Three Years into SCHIP: What States Are and Are Not Spending." Washington, D.C.: The Urban Institute. *Assessing the New Federalism* Policy Brief A-44.

Krebs-Carter, Melora, and John Holahan. 2000. *State Strategies for Covering Uninsured Adults*. Washington, D.C.: The Urban Institute. *Assessing the New Federalism* Discussion Paper 00-02.

Kulp, Russ. 2002. "Changes to MassHealth Basic and MassHealth Buy-In Eligibility Rules." Eligibility Operations Memo 02-20. http://www.state.ma.us/dma /publications/EOMs/EOM02-20.pdf. (Accessed January 28, 2003.)

Legal Services of New Jersey. 2002. http://www.lsnj.org/keyRecentDevelopments /NJFamCareCap053002.htm. (Accessed January 28, 2003.)

Maloy, Kathleen A., Kyle Anne Kenney, Julie Darnell, and Soeurette Cyprien. 2002. *Can Medicaid Work for Low-Income Working Families?* Washington, D.C.: The Kaiser Commission on Medicaid and the Uninsured.

Minnesota Department of Human Services. 2003a. "DHS/Health Care: History of Minnesota Care." http://www.dhs.state.mn.us/HealthCare/MinnesotaCare/history.htm. (Accessed April 28, 2003.)

———. 2003b. "Minnesota's Home and Community-Based Waivers." http://www.dhs .state.mn.us/Contcare/disability/hcbwaiver.htm. (Accessed April 28, 2003.)

Nichols, Len, Leighton Ku, Stephen Norton, and Susan Wall. 1997. *Health Policy for Low-Income People in Washington*. Washington, D.C.: The Urban Institute. *Assessing the New Federalism* State Report.

Ross, Donna Cohen, and Laura Cox. 2000. *Making It Simple: Medicaid for Children and CHIP Income Eligibility Guidelines and Enrollment Procedures*. Washington, D.C.: The Kaiser Commission on Medicaid and the Uninsured.

Smith, Vernon K., and David M. Rousseau. 2002. *SCHIP Program Enrollment: December 2001 Update*. Washington, D.C.: The Kaiser Commission on Medicaid and the Uninsured.

Sparer, Michael S. 1999. *Health Policy for Low-Income People in Oregon*. Washington, D.C.: The Urban Institute. *Assessing the New Federalism* Occasional Paper No. 31.

Spillman, Brenda C. 2000. "Adults Without Health Insurance: Do State Politics Matter?" *Health Affairs* 19(4): 178–87.

TennCare. 2002. "TennCare Program Design and Waiver Modifications, State of Tennessee, Don Sundquist." Submitted to Secretary Tommy Thompson, Department of Health and Human Services, February 12, 2002. http://www.state.tn.us /tenncare/waiver2-11.pdf. (Accessed February 21, 2002.)

Ullman, Frank, and Randy Bovbjerg. 2002. *Recent Changes in Health Policy in New Jersey*. Washington, D.C.: The Urban Institute. *Assessing the New Federalism* State Update No. 21.

U.S. General Accounting Office (GAO). 1999. *Children's Health Insurance Program: State Implementation Approaches Are Evolving*. GAO/HEHS-99-165. Washington, D.C.: General Accounting Office.

U.S. House of Representatives. 1998. Committee on Ways and Means. *1998 Green Book*. Washington, D.C.: U.S. Government Printing Office.

Washington State Health Care Authority. 2002. "Basic Health History." http://www.basichealth.hca.wa.gov/bhhistory.shtml. (Accessed April 28, 2003.)

———. 2003. "Recommendation Summary." http://www.ofm.wa.gov/budget03 /recsum/107rs.htm. (Accessed January 30, 2003.)

7

Medicaid Managed Care
State Flexibility in Action

Robert E. Hurley
Stephen Zuckerman

The rapid expansion of managed care in state Medicaid programs over the past decade presents a unique opportunity to examine how sweeping programmatic change was promoted, shaped, and constrained by the evolving federal-state relationship. Nearly all of the states launched managed care, displaying in the process characteristic diversity of motives, methods, and achievements. Most states had to petition federal officials for permission to do so, because the move to managed care usually required the states to deviate from Medicaid requirements. The dramatic growth of the new models of care quickly immersed state agencies in complex administrative responsibilities stemming from managed care purchasing. This growth also exposed the states and their Medicaid beneficiaries to the vicissitudes of the turbulent health care marketplace. And, not surprisingly, the move to managed care was marked by highly visible successes and failures that have engaged the attention of policymakers, advocates, and the general public.

The managed care experiences of the 1990s have reinvigorated the debate over whether Medicaid is a national program built around a federal-state partnership or essentially a state-based program with federally imposed conditions that must be met in order to garner matching funds. Notwithstanding the debate, at the heart of efforts to pursue new ways of paying for and delivering health care has been the desire to make Medicaid a better program. One should not disregard this goal in reflecting on the broader policy question of federalism. In fact, determining the ways in which managed care may have improved Medicaid is directly pertinent to federalism. Positive and negative impacts on beneficiaries are important to both federal and state governments, but the significance of cost savings, administrative burden, and reduced program uniformity may be seen differently from federal and state vantage points.

This chapter examines how managed care implementation and growth have been a revealing experience for students of federalism. It explores why and how most state Medicaid agencies came to see managed care as a valuable development and how their aims for this model of care have changed over time. In examining the regulatory context of change, the chapter focuses on whether states have in fact had the necessary flexibility to proceed. It assesses whether all states acted responsibly and whether federal agencies exercised due discretion while nurturing creativity, particularly given that managed care is a market-based strategy with considerable risks and uncertainties. Next, the chapter appraises the extent to which states have succeeded in transforming their Medicaid programs and examines empirical evidence of program effects. Finally, because managed care has proven to be so controversial in its own right, it offers some thoughts on generalizing this particular experience to other policy developments. The chapter concludes with several important lessons to be gleaned from this era of experimentation.

Origins of Managed Care in Medicaid

The antecedents of recent managed care experimentation can be traced back to the 1980s, when some states petitioned federal officials for permission to introduce mandatory enrollment in prepaid health plans. This idea had been seriously discredited by experiences in California in the 1970s, when contracting with health plans encountered numerous problems, including fraud, marketing abuses, and financial failure (Chavkin and Treseder 1977). Most notable among the pioneer states was Arizona. The last state to implement a Medicaid program, it launched the Arizona Health Care Cost Containment System—built entirely around prepaid health plans—in 1982 (McCall et al. 1985). Other states followed suit, devising demonstration programs in one or more counties that included features of the emerging concept of managed care (Freund et al. 1988). Among the innovators were

- California, where the state Medi-Cal agency contracted with quasi-governmental authorities in Santa Barbara and Monterey to develop county-based managed care programs for which the local authority would assume full financial risk;
- Missouri, where the Medicaid agency contracted with four prepaid health plans created to serve beneficiaries in the Kansas City area;
- Minnesota, where a portion of Medicaid beneficiaries in the greater Twin Cities area were randomly assigned to enroll in existing and new health maintenance organizations (HMOs);
- New York, where a mandatory HMO enrollment program was implemented in Monroe County (Rochester); and
- New Jersey, which implemented a managed care program featuring voluntary enrollment and partial capitation (i.e., payment on a per capita basis) in selected counties.

This first generation of programs aimed to improve access to care and to make future program costs more predictable. In the early 1980s, there was virtually no evidence from commercial managed care plans to support the belief that substantial cost savings could be realized in Medicaid managed care programs; however, setting or negotiating per capita rates in prepaid health plans intuitively suggested that some measure of control could be exerted over future costs. Obtaining a contractually assured medical home for beneficiaries was widely espoused by pioneering states (Freund and Hurley 1987). Other states climbed aboard this bandwagon in the mid-1980s, including some that decided on other ways to achieve the virtues of coordinated care and guaranteed access. Utah and Michigan were among the first states to develop primary care case management (PCCM), an early version of what later became known as gatekeeping (Freund 1984).

It was not until the late 1980s, when fragmentary evidence of cost savings began to accumulate from these programs, that cost control began to compete with access improvement as a reason for managing care (Freund et al. 1988). The next few years brought steeply escalating Medicaid expenditures. Many more states turned to managed care, first with hesitancy and then with enthusiasm, as they heard informed or misinformed claims of savings (Hurley, Freund, and Paul 1993). The desire of some states to parlay presumed savings into expanded eligibility propelled even more dramatic growth in managed care. By the mid-1990s, access and cost-saving objectives were joined by rising expectations that managed care could improve the accountability of managed care vendors as well as clinical quality and beneficiaries' satisfaction with medical care (Davidson and Somers 1998). Managed care seemed to be a panacea for Medicaid (Hurley 1998).

Medicaid managed care increased roughly ninefold in the 1990s, with coverage leveling off at approximately 55 percent of all beneficiaries (figure 7-1) (National Academy for State Health Policy 2001). The number of states with managed care programs grew from 29 to 49, as nearly every Medicaid agency offered some kind of managed care in at least part of the state. Because the bulk of Medicaid enrollees are low-income women and children, managed care is now the dominant form of care for this group. Enrollment of aged and disabled beneficiaries into Medicaid managed care has lagged. Managed care also dominates the private health insurance market.

Essentially, states offered two managed care models: fully capitated HMOs and PCCM programs that retained fee-for-service payments and relied on the primary care physician to coordinate and authorize care. Enrollment grew in both types of programs throughout the decade (figure 7-2), but by 2000, nearly 70 percent of all beneficiaries in managed-care arrangements were enrolled in HMOs (Centers for Medicare and Medicaid Services [CMS] 2001). Most states mandate enrollment for eli-

Figure 7-1. *Medicaid Managed Care Enrollment, 1981–2000*

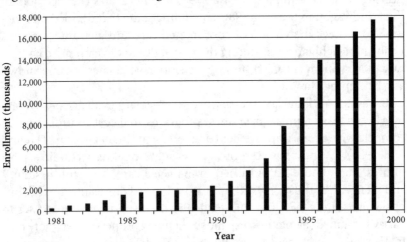

Source: Centers for Medicare and Medicaid Services (2001).

Figure 7-2. *Enrollment by Model Type, Selected Years*

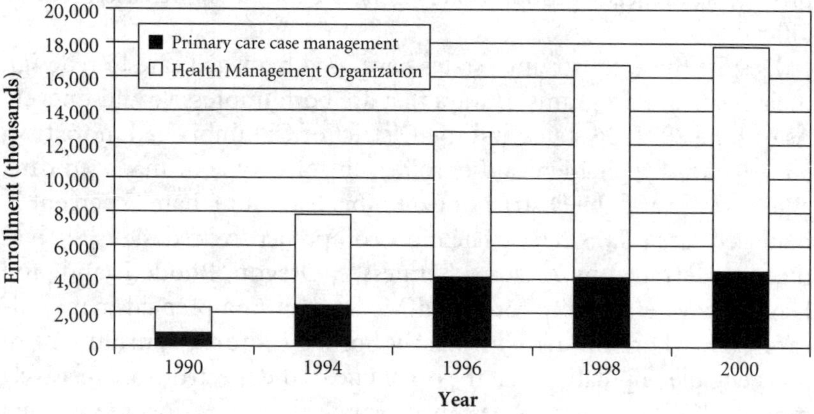

Source: National Academy for State Health Policy (2001).

gible populations, although voluntary programs have persisted for several groups that have special needs and present particular challenges to both state agencies and managed care plans. These smaller groups reveal one of the ragged edges of federal-state relations in the managed care experience and are discussed below.

As they adopted and adapted managed care models, states discovered that they faced a particularly thorny set of problems and constraints that private purchasers of health services did not (Coughlin et al. 1999; Hurley and Wallin 1998). To begin with, Medicaid had already achieved savings through its administered pricing, such as fee schedules that were below market rates for many services and thus not amenable to further discounting. But most problems arose because Medicaid does much more than just purchase health services for beneficiaries. It provides targeted support for safety net providers; in fact, Medicaid revenues are often critical to financially vulnerable providers such as public hospitals. Medicaid also makes major contributions to medical education through its support of teaching hospitals. Medicaid agencies function as pass-through entities, drawing down federal matching funds to support state facilities for institutionalized populations and programs managed by other state agencies. These and other functions impede states' ability to contract aggressively for care, promote new models of financing and delivery, and extract substantial cost savings. Many states realized that their maneuverability was limited or had to be implemented cautiously. Other states were reminded of confounding responsibilities by providers, advocacy groups, sister agencies, and, in some cases, federal officials.

Despite these constraints, states have used managed care to redesign their Medicaid programs in ways that are both impressive and uneven. As of June 2001, 36 states and the District of Columbia had more than 50 percent of their Medicaid enrollees in some type of managed care, and 13 states and the District of Columbia had more than 75 percent in managed care (CMS 2001). The most comprehensive redesigns, such as those undertaken by Arizona, Tennessee, Oregon, Rhode Island, and Hawaii, have essentially converted Medicaid into a prepaid managed-care-everywhere model with nearly border-to-border enrollment of most eligible populations. At the other end of the spectrum are relatively modest PCCM programs designed primarily for low-income women and children (as in Georgia) or for chronically ill and disabled beneficiaries as well as low-income women and children (as in North Carolina and Arkansas). Such states continue to rely on a traditional Medicaid administrative structure but appear over time to enhance programs and to add new functions (such as case and disease management).

In the middle range are a large number of mixed models of managed care and varied combinations of eligible populations. These models typically feature HMOs in urban areas and PCCM programs in rural areas (as in Pennsylvania, New York, and Virginia) or prepaid enrollment for low-income women and children, but principally PCCM for populations with special needs (as in Massachusetts). Such states maintain many features of the traditional Medicaid program while assuming the additional functions of prepaid managed care systems. Adding to this structural diversity is the dynamic nature of the managed care market, which has compelled states to adapt their strategies to changing market conditions.

Federalism and Experimentation— Waivers as a Framework for Innovation

The story of Medicaid managed care has been a saga of waivers sought and largely granted (Freund and Hurley 1987; Holahan et al. 1995). The waiver process epitomizes the federal-state relationship in Medicaid: It is the vehicle states use to seek relaxation of federal rules and regulations in order to undertake experimentation and still qualify for matching funds. In principle, states could (and a few did) allow beneficiaries to enroll voluntarily in HMOs without waivers. But to pursue managed care strategies aggressively, states had to request permission to abridge such Medicaid features as freedom of choice, statewide availability of programs, uniformity of policies such as provider payment, and strictures against releasing personal information about beneficiaries to non–state agency personnel. In return, states had to abide by certain conditions imposed through the waivers, notably protection of beneficiaries (discussed below) and budget-neutrality—that is, the innovation could not be expected to cost the federal government more than the traditional Medicaid program would have cost.

The waiver process has come to exemplify the debate over whether Medicaid is fundamentally a state or a national program, and how federal officials should control and influence the activities of the states. Two broad types of waivers have been employed to implement managed care (Freund and Hurley 1987): research and demonstration waivers (Section 1115) and programmatic waivers (Section 1915(b)). In both cases, waivers represent state use of regulatory authority vested in the Health Care Financing Administration (now the Centers for Medicare and Medicaid Services, or CMS). The authority allows states to operate their Medicaid programs in a fashion that would not otherwise qualify for federal matching funds.

The differences between the two types of waivers are significant in principle, if not always in practice. Section 1115 waivers were originally conceived to create and test new models of financing and delivery. In return for greater flexibility, states were expected to comply with detailed reporting and oversight requirements (Freund and Hurley 1987). The requirements are designed to facilitate research and evaluation, thus generating knowledge that could benefit other states and the Medicaid program in general. Arizona's Medicaid program, now nearly 20 years old, is the classic example: A Section 1115 waiver allowed that state to create a program that relies exclusively on prepaid health plans. Early Section 1115 waivers, implemented in the 1980s in Arizona, California, Missouri, Minnesota, New York, and New Jersey, yielded considerable information (Freund et al. 1988).

Section 1915(b) waivers had a narrower aim—to give states the opportunity to enhance their individual Medicaid programs (Freund and Hurley 1987). These waivers are often characterized as freedom of choice waivers, but they typically waive other regulations as well. Although expectations and requirements of these waivers were normally more modest, many states transformed their existing Medicaid program into a managed care arrangement with them. Evaluation and assessment demands were more limited and focused on state-specific experience in regard to cost of care and access to care. The assumption underlying both types of waivers was that guided flexibility would enable states to introduce program variations that would yield gains for beneficiaries and the state alike. The gains were expected to at least offset the loss of intra- or interstate uniformity and, in some cases, the risk associated with restricted freedom of choice as well.

Several states, beginning with Oregon, Tennessee, and Hawaii, seized upon the Section 1115 waiver as the instrument through which they could pursue more extensive reforms, such as coverage expansions (Holahan et al. 1995). The states' increasingly aggressive use of the waivers in the 1990s reflected the confluence of several forces: a loss of faith in the likelihood of federal reform; a sense in many states that dramatic steps were necessary to control costs or expand coverage, or both; and a renewal of states' rights sentiments that was finding its voice in the promotion of block grants for Medicaid. Some states used waivers as an interim strategy while they awaited the block grants they believed would reconfigure the federal-state relationship. Block grants were expected to give each state a fixed amount of money, based on its past expenditures, and to provide a minimum set of federal rules that the states would have to follow.

Federal officials were initially hesitant to throw open the door to waivers, but a changing policy environment led to a softening of resistance, and by 1997 more than 15 new Section 1115 waivers were granted (Iglehart 1999). While some programs maintained a semblance of their original research and demonstration function, waivers increasingly authorized highly idiosyncratic models of reform and programmatic changes, nearly always with a managed care component.

The Federal-State Cold War over Medicaid Waiver Policy

The federal posture toward waivers has gone through several phases, reflecting policy priorities, program interests and concerns, and political considerations. Throughout the past two decades, simmering tensions between the federal government and the states have sometimes flared into open warfare. In the early 1980s, states were encouraged to pursue experimentation and program innovations, particularly as waiver authority was liberalized in the Omnibus Budget Reconciliation Act (OBRA) of 1981, which added Section 1915(b) to the Social Security Act (Freund and Hurley 1987). Though support for expansion of managed care had leveled off by the late 1980s, Medicaid programs faced renewed cost pressures triggered by eligibility expansions under OBRA 1989 (Kaiser Family Foundation 1993). The eligibility expansions coincided with the surge in Medicaid managed care enrollment in the 1990s (figure 7-1), putting to the test policymakers' belief—despite very scant evidence—that managed care could produce and sustain large savings (Hurley 1998). CMS officials initially displayed sympathy for the financial distress of state Medicaid programs. They typically supported states in their efforts to expand managed care, particularly for women and children, despite the fact that some of the programs had been singled out for harsh criticism, notably those in Philadelphia and Chicago (U.S. General Accounting Office [GAO] 1987, 1990).

This supportive posture continued well into the 1990s, particularly once the Clinton administration's efforts to reform health care came to naught and the mantle of reform was donned by the states. Congressional pressure began to build for more sweeping reforms, like block grants for Medicaid, that would render waiver-granting authority virtually moot. The controversial features of the Oregon waiver, which limited coverage to certain diagnoses and treatment groups, were a lightning rod for concerns about granting states too much leeway in Medicaid reform, and the plan's protracted review and ultimate approval spanned two administrations (Brown et al. 2001; GAO 1992). However, approval of Tennessee's plan was swift and cleared the way for several other states to expand Medicaid managed care and, presumably, use the savings to expand coverage to previously uninsured persons (Conover and Davies 2000). Federal support of greatly increased state flexibility was so strong that it did not flag measurably when Tennessee's program encountered serious difficulties.

By the mid-1990s, consumer advocates were challenging the suitability of conventional managed care for some Medicaid-eligible populations, particularly persons with special needs. Their challenges were launched on the state front, in attempts to influence decisions about the nature of managed care programs and the pace of implementation, and on the federal front, in attempts to influence the waiver granting or renewal process (Bazelon Center for Mental Health Law 2001). In response, federal officials required states seeking waivers to conduct public hearings. Some states saw this as a change of direction, and the federal government's waiver-granting authority was criticized as an impediment to innovation and a source of frustration for proponents of devolution. The multiyear review process of New York's mandatory managed care waiver reveals a number of these sentiments and tensions (Coughlin, Long, and Holahan 2001).

The passage of the Balanced Budget Act (BBA) of 1997 was expected to alter the perception of waivers as barriers by enabling states to undertake mandatory managed care programs as a "state plan amendment." States would not have to request a federal waiver as long as their proposed programs complied with new regulations called for in the act. But states' hopes for a more liberal policy faded when it became apparent that the new requirements, when translated into proposed regulations, raised the bar on what states had to do in order to launch managed care programs without a waiver (Beronja, Chimento, and Forbes 2000). States would be required to improve beneficiary information and notification, health plan reporting, and health plan quality. Moreover, certain groups were granted special protection—namely, disabled persons who were covered by both Medicare and Medicaid, Native Americans, and children with special health care needs—and states had to continue to request waivers if their managed care programs aimed to cover these groups.

Controversy surrounded the proposed regulations for several years. States and their health plan contractors contended that the regulations were burdensome, overly prescriptive, and would contribute to health plan withdrawals from Medicaid. The Bush administration proposed alternative regulations that were finally issued in mid-2002. By that time, however, a number of the 1997 act's original provisions had effectively been implemented through CMS directives to states (Beronja et al. 2000). In sum, the BBA that was expected to liberate states from some of the obstacles to managed care failed to do so in the eyes of most states and many in Congress.

Beneficiary Protection: By Whom and from Whom?

One interpretation of the waiver process is that it positions the federal Medicaid agency to review significant deviations from traditional Medicaid policies and practices in the interest of ensuring that beneficiaries' well-being is not jeopardized. Concern about adverse impacts arose both from the restricted choice associated with most managed care models and from the potential for prepayment to adversely affect access to and quality of care—particularly because Medicaid's payment rates are low. But federal oversight implies that the states, if left to their own devices, might put beneficiaries at risk or, for that matter, that traditional Medicaid arrangements are less threatening than new models of financing and delivery.

Not surprisingly, states have found this insinuation insulting and unjustified. Many state officials contend that the federal government's monolithic, inflexible approach to Medicaid is a far greater threat to beneficiaries' well-being because it impedes innovation and inhibits states from responding to changing market conditions and opportunities. Moreover, some states believe, and point to credible evidence, that managed care arrangements have improved access to primary care, increased vendor accountability, and reduced costs or increased value for current expenditures.

The importance of these contrasting positions cannot be overstated. They have consistently been at the root of federal-state tensions surrounding Medicaid managed care and the devolution of authority to the states. Moreover, other parties that are opposed to managed care or its extension to certain populations have played upon the federal-state friction. Some contend that, rather than acting as responsible experimenters, states may jeopardize the well-being of Medicaid beneficiaries by pursuing short-term cost-containment goals. States counter that this view distorts their motives and fails to acknowledge that managed care models can enable them to improve their Medicaid programs. The states argue further that federal preoccupation with program uniformity prevents them from engaging in creative, customized solutions to their particular problems.

States also argue that they are fully capable of dealing with state and local interests and pressures as they design programs. They point to California, for example, where the state agency responsible for managed care planning in the early 1990s unleashed a storm of protest from safety net providers and local officials who opposed the state's plan to rely principally upon private health plans for expansion (Draper and Gold 2000). The ensuing debate led to a major program redesign and the subsequent introduction in a dozen major counties of the two-plan model, which gives safety net providers an explicit role in locally developed health plans. This accommodation defused opposition and has led to what is now seen as a particularly successful innovation (Draper and Gold 2000; McCall et al. 2000).

Another bone of contention has been the inclusion of persons with chronic illnesses and disability in Medicaid managed care programs. While the number of states that include these persons has increased steadily over time, enrollment of chronically ill and disabled persons in managed care has typically been limited and voluntary (Regenstein and Anthony 1998). Nearly 70 percent of Medicaid spending is for chronically ill and disabled persons, so excluding them from managed care programs sharply curtails the state's ability to lower overall Medicaid expenditures. But the states' hesitancy to include these populations also reflects legitimate concerns about how well conventional managed care models can be adapted to persons with serious, complex health problems. Moreover, many persons with chronic disease or disability, their advocates, and their service providers fear that they may be ill-served or underserved by managed care plans (Battaglia 1993; Tanenbaum and Hurley 1995). The states' track records have been uneven. Some, like Tennessee, moved quickly to include these populations on a mandatory basis (Conover and Davies 2000), while others, like Minnesota and Wisconsin, moved far more slowly, despite having mature programs in place for low-income women and children.

The federal government typically did not intervene in questions about managed care for persons with chronic illnesses and disability unless problems erupted. Such was the case recently with New Mexico's managed-care program for behavioral health (Bazelon Center for Mental Health Law 2001). Several advocacy organizations voiced concerns about program deficiencies, threatening and ultimately delaying renewal of the state's waiver. The federal government has been criticized by people who think a more vigilant role is justified. For example, a number of states have received waivers for prepaid managed care programs for these high-cost beneficiaries without having first determined whether per capita rates had been adjusted appropriately. In light of the great cost variations that have been documented for some groups, it could be argued that waivers ought not to be granted until a credible risk-adjustment scheme has been put in place (Hurley and Draper 1998).

The process of granting waivers has been greatly complicated in recent years by the breadth and ambition of the reform efforts that waivers encompass. Most Section 1115 waivers incorporate such diverse features as eligibility expansions, modifications in payment strategies, and program design and management issues (Holahan et al. 1995). These multiple, concurrent changes make it difficult to disentangle the expected contribution of managed care to state Medicaid endeavors and to determine whether, or to what extent, a waiver is budget-neutral. States have employed considerable ingenuity and artfulness to assert that their waiver programs adhere to budget-neutrality requirements and that Medicaid beneficiaries' access to and quality of medical care have not been degraded.

States as Laboratories for Innovation: An Operational Appraisal

First-generation managed care programs were venturesome but not always successful, as evidenced by the failure of Section 1115 demonstration programs in the 1980s in California and New Jersey. Later programs drew upon the successes and failures of their predecessors, offering a glimpse into the extent to which states have engaged in collateral or cross-state learning. Some states redesigned their programs, notably California, with its multiple model approach, and Florida, with its dual emphasis on HMOs and PCCM plans. Other states shifted sequentially from one phase to another, as Maryland and Michigan did when they replaced PCCM programs with prepaid arrangements. A number of states offer multiple models based on within-state market variation (typically rural versus urban), among them Texas, Virginia, and New York. The ability to refine strategies and adapt them to local conditions is necessary for a market-based initiative like managed care.

Experimentation has been opportunistic, at least in part because of the evolving nature of managed care and changing ideas about what it may contribute. Many states moved from traditional fee-for-service care to PCCM programs until prepaid managed care became more broadly available and vendors became more willing to venture into the risky Medicaid market. Likewise, as managed care plans, especially the predominantly commercial ones, withdrew from Medicaid in the late 1990s, states had to reconsider the importance of keeping prepaid arrangements (Felt-Lisk 1998; McCue et al. 1999). Some states, such as New York, responded by increasing payment rates and relying more heavily on health plans sponsored by safety net providers (Coughlin et al. 2001). Others, such as New Jersey, Maryland, and Washington, found that contracting with fewer plans, and typically those that serve only the Medicaid population, was an effective response (Hurley and McCue 2000). Still others, such as Georgia and Vermont, reverted back to PCCM programs (National Academy for

State Health Policy 2001). Proponents of maximum state flexibility point to these varied responses as proof that program managers can adjust to market signals and modify programs appropriately.

One of the most interesting aspects of the Medicaid managed care experience is the extent to which state agencies had to transform themselves to take on their new role as prudent, value-based purchasers of managed care services (Fossett et al. 2000). Given their history as passive, bill-paying organizations that were expected *not* to alter care delivery, Medicaid agencies lacked the personnel, expertise, and infrastructure to engage in the design, procurement, rate setting, negotiation and bidding, contract execution, and monitoring activities required to launch managed care. Add the political context to this mix, and one cannot help but be impressed with how much success a number of states have had. They hired contractors for much of the work (figure 7-3), a fact the states point to as indicative of their resourcefulness in taking on new responsibilities (National Academy for State Health Policy 2001).

Figure 7-3. *Selected Functions Performed Fully or in Part by Contractors, 2000*

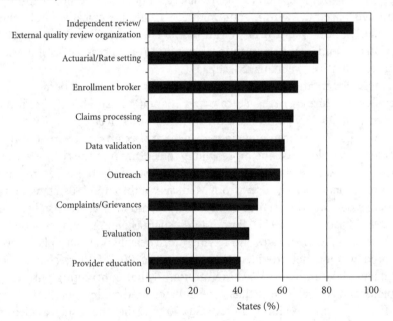

Source: National Academy for State Health Policy (2001).

In truth, most states struggled mightily with their new roles and responsibilities (Fossett et al. 2000). The more dependent a state was on prepaid managed care contracting, the greater the demands on the state to develop sufficient expertise and infrastructure to administer its Medicaid program. Particularly notable was the lack of expertise in contracting with health plans. A massive study revealed just how primitive Medicaid contracts were in most states (Rosenbaum et al. 1997). Often the documents had been created by literally cutting and pasting together versions of contracts developed by innovative states such as Wisconsin (Hurley 1998). Rather than viewing the contracting study as an indictment, many states and advocates came to see it as an opportunity to create far more explicit, demanding agreements. Such agreements could extract better performance from health plans and allow states to intensify their efforts to improve monitoring and quality of care (Landon, Tobias, and Epstein 1998).

Rate setting was another area in which states floundered, not only because they lacked experience and sophistication, but also because they worked from low fee-for-service bases and had severe data problems. Some states spent years refining their rates to avoid systematically overpaying plans because of favorable selection associated with voluntary enrollment or the state's practice of offering multiple models of managed care side-by-side. More generally, states and managed care plans had almost no sound data on which to debate rates until an Urban Institute study in 1999 (Holahan, Rangarajan, and Schirmer 1999). Alternative methods of devising rates, such as pure or modified competitive bidding or rate negotiation, have produced uneven and sometimes disruptive experiences across and within states, suggesting that to date there is no best way of establishing fair rates.

Despite its importance, the issue of adequate rates was rarely raised in the waiver review process, much to the consternation of many health plans and providers. The final version of the BBA regulations imposed a standard of "actuarial soundness" on states' capitation rates, but because this particular requirement was not scheduled to take effect until mid-2003, its implications remain uncertain.

Learning about other states' problems and responses was more successful in other areas. The enormous problems Tennessee encountered when it implemented TennCare just 45 days after its waiver was granted persuaded other states that this strategy of bulldozing opposition before it could become entrenched was both ill-advised and likely to result in many years' work to repair damaged relationships (Hurley 1998). Florida's problems with health plan marketing abuses influenced other states to turn to enrollment brokers, which have proved to be one of Medicaid managed care's most valuable innovations (Kenesson 1997). Several states had serious difficulty designing behavioral health programs, especially services for the chronically mentally ill (Mechanic 1998); consequently, these states are very cautious about program strategies and their potentially adverse impact on existing providers of services (Savela, Robinson, and Crow 2000). In general, states have learned from successful programs, like those in Wisconsin and Massachusetts, that getting interested parties involved in program design, development, and implementation can build coalitions and effectively defuse opposition (Perkins et al. 1996).

States have been truly innovative in three areas, particularly when contrasted with managed care plans in the private sector and traditional Medicare programs. First, because so many populations with special needs are eligible for Medicaid, states have been at the forefront of devising ways to promote care management features without undermining existing relationships or the specialized expertise of providers who serve these populations (e.g., Massachusetts, Wisconsin, and Ohio). The states have designed unique partnerships and collaborations to mesh the resources of clinical service providers and care management organizations with the interests of persons with chronic conditions and disabilities, including those with HIV/AIDS, severe physical and developmental disabilities, and severe and persistent mental illness (Master 1998; Pandey et al. 2000). It became clear that, in prepaid medical programs, the development of risk-adjustment mechanisms was crucial to engaging plans and nurturing constructive long-term relationships (Kronick and Drefus 1997). Medicaid agencies have devoted considerable attention to these issues (figure 7-4). Several states, notably Colorado, Washington, and Maryland, have been on the front lines of testing the suitability and effectiveness of these schemes. By using either newly developed methods or new sources of data, they are in advance of most private and traditional Medicare plans (Payne et al. 2000; Tollen and Rothman 1998; Weiner et al. 1998).

Second, nearly two-thirds of Medicaid programs employ enrollment brokers to help beneficiaries select health plans or physicians, or to assign beneficiaries who fail to make a choice (Kenesson 1997). This practice, invented in response to marketing abuses in a number of states, imposes more structure and objectivity on the plan selection process. In some states, brokers simply augment existing state staff and provide the expertise, customer service resources, and infrastructure needed to build pro-

Figure 7-4. *Factors Used in Setting Capitation Payments*

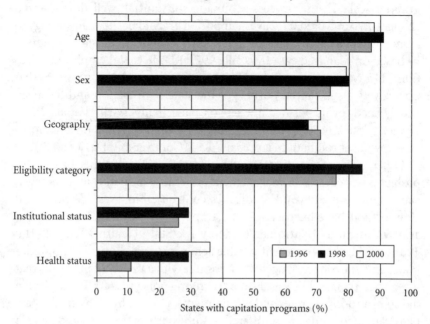

Source: National Academy for State Health Policy (2001).

grams quickly or make changes expeditiously. In other states, brokers have been instrumental in ensuring smooth transitions when plans withdrew from Medicaid (Tucker 2001).

Third, PCCM is one of the few managed care models that has proved feasible and sustainable in rural areas (Felt-Lisk et al. 1999, Silberman et al. 2002). Despite their relatively low aspirations and limited enhancements in most states, these programs have delivered stable medical homes and bolstered rural health care providers whose patients might otherwise have had to enroll in urban HMOs. Some states have succeeded in ramping up these programs to the point where they have a number of the desirable features of more comprehensive and integrated health care delivery systems (Smith, Des Jardins, and Peterson 2000). Arizona and Tennessee have attempted to extend prepaid medical care to every part of the state and in so doing have become market shapers. Other states have concluded that offering HMO and PCCM options within the state enables them to conform Medicaid to the financing and delivery systems in local markets, just as most private purchasers have chosen to do.

Some states have used managed care to transform Medicaid on a grander scale, in the process achieving substantial, well-documented changes. Arizona used its waiver-supported prepaid health plan strategy to launch what has been characterized as the first state Medicaid program to be based on managed care (McCall 1997). Rhode Island employed a Section 1115 waiver to devise an HMO-based managed care program that now covers a substantial portion of the state's population and has been widely cited for its positive impacts on participants (Griffin et al. 1999). TennCare's nearly 50 percent eligibility expansion was built on a platform of statewide enrollment in a prepaid plan (Conover and Davies 2000).

Other managed care strategies have fared less well, either because of problems with design or management or because of market and managed care sector forces beyond Medicaid's control. Ohio, West Virginia, and Connecticut have been seriously hampered by health plan instability and withdrawals (National Academy for State Health Policy 2001). TennCare has had persistent trouble achieving a solid financing foundation. Some states have struggled successfully with a variety of problems that threatened their viability and support among policymakers. Pennsylvania did so by modifying rates and requirements, Oregon by allowing for partially capitated models to be offered in some parts of the state, and Florida and Texas by permitting PCCM programs to compete directly with HMOs to ensure that alternatives remain available. Some observers would add Tennessee to this cluster of states, given its adroitness in maintaining TennCare despite the swirl of criticism surrounding it.

The states' performance as experimenters in managed care must also be compared with that of other purchasers. Large private purchasers have encountered many of the same challenges as the states in the past decade, with comparable ups and downs. However, private buyers are far less constrained than Medicaid agencies, mainly because they are not expected to protect the well-being of the insured. Private purchasers have far greater maneuverability in designing products and promoting consumer choice than Medicaid agencies because, unlike those agencies, they can use substantial cost sharing to influence behavior.

Compared with Medicare's foray into managed care, a number of Medicaid agencies have fared well, at least as measured by enrollment growth and market stability (Felt-Lisk 2001; Gold 2001). Certainly, Medicaid's ability to mandate enrollment in managed care makes a major difference. But the monolithic design of Medicare, its centralized and relatively inflexible administration, and its relative inability to engage in experimentation distinguish it from Medicaid in areas that are critical to success in managed care. Supporters of state flexibility contend that these differences allow states to adapt to market changes in a way that the federal government cannot. Elasticity enabled New York to make major rate adjustments to reinvigorate its program and enabled California to devise three distinct program models for three substantially different types of local markets. Despite Medicaid's greater flexibility, however, prepaid managed care efforts in Ohio, Georgia, and Kentucky have encountered difficulties fully equal to those of Medicare. Moreover, Medicaid managed care programs are not as consistent in performance reporting, dissemination of information to consumers, and regulatory oversight as the Medicare+Choice program.

States as Laboratories for Innovation:
An Evidence-Based Appraisal

Any assessment of the success or failure of mounting massive managed-care initiatives certainly requires a careful look at the empirical evidence. The evolution of Medicaid managed care over the past two decades has required administrative changes in many states, new approaches to purchasing health care through plans as opposed to providers, and fundamental shifts in the role played by the federal government as the overseer of Medicaid. The enthusiastic march of one state after another into the managed care arena and the willingness of the federal government to grant waivers grew out of the widely held belief that fee-for-service payments led to excessive utilization of services and added to program costs. However, most of the assumptions about *likely* savings or improved access associated with managed care in any particular state were rarely based on solid research findings. The notion that research evidence from the early innovators shaped the design of later Medicaid managed care programs is hard to prove. However, a large body of research has emerged that assesses how managed care has transformed Medicaid through its impacts on costs and on beneficiaries' access to and use of health services—the two areas that states have identified as their primary motivation for choosing managed care.

Synthesizing evidence into a broad overview of Medicaid managed care is challenging, because most studies have focused on single states or small groups of states and have limited their scope to specific populations or health outcomes. Over the years, several researchers have met this challenge by summarizing findings and drawing conclusions from a meta-analysis of them (Brown et al. 2001; Hurley et al. 1993; Rowland et al. 1995). Many of the studies cited in their reports are derived from specific evaluations of the Section 1915(b) and Section 1115 waivers granted to states by the federal government.

More recent studies have used nationally representative data to draw broader conclusions about the impact of Medicaid managed care (Garrett, Davidoff, and Yemane 2003; Zuckerman, Brennan, and Yemane 2002). The ongoing reviews of research by Miller and Luft, which look at managed care in general (private sector, Medicare, and Medicaid), have never found strong evidence that managed care creates problems for patients. Recently, the reviews suggest that expanded managed care has resulted in patients both within and outside of managed care plans being seen by the same providers—and, as a result, patterns of care are converging (Miller and Luft 2001). This section focuses on research related to the effects of managed care on Medicaid program costs and beneficiaries' access to and use of health services.

Program Costs

As states moved to expand Medicaid managed care, officials expected a 5 to 10 percent savings relative to fee-for-service programs (Holahan et al. 1998). This expectation was based on evidence from earlier studies (Hurley et al. 1993), and state officials based their initial per capita payment rates on these projections. Moreover, all of the Section 1115 waivers were supposed to be budget-neutral, although CMS did not insist on evaluations to confirm their neutrality. In part, the movement away from a strict budget-neutrality test may have been motivated by the difficulty of making and justifying assumptions related to expected trends in costs.[1]

Lacking a state-specific analysis of budget-neutrality, one turns to a study that compares the cost experiences of the states operating under waivers with the national average (Ormond, Ku, and Bruen 2001). This analysis showed that managed care did not translate into dramatically slower growth in program costs per beneficiary. In Hawaii, Oklahoma, Rhode Island, and Tennessee, overall expenditures grew at or near the national average through 1998. Findings such as these should not have been entirely surprising, given that Medicaid programs already had low provider payments (Norton 1995) and, in some instances, had imposed controls on beneficiaries' use of services (Zuckerman 1987). Maryland was an exception: Real costs per beneficiary did not change between 1996 and 1998 (the first two years of the state's 1115 waiver), while costs rose nationally by about 2.6 percent per year.

Given the importance of cost savings in motivating the expansion of Medicaid managed care, it is remarkable that there have not been more attempts to measure the extent to which savings did or did not materialize. The question of whether initial savings can be sustained is important for policymakers. States became concerned that mainstream commercial plans would withdraw from Medicaid (Coughlin et al. 2001), and this fear may have contributed to the much faster growth of capitation rates under Medicaid than Medicare between 1998 and 2001 (Holahan and Suzuki 2003). Studies that focus on long-term cost savings are needed to assess the extent to which initial savings may have eroded. At present, these studies do not exist. However, the apparently waning ability of commercial managed care to sustain its cost successes of the mid-1990s (Levit et al. 2002) may not bode well for future savings in Medicaid managed care.

Beneficiary Access and Use

Without some reasonable expectation of savings, states may lose their enthusiasm for Medicaid managed care. They may decide that the effort required to contract with plans and keep them in the program is no longer worthwhile. In the end, this major change in the Medicaid program may be justifiable only on the grounds of being better for beneficiaries—and the evidence on this point is mixed.

Most research on impacts has focused on how Medicaid managed care has affected access to and use of care. Some attempts have been made to examine health outcomes, quality of care, and patient satisfaction. Although the bulk of the research has focused on the impact of moving from fee-for-service to managed care, one recent study has examined the influence of various characteristics of managed care plans.

One of the first major reviews of Medicaid managed care research (Hurley et al. 1993) examined evidence from 25 programs that varied in whether they included PCCMs or HMOs, required providers to share financial risks, and relied on voluntary or mandatory enrollment. The evidence suggested that, in the early days, Medicaid managed care was associated with reduced use of emergency rooms, prescription drugs, and hospital care, compared to the fee-for-service program. There was no widespread evidence to suggest that use of physician services had decreased. The authors suggested this was because PCCM programs, which feature fee-for-service payment, provided incentives for more physician visits.

Research on Medicaid managed care grew throughout the 1990s. In 1995, the Kaiser Commission on the Future of Medicaid reviewed 130 studies (Rowland et al. 1995). That review confirmed the earlier synthesis showing that Medicaid managed care reduced emergency room use and had no effect on physician visits. However, the 1995 review found reduced use of specialists and only minimal changes in preventive care or hospital use. In addition, where satisfaction with Medicaid managed care was high, it appeared to be because beneficiaries were able to enroll without having to change providers.

Findings from Section 1115 waiver programs that started in the mid-1990s did not always confirm the benefits seen in many of the earlier and smaller evaluations (e.g., Coughlin and Long 2000; Mitchell et al. 1999). However, it is difficult to develop methods for assessing the effects of moving from fee-for-service Medicaid to managed care (Gold 1999), and, as a result, the findings may not be robust. There are other reasons to expect differing effects in the earlier and later Medicaid managed care programs. First, in the 1980s, Medicaid was implementing managed care in a largely fee-for-service health care market; thus, it was easier to induce providers to treat Medicaid managed care enrollees differently from patients covered under fee-for-service arrangements and easier to detect those differences than in the 1990s, when managed care was widely implemented by all private and public purchasers of health care. Second, by the late 1990s, overall savings from managed care had leveled off (Gabel et al. 2001). Third, in the 1990s, Medicaid managed care was often part of a broader reform of the Medicaid program that included eligibility expansions; as a result, isolating the effects of managed care became more difficult.

The complexities of assessing the impact of the later Section 1115 waivers can be illustrated by the experience of Tennessee. In creating its TennCare program, the state moved all of its Medicaid population into managed care and used the projected savings to expand eligibility to roughly 400,000 uninsured Tennesseans (Conover and Davies 2000). The federally funded evaluation of TennCare and a variety of other studies have given analysts and policymakers a great deal of information about the effects of this program. However, none of the available studies has been able to separate the effects of managed care from the effects of the eligibility expansion. In fact, to the extent that expectations of savings from Medicaid managed care convinced policymakers to move ahead with the eligibility expansion, the most profound effect of Medicaid managed care under TennCare may have been on the previously uninsured, not on the people who were already Medicaid beneficiaries. For the newly insured, out-of-pocket costs fell, preventive care increased, and satisfaction with care improved (Brown et al. 2001).[2]

In more recent studies of national data, researchers have compared traditional Medicaid with PCCMs and HMOs and assessed the effects of these approaches on adults and on children. Two such studies (Garrett et al. 2003; Zuckerman et al. 2002) report that HMOs improve health care utilization for adults and for children, compared with traditional Medicaid.[3] Some evidence shows that PCCMs connect beneficiaries with providers better than traditional Medicaid programs do, but the improved access has limited effects on patterns of use.[4] Although these findings raise questions about the value of the PCCMs in place by the mid-1990s, they are not particularly useful for assessing the enhanced PCCMs that some states have turned to recently after encountering difficulties in contracting with HMOs.[5] Despite the advantages of the research methods employed in these studies, the results are not always consistent with expectations. For example, there is little evidence that HMOs reduce rates of hospitalizations, regardless of widely held views to the contrary (Zuckerman et al. 2002).

Given the foothold that managed care has gained within Medicaid and the difficulty of developing comparisons with beneficiaries' fee-for-service experience, one major evaluation tried to examine the effects of differences in plan characteristics (Moreno et al. 2001). Such information, the researchers argued, might be more useful to states than contrasts with fee-for-service Medicaid. However, small samples of enrollees in various types of plans produced statistically insignificant results that were not generally consistent for adults and children. With this caution in mind, the results may ease some concerns about poor care being delivered in plans that provide financial incentives to skimp on care or that serve a predominantly Medicaid clientele. But the study also suggests a need for uneasiness about plans that use safety net providers as primary care gatekeepers. Holding constant a range of demographic, economic, and health status indicators, the study found that beneficiaries in these plans reported less satisfaction with and less access to health care. Inasmuch as states are becoming more dependent on plans organized around safety net providers (Coughlin et al. 2001), this evidence of poor service delivery (Moreno et al. 2001) implies the need for careful monitoring of such plans.

Vulnerable Populations

Most of the early studies of the effects of Medicaid managed care were based on low-income families and did not cover the elderly or disabled beneficiaries. In fact, by the time the Kaiser Family Foundation review was prepared in 1995 (Rowland et al. 1995), research was pointing to the potential problems that could arise in trying to bring elderly and disabled Medicaid beneficiaries into managed care (e.g., Fox, Wicks, and Newacheck 1993; Newacheck et al. 1994). Such studies noted that states were excluding these vulnerable populations from managed care enrollment or paying for extra services that might be required outside the basic managed care contracts.

As a result, Medicaid has not yet demonstrated its ability to manage care in a way that will improve health care access and quality or control costs for elderly and disabled beneficiaries. Because these are the groups with the greatest service needs and the highest costs, this is an important missed opportunity. But states have generally been hesitant to mandate enrollment, because beneficiaries and their families are concerned that services might be withheld and because it is difficult to adjust payments to appropriate levels.

Under TennCare, people receiving Supplemental Security Income (SSI) were required to enroll in managed care, although behavioral health care was delivered through separate plans. Evidence shows that the SSI population was less satisfied with their care than other Medicaid beneficiaries and that people with mental illness reported little use of services and many unmet needs (Hill and Wooldridge 2001). This finding suggests that earlier concerns about the adverse effects of Medicaid managed care on these groups may have been warranted and that states need to be cautious and attentive to problems as they attempt to enroll these groups in managed care.

The Overall Role of the Evidence

Although studies of elderly and disabled populations may have slowed the expansion of Medicaid managed care to these groups, general evaluations do not seem to have influenced the policy process a great deal. The states that combined Medicaid managed care with eligibility expansions in the 1990s (such as Tennessee, Oregon, and Hawaii) had no credible research roadmap based on the managed care programs of the 1980s to guide their policy design. The conflicting evidence derived from different states, different time periods, different data sources, and different methodological approaches made it nearly impossible to draw any firm conclusions about how Medicaid managed care would work in any particular state. Instead of using research findings to guide policy, states seem inclined to monitor broad indicators of program performance, such as self-enrollment rates, plan participation, and provider availability, to identify immediate problems.

Thus research plays a secondary, quality assurance role of identifying egregious problems that would not be detected otherwise. As long as no evidence of such problems is uncovered, the federal government renews waivers, and states continue to rely on Medicaid managed care. Year-to-year decisions are more likely to be driven by political considerations and market conditions than by research evidence, which takes longer to develop. In fact, the recognition that research evidence plays a small role in federal policy decisions may have made some states reluctant to invest in the potentially costly encounter data studies needed to compare Medicaid managed care with fee-for-service Medicaid. However, after more than two decades of research on Medicaid managed care programs, there is little definitive evidence that harm is being done to beneficiaries—and this should assuage most concerns about the limited role that empirical evidence has played in policy development.

Summing Up: A Balanced Scorecard on an Age of Innovation

While the past decade of intensified interest in federalism and devolution has been an especially active one for Medicaid managed-care initiatives, innovation in this realm is now really two decades old. Consequently, it is possible to weigh considerable evidence obtained over a lengthy period in assessing the durability of state efforts to use waivers to "remake Medicaid" (Davidson and Somers 1998). Evidence and observations permit the following conclusions to be drawn.

States have navigated the waiver process successfully, and several have introduced genuine innovations to enhance the operations and effectiveness of their Medicaid programs. In part, the cumbersome nature of the waiver process is purposeful: Protracted, interactive review can increase attention to operational detail and uncover potential unintended consequences. CMS interrogatories and requirements have in many instances strengthened programs or forced better planning and preparation, thereby increasing the likelihood of success. The small number of waiver renewals denied is a particularly telling indication of federal officials' reluctance to interfere with programs once they are under way. That reluctance has probably provoked more searching reviews of initial submissions. Operationally, CMS has been vulnerable to legitimate criticism about the timeliness of its actions, in no small part because of the limited resources available to respond to the large volume of waiver requests submitted in recent years. However, the complaints raised by many state officials and some members of Congress are to be expected, given inherently conflicting viewpoints about the philosophical underpinnings of Medicaid, which are likely to remain irreconcilable.

Most states have proven themselves to be responsible, although at times overly ambitious, innovators. The success of several states in broadening Medicaid coverage challenges the assertion that cost control is the only interest of state policymakers. In addition, as managed care became the mainstream delivery system for most persons with private coverage, the aspersions cast on states that pursued managed care initiatives as "peddling the poor to the lowest bidder" have largely disappeared. States appear to have won over many, though not all, critics who doubted their motives for undertaking managed care or questioned their capacity to select and contract with creditable managed care vendors. States have not been uniformly successful in their endeavors. Their lack of success in enrolling the most costly beneficiaries, thereby limiting the potential for savings, is perhaps the most notable shortfall. But they have displayed impressive resilience and resourcefulness when encountering obstacles. Nearly every state that implemented a mandatory managed care program has stayed the course, though a few have been unable to achieve or sustain their preferred models. Many states have chosen to step back from excessively ambitious timetables or have curtailed extension of their programs, sometimes in response to federal pressure and sometimes to avoid engendering local resistance. On balance, states have exhibited the responsible innovation they contend is their aim and forte. However, permitting rather than requiring states to adopt innovations like managed care means that little change will occur in states that lack the interest or resources, or both, to pursue new initiatives in their Medicaid programs.

Medicaid's experience as a purchaser of managed care services has been an uneven one. The difficult new roles and responsibilities associated with purchasing care can handicap state efforts to make Medicaid a better program through managed care. As empirical studies show, experience to date with managed care programs has been decidedly mixed across states, models, populations, and performance indicators. The same would be true of the fee-for-service experience of states and their beneficiaries. States have generally succeeded in moving their Medicaid programs to the point of operational stability, thus making improved outcomes more likely, as indicated in some of the mature programs. In addition, the durability and relative stability of most Medicaid managed care programs can be contrasted with the instability and impermanence of many Medicare managed care plans (Felt-Lisk 2001; Gold 2001). Medicaid programs have generally reacted quickly and successfully to developments that jeopardized their viability, and, by many accounts, a number are shifting toward long-term relationships with their remaining managed care contractors. States are generally achieving cost neutrality or generating small savings, whereas the Medicare HMO program has been demonstrated to cost more than fee-for-service because less costly beneficiaries have enrolled.

States have been discriminating in learning from the experience of other states. Given the general unfamiliarity with managed care in the early years of innovation, it is hardly surprising that many first-generation programs made some ill-considered attempts to imitate what was done in other states. The limited availability of timely research and evaluation made it difficult to determine what was working and what was not, leaving states to operate in the dark at times. This state of affairs changed substantially in the 1990s as experience broadened, exchange among states improved, and more and better evidence began to be disseminated. Innovations regarding enrollment brokers, rate setting, and risk adjustment illustrate how states became more operationally astute, in part by finding out what did and did not work in other states. States today are rightly leery of adopting managed care approaches that are not consonant with local market conditions and provider sentiment. This caution seems to reveal how well they—and their health plan contractors—have learned that local delivery systems are much more resistant to change than once thought.

The fact that almost all rural Medicaid managed care is built on PCCM programs speaks clearly to this point.

Managed care is an especially challenging enterprise for states because of its instability and the turmoil it has provoked and experienced in health care markets. The meteoric rise of managed care models between the mid-1980s and the 1990s created powerful pressures on state Medicaid programs to conform their payment and delivery systems to developments in the private sector. Although initially lagging behind private markets, state Medicaid programs caught up in the late 1990s, just as the managed care backlash was building and private health plans lost traction in their attempts to contain costs. Many private plans acceded to member demands for less restrictive products, and a number of plans introduced practices and payment methods that they hoped their providers would find less odious. Such developments are daunting to Medicaid programs, which cannot rely on products that have substantial cost-sharing features, cannot afford sustained double-digit premium increases, and expect to continue to rely on tight provider networks to control costs. However, most states do not want to return to unmanaged fee-for-service care for their Medicaid beneficiaries, even if providers do. Consequently, Medicaid plans, models, and methods of managed care may need to be more customized if the managed care market drifts away from what Medicaid can and wants to purchase.

The trial-and-error and opportunistic nature of reform on the state level invariably leads to controversy and disputes over the methods and pace of change. A continuing theme in the debate between the states and federal officials is that the practical demands of meeting citizens' needs are much more acutely felt at the state and local levels. While states may be interested in the ideological debates in Washington over state and federal rights and roles, they feel compelled to do something. Invariably, this adds a certain iterative trial-and-error dimension to state innovation. It also means that state officials must seize any moment that provides them with a policy window or a favorable alignment of circumstances. Turbulent private health care markets and cyclical state revenues introduce additional uncertainty and undermine better, or at least more deliberate, strategizing. This sensitivity to timing contributes to state officials' legitimate frustration with the slow pace of the waiver process. Expediting reviews and renewals is one remedy that has already been tried, and additional flexibility, such as the originally intended relaxation of waiver requirements in the BBA 1997, is a reasonable next step. But continued conflict on this front seems inevitable.

Variation among state Medicaid programs has probably been amplified by forays into managed care. Medicaid programs have certainly become more diverse since managed care was introduced. This is true not only because the structure and operational requirements of managed care programs differ from those of traditional fee-for-service arrangements, but also because states with managed care plans are far more subject to market forces. In some respects, the states' managed care experience parallels Medicare's—that is, concerns over equity have risen because some beneficiaries in some locales have access to services and benefits that are not available to others. The fact that Medicare's managed care enrollment is voluntary and Medicaid's is typically mandatory intensifies these concerns.

While variation across states is endemic to the Medicaid program, differential employment of waivers promotes even greater variation. This has clearly been the case in the managed care experience. A more trenchant argument is that releasing states from the strictures of uniformity allows them, or at least the venturesome among them, to improve their Medicaid programs beyond what other states are doing to meet minimum requirements. By implication, if improvements can be substantiated, other states will follow suit as their interests and opportunities allow. But some states will not, and state-to-state variation will grow. Fundamentally, however, waivers foster an ethos of program improvement, and this ethos underlies the past two decades of Medicaid managed care expansion.

Conclusion

The past decade of dramatic growth in Medicaid managed care reveals much about how states and federal officials have found a measure of accommodation and collaboration through the waiver-granting process. Although the process is subject to contentiousness, because of specific issues and the general political climate, states have exploited the opportunities that waivers have given them to launch initiatives and to introduce and refine creative programs and practices. While most states have experimented responsibly with new models of payment and delivery, the impacts of these arrangements have been uneven and will require more time to appraise fully. Moreover, waivers have led to more variation in Medicaid programs, both by design and necessity. Advocates of greater devolution to the states contend that it is by permitting and promoting variation that program improvements are made.

NOTES

1. For example, studies of TennCare and other Section 1115 waivers have concluded that original projections of costs without the waiver do not represent a valid comparison because of changes in medical cost inflation that occurred independent of the waiver (Brown et al. 2000; Conover and Davies 2000).

2. However, actual savings under TennCare managed care were not as great as expected, and expansion was slowed when the state was forced to freeze enrollment in 1995; it subsequently opened the program to new enrollment in 1997. Recent budgetary concerns have led to a new round of enrollment freezes and proposals to roll back eligibility or increase costs to beneficiaries.

3. These conclusions are based on data and models that include enrollees in PCCM, HMO, and fee-for-service arrangements. Earlier studies often made such comparisons by linking studies from different states that may have used fundamentally different types of data.

4. Zuckerman, Brennan, and Yemane (2002) found that, for children, the probability of seeing a physician or other health professional was increased in comparison with traditional Medicaid, but that there was no effect on preventive care. There were no effects related to care provided to adults.

5. Enhanced PCCMs are programs in which state Medicaid agencies try actively to manage their provider networks, using care management, incentives, and oversight similar to those employed by private health plans.

REFERENCES

Battaglia, Andrew I. 1993. "Health Care Reform and People with Disabilities." *Health Affairs* 12(1): 40–57.

Bazelon Center for Mental Health Law. 2001. http://www.bazelon.org/newmexico.html. (Accessed April 30, 2003.)

Beronja, Nancy, Lisa Chimento, and Moira Forbes. 2000. *Impact of the Proposed Medicaid BBA Regulation on Medicaid Managed Care.* Princeton, N.J.: Center for Health Care Strategies.

Brown, Randall, Judith Wooldridge, Sheila D. Hoag, and Lorenzo Moreno. 2001. *Reforming Medicaid: The Experiences of Five Pioneering States with Mandatory Managed Care and Eligibility Expansions.* Princeton, N.J.: Mathematica Policy Research, Inc.

Centers for Medicare and Medicaid Services (CMS). 2001. "2000 Medicaid Managed Care Enrollment Report." http://cms.hhs.gov/medicaid/managedcare/mmcss00.asp. (Accessed April 30, 2003.)

Chavkin, David F., and Anne Treseder. 1977. "California's Prepaid Health Plan Program: Can the Patient Be Saved?" *Hastings Law Journal* 28: 685–760.

Conover, Christopher J., and Hester H. Davies. 2000. *The Role of TennCare in Health Policy for Low-Income People in Tennessee.* Washington, D.C.: The Urban Institute. *Assessing the New Federalism* Occasional Paper No. 33.

Coughlin, Teresa A., and Sharon K. Long. 2000. "Effects of Medicaid Managed Care on Adults." *Medical Care* 38(4): 433–46.

Coughlin, Teresa A., Sharon K. Long, and John Holahan. 2001. "Commercial Health Plan Participation in Medicaid Managed Care: An Examination of Six Markets." *Inquiry* 38(1): 22–34.

Coughlin, Teresa A., Stephen Zuckerman, Susan Wallin, and John Holahan. 1999. "A Conflict of Strategies: Medicaid Managed Care and Medicaid Maximization." *Health Services Research* 34(1, Part 2): 281–93.

Davidson, Stephen, and Stephen A. Somers. 1998. *Remaking Medicaid: Managed Care for the Public Good.* San Francisco: Jossey-Bass.

Draper, Debra A., and Marsha R. Gold. 2000. "Customizing Medicaid Managed Care— California Style." *Health Affairs* 19(5): 233–38.

Felt-Lisk, Suzanne. 1998. *The Changing Medicaid Managed Care Market: Trends in Commercial Plans' Participation.* Washington, D.C.: Kaiser Commission on Medicaid and the Uninsured.

———. 2001. *Trends in Health Plan Participation in Medicaid Managed Care.* Menlo Park, Calif.: The Henry J. Kaiser Family Foundation.

Felt-Lisk, Suzanne, Pam Silberman, Sheila Hoag, and Rebecca Slifkin. 1999. "Medicaid Managed Care in Rural Areas: A Ten-State Follow-up Study." *Health Affairs* 18(2): 238–45.

Fossett, James W., Malcolm Goggin, John S. Hall, Jocelyn Johnston, L. Christopher Plein, Richard Roper, and Carol Weissert. 2000. "Managing Medicaid Managed Care: Are States Becoming Prudent Purchasers?" *Health Affairs* 19(4): 36–49.

Fox, Harriette B., Lori B. Wicks, and Paul W. Newacheck. 1993. "State Medicaid Health Maintenance Organization Policies and Special-Needs Children." *Health Care Financing Review* 15(1): 25–37.

Freund, Deborah. 1984. *Medicaid Reform: Four Studies of Case Management.* Washington, D.C.: American Enterprise Institute.

Freund, Deborah, and Robert E. Hurley. 1987. "Managed Care in Medicaid: Selected Issues in Program Origins, Design, and Research." *Annual Review of Public Health* 8: 137–63.

Freund, Deborah, L. Rossiter, Peter D. Fox, J. Meyer, Robert E. Hurley, T. Carey, and J. Paul. 1988. *Nationwide Evaluation of Medicaid Competition Demonstrations, Volume 1: Integrative Final Report.* Research Triangle Park, N.C.: Research Triangle Institute.

Gabel, Jon R., Paul B. Ginsburg, Jeremy D. Pickreign, and James D. Reschovsky. 2001. "Trends in Out-of-Pocket Spending by Insured American Workers, 1990–1997." *Health Affairs* 20(2): 47–57.

Garrett, Bowen, Amy Davidoff, and Alshadye Yemane. 2003. "Effects of Medicaid Managed Care Programs on Health Services Access and Use." *Health Services Research* 38(1): 575–94.

Gold, Marsha. 1999. "Making Medicaid Managed Care Relevant." *Health Services Research* 33(3): 1639–50.

———. 2001. "Medicare+Choice: An Interim Report Card." *Health Affairs* 20(4): 120–38.

Griffin, Jane F., Joseph W. Hogan, Jay S. Buechner, and Tricia M. Leddy. 1999. "The Effect of a Medicaid Managed Care Program on the Adequacy of Prenatal Care Utilization in Rhode Island." *American Journal of Public Health* 89(4): 497–501.

Hill, Steven S., and Judith Wooldridge. 2001. *SSI Enrollees in TennCare: Room for Improvement*. Princeton, N.J.: Mathematica Policy Research, Inc.

Holahan, John, and Shinobu Suzuki. 2003. "Medicaid Managed Care Payment Methods and Capitation Rates in 2001." *Health Affairs* 22(1): 204–18.

Holahan, John, Suresh Rangarajan, and Matthew Schirmer. 1999. "Medicaid Managed Care Payment Rates in 1998." *Health Affairs* 18(3): 217–27.

Holahan, John, Stephen Zuckerman, Alison Evans, and Suresh Rangarajan. 1998. "Medicaid Managed Care in Thirteen States." *Health Affairs* 17(3): 43–63.

Holahan, John, Teresa A. Coughlin, Leighton Ku, Debra J. Lipson, and Shruti Rajan. 1995. "Insuring the Poor Through Section 1115 Waivers." *Health Affairs* 14(1): 199–216.

Hurley, Robert E. 1998. "Reflections on Medicaid Managed Care: Have We Overdosed on a Panacea?" In *Remaking Medicaid: Managed Care and the Public Good*, edited by Stephen Davidson and Stephen A. Somers (20–40). San Francisco: Jossey-Bass.

Hurley, Robert E., and Debra A. Draper. 1998. "Special Plans for Special Persons: The Elusive Pursuit of Customized Managed Care." In *Remaking Medicaid: Managed Care and the Public Good*, edited by Stephen Davidson and Stephen A. Somers (245–75). San Francisco: Jossey-Bass.

Hurley, Robert E., and Michael A. McCue. 2000. *Partnership Pays: Making Medicaid Managed Care Work in a Turbulent Environment*. Princeton, N.J.: Center for Health Care Strategies.

Hurley, Robert E., and Susan Wallin. 1998. "Adopting and Adapting Managed Care for Medicaid Beneficiaries: An Imperfect Translation." Washington, D.C.: The Urban Institute. *Assessing the New Federalism* Policy Brief A-7.

Hurley, Robert E., Deborah Freund, and John E. Paul. 1993. *Managed Care in Medicaid: Lessons for Policy and Program Design*. Ann Arbor, Mich.: Health Administration Press.

Iglehart, John K. 1999. "The American Health Care System—Medicaid." *New England Journal of Medicine* 340(5): 403–8.

Kaiser Family Foundation. 1993. *The Medicaid Cost Explosion: Causes and Consequences*. Prepared by the Kaiser Commission on the Future of Medicaid. Menlo Park, Calif.: The Henry J. Kaiser Family Foundation.

Kenesson, Mary. 1997. *Medicaid Managed Care Enrollment Study: Report of Findings from the Survey of State Medicaid Managed Care Programs*. Princeton, N.J.: Center for Health Care Strategies.

Kronick, Richard, and Tony Drefus. 1997. *The Challenge of Risk Adjustment for People with Disabilities: Health-Based Payment for Medicaid Programs—A Guide for State Medicaid Programs, Providers, and Consumers*. Princeton, N.J.: Center for Health Care Strategies.

Landon, Bruce E., Carol Tobias, and Arnold M. Epstein. 1998. "Quality Management by State Medicaid Agencies Converting to Managed Care: Plans and Current Practice." *Journal of the American Medical Association* 279(3): 211–16.

Levit, Katharine, Cynthia Smith, Cathy Cowan, Helen Lazenby, Art Sensenig, and Aaron Catlin. 2002. "Trends in U.S. Health Care Spending, 2001." *Health Affairs* 22(1): 154–64.

Master, Robert J. 1998. "Massachusetts Medicaid and the Community Medical Alliance: A New Approach to Contracting and Care Delivery for Medicaid-Eligible Populations with AIDS and Severe Physical Disability." *American Journal of Managed Care* 4 (Special Issue): SP90–8.

McCall, Nelda. 1997. "Lesson from Arizona's Medicaid Managed Care Program." *Health Affairs* 16(4): 194–99.

McCall, Nelda, Jodi Korb, Pamela Turner, and Andrew Petersons. 2000. *The Medi-Cal Market: 1996–1998.* Oakland, Calif.: The Medi-Cal Policy Institute.

McCall, Nelda, D. Henton, M. Crane, S. Haber, Deborah Freund, and W. Wrightson. 1985. "Evaluation of the Arizona Health Care Cost Containment System (AHC-CCS): The First Eighteen Months." *Health Care Financing Review* 7(2): 77–88.

McCue, Michael J., Robert E. Hurley, Debra A. Draper, and Michael Jurgensen. 1999. "Reversal of Fortune: Commercial HMOs in the Medicaid Market." *Health Affairs* 18(1): 223–30.

Mechanic, David, ed. 1998. *Managed Behavioral Health Care: Current Realities and Future Potential.* San Francisco: Jossey-Bass.

Miller, Robert H., and Harold S. Luft. 2001. "HMO Plan Performance Update: An Analysis of Recently Published Literature." Paper presented at Robert Wood Johnson Foundation Future of Managed Care Conference, Princeton, N.J., May 18.

Mitchell, Janet B., Susan G. Haber, Galina Khatusky, and Suzanne Donoghue. 1999. "Children in the Oregon Health Plan: How Have They Fared?" Paper presented at the Association of Public Policy and Management Conference, Washington, D.C., November.

Moreno, Lorenzo, Sheila D. Hoag, Leslie Foster, and Carol Razafindrakoto. 2001. *HMO Characteristics and the Experiences of Medicaid Beneficiaries: An Analysis from Four States.* Princeton, N.J.: Mathematica Policy Research, Inc.

National Academy for State Health Policy. 2001. *Medicaid Managed Care: A Guide for States,* 5th ed. Portland, Maine: National Academy for State Health Policy.

Newacheck, Paul W., Dana C. Hughes, Jeffrey J. Stoddard, and Neal Halfon. 1994. "Children with Chronic Illness and Medicaid Managed Care." *Pediatrics* 93(3): 497–500.

Norton, Stephen A. 1995. "Medicaid Fees and the Medicare Fee Schedule: An Update." *Health Care Financing Review* 17(1): 167–81.

Ormond, Barbara A., Leighton Ku, and Brian Bruen. 2001. *Engine of Change or One Force Among Many? Section 1115 Demonstration Projects and Trends in Medicaid Expenditures.* Washington, D.C.: The Urban Institute.

Pandey, S. K., M. G. Mussman, H. W. Moore, J. G. Folkemer, and J. J. Kaelin. 2000. "An Assessment of Maryland Medicaid's Rare and Expensive Case Management Program." *Evaluation & the Health Professions* 23(4): 457–79.

Payne, Susan M. C., Randall D. Cebul, Mendel E. Singer, Jaikumar Krishnaswamy, and Katherine Gharrity. 2000. "Comparison of Risk-Adjustment Systems for the Medicaid-Eligible Disabled Population. *Medical Care* 38(4): 422–32.

Perkins, Jane, Kristi Olson, Lourdes Rivera, and Julie Skatrud. 1996. *Making the Consumers' Voice Heard in Medicaid Managed Care: Increasing Participation, Protection and Satisfaction.* Report on Required and Voluntary Mechanisms, National Health Law Program. Chapel Hill, N.C.: Sheps Center.

Regenstein, Marsha, and Stephanie E. Anthony. 1998. *Medicaid Managed Care for Persons with Disabilities.* Washington, D.C.: Economic and Social Research Institute.

Rosenbaum, Sara, Peter W. Shin, B. Smith, Elizabeth Wehr, Phyllis C. Borzi, Marcie Zajeim, Karen Shaw, and K. Silver. 1997. *Negotiating the New Health Care System: An Analysis of Contracts Between State Medicaid Agencies and Managed Care Organizations.* Washington, D.C.: George Washington University Medical Center, Center for Health Policy Research.

Rowland, Diane, Sara Rosenbaum, Lois Simon, and Elizabeth Chait. 1995. *Medicaid and Managed Care: Lessons from the Literature.* Menlo Park, Calif.: The Henry J. Kaiser Family Foundation.

Savela, Terry, Gail Robinson, and Sarah Crow. 2000. *Contracting for Public Mental Health Services: Opinions of Managed Care Behavioral Health Care Organizations.* DHHS Publication No. (SMA) 00-3438. Rockville, Md.: Center for Mental Health Services, Substance Abuse and Mental Health Services Administration.

Silberman, Pam, Stephanie Poley, Kerry James, and Rebecca Slifkin. 2002. "Tracking Medicaid Managed Care in Rural Community: A Fifty-State Follow-Up." *Health Affairs* 21(4): 255–63.

Smith, Vernon K., Terrisca Des Jardins, and Karin A. Peterson. 2000. *Exemplary Practices in Primary Care Case Management Programs.* Report for the Center for Health Care Strategies, Princeton, N.J.

Tanenbaum, Sandra J., and Robert E. Hurley. 1995. "The Disabled and the Managed Care Frenzy: A Cautionary Note." *Health Affairs* 14(4): 213–19.

Tollen, Laura, and Michael Rothman. 1998. "Case Study: Colorado Medicaid HMO Risk Adjustment." *Inquiry* 35(2): 154–70.

Tucker, Alan. 2001. *Transitioning Clients When Plans Exit Medicaid Managed Care.* Princeton, N.J.: Center for Health Care Strategies.

U.S. General Accounting Office (GAO). 1987. *Medicaid: Early Problems in Implementing the Philadelphia HealthPASS Program.* HRD-88-37. Washington, D.C.: General Accounting Office.

———. 1990. *Medicaid: Oversight of Health Maintenance Organizations in the Chicago Area.* HRD-90-81. Washington, D.C.: General Accounting Office.

———. 1992. *Medicaid: Oregon's Managed Care Program and Implications for Expansions.* HRD-92-89. Washington, D.C.: General Accounting Office.

Weiner, Jonathan P., A. M. Tucker, Anthony M. Collins, H. Fakhraei, R. Lieberman, Chad Abrams, G. R. Trapnell, and J. G. Folkemer. 1998. "The Development of a Risk-Adjusted Capitation Payment System: The Maryland Medicaid Model." *Journal of Ambulatory Care Management* 21(4): 29–52.

Zuckerman, Stephen. 1987. "Medicaid Hospital Spending: Effects of Reimbursement and Utilization Control Policies." *Health Care Financing Review* 9(3): 65–77.

Zuckerman Stephen, Niall Brennan, and Alshadye Yemane. 2002. "Has Medicaid Managed Care Affected Beneficiary Access and Use?" *Inquiry* 39(3): 221–42.

8

Long-Term Care
Can the States Be the Engine of Reform?

Joshua M. Wiener
Jane Tilly

L ong-term care is a key area of state health policy and spending. It
accounted for 27 percent of state and local spending on personal
health services in 2000.[1] Excluding disproportionate share hospital
(DSH) payments, it accounted for almost 38 percent of Medicaid expenditures on personal health services in fiscal year (FY) 2001, and in some
states it accounted for a majority of all Medicaid expenditures (Bruen
and Holahan 2002). Adults with physical and mental disabilities rely
heavily on publicly funded programs for supportive services such as personal care, adult day care, homemaker services, and nursing home care.
In 1999–2000, 76 percent of nursing home residents depended on public
programs to pay for their care (American Health Care Association 2001).

Medicaid bears the primary financial responsibility for long-term care
of low-income elderly persons and disabled persons, but at least four
other federal programs also provide significant funding—Medicare, the
Social Services Block Grant (SSBG), the Older Americans Act, and the
Rehabilitation Act. These programs vary in how responsibility is divided
between the federal and state governments. In addition, many states have
their own programs.

There has been a long-standing debate about whether the federal government or the states should play the larger role in financing, designing,
and administering Medicaid's long-term care programs. The principal
argument in favor of a larger federal role is that the other main programs

249

for older people and for persons with disabilities—Medicare, Social Security, Supplemental Security Income (SSI), and Disability Insurance—are almost entirely federal. Federalizing long-term care might increase coordination among these programs and result in a less fragmented approach to the needs of beneficiaries. Moreover, the federal government is arguably better equipped financially to cope with the skyrocketing demand for long-term care that will certainly accompany the aging of the baby boom generation.

The main argument in favor of an increased state role—in program design, if not financing—is that the states are much more heavily involved in the day-to-day management of the long-term care system than the federal government is. States set reimbursement rates for Medicaid and other public programs, control supply through certificate-of-need programs and moratoriums on new construction, decide what services will be available through Medicaid and their own programs, and assess clients and determine what services they will receive. State control of the policy levers would also be consistent with the notion that long-term care is local and highly idiosyncratic, because it is largely about how individuals choose to live their lives. Arguably, states are better able to respond to local preferences and norms. Indeed, in most developed countries, local or subnational governments and organizations play a major role in financing and delivering long-term care services (Wiener 1996a).

This chapter examines how states have responded to the flexibility available in some federal programs and how they have coped with the rigidity of others—and to what extent they have simply gone their own way through state-funded programs. It addresses the financing of long-term care, integrating health and long-term care programs, providing home and community services, allocating resources and containing costs, and ensuring quality of care. Policymakers' approaches to these challenges differ, depending on the federal-state division of responsibility and the subject under consideration. While not the sole focus, much of the analysis in this chapter focuses on the 13 states in the *Assessing the New Federalism* (ANF) project. These states accounted for 53 percent of Medicaid long-term care expenditures in FY 2001 and 44 percent of all nursing facility beds.[2]

Background

The major sources of federal funding for long-term care are Medicare, Medicaid, the Older Americans Act, the SSBG, and the Rehabilitation Act.

Medicare

Medicare funds much of the health care for almost all Americans age 65 and older and for part of the younger disabled population, and it covers a limited amount of skilled nursing facility services and medically related home health care. Funding for Medicare comes entirely from federal sources through payroll taxes and general revenues. The federal government sets the program's rules, including those governing benefits and cost sharing with beneficiaries.

Medicare is not designed to cover most long-term care services. In fact, the program's rules limit long-term care to medically related services. Specifically, Medicare covers skilled nursing facility services only when a beneficiary has spent three days in a hospital, is admitted to the nursing facility within 30 days of the hospitalization, and needs skilled nursing or rehabilitation services. Coverage is limited to 100 days, but the average length of a Medicare-covered stay is only about 30 days (U.S. House of Representatives, Committee on Ways and Means 2000). The home health benefit is available to homebound beneficiaries who need intermittent or part-time skilled nursing or rehabilitation services. Medicare spent about $12.6 billion on skilled nursing facility benefits and $13.0 billion for home health care in FY 2000 (U.S. House of Representatives, Committee on Ways and Means 2000). Medicare is a relatively small source of financing for skilled nursing facilities, although its importance grew dramatically during the 1990s; it is a much more important source of financing for skilled home health care.

Expenditures on Medicare skilled nursing facility and home health care vary markedly by state (table 8-1). In 1998, Medicare spent the most per beneficiary on skilled nursing facility services in Florida, Massachusetts, and Texas; spending ranged from $241 per Medicare beneficiary in Minnesota to $435 in Massachusetts. For home health in that year, Medicare spent the most per beneficiary in Texas, Mississippi, and Massachusetts, with spending per beneficiary ranging from $110 in Minnesota to $616 in Texas.

In states where Medicare spending on skilled nursing facilities and home health services are relatively high and spending on Medicaid home and community services comparatively low, most of the publicly funded services available to residents are medically related rather than nonskilled or custodial. Southern states, in particular, have long had a high utilization of Medicare home health, possibly using it as a substitute for Medicaid home health or other home care services (Schore 1995).

Table 8-1. *Medicare Spending on Skilled Nursing Facility
and Home Health Benefits, by State, 1998*

| | Skilled Nursing Facility | | Home Health | |
| | Total Spending ($ thousands) | Spending per Beneficiary ($) | Total Spending ($ thousands) | Spending per Beneficiary ($) |
State				
Alabama	157,455	235.01	229,162	342.03
California	1,035,586	271.66	741,481	194.51
Colorado	131,132	288.20	82,019	180.26
Florida	934,341	337.55	792,866	286.44
Massachusetts	413,666	435.44	375,162	394.91
Michigan	334,032	242.40	370,545	268.90
Minnesota	154,733	240.64	70,905	110.27
Mississippi	124,977	304.08	241,196	586.85
New Jersey	316,323	264.26	238,940	199.62
New York	814,754	306.18	605,548	227.56
Texas	832,906	379.63	1,351,092	615.81
Washington	186,762	260.48	84,344	117.63
Wisconsin	239,522	311.88	108,976	141.90
United States	11,180,561	294.09	10,398,247	273.51

Source: Urban Institute calculations based on U.S. Department of Health and Human Services (2001).

Medicaid

Medicaid funds long-term care for persons who have low incomes or who have been impoverished by the high costs of acute and long-term care. Although largely forgotten, the federal role in financing long-term care, especially nursing home care, preceded Medicaid by many years, beginning with the Social Security Amendments of 1950 (Stevens and Stevens 1974).

In FY 2001, Medicaid (including both federal and state funds) spent $75.2 billion for long-term care, including $42.7 billion for nursing facility care, $10.3 billion for services in intermediate care facilities for the mentally retarded, and $22.2 billion for home and community services.[3] This is almost three times the amount Medicare spends on skilled nursing facility and home health care, making Medicaid the largest public funder of long-term care services. Medicaid expenditures for long-term care vary significantly (table 8-2). While total expenditures averaged $264 per capita, they varied from $709 per capita in New York to $147 per capita in California.

In contrast to Medicare, Medicaid funding comes largely from federal and state revenues. The federal government sets broad guidelines under which the states operate. While states must provide nursing facility and home health services, they can limit the amount, duration, and scope of those services. Coverage of intermediate care facilities for the mentally retarded is optional, but all states include it. States may provide a range of optional home and community services. They may also offer personal care and case management, as well as adult day care, under the clinic service option. Home and community services waivers give states even more flexibility. Under waivers, states can provide a broad package of services that

Table 8-2. *Medicaid Long-Term Care Expenditures by State, FY 2001*

| | Overall Spending ($ millions) | | | | Per Capita Spending | | |
State	Total Long-Term Care	Home Care[a]	Nursing Homes	ICF/MR[b]	Total	Home Care	Institutional Care[c]
Alabama	927	192	674	62	208	43	165
California	5,066	2,048	2,598	420	147	59	87
Colorado	768	393	360	16	174	89	85
Florida	2,648	655	1,703	291	162	40	122
Massachusetts	2,450	815	1,423	212	384	128	256
Michigan	2,385	610	1,744	31	239	61	178
Minnesota	1,916	797	901	218	385	160	225
Mississippi	646	60	416	170	226	21	205
New Jersey	3,192	578	2,193	421	376	68	308
New York	13,469	4,918	6,392	2,159	709	259	450
Texas	3,288	960	1,604	725	154	45	109
Washington	1,427	683	614	131	238	114	124
Wisconsin	1,813	647	960	206	336	120	216
United States	75,288	22,210	42,728	10,351	264	78	186

Source: Urban Institute calculations on Health Care Financing Administration (HCFA) 64 data presented in Burwell, Eiken, and Sredl (2002).

a. Home care includes personal care, home and community services waivers, and home health.

b. Intermediate care facilities for the mentally retarded.

c. Institutional care includes nursing homes and ICF/MRs.

Medicaid does not routinely cover, and they can exert far greater fiscal control than they can under the regular Medicaid program.

In contrast to Medicaid spending on acute care, the vast majority of Medicaid spending on long-term care is for optional services or groups (Kaiser Commission on Medicaid and the Uninsured 2001). In 1998, only 10 percent of Medicaid expenditures on long-term care were for mandatory services to populations that federal law requires the states to cover. Long-term care expenditures are overwhelmingly on optional services for mandatory eligibility groups (24 percent) and mandatory and optional services for optional eligibility groups (66 percent), primarily people who spend down to Medicaid in nursing homes and other institutions. Although many states complain about the high costs of long-term care, they mostly incur these expenditures as a result of state choices, not federal mandates.

Other Long-Term Care Programs

Although Medicaid provides the bulk of long-term care funding to states, several other federal programs are designed to serve the aged and disabled populations. Funding for these programs is very small relative to Medicare and Medicaid. Moreover, most states supplement these programs with state-only funded programs.

The Older Americans Act requires states to designate state and regional agencies on aging. These agencies receive federal funding for small amounts of home and community services for persons age 60 and over. The agencies plan, coordinate, and develop service systems and administer a new family caregiver support program. They also advocate on behalf of older persons at the state and local levels. Appropriations for home and community services, including caregiver support, ranged from $4.2 million in Mississippi to $41.6 million in California in FY 2001 (table 8-3).

The Rehabilitation Act supports statewide Independent Living Councils and regional centers for independent living, both of which serve younger adults with disabilities. The Councils and centers' activities promote the independence of individuals with disabilities and help integrate them into mainstream society by providing a range of services, including home and community services. Rehabilitation Act funding for independent living grants in the 13 ANF states ranged from about $300,000 in four states to about $2 million in California in FY 2001.

The SSBG gives states funds that they may use for a wide range of social services, including those related to long-term care. In FY 2001, these fed-

Table 8-3. *Federal Grant Programs for Home and Community Services for the Aged and Disabled, by State, FY 2001*

State	Older Americans Act Supportive Services & Family Caregiver Support ($)	Rehabilitation Act Independent Living State Grants ($)	Social Services Block Grant ($)
Alabama	6,778,605	297,581	27,618,589
California	41,642,576	1,986,795	207,310,764
Colorado	4,887,336	297,581	25,200,693
Florida	30,748,826	907,184	94,659,667
Massachusetts	10,833,608	373,858	39,009,988
Michigan	14,576,777	597,066	62,300,479
Minnesota	7,172,360	297,581	29,985,715
Mississippi	4,247,979	297,581	17,464,696
New Jersey	4,582,078	493,551	51,499,276
New York	31,475,723	1,105,395	115,341,878
Texas	23,758,762	1,201,794	125,400,578
Washington	7,629,589	346,002	36,103,436
Wisconsin	8,483,508	317,721	33,152,461
United States	450,075,000	22,296,000	1,725,000,000

Sources: U.S. Department of Health and Human Services (2002c); U.S. Department of Education (2002).

eral grants ranged from $17.5 million in Mississippi to $207.3 million in California. Very few guidelines have been established for spending SSBG funds, and the proportion devoted to home and community services for the aged and disabled is unknown.

Many states use their own funds to provide home and community services that federal programs may not cover or to provide services to persons who do not qualify for Medicaid. Wisconsin's Community Options Program, for example, provides virtually any service that a person needs to remain at home.

Financing Long-Term Care

Over the past 10 years, states have demanded greater flexibility in the operation of Medicaid and other programs. At the same time, Medicaid and Medicare have become more important sources of financing for long-term care. As a result, the federal government has been shouldering a larger proportion of the spending on long-term care. Under some state financing strategies, even more expenditures have been shifted to the federal government, sometimes with few, if any, new services being provided (see Chapter 5). States have also tried to shift costs to the private sector by encouraging private long-term care insurance.

The growing importance of federal financing has come about in several ways. First, although Medicare's skilled nursing facility and home health expenditures fell in the aftermath of the provisions of the Balanced Budget Act (BBA) of 1997, they increased dramatically between 1988 and 2001. Medicare's home health expenditures increased from $1.9 billion in 1985 to $9.7 billion in 2000, and skilled nursing facility expenditures increased from $0.8 billion in 1985 to $12.6 billion in 2000 (U.S. House of Representatives, Committee on Ways and Means 2000). For home health care in particular, this increase resulted from a shift in Medicare's orientation from caring just for persons with short-term needs to providing more services to people with chronic disabilities (Leon, Neuman, and Parents 1997).

Second, Medicare is the first payer for services covered by both Medicare and Medicaid. States had long sought to shift Medicaid and state-funded long-term care expenditures to Medicare, but until the late 1980s, they were frustrated by the narrow range of Medicare coverage for nursing home and home health care. That situation changed dramatically when Medicare's coverage rules for post-acute care were liberalized. In response, some states, including Massachusetts, New York, and Wisconsin, implemented Medicare maximization policies to ensure that Medicare pays for home health and nursing facility care wherever possible (Wiener and Stevenson 1998a). Their efforts take the form of educating providers about Medicare benefits, improving the Medicaid data system to identify persons eligible for benefits under both Medicare and Medicaid (so-called dual eligibles), and making sure Medicare gets billed first. In addition, many states require that all long-term care providers be certified by both Medicare and Medicaid and that they bill Medicare whenever there is the slightest chance of reimbursement. Partly reflecting these initiatives, one study of home health expenditures found an inverse relationship between Medicare and Medicaid home health spending (Kenney, Rajan, and Soscia 1998).

Third, states have shifted much of their state-funded home care programs into Medicaid, thus obtaining a federal match for at least half of their costs. California, Washington, and Wisconsin are states that have done so. California's In-Home Supportive Services program, one of the biggest home and community services programs in the country, began as an exclusively state-funded program and is now funded under the Medicaid personal care option.

In addition, some states depend on county-run nursing homes to draw down additional federal funds without having to increase state funding. They do this through the upper payment limit (UPL) strategy, which is discussed in greater detail in Chapter 5. Federal law stipulates that Medicaid payments can be no higher than the amount that Medicare would have paid for the same service—the UPL. However, until recently, federal regulations contained a loophole that allowed states to pay far higher amounts to public facilities, such as county nursing homes (Coughlin, Bruen, and King 2003). Under a typical UPL program, states determine what would have been paid by Medicare to both public and private facilities and then make a UPL payment, which is over and above regular Medicaid reimbursement, just to the publicly owned nursing homes. Public facilities are used because they generally provide the state Medicaid share through intergovernmental transfers of funds. The facilities then return much, if not all, of the payment to the state. Meanwhile, the state collects the federal Medicaid matching payment. So, at the end of the transaction, the federal government has made additional nursing home payments without any real state spending and usually with very little of the UPL funds being kept by nursing homes.

States have used a variety of such mechanisms to increase substantially the federal funds flowing to them. Michigan's UPL strategy involves payments to county-owned medical care facilities and hospital chronic care units; in FY 2001, Michigan made $350 million in such payments. New York's nursing home UPL program, which began in 1995, involved nearly $1 billion in combined federal-state Medicaid funds in FY 2000. Washington's UPL strategy involves 14 government-owned nursing homes; the state anticipates receiving more than $450 million in new federal dollars in 2002 and 2003 and retroactive payments for 2000 and 2001, much of which will be transferred to the general fund to help the state balance its budget. Since 1985, Wisconsin has used local contributions to nursing homes owned by local governments to claim federal funds. With the changes enacted in 2001, Wisconsin's program could bring in $604 million in federal funds during the state's 2001–03 biennium, most of which will be used to fund rate increases for nursing homes.

The use of UPL strategies is sure to decline, because Congress passed the Benefits Improvement and Protection Act of 2000, which phases out the use of UPL strategies, and because the Bush administration is determined to end these practices. However, it is unclear whether these strategies, which are politically popular at the state level, will actually be eliminated, especially in a time of state fiscal pressure.

Some states have sought to promote private long-term care insurance as a way of preventing the impoverishment of the middle class as a result of use of nursing home and home care services, and the subsequent Medicaid expenditures on people who have exhausted their personal resources. Whether long-term care insurance can reach far enough down the income distribution to reduce Medicaid expenditures is highly controversial (Cohen, Kumar, and Wallack 1994; Wiener, Illston, and Hanley 1994). Among the ANF states, California and New York operate so-called partnership programs, which provide easier access to Medicaid for individuals who purchase state-approved private long-term care insurance policies (McCall 2001: 243–59). In essence, purchasers may keep far more in assets and still qualify for Medicaid than would otherwise be the case. Despite a number of years of effort, however, only about 19,000 policies were in force in California and 30,000 in New York as of 2000 (Laguna Research Associates 2002).

In addition, a number of states have enacted tax incentives to encourage the purchase of long-term care insurance, something that has been proposed at the federal level but not enacted. As of 1999, 18 states provided tax deductions or credits to purchasers of private long-term care insurance, including Alabama, Colorado, Minnesota, New York, and Wisconsin (Wiener, Tilly, and Goldenson 2000). In almost all cases, however, the tax incentive is very small, making it unlikely to substantially increase the affordability of private long-term care insurance.

Integrating Acute and Long-Term Care Programs

People with disabilities currently receive acute and long-term care in a splintered, uncoordinated financing and delivery system (Wiener 1996b). Almost all older Medicaid beneficiaries are also eligible for Medicare, as are about a quarter of Medicaid beneficiaries with disabilities (Schneider 2002). Because of the multiplicity of funding sources for acute and long-term care, each with its own eligibility and coverage criteria and set of services, states face a major task in coordinating and integrating services. Most of the ANF states have taken the path of least resistance by not attempting to integrate Medicare and Medicaid and by allowing multiple, independent state agencies to manage the various long-term care programs. Generally, departments of medical assistance or health have administrative responsibility for Medicaid programs; departments of aging are responsible for administering Older Americans Act programs; departments of social services for SSBG programs; and departments of vocational rehabilitation for Rehabilitation Act programs.

A few states have attempted to improve service delivery and program administration by integrating services and financing. In general, they hope to provide higher quality care, save money, and increase funding for long-term care at no additional cost by substituting less costly nursing home and home care for hospital and other acute care. At least three ANF states—Minnesota, Massachusetts, and Wisconsin—have integrated health and long-term care services for beneficiaries dually eligible for Medicare and Medicaid. The initiatives are designed to minimize barriers between Medicare and Medicaid, improve coordination of health and long-term care services, and thus reduce unnecessary institutionalization. In 1995, Minnesota received Medicare and Medicaid waivers to implement the Minnesota Senior Health Options demonstration (Minnesota Department of Human Services 2003). The demonstration provides coordinated primary, acute, and long-term care to older people enrolled in both Medicare and Medicaid, operates in 10 counties, and, as of 2001, had voluntarily enrolled about 4,000 people. The state has received federal approval to extend this program to younger, disabled Medicaid beneficiaries who are also eligible for Medicare.

Massachusetts has received federal approval to offer senior care organizations to dual Medicare-Medicaid beneficiaries. The organizations will provide health and long-term care services in return for risk-adjusted per capita payments. The Wisconsin Partnership Program, which operates under Medicare and Medicaid waivers, is a capitated program of acute and long-term care services that are coordinated by an interdisciplinary team. The program offers two models—one for the older population and one for younger people with disabilities. The Wisconsin Partnership Program is modeled, in part, on the Program of All-inclusive Care of the Elderly (PACE) but without the reliance on adult day care.

While the foregoing programs result from state waiver initiatives, PACE programs are a regular part of Medicare and Medicaid and provide an integrated, comprehensive array of health and long-term care services to dual-eligible persons (Branch, Coulam, Zimmerman 1995). Enrollees must need a nursing home level of care and receive many of their services in adult day care centers. Medicare and Medicaid provide per capita payments to PACE programs, which are at financial risk. In some ways, PACE is a textbook example of how local innovation can work its way into national legislation. It started as a Section 1115 and Section 222 Medicare and Medicaid demonstration in San Francisco, was replicated in a national demonstration supported in part by the Robert Wood Johnson Foundation, and finally codified as a Medicare benefit and an optional Medicaid service. In 2000, the program served 6,575 persons in 24 fully capitated sites across the country (National PACE Association 2001).

In all, these programs are quite small, and their potential to change the financing and delivery of health and long-term care services for the aged and the disabled on a wider basis has yet to be realized. Although a great deal of interest and discussion has focused on integrating acute and long-term care services, states have been slow to act, for several reasons.

First, overcoming the fragmentation of the existing system of financing and delivery is simply more difficult than states initially realized. Moreover, integration is not well-defined and there is little understanding of how to go about it (Wiener and Skaggs 1995).

Second, the federal government has had reservations about granting waivers for integration, at least as states have proposed them (Wiener and Stevenson 1998c). To maximize their leverage over providers, states have wanted control over the Medicare payments, but federal officials have worried that states will shift the costs of these projects from Medicaid to Medicare. Moreover, several states feared, initially at least, that participation in integrated systems would be modest unless enrollment was mandatory. The Centers for Medicare and Medicaid Services (CMS) has insisted, however, that dual-eligibles are Medicare beneficiaries first and foremost and that they are entitled to freedom of choice of providers; thus, mandatory enrollment for Medicare services is not permitted for dual-eligibles.

Third, while there are many reasons to support the integration of acute and long-term care services, there are also reasons to be concerned about possible negative effects, especially from a long-term care perspective. Indeed, these concerns derailed an ambitious plan in Wisconsin to integrate the two sets of services in 1997 (Coughlin et al. 1998). Opponents of the plan were critical of the state's reliance on managed care organizations that they said had little experience or skill with older people or with long-term care. Critics also worried that fiscal pressures within the integrated system could short-change long-term care if providers did not view it as a priority or if acute care overran its budget. In addition, long-term care could become overmedicalized and services could become less consumer-directed if the balance of power shifted from the individual client and his or her chosen provider to the managed care organization. Home care providers were concerned about their negotiating strength and the potential bias of managed care toward institutional services.

While no ANF state has tackled integration of Medicare and Medicaid on a large scale, several states have combined their long-term care programs serving the aged or disabled population into single administrative entities at the state or local level. Colorado, New Jersey, and Washington have local, single-point-of-entry systems that provide information about programs, assess the need for services, establish Medicaid eligibility, and determine what setting would be most appropriate for aged or disabled applicants. In addition, Washington's Aging and Adult Services Administration coordinates all programs serving adults with disabilities at the state level. Michigan recently combined its long-term care programs at the state level through its Long-Term Care Initiative.

Wisconsin has perhaps gone further than any other state to integrate long-term care services. Its Family Care demonstration program has been implemented in several counties, including Milwaukee (Alecxih et al. 2000, 2001). The project combines funds from Medicaid and state and county programs for long-term care. From a Medicaid perspective, it operates as one of the few combination freedom-of-choice and home and community-based services waivers. Family Care's local aging and disability resource centers offer one place for consumers to receive information and counseling on all long-term care services and providers. The centers also conduct functional assessments and determine financial eligibility for Family Care and other public programs; if appropriate, they assist beneficiaries with enrollment in a care management organization.

Care management organizations receive capitated payments in return for managing the entire range of long-term care services for beneficiaries, including institutional care. The capitation payment is based on the individual's functional disability, and the state and the care management organization share financial risk. Family Care provides beneficiaries with an entitlement to a comprehensive array of flexible long-term care services. The state plans to increase the number of people receiving home and community services without dramatically increasing expenditures by reducing the number of people using nursing home care. Budget constraints have stopped expansion of the program to other counties.

Home and Community Services

Long-term care funding for adults with disabilities has long been devoted primarily to nursing facilities and intermediate care facilities for the mentally retarded, despite the strong preference of people with disabilities to live in the community. As a consequence of various pressures and incentives, most ANF states have spent a slowly increasing proportion of their long-term care funding on home and community services, through personal care and home health, consumer-directed programs, assisted-living facilities, and nursing home transition programs. Indeed, in virtually all states, a major policy goal is to create a more balanced delivery system, which generally means putting more emphasis on home and community services. It is in this area that states have been most innovative, although only a modest number of ANF states, notably Washington and Wisconsin, can truly be considered highly innovative.

Pressures to Increase Provision of Innovative Home and Community Services

States began shifting their long-term care resources and policy attention to home and community services for adults with disabilities in response to rising nursing home costs, beneficiaries' strong preference for remaining in their homes and communities, the U.S. Supreme Court's *Olmstead* decision, and recent federal initiatives to provide home and community services.

Medicaid nursing home costs totaled $42.7 billion in FY 2001 and accounted for about 21 percent of Medicaid expenditures (excluding administration and DSH payments, but including UPL payments) (Burwell, Eiken, and Sredl 2002). States fear that increases are inevitable because of the rising number of older persons at risk of institutionalization. As a result, the states are interested in less costly alternatives.

The independent living movement, which has been led by younger adults with disabilities, asserts that people with disabilities have the right to receive and manage their own services in home and community settings and to become part of mainstream society (Tilly and Wiener 2001). Not surprisingly, advocates for people with disabilities strongly dislike institutions because they separate the individual from the rest of society (Wiener and Sullivan 1995). The movement puts political pressure on states to let individuals with disabilities make the decisions about the supportive services that affect their lives. Although there are barriers to adoption of the independent living movement's precepts by the aging advocacy community, there is growing interest in applying these concepts to the older population (Tilly and Wiener 2001).

Another push for home and community services came from the Supreme Court's 1999 *Olmstead* decision (*Olmstead v. L.C. ex. rel. Rimring*, 119 S. Ct. 2176 (1999)), which found that unnecessary institutionalization of people with disabilities is a violation of the Americans with Disabilities Act and, within limits, that they have a right to home and community services. The states' reactions to this decision have varied. New York, Wisconsin, and Washington, with relatively large home and community services systems, believe they are not likely to be vulnerable to lawsuits based on the *Olmstead* decision. However, Mississippi and Texas have developed plans to expand their home and community services systems in direct response to the Supreme Court's mandate.

While most pressures to increase funding for home and community services have come at the state level or from the federal courts, some recent federal legislation promotes a more balanced system of care. New initiatives to promote home and community services include a program of grants for family caregivers and a program of planning grants for home and community services. Congress created the National Family Caregiver Program as part of the Older Americans Act Amendments of 2000. Through this new authority, the Administration on Aging gives states grants for services such as information and assistance, counseling, support groups and training, and respite services. Funding for the new initiative was $141.5 million in FY 2002 (U.S. Department of Health and Human Services [HHS] 2002b).

In addition, Systems Change Grants for Community Living are federal funds to help states improve their community services and promote consumer choice. Congress appropriated $64 million for this initiative in FY 2001 and an additional $55 million in FY 2002 (HHS 2002a). States compete for grants designed to help them improve their home and community services and consumer-directed programs and to help bring nursing home residents into the community. While funding is not large enough to pay for services, it does provide resources to hire staff dedicated to the task of expanding services.

State Responses to Pressures and Incentives

Since the latter half of the 1990s, states have responded to these pressures and to federal initiatives with increased funding for home and community services as well as with innovative programs. Some states have made more progress than others in opening up home and community services to aged and disabled beneficiaries. Thus, residents of innovative states may have far more access to flexible home and community services than those who live in less innovative states.

INCREASED FUNDING

States have been steadily increasing their funding for home and community services and decreasing their dependence on institutional services. While state-funded programs perform important functions, the vast bulk of funding for home care is through Medicaid. Total Medicaid home and community services expenditures increased from $9.4 billion in FY 1995 to $22.2 billion in FY 2001 (table 8-4) (Burwell et al. 2002). The majority of these funds were for people with developmental disabilities rather than for older people or younger persons with physical disabilities. Viewed from another perspective, 80 percent of all Medicaid long-term care spending in FY 1995 was for nursing facilities and intermediate care facilities for the mentally retarded; by FY 2001, the percentage had dropped to 71 percent. During this period, the proportion of Medicaid long-term expenditures dedicated to facilities for the mentally retarded declined more rapidly than the proportion dedicated to nursing facilities.

All but one of the ANF states devoted more than half of their Medicaid long-term care funding (including services for people with developmental disabilities) to institutions in FY 2001. The proportion of spending on institutions ranged from 49 percent in Colorado to 91 percent in Mississippi (Burwell et al. 2002). California, Colorado, Minnesota, and Washington all dedicated less than 60 percent of Medicaid long-term care funding to institutions, while Alabama, Florida, Mississippi, and New Jersey devoted more than 75 percent to institutions. Florida is striking in that it has the oldest population in the country, but Florida, along with other southern ANF states, relies heavily on institutions and Medicare home health to serve persons with disabilities.

Table 8-4. *Medicaid Home and Community Services Expenditures, by State, FY 2001*

State	Overall Spending ($ millions)				Per Capita Spending			
	Total Home Care	Personal Care	Home & Community Services Waivers	Home Health	Total Home Care	Personal Care	Home & Community Services Waivers	Home Health
Alabama	192	N/A	153	39	43	N/A	34	9
California	2,048	1,376	526	146	59	40	15	4
Colorado	393	N/A	320	73	89	N/A	72	17
Florida	655	18	551	86	40	1	34	5
Massachusetts	815	242	508	66	128	38	80	10
Michigan	610	183	412	14	61	18	41	1
Minnesota	797	129	610	59	160	26	123	12
Mississippi	60	N/A	49	11	21	N/A	17	4
New Jersey	578	198	326	53	68	23	38	6
New York	4,918	1,870	2,011	1,037	259	98	106	55
Texas	960	267	692	—	45	13	32	—
Washington	683	153	517	13	114	26	86	2
Wisconsin	647	104	488	55	120	19	90	10
United States	22,210	5,254	14,383	2,573	78	18	51	9

Source: Urban Institute calculations on HCFA 64 data presented in Burwell et al. (2002).
Note: N/A = not applicable.

Medicaid funding has eclipsed state funding of home care programs in all but a few states because of the desire for federal Medicaid matching dollars, though at the price of complying with federal rules and regulations. States are required to provide home health care to people who require a nursing facility level of care, and they may provide it to other groups as well—and virtually all states do. In addition, states may choose to offer personal care and adult day care, usually as part of the clinic benefit within the regular Medicaid program.

Offering home health and optional services under the regular Medicaid program can be done with administrative ease, but it entails important constraints. States must offer home health, personal care, adult day care, and other services as an open-ended entitlement—a legal obligation on the part of government to provide services to individuals who meet established criteria, regardless of the cost. This characteristic opens states up to large increases in spending due to increased demand by the high percentage of disabled people in the community who are not receiving paid services (Liu, Manton, and Aragon 2000). In addition, these options constitute a fairly narrow range of services and may not effectively maintain people with disabilities in the community.

The potential fiscal exposure combined with limited services has prompted states to rely upon waivers to finance their noninstitutional long-term care. Under Section 1915(c) of the Social Security Act, states may apply to the U.S. Department of Health and Human Services (HHS) for Medicaid home and community services waivers that are designed to give them greater flexibility in meeting the needs of persons with disabilities living in the community. In 2002, all 50 states and the District of Columbia had a Medicaid home and community services waiver for older people, for younger persons with disabilities, and for persons with developmental disabilities (principally mental retardation). However, states vary in the degree to which they used waivers to fund home and community services.

Because the waivers are intended to substitute noninstitutional care for institutional care, states must limit their programs to beneficiaries with relatively severe disabilities—that is, people who meet the state's criteria for nursing home care, intermediate care facilities for the mentally retarded, or hospital services, criteria that vary greatly across states (O'Keeffe 1996, 1999). For the older population and for younger adults with physical disabilities, the comparison institution is almost always a nursing home. Programs have to be budget-neutral; that is, average

Medicaid expenditures for waiver beneficiaries may be no greater than they would be without the waiver. In addition, states must limit in advance the number of people they will serve during a year and may establish waiting lists for waiver programs. Thus, waiver programs are not an entitlement, unlike regular Medicaid services, which must be provided to all who qualify. States may also limit services to certain populations (e.g., older people, younger people with disabilities, people with developmental disabilities) and operate the waiver on less than a statewide basis.

Under waivers, states may cover a very wide range of services, including case management, homemaker–home health aide services, personal care services, habilitation, respite care, nonmedical transportation, home modifications, adult day care, and other services approved by the Secretary of HHS. Many of these services are not strictly medical in nature and are not usually covered by Medicaid. In addition, states may extend Medicaid eligibility to community beneficiaries with incomes up to 300 percent of the federal SSI cash assistance level ($1,656 a month for an individual in 2003), which many states use as their institutional income eligibility standard (Bruen, Wiener, and Thomas 2003).

During the administrations of Presidents Ronald Reagan and George H. W. Bush, strict federal rules made it quite difficult for states to obtain Medicaid home and community services waivers (Lutzky et al. 2000). The federal government, especially the Office of Management and Budget, feared that waiver services would supplement rather than replace institutional services, increasing overall Medicaid expenditures. To maximize savings or at least prevent increases in spending, federal regulations imposed a very strict cost-effectiveness test, essentially requiring that institutional beds be closed or otherwise remain empty, the so-called cold bed rule. Because of the difficulty of meeting this criterion, waiver programs tended to be small and to be used more often for persons with developmental disabilities than for older people and younger persons with physical disabilities. As a result, expenditures were low, reaching only $1.3 billion by 1990 (Miller 1992).

In 1994, the Clinton administration eliminated the cold bed requirement, making it much easier for states to meet the budget-neutrality requirement (Lutzky et al. 2000). Current rules only require that states ensure that the average costs with the waiver are less than the average Medicaid costs of the comparison institutional provider—nursing facilities, intermediate care facilities, or hospitals. These rules are much less stringent and easy for states to comply with. With cost neutrality removed as a barrier, states have aggressively expanded services. Indeed, while some ANF states cited lack of state funds as a problem, none identified lack of federal waiver approval as a barrier to the expansion of home and community services.

With federal approval easier to obtain, expenditures under Medicaid home and community services waivers soared to $14.1 billion in FY 2001 (Eiken and Burwell 2002). Nationally, spending under these waivers rose from 32 percent of Medicaid spending on home and community services in FY 1990 to 65 percent in FY 2001 (Eiken and Burwell 2002). During FY 2001, only 26 percent of expenditures under the home and community services waivers were for aged and younger, physically disabled persons, while 74 percent were for people with developmental disabilities. Yet people with developmental disabilities represented only about 38 percent of beneficiaries covered under these waivers (Burwell 2001).

CONSUMER DIRECTION

A key issue in the design of home and community services programs is the extent to which clients control their services. Consumer involvement in managing Medicaid and state-funded services ranges from very little to virtually complete control. The vast majority of home care services are provided by agencies, which assume responsibility for hiring, training, directing, scheduling, and firing workers. Under a consumer-directed model of care, the individual client has responsibility for these functions.

An increasing number of states, including Washington, Wisconsin, Michigan, and California, give disabled beneficiaries of all ages, even those with severe disabilities and cognitive impairments, the ability to choose and direct independent providers; beneficiaries with cognitive impairments are usually assisted by informal caregivers or surrogate decisionmakers (Tilly and Wiener 2001). New Jersey participates in the HHS-sponsored cash and counseling demonstration, which uses Medicaid funds to provide cash payments to beneficiaries, who then hire their own workers. Although client empowerment as a policy goal is an important motivator of state action, the opportunity for savings also attracts state policymakers. Payment rates for independent providers are usually far less than for agencies, in part because they have fewer employment benefits (including health insurance) and overhead costs.

While the ideology of consumer-directed services emphasizes individuals going into the competitive marketplace to choose their workers, a high proportion of beneficiaries pick family members or other persons they know (Wiener, Tilly, and Alecxih 2002). Family members constitute about one-half of the independent providers in Washington and Michigan. In California, about 75 percent of independent providers knew the consumer before they started work (Doty et al. 1999). Some public officials are concerned about quality of care under consumer direction and the possibility that payments to relatives may function more as an income supplement for the family than as a mechanism of providing care to the beneficiary.

GROUP RESIDENTIAL SETTINGS

Several states have embraced assisted-living facilities and other group residential settings as alternatives to nursing homes. Ideally, these facilities provide the economies of scale available in congregate facilities without the institutional, more medical atmosphere of a nursing home. Group residential settings are especially useful for people who need a great deal of supervision but not a great deal of hands-on care, such as many people with Alzheimer's disease. Services in these facilities, but not room and board, may be covered under Medicaid home and community services waivers.

Because it is sometimes difficult to distinguish group residential settings from institutions, states diverge on how enthusiastically they have embraced this approach. Washington views residential providers as a key component of its strategy of deinstitutionalization and as a means of decreasing growth of long-term care costs. Strong political support and funding fueled the increasing numbers of adult family homes, boarding homes, and assisted-living facilities in the 1990s, while restrictions on nursing home growth and payments constricted the supply of nursing facility services. On the other hand, while group residential facilities are a major component of Wisconsin's Community Options Program, the state has been ambivalent about using them because the program is supposed to support "home care." Several Wisconsin observers criticized residential facilities, saying that they were too large and too much like "little nursing homes."

NURSING HOME TRANSITION PROGRAMS

One strategy for increasing the substitution of home and community services for institutional care has been to aggressively identify nursing home residents who do not need institutionalization and relocate them into the community. Michigan, New Jersey, Texas, and Washington have implemented such programs. New Jersey's Community Choice Counseling

Program is one of the most ambitious. Begun in 1998, the program makes several types of services available to former nursing home residents, including case management, placement in adult foster homes or assisted-living facilities, and some in-home services. According to the state budget, Eldercare placed 2,400 nursing home residents in the community between April 1998 and October 2000.

Difficulties in implementing the program have included the time needed to ensure sufficient high-quality services and difficulties in getting assisted-living facilities to participate in Medicaid because of payment and other regulatory issues. A Rutgers University survey of program participants found that 81 percent were living in home-based settings and about 33 percent were living alone; 95 percent were satisfied with their current living situation (Howell-White, Palmer, and Bjerklie 2001). By the end of 2002, New Jersey officials expected to interview 43,000 older people in hospitals and nursing homes and help as many as possible move into the community (Whitman 1999).

Allocating Resources and Containing Costs

States can only react to federal actions regarding skilled Medicare nursing facility and home health services. But states can use a number of tools to allocate Medicaid and other programs' long-term care funds to those most in need and to contain costs. These tools include setting eligibility standards for Medicaid services and controlling use of and payment for nursing homes and home and community services. The ANF states have restricted financial and functional eligibility for services, but their standards and methods vary markedly. Most states have controlled growth in the number of nursing home beds to some extent or have limited reimbursements to nursing homes. Although many states' primary target for cost containment is nursing homes, ANF states have controlled growth in home and community expenditures through the use of waivers and waiting lists, as well as payment rate limits.

A major constraint on expansion of services and efforts to control payment rates is the shortage of nurses and paraprofessional workers. Labor shortages among long-term care providers have caused Colorado to increase certain payment rates and have raised state officials' concern about the quality of care, particularly in the home and community. For example, the labor shortage could lead to missed visits, which could complicate medication management for older Medicaid beneficiaries living at home. In Minnesota, some nursing homes have been forced to eliminate beds or even close entire wings as a result of the worker shortage. This has contributed to waiting lists for some nursing homes (*American Health Line* 2001). The state has increased payments to long-term care providers and relaxed staff certification requirements to increase the number of long-term care workers available. New York's response to its labor shortage was to focus on substantial additional funding to increase workers' wages.

Eligibility for Medicaid and Other Long-Term Care Services

Long-term care is expensive. The average cost of a year of nursing home care in 2000 was $49,000 (National Statistics Group 2002). To make sure that limited resources are targeted to the populations most in need, states have developed various mechanisms for allocating resources. Applicants for public programs must be assessed to determine whether their incomes and assets are low enough to meet financial eligibility criteria and whether their disabilities are severe enough to meet functional eligibility tests. To limit expenditures, Medicaid programs are limited to the low-income population, and home and community services waivers are restricted to people with relatively severe disability; state programs are often far more liberal in terms of both financial and functional eligibility.

Theoretically, financial eligibility for Medicaid is governed by rigid federal guidelines because of the program's close link to SSI, the federal cash assistance program for older people and persons with disabilities. However, states have great legal flexibility in the methodologies by which income and assets are counted (Bruen et al. 2003). Under Section 1902(r)(2) of the Social Security Act, states may use less restrictive income and resource methodologies than those used by SSI for the aged, blind, and disabled. By excluding certain income and assets in determining eligibility, the effective standard can be higher than the nominal one. Nonetheless, states generally adhere fairly closely to SSI regulations (Bruen et al. 2003). Nine ANF states (New Jersey, New York, California, Massachusetts, Florida, Michigan, Washington, Wisconsin, and Minnesota) allow aged and disabled individuals to qualify for Medicaid by spending down their income on medical expenses until they reach the "medically needy" income level. However, this income level is usually less than the SSI payment level.

Financial eligibility for Medicaid nursing home services is set at 300 percent of the SSI cash assistance level (or $1,656 a month for an individual in 2003) or at the medically needy level (Bruen et al. 2003). Financial eligibility for home and community services waivers is usually the same as that for nursing home care—a far higher income level than would normally be allowed in the community. Raising the eligibility level for services offered under waivers is designed to level the playing field between institutional and noninstitutional care; otherwise, states might be biased in favor of institutional care because Medicaid eligibility standards are more liberal for institutional care. In all but a few ANF states, aged and disabled beneficiaries find it easier to qualify financially for waiver or nursing home services than for home health and personal care.

In contrast to the heavy federal influence in setting rules on Medicaid financial eligibility, states have almost complete control over functional eligibility standards for optional long-term care, nursing home care, and services offered under waivers. States universally consider nursing needs and physical and mental functioning when determining whether a person qualifies for nursing home care, but no commonly accepted practice or standards exist for determining functional eligibility (O'Keeffe 1996, 1999). Approaches vary from numerical scoring systems to reliance on professional judgment.

Federal rules require states to use the same level-of-care criteria for determining eligibility for services under waivers as they do for establishing nursing home eligibility. As a result, states cannot expand functional eligibility for the waivers without also liberalizing eligibility for institutional care, creating a dilemma for states that wish to use waivers to cover a broader population. Functional eligibility standards for optional long-term care services under Medicaid, such as personal care, are usually less stringent than eligibility standards for waiver services. As a result of the variation across states, people with the same level of functioning may be eligible for Medicaid long-term care services in one state but denied them in another.

Controlling Nursing Home Expenditures

States use three basic methods to control nursing home costs—controlling the supply of beds, limiting Medicaid reimbursement rates, and expanding home and community services. States currently have complete flexibility in the first two areas, although the federal government strongly promoted health planning in the 1970s and had minimum standards for Medicaid reimbursement rates from 1980 until 1997. As discussed above, states have considerable flexibility in fashioning their home and community services programs under Medicaid.

The use of supply constraints as a cost-control strategy is based on the notion that nursing home utilization (and consequently Medicaid spending) rises when the supply of beds increases, independent of need (Wiener, Stevenson, and Goldenson 1999). Controlling the supply of nursing home beds can involve requiring providers to demonstrate the need for beds through a certificate-of-need process, placing moratoriums on new beds, and offering incentives for facilities to close beds. Although state certificate-of-need requirements for acute care services such as hospitals have declined drastically over the past 20 years, all but four of the ANF states (California, Colorado, Texas, and Minnesota) have maintained their requirement in the case of nursing homes. In recent years, at least four ANF states (Alabama, Mississippi, Texas, and Wisconsin) have used moratoria on construction or Medicaid certification of new nursing home beds to limit supply.

A less frequent strategy has been the use of mechanisms that allow nursing homes to close beds without permanently losing control of those resources. In 2000, Minnesota established a process for closing nursing homes by allowing providers to place a limited number of beds on layaway, for potential return to use at a later date. Washington has a program that allows facilities to set aside, or bank, beds through two mechanisms— one for facilities that are closing and would like to retain or sell the rights to their beds, and one for facilities that would like to convert beds to another use. Wisconsin has a similar program.

State restrictions on new construction and funding policies determine the supply of nursing home and group residential care beds (table 8-5). In 1998, five of the ANF states had fewer than the national average. Three of the states, Alabama, Florida, and Mississippi, are located in the South, which historically has had low levels of public funding for long-term care; the other two, New Jersey and New York, devote relatively large amounts of funding to home and community services, which may have reduced their dependence on facility-based care. California, Washington, and Michigan had low supplies of nursing home beds and high supplies of residential beds. In Washington, at least, the large number of residential beds resulted from the state's decision to reduce dependence on nursing homes and increase the availability of residential alternatives. These findings indicate that people with disabilities have marked differences in access to nursing home and assisted-living facility beds.

Table 8-5. *Supply of Nursing Home and Group Residential Setting Beds, by State, 1998*

State	Nursing Facility Beds (per 1,000 age 65+)	Other Licensed Residential Care Beds (per 1,000 age 65+)
Alabama	45.3	12.4
California	36.5	46.8
Colorado	51.5	27.1
Florida	29.7	24.8
Massachusetts	63.7	11.8
Michigan	42.4	37.8
Minnesota	75.1	29.9
Mississippi	52.1	10.2
New Jersey	45.1	17.4
New York	49.0	17.1
Texas	65.6	14.9
Washington	41.7	49.2
Wisconsin	69.7	34.5
U.S. average	52.5	25.5

Source: Harrington et al. (1999).

From 1980 to 1997, federal Medicaid law required that state Medicaid programs pay nursing home providers enough "to meet the costs which must be incurred by efficiently and economically operated facilities" that meet federal and state regulations and standards of quality and safety. State Medicaid officials came overwhelmingly to oppose this requirement, known as the Boren amendment, believing that they were forced by the courts to spend too much on nursing homes at the expense of other services (Wiener and Stevenson 1998b). Repeal of the amendment by the BBA in 1997 eliminated virtually all federal rules and allows states to modify provider payment systems any way they like. By eliminating the requirement that rates be "reasonable," the act also paved the way for the extraordinarily high payments to some public nursing facilities that are a key component of many UPL strategies.

At the time of the repeal, the nursing home industry warned that Medicaid reimbursement was already too low and that further reductions would adversely affect the quality of care. In 1998, the national average Medicaid nursing facility rate was $95.72 per day (table 8-6). Among ANF

Table 8-6. *Average Medicaid Nursing Facility Rates, Freestanding Facilities, 1998*

State	Daily Rate ($)
Alabama	98.69
California	83.12
Colorado	101.55
Florida	97.99
Massachusetts	116.63
Michigan	96.05
Minnesota	106.65
Mississippi	80.60
New Jersey	115.76
New York	158.93
Texas	70.83
Washington	116.00
Wisconsin	91.70
U.S. average	95.72

Source: Harrington et al. (1999).

states, it ranged from $70.83 in Texas to $158.93 in New York (Harrington et al. 1999). Because Medicare usually pays higher rates than Medicaid, nursing homes have argued that Medicare has traditionally subsidized low Medicaid payment rates in many states. Medicare payments for skilled nursing facility services grew rapidly until 1997, when the BBA radically changed reimbursement methods and reduced payment levels. The reductions were largely offset through a series of time-limited add-ons by the Balanced Budget Refinement Act of 1999 and the Medicare, Medicaid, and State Children's Health Insurance Program (SCHIP) Benefits Improvement and Protection Act of 2000, some of which expired in 2002.

In the period immediately following the repeal of the Boren amendment, several states, including Wisconsin, Texas, New Jersey, and Washington, took advantage of their new flexibility to trim Medicaid's nursing home reimbursement, most commonly by reducing inflation updates and lowering the ceilings for cost centers (Holahan et al. 2002). Some states, including New Jersey, contended that they could have done this even if the Boren amendment had not been repealed. In New York, the governor proposed major cuts in nursing home reimbursement, but they were rejected by the legislature. The lack of large across-the-board cuts in nursing home rates is attributable in part to the excellent financial condition of the states in the late 1990s. In addition, the nursing home industry is powerful at the state level and usually more successful than home and community services providers at obtaining reimbursement rate increases.

In 2000 and 2001, several states, including California, Florida, Texas, Wisconsin, Minnesota, and Massachusetts, increased Medicaid reimbursement rates in response to a perceived deterioration in the financial status of nursing homes and concerns about inadequate quality of care and difficulty of attracting long-term care workers. Rather than giving unfettered increases, the higher rates were targeted at raising the wages of nursing home workers or increasing staff. As a practical matter, however, tracking the funds to make sure they resulted in wage increases has proved difficult. Moreover, some of the wage pass-through requirements are complicated. Providers argue that they have not been fully reimbursed for their increased costs: Although the higher rates apply only to Medicaid beneficiaries, workers must be paid those rates regardless of the payment source. While workers have received some wage increases, few were large enough to significantly change the pay scale in the industry.

With continued economic problems in 2002 and 2003, and the sharp downturn of the stock market, states face serious economic difficulties (Holahan et al. 2003; Lav and Johnson 2002). On the one hand, cutting nursing home rates has traditionally been a quick way to slow the growth of Medicaid expenditures. On the other hand, the availability of federal matching funds, the potential of undermining what is already a problematic quality of care, and the political strength of the nursing home industry make cutting rates a struggle. Nonetheless, in FY 2003, many states have achieved Medicaid savings by cutting, freezing, or not making inflation adjustments in provider payment rates (Holahan et al. 2003).

Most of the ANF states use case-mix reimbursement systems for nursing homes. Case-mix systems pay more for nursing home residents who are severely disabled and need more services. They are designed to give nursing homes an incentive to take residents whom the facilities might try to avoid under average cost or flat-rate payment systems. The movement to case-mix payments under Medicaid was probably influenced by the federal government's decision to use case-mix reimbursement for Medicare skilled nursing facility payments and its funding of demonstration projects designed to determine the effects of this form of nursing home payment. The federal demonstration projects, in turn, were influenced by state efforts to establish case-mix reimbursement systems in the 1980s and early 1990s. Thus, case-mix reimbursement is one policy area in which the interaction between the states and the federal government has moved policy at both levels of government.

Most state officials view expansion of home and community services as a cost-effective alternative to nursing home care, despite a substantial amount of rigorous research on older people with disabilities which finds that expanding home care increases rather than decreases aggregate costs (Weissert and Hendrick 1994; Wiener and Hanley 1992). Expenditures rise because most of the people studied receive home and community services in lieu of no paid services, not in lieu of nursing home care. Thus, large increases in the use of home and community services more than offset relatively small reductions in nursing home use. This research is 20 years old, however, and states argue that they have learned a lot about how to manage home and community services cost-effectively in the ensuing years.

Containing the Costs of Home and Community Services

All states and the federal government face the challenge of controlling spending on popular home and community services. Many government officials fear that the large number of disabled persons who do not now receive any paid services will begin to use home and community services if they are made available. The federal government controls Medicare home health spending through restrictions on coverage and through recent changes in reimbursement methodologies.

The federal role in containing the cost of Medicaid home and community services primarily involves restricting the number of waiver slots they allow. The states can contain costs in several ways—by capping the number of beneficiaries served under waivers, limiting the average cost per beneficiary, restricting coverage and payment for services, and establishing waiting lists.

States choose the number of people they serve under a Medicaid waiver, and their spending must not exceed a federally imposed average per beneficiary. These mechanisms combine to place an absolute limit on the states' financial liability for Medicaid waivers. States generally limit their average home and community services costs to some percentage of average nursing home costs and then monitor the statewide or countywide cost per waiver beneficiary.

Because programs operated under Medicaid waivers and state-funded programs are not open-ended entitlements, many states establish waiting lists when demand for services exceeds funding. For example, Alabama and Wisconsin have older people and younger adults with physical disabilities on waiting lists for Medicaid home and community services. Waiting lists of people with developmental disabilities are very common. Concerns about waiting lists have heightened because slow-moving lists could be a red flag, indicating possible discrimination against people with disabilities under the Supreme Court's *Olmstead* decision.

States also can contain Medicaid home and community services expenditures by limiting the amount and type of services covered. For example, Alabama does not cover Medicaid personal care services outside of its waivers, thus limiting the number of people who can qualify for services. For covered services, states can limit the number of visits and require prior authorization. Again, Alabama limits Medicaid home health visits to 104 a year, with skilled nursing and home health aide visits counted separately.

Providers in almost every state consider Medicaid reimbursement rates to be very low. Alabama's home health payment rates have increased only marginally since the late 1980s. Lower payment rates are part of the attraction of consumer-directed care for some state policymakers. Washington requires that all clients needing more than 112 hours of care a month use consumer-directed services, which are about half the cost of agency-directed care. Low rates may be a major impediment to recruiting and retaining long-term care workers—it is commonly observed that workers can obtain better wages and benefits working for fast-food restaurants. As with nursing homes, the federal government does not set minimum payment rates for Medicaid home and community-based services.

Quality Assurance for Long-Term Care Services

The federal and state governments share responsibility for ensuring the quality of the long-term care services that Medicare and Medicaid fund. The federal government dominates the quality assurance standards and process for nursing homes and home health agencies, but states play an important role in carrying out the federal mandates. Because states actually inspect nursing homes, have day-to-day contact with facilities, and initiate enforcement actions, their role is much larger than just a mechanical implementer of the federal rules. In addition, states have virtually complete autonomy in ensuring the quality of nonskilled home and community services, but they have focused more on expanding services than regulating their quality.

Nursing Homes

The federal government sets the quality and safety rules for nursing homes that participate in Medicare and Medicaid, and states determine compliance with these rules through their survey and certification activities. The strong federal role is due both to the large amount of federal money paid to nursing homes and to the steady stream of reports of poor quality of care in nursing homes (Administration on Aging 2001; U.S. General Accounting Office [GAO] 1998, 1999b, 1999c, 2000). There is some evidence that the federal standards established by the Omnibus Budget Reconciliation Act of 1987 have led to improvements in nursing home quality across the country (Hawes et al. 1997), but both the federal government and the states have been criticized for lax regulatory oversight. The federal government has been reluctant to devolve responsibility for quality assurance to the states because of concern that the fiscal demands of balanced budgets will cause states to skimp on quality. Indeed, some observers claim that fears about what would happen to the quality of care in nursing homes was a major factor in the defeat of the proposed Medicaid block grant in 1996 (Feder 2003).

Even with relatively detailed federal regulations, there are wide variations in deficiency rates among the ANF states (table 8-7). In 2000, the average number of deficiencies per nursing home ranged from 3 in Wisconsin to 11 in California; the U.S. average was 6 (Harrington, Carrillo, and Wellin 2001). The percentage of facilities cited for harm to residents or placing them in immediate jeopardy ranged from 17 percent in Florida to 39 percent in Washington, and the percentage of facilities with no deficiencies ranged from 3 percent in Michigan to 39 percent in Texas. While some of the differences may reflect variation in nursing home quality, most of them probably result from divergent state approaches to inspections.

While federal rules dominate the quality assurance process, most states have taken action in recent years to augment the resources devoted to survey and certification. For example, the quality of care in Michigan's nursing homes has been the subject of both federal and state criticism

Table 8-7. *Nursing Home Deficiencies, 2000*

State	Deficiencies per Nursing Home (Average)	Nursing Homes Receiving a Deficiency for Actual Harm to or Jeopardy of Residents (%)	Nursing Homes with No Deficiencies (%)
Alabama	7.4	26.2	3.2
California	11.3	17.3	5.4
Colorado	4.6	23.1	18.1
Florida	6.4	17.0	8.0
Massachusetts	4.3	25.7	24.0
Michigan	9.6	34.7	3.1
Minnesota	4.9	21.9	12.1
Mississippi	7.5	20.9	7.7
New Jersey	4.0	22.3	22.6
New York	4.6	34.3	16.9
Texas	4.1	19.9	39.1
Washington	9.3	39.0	5.8
Wisconsin	3.1	14.1	27.5
U.S. average	5.9	23.5	16.6

Source: Harrington, Carrillo, and Wellin (2001).

(Scanlon 1999). In response, the state created more jobs for inspectors and worked to fill existing vacancies; implemented an early review process to detect problems at facilities between surveys; hired a contractor to consult with homes that are not in compliance with quality standards; created the Quality Improvement Nurse Program, in which nurses provide technical assistance to borderline facilities; and established awards for innovative quality improvement projects (Scanlon 1999). New Jersey has responded to similar concerns about quality with several initiatives, among them establishing nursing home report cards based on survey results, experimenting with continuous quality improvement in 20 nursing homes under a Robert Wood Johnson Foundation grant, and providing grants to nursing homes interested in the Eden Alternative, which emphasizes holistic methods of care (Howell-White 2000).

Liability insurance for nursing homes has been a major issue in only a few states, and it has not yet resulted in any federal legislation. In Florida and Texas, however, a substantial number of civil lawsuits alleging poor quality of care ended with large judgments against several nursing homes. Liability insurance premiums rose dramatically and insurers left the market. Reportedly, many facilities have decided to forgo liability insurance coverage altogether. Consumer advocates and trial lawyers blamed chronically poor quality of care in nursing homes for these problems, while the nursing home industry held trial lawyers responsible. After a major political battle in 2001, Florida passed significant tort reform, limiting awards on punitive and compensatory damages as well as initiating a number of mechanisms to improve quality of care, such as requiring more staff. Texas has addressed only the availability of insurance, allowing nursing homes into a state-sponsored, medical malpractice high-risk pool.

Home and Community Services

In contrast to nursing homes, states are almost entirely responsible for regulating the quality of care provided by assisted-living facilities and home care agencies that provide nonskilled services. Federal standards dominate the regulation of home health agencies, but inspections and enforcement are a low priority for both federal and state governments (GAO 2002). Federal Medicaid rules do not establish quality of care standards for personal care or adult day care. For care provided under the Medicaid home and community services waivers, states are required to have a quality assurance plan as part of their waiver program, but the content of that plan is up to each state (Smith et al. 2000). The CMS has recently developed protocols for its regional offices to use when assessing state waiver programs.

As states have expanded home and community services, attention has focused on quality assurance. States are not uniform in their approach to regulation. Washington licenses all home health and home care agencies, whereas Michigan does not regulate home care agencies. Michigan ensures the quality of waiver services by onsite monitoring of providers, audits, and special studies.

Most states have modest quality assurance activities, especially outside Medicaid home and community services waiver programs, and rely heavily on informal mechanisms (Wiener et al. 2002). Case managers typically play a key role in quality assurance. In addition to developing service plans and arranging for and ensuring that providers deliver services, case managers monitor the quality of services, respond to complaints, and take action to resolve problems with agencies and their workers. Some states, such as Wisconsin, Indiana, and Alabama, conduct consumer satisfaction surveys. In most consumer-directed programs, states consider the consumer who hires and fires the worker to be primarily responsible for quality assurance. However, there are concerns that the tight labor supply and the heavy use of family caregivers could inhibit the ability of dissatisfied clients to fire their workers.

Most of the ANF states had minimal entry-level training requirements for paraprofessional workers and some level of criminal background check to weed out potentially abusive providers. The lack of extensive training requirements raises some concern that individual workers, in particular, do not receive enough training. Washington has among the strictest requirements regarding staff training, requiring all workers to complete 22 hours of training, pass a written and a hands-on competency test, and complete 10 hours of continuing education annually.

In contrast to the extensive federal rules governing nursing home care, there are no federal standards for assisted-living facilities. While the federal government finances the services component of this care to a small extent through Medicaid home and community services waivers, its quality assurance role is very limited. To date, no widespread scandals have occurred in these facilities, although at least three ANF states have experienced quality problems. Following a number of deaths in Alabama's assisted-living facilities, the state's Department of Public Health strengthened its oversight and regulation of licensure, facility administration, personnel and training, storage of medications, care of residents, and facilities' physical requirements (Health Policy Tracking Service, National Conference of State Legislatures 2000). In Washington, concerns included alleged abuse of residents by staff. Media stories in Wisconsin have reported that the majority of assisted-living facilities have been cited for caregiving issues (Zahn 2001).

There are several reasons why federal and state governments are less involved in regulation of home and community services. First, Medicare funding of such services is limited to home health; it does not cover personal care, adult day care, homemaker services, or assisted living. Moreover, home health agencies are not major providers of long-term care. Second, a major premise of the expansion of home and community services is that the quality of care they offer is better than that in nursing homes. In fact, there have been relatively few scandals among such providers (GAO 1999a; Wiener and Lutzky 2001), but whether that stems from better quality of care or merely the paucity of data is difficult to tell. Third, the physically dispersed location of home care clients and the lack of ways to measure quality make regulation difficult. States have a hard time holding providers accountable for adverse outcomes because the home care workers and agencies spend only a limited amount of time in a consumer's home, unlike the situation in nursing homes (Kane et al. 1994).

The Federal-State Mix in Long-Term Care

Long-term care is a shared responsibility. The federal government provides most of the money through Medicare and Medicaid, establishes minimum quality standards for nursing homes and home health agencies, and sets some general rules for states under Medicaid. States put up some of the money for Medicaid, inspect nursing homes, have almost total responsibility for quality of nonskilled home care, decide what home and community services will be covered, set eligibility standards, assess the financial and functional status of beneficiaries, and pay providers. How has this allocation of responsibilities worked out?

First, long-term care gets more attention at the state level than it does at the federal level. This is because long-term care is of relatively greater fiscal importance to the states and because the states have more day-to-day responsibility for operating the system. As the population ages and demand for long-term care increases, federal participation may increase, but that is not likely to occur for some time. For the time being, the federal debate on long-term care is stymied by ideological conflicts between those who believe that the ultimate financing solution lies with private long-term care insurance and those who believe that public programs will always be the dominant source of funding. The issue of quality of care in nursing homes is an exception, receiving substantial federal consideration in the form of standards, inspections, and enforcement.

Second, despite the large federal role in financing long-term care, states are fearful of what the aging population will mean for them fiscally. Ironically, even as states have demanded more flexibility in operating Medicaid and other programs, they have become more dependent on federal financing, shifting costs onto Medicare, moving state-funded programs into Medicaid, using Medicaid funding to expand home and community services, and engaging in UPL schemes. A major question is whether states will be willing and able to invest the financial resources needed to support the vastly increased demand for long-term care in the future (Wiener et al. 1994). In particular, will states be willing to invest the financial resources necessary to expand home and community services? Lack of state funding has always been a major barrier to creating a more balanced delivery system, but the current economic downturn, tax cuts, and the terrorist attacks of September 11 have put additional strains on state budgets (see Chapter 3).

Third, in areas of long-term care where states have flexibility, there is a lot of variation in state actions. Because there is little guidance regarding functional eligibility for Medicaid nursing home and waiver services, each state has developed its own approach. A few very innovative ANF states have used the flexible Medicaid home and community services waivers to provide extensive services to beneficiaries and to integrate programs and services for aged and disabled people; other states offer primarily nursing home and some home health services. Some states spend a lot on home and community services for people with disabilities, others do not.

The wide variation in eligibility and covered services raises the issue of horizontal equity. People with the same degree of disability qualify for services in some states but not in others. Medicaid beneficiaries in Washington have access to a wide variety of home, community, and assisted-living facility services that are fairly closely regulated, while beneficiaries in many of the southern states are limited primarily to nursing home care or medically related home health services under Medicare.

While some states have been innovative in terms of service delivery, they have not experimented very much in the area of financing. No state has tried to move dramatically toward either private or social insurance; they have generally stayed within the given structures of the Medicaid program. In contrast, states have tried a variety of financing mechanisms to expand health insurance coverage of acute care for children and nondisabled adults.

Fourth, the differences in eligibility criteria, locus of primary responsibility, administration, and program philosophy are likely to continue hampering efforts to integrate Medicare and Medicaid for people with disabilities. Although the dominant mode of dealing with separate funding sources is to maintain them in different parts of state government—which exacerbates the effects of fragmented financing—some states are beginning to integrate funding at the state or local level. Colorado, New Jersey, Washington, and Wisconsin have single points of entry into their long-term care systems, giving beneficiaries access to a range of services and streamlining program management.

Fifth, quality assurance is one of the most daunting challenges the federal government and the states face. The federal government has very detailed rules governing nursing home quality but few standards governing most home and community services. The result is comprehensive regulation of nursing home care but little regulation of most home and community services. Moreover, despite 15-year-old nursing home quality standards at the federal level, almost every state has experienced major problems. The causes are shoddy provider practices, a shortage of workers, and, perhaps, low reimbursement. A relatively strong federal presence has not resulted in high-quality care.

While they have expanded home and community services, states have not focused very much on the quality of those services, although problems surrounding the quality of assisted-living facilities have begun to arise in some states. Quality assurance in home care is complex and difficult because such care is delivered one-on-one in people's homes. As more persons with severe disabilities receive care in the community, the fiduciary responsibility of the states—and the federal government—may lead them to play a more active role in monitoring the quality of home and community services.

Conclusions

As policymakers consider the future of long-term care, a key issue will be the relative roles of the state and federal governments, especially in terms of financing. A number of options are possible. One is to retain the status quo, with the pros and cons described above. Another is to retain the current financing structure but to impose more or fewer federal requirements, to give states more or less flexibility. A block grant to the states for long-term care has been considered on numerous occasions, always failing because of fears about what would happen to the level of federal and state funding and to the quality of care. Additional federal mandates may achieve certain goals, but they may also strain state financial resources and restrict innovation.

Two new options are to give people with disabilities cash instead of services and to establish a program for home and community-based services similar to SCHIP. These options are not mutually exclusive. Under the first option, beneficiaries would receive cash benefits, and the choice of services would be left entirely to them and their support networks, leapfrogging over the states. States could become largely irrelevant, except for determining eligibility and level of benefits. Austria and Germany have long-term care systems configured largely in this fashion, although much of the cash ends up supporting informal caregivers rather than purchasing formal services (Cuellar and Wiener 2000; Tilly, Wiener, and Cuellar 2000). Cash payments in these countries are very popular and include people with very severe disabilities.

Proposals by Presidents Bill Clinton and George W. Bush to provide tax benefits to informal caregivers are steps in this direction. Important issues that must be addressed include adequacy of benefits, the ability of severely disabled individuals to manage cash benefits, and incentives for applicants to overstate disability in order to qualify for higher benefits. An additional concern is that without a direct link to services, there is substantial risk that cash payments will not keep pace with the cost of care. Tax proposals to support private long-term care insurance are another policy option that bypasses the states and deals directly with individual consumers.

The second new option, one that builds on state expertise in long-term care, would establish a new federal program for home and community services as a way of providing additional funding for noninstitutional services. This approach would give states strong financial incentives for creating a balanced delivery system with more home and community services. SCHIP provides a rough blueprint for how this could be done (see Chapter 9 for a discussion of SCHIP). The new program would incorporate the three main characteristics of SCHIP that make it popular with the states. First, the federal government would provide very high matching rates, much higher than current Medicaid matching rates. Consequently, the program would be funded with a great deal of federal money and only limited state funds. Second, in order to give states a strong sense of ownership, they would have considerable flexibility in how they design and administer the program. And third, states would not have to operate the new program as an individual entitlement program, which would take away the fear of runaway costs. Although the new program would have many similarities to SCHIP, this approach can also be seen as a scaled-down version of the long-term care program proposed by President Bill Clinton in 1993–94 (Wiener et al. 2001). The key to this new program would be a substantial infusion of new federal funds.

Applying these program features to a new long-term care program for home and community services sitting on top of the existing Medicaid program could help change the balance of the delivery system and even out interstate disparities in coverage. In particular, it would create strong incentives for states to use home and community services rather than institutional care. Issues include coordination between Medicaid and the new program and the potential that the new capped program would be inadequately funded.

As the population ages, the need for additional long-term care services is inevitable. Under the current system, both the federal government and state governments play major roles in financing care, organizing services, and monitoring quality. States have been the locus of innovation, but new approaches, such as consumer-directed home care and assisted-living facilities, have been limited to a modest number of states. The states are increasingly dependent on federal financing and will probably need additional federal money if they are to make further progress in reforming the long-term care system. How these two levels of government work together, and do not work together, has major consequences for a large and growing number of people with disabilities.

NOTES

1. Urban Institute calculations based on Centers for Medicare and Medicaid Services (CMS) estimates of national health expenditures for 2000 and Health Care Financing Administration (HCFA) 64 data for 2000 and 2001 (Burwell, Eiken, and Sredl 2002; CMS 2003).

2. Authors' calculations based on HCFA 64 data provided in Burwell et al. (2002) and Nawrocki and Gregory (2000).

3. Urban Institute calculations based on HCFA 64 data (Burwell et al. 2002).

REFERENCES

Administration on Aging. 2001. "2000 National Ombudsman Reporting System Data Tables." Washington, D.C.: U.S. Department of Health and Human Services. http://www.aoa.gov/ltcombudsman/2000nors/default.htm. (Accessed February 18, 2002.)

Alecxih, Lisa Maria B., Karen Linkins, Sharon Zeruld, and Christina Neill. 2001. *Wisconsin Family Care Implementation Process Evaluation, Report II, Final Report.* Prepared for the Wisconsin Legislative Audit Agency. Fairfax, Va.: The Lewin Group.

Alecxih, Lisa Maria B., Steven Lutzky, Karen Linkins, Sharon Zeruld, and Christina Neill. 2000. *Wisconsin Family Care Implementation Process Evaluation Report.* Prepared for the Wisconsin Legislative Audit Bureau. Fairfax, Va.: The Lewin Group.

American Health Care Association. 2001. *Facts and Trends: Nursing Facility Sourcebook, 2001.* Washington, D.C.: American Health Care Association.

American Health Line. 2001. "Minnesota: Long-Term Care Worker Salary Hike Considered." March 7.

Branch, Laurence G., Robert F. Coulam, and Yvonne A. Zimmerman. 1995. "The PACE Evaluation: Initial Findings." *Gerontologist* 35(3): 349–59.

Bruen, Brian, and John Holahan. 2002. "Acceleration of Medicaid Spending Reflects Mounting Pressures." Washington, D.C.: The Henry J. Kaiser Family Foundation. http://www.kff.org/content/2002/20020611/4056.pdf#note1. (Accessed May 5, 2003.)

Bruen, Brian, Joshua M. Wiener, and Seema Thomas. 2003. *Medicaid Eligibility Policy for Aged, Blind and Disabled Beneficiaries.* Washington, D.C.: American Association of Retired Persons.

Burwell, Brian. 2001. "Home and Community Based Services Waiver Data." Presentation at the 19th Annual National Home and Community-Based Services Waiver Conference, Arlington, Va., October 22.

Burwell, Brian, Steve Eiken, and Kate Sredl. 2002. *Medicaid Long-Term Care Expenditures in FY 2001.* Memo, May 10. Cambridge, Mass.: The MEDSTAT Group, Inc.

Centers for Medicare and Medicaid Services (CMS). 2003. "Table 9: Personal Health Care Expenditures, by Type of Expenditure and Source of Funds, Calendar Years 1993–2001." http://www.cms.hhs.gov/statistics/nhe/historical/t9.asp. (Accessed May 5, 2003.)

Cohen, Marc A., Nanda Kumar, and Stanley S. Wallack. 1994. "Long-Term Care Insurance and Medicaid." *Health Affairs* 13(3): 127–39.

Coughlin, Teresa A., Brian K. Bruen, and Jennifer King. 2003. *State Use of Medicaid UPL and DSH Financing Mechanisms.* Washington, D.C.: The Henry J. Kaiser Family Foundation.

Coughlin, Teresa A., Joshua M. Wiener, Jill Marsteller, Stephanie Soscia, and Debra J. Lipson. 1998. *Health Policy for Low-Income People in Wisconsin.* Washington, D.C.: The Urban Institute. *Assessing the New Federalism* State Reports.

Cuellar, Alison Evans, and Joshua M. Wiener. 2000. "Can Social Insurance for Long-Term Care Work? The Case of Germany." *Health Affairs* 19(3): 8–25.

Doty, Pamela, A. E. Benjamin, Ruth E. Matthias, and Todd M. Frankle. 1999. "Summary: In-Home Supportive Services for the Elderly and Disabled: A Comparison of Client-Directed and Professional Management Models of Service Delivery." http://aspe.hhs.gov/daltcp/reports/ihss.htm. (Accessed July 15, 2002).

Eiken, Steve, and Brian Burwell. 2002. *Medicaid HCBS Waiver Expenditures, FY 1995 through FY 2001.* Memo. Cambridge, Mass.: The MEDSTAT Group.

Feder, Judith. 2003. "Perspective on the Politics of Long-Term Care." In *Long-Term Care and Medicare Policy: Can We Improve the Continuity of Care?*, edited by David Blumenthal, Cristina Boccuti, Marilyn Moon, and Mark Washawsky. Washington, D.C.: Brookings Institution Press.

Harrington, Charlene, Helen M. Carrillo, and Valerie Wellin. 2001. *Nursing Facilities, Staffing, Residents, and Facility Deficiencies, 1994 through 2000.* San Francisco: University of California at San Francisco.

Harrington, Charlene, James H. Swan, Valerie Wellin, Wendy Clemena, and Helen M. Carrillo. 1999. *1998 State Data Book on Long-Term Care Program and Market Char-

acteristics. San Francisco: University of California at San Francisco. http://www.cms .gov/medicaid/services/998sdbltc.pdf. (Accessed September 6, 2002.)

Hawes, Catherine, Vincent Mor, Charles D. Phillips, Brant E. Fries, John D. Morris, Eliana Steel-Friedlob, Angela M. Greene, and Marianne Nennestiel. 1997. "The OBRA-87 Nursing Home Regulations and Implementation of the Resident Assessment Instrument: Effects on Process Quality." *Journal of the American Geriatrics Society* 45(8): 977–85.

Health Policy Tracking Service and National Conference of State Legislatures. 2000. *Major Health Care Policies: Fifty State Profiles.* Washington, D.C.: National Conference of State Legislatures.

Holahan, John, Joshua M. Wiener, and Amy Westpfahl Lutzky. 2002. "Health Policy for Low-Income People: State Responses to New Challenges." *Health Affairs* (web exclusive). http://www.healthaffairs.org/WebExclusives/2104Holahan2.pdf. (Accessed May 5, 2003.)

Holahan, John, Joshua M. Wiener, Randall R. Bovbjerg, Barbara A. Ormond, and Stephen Zuckerman. 2003. *The State Fiscal Crisis and Medicaid: Will Health Programs Be Major Budget Targets?* Washington, D.C.: The Henry J. Kaiser Family Foundation.

Howell-White, Sandra. 2000. *The Eden Alternative™ Grant Program Evaluation Report.* Submitted to the New Jersey Department of Health and Senior Services, September 21. New Brunswick: The Center for State Health Policy, Rutgers, The State University of New Jersey.

Howell-White, Sandra, Suzanne Palmer, and J. R. Bjerklie. 2001. *Transitions to the Community: A Survey of Former Nursing Home Residents Discharged after Community Choice Counseling.* New Brunswick: The Center for State Health Policy, Rutgers, The State University of New Jersey.

Kaiser Commission on Medicaid and the Uninsured. 2001. *Medicaid "Mandatory" and "Optional" Eligibility and Benefits.* Washington, D.C.: The Henry J. Kaiser Family Foundation.

Kane, Rosalie A., Robert L. Kane, Laurel Hixon Illston, and Nancy N. Eustis. 1994. "Perspectives on Home Care Quality." *Health Care Financing Review* 16(1): 69–90.

Kenney, Genevieve, Shruti Rajan, and Stephanie Soscia. 1998. "State Spending for Medicare and Medicaid Home Care Programs." *Health Affairs* 17(1): 201–12.

Laguna Research Associates. 2002. *Partnership for Long-Term Care: National Evaluation Summary Statistics as of December 31, 2000.* San Francisco: Laguna Research Associates.

Lav, Iris J., and Nicholas Johnson. 2002. *State Budget Deficits for Fiscal Year 2004 Are Huge and Growing.* Washington, D.C.: Center on Budget and Policy Priorities.

Leon, Joel, Patricia Neuman, and Stephen Parents. 1997. *Understanding the Growth of Medicare's Home Health Expenditures.* Washington, D.C.: The Henry J. Kaiser Family Foundation.

Liu, Korbin, Kenneth G. Manton, and Cynthia Aragon. 2000. "Changes in Home Care Use by Disabled Elderly Persons: 1982–1994." *Journal of Gerontology: Social Sciences* 55B(4): S245–S253.

Lutzky, Steven, Lisa Maria B. Alecxih, Jennifer Duffy, and Christina Neil. 2000. "Review of the Medicaid 1915(c) Home and Community-Based Services Waiver Program Literature and Program Data." Prepared for the Health Care Financing Administration. http://www.cms.gov/medicaid/services/hcbsprog.pdf. (Accessed July 24, 2002.)

McCall, Nelda, ed. 2001. *Who Will Pay for Long-Term Care? Insights from the Partnership Programs*. Chicago: Health Administration Press.

Miller, Nancy A. 1992. "Medicaid 2176 Home and Community-Based Care Waivers: The First Ten Years." *Health Affairs* 11(4): 162–71.

Minnesota Department of Human Services. 2003. "Minnesota Senior Health Options (MSHO): Project Summary." http://www.dhs.state.mn.us/HealthCare/msho-mndho/MSHO.htm. (Accessed May 5, 2003.)

National PACE Association. 2001. "PACE Profile 2001." http://www.npaonline.org /content/research/profile/profile2.asp. (Accessed April 11, 2002.)

National Statistics Group, Office of the Actuary. 2002. *Estimated Spending for Freestanding Nursing Home Care, Calendar Years 1960–2000*. Unpublished data. Baltimore: Centers for Medicare and Medicaid Services.

Nawrocki, Heather, and Steven R. Gregory. 2000. *Profiles of Long-Term Care Systems: Across the States, 2000*. Washington, D.C.: American Association of Retired Persons.

O'Keeffe, Janet. 1996. *Determining the Need for Long-Term Care Services: An Analysis of Health and Functional Eligibility Criteria in Medicaid Home and Community-Based Waiver Programs*. Washington, D.C.: American Association of Retired Persons.

———. 1999. *People with Dementia: Can They Meet Medicaid Level-of-Care Criteria for Admission to Nursing Homes and Home and Community-Based Waiver Programs?* Washington, D.C.: American Association of Retired Persons.

Scanlon, William. 1999. *Nursing Homes: Stronger Complaint and Enforcement Practices Needed to Better Ensure Adequate Care*. Congressional Testimony, March 22. Washington, D.C.: U.S. General Accounting Office.

Schore, Jennifer. 1995. "Regional Variation in the Use of Medicare Home Health Services." In *Persons with Disabilities: Issues in Health Care Financing and Service Delivery*, edited by Joshua M. Wiener, Steven C. Clauser, and David L. Kennell (267–90). Washington, D.C.: The Brookings Institution.

Schneider, Andy. 2002. *The Medicaid Resource Book*. Washington, D.C.: The Henry J. Kaiser Family Foundation.

Smith, Gary, Janet O'Keeffe, Letty Carpenter, Pamela Doty, Gavin Kennedy, Brian Burwell, Robert Mollica, and Loretta L. Williams. 2000. "Understanding Medicaid Home and Community Services: A Primer." Prepared for the Office of the Assistant Secretary for Planning and Evaluation/U.S. DHHS by the George Washington University Center for Health Policy Research. http://aspe.hhs.gov/search/daltcp/Reports/primerpt.htm. (Accessed August 10, 2002.)

Stevens, Robert, and Rosemary Stevens. 1974. *Welfare Medicine in America: A Case Study of Medicaid*. New York: The Free Press.

Tilly, Jane, and Joshua M. Wiener. 2001. "Consumer-Directed Home and Community Services Programs in Eight States: Policy Issues for Older People and Government." *Journal of Aging and Social Policy* 12(4): 1–26.

Tilly, Jane, Joshua M. Wiener, and Alison Evans Cuellar. 2000. "Consumer-Directed

Home and Community-Based Services Programs in Five Countries: Policy Issues for Older People and Government." *Generations* 24(3): 74–84.

U.S. Department of Education. 2002. *Budget for FY 2003.* Washington, D.C.: U.S. Department of Education.

U.S. Department of Health and Human Services (HHS). 2001. "Medicare and Medicaid Statistical Supplement, 2000." *Health Care Financing Review* (June).

———. 2002a. "Administration Announces Steps to Promote Community Living for People with Disabilities." March 25, 2002. http://www.hhs.gov/news. (Accessed April 11, 2002.)

———. 2002b. "HHS Awards $128 Million in Grants to Help Family Caregivers." http://www.hhs.gov/news. (Accessed April 10, 2002.)

———. 2002c. *Justifications for Estimates for Appropriations Committees for FY 2003.* Washington, D.C.: U.S. Department of Health and Human Services.

U.S. General Accounting Office (GAO). 1998. *California Nursing Homes: Care Problems Persist Despite Federal and State Oversight.* GAO/HEHS-98-202. Washington, D.C.: U.S. General Accounting Office.

———. 1999a. *Assisted Living: Quality of Care and Consumer Protection Issues.* GAO/T-HEHS-99-111. Washington, D.C.: U.S. General Accounting Office.

———. 1999b. *Nursing Homes: Additional Steps Needed to Strengthen Enforcement of Federal Quality Standards.* GAO/HEHS-99-46. Washington, D.C.: U.S. General Accounting Office.

———. 1999c. *Nursing Homes: Complaint Investigation Processes Often Inadequate to Protect Residents.* GAO/HEHS-99-80. Washington, D.C.: U.S. General Accounting Office.

———. 2000. *Nursing Homes: Sustained Efforts Are Essential to Realize Potential of the Quality Initiatives.* GAO/HEHS-00-197. Washington, D.C.: U.S. General Accounting Office.

———. 2002. *Medicare Home Health Agencies: Weaknesses in Federal and State Oversight Mask Potential Quality Issues.* GAO-02-382. Washington, D.C.: U.S. General Accounting Office.

U.S. House of Representatives, Committee on Ways and Means. 2000. *The 2000 Green Book: Background Material and Data within the Jurisdiction of the Committee on Ways and Means.* Washington, D.C.: U.S. Government Printing Office.

Weissert, William G., and Susan C. Hendrick. 1994. "Lessons Learned from Research on Effects of Community-Based Long-Term Care." *Journal of the American Geriatrics Society* 42: 348–53.

Whitman, Christine Todd. 1999. Governor of New Jersey. *State of the State.* January 12. Trenton.

———. 1996a. "Long-Term Care Reform: An International Perspective." In *Health Care Reform: The Will To Change.* Health Policy Studies No. 8 (67–79). Paris: Organization for Economic Cooperation and Development.

———. 1996b. "Managed Care and Long-Term Care: The Integration of Financing and Services." *Generations* 20(2): 47–52.

Wiener, Joshua M., and Raymond J. Hanley. 1992. "Caring for the Disabled Elderly: There's No Place Like Home." In *Improving Health Policy and Management,* edited by Stephen Shortell and Uwe Reinhardt (75–110). Ann Arbor, Mich.: Health Administration Press.

Wiener, Joshua M., and Steven M. Lutzky. 2001. "Home and Community-Based Services for Older People and Younger Persons with Physical Disabilities in Washington." Washington, D.C.: The Urban Institute.

Wiener, Joshua M., and Jason Skaggs. 1995. *The Integration of Acute and Long-Term Care.* Washington, D.C.: American Association of Retired Persons.

Wiener, Joshua M., and David G. Stevenson. 1998a. "Assessing the New Federalism: Long-Term Care and State Health Policy." Washington, D.C.: The Urban Institute.

———. 1998b. "Repeal of the 'Boren Amendment': Implications for Quality of Care in Nursing Homes." Washington, D.C.: The Urban Institute. *Assessing the New Federalism* Policy Brief A-30.

———. 1998c. "State Policy on Long-Term Care for the Elderly." *Health Affairs* 17(3): 81–100.

Wiener, Joshua M., and Catherine M. Sullivan. 1995. "Long-Term Care for the Younger Population: A Policy Synthesis." In *Persons with Disabilities: Issues in Health Care Financing and Service Delivery,* edited by Joshua M. Wiener, Steven B. Clauser, and David L. Kennell (291–324). Washington, D.C.: The Brookings Institution.

Wiener, Joshua M., Laurel Hixon Illston, and Raymond J. Hanley. 1994. *Sharing the Burden: Strategies for Public and Private Long-Term Care Insurance.* Washington, D.C.: The Brookings Institution.

Wiener, Joshua M., David G. Stevenson, and Susan M. Goldenson. 1999. "Controlling the Supply of Long-Term Care Providers at the State Level." *Journal of Aging and Social Policy* 10(4): 51–72.

Wiener, Joshua M., Jane Tilly, and Lisa Maria B. Alecxih. 2002. "Home and Community-Based Services in Seven States." *Health Care Financing Review* 23(3): 89–114.

Wiener, Joshua M., Jane Tilly, and Susan M. Goldenson. 2000. "Federal and State Initiatives to Jump Start the Market for Private Long-Term Care Insurance." *The Elder Law Journal* 8(1): 57–102.

Wiener, Joshua M., Carroll L. Estes, Susan M. Goldenson, and Sheryl L. Goldberg. 2001. "What Happened to Long-Term Care in the Health Reform Debate of 1993–1994? Lessons for the Future." *The Milbank Quarterly* 79(2): 207–52.

Zahn, Mary. 2001. "Lapses in Care Lead to Deaths, Records Show." *Milwaukee Journal Sentinel,* August 25.

9

The State Children's Health Insurance Program

A New Approach to Federalism

Alan Weil
Ian Hill

Periodic efforts to rationalize the structure of American government have called for greater differentiation of tasks between the federal and state governments. Clean divisions of responsibility are thought to improve accountability and yield more rational allocation of resources (see, for example, Committee on Federalism and National Purpose 1985). Nonetheless, politicians continue to design programs that share responsibility between the federal government and the states. The resulting marble cake federalism,[1] while messy, is appealing. In theory, it allows a national objective to be implemented in a manner that fits the varied circumstances and values that exist around the country (see Chapter 2).

The largest combined federal-state program—Medicaid—demonstrates the strengths and weaknesses of shared responsibility. Medicaid is characterized by a federally mandated, uniform core of benefits and eligible groups, supplemented by states' optional expansions. With this structure, Medicaid has achieved national objectives, such as guaranteeing all poor children and the frail elderly eligibility for a comprehensive set of health benefits. At the same time, state flexibility has yielded considerable variation in covered services, participation by those who are eligible, payment rates for providers, reliance upon managed care, and many other matters. Shared state and federal roles have led to recurrent tension over program costs and administrative control.

The State Children's Health Insurance Program (SCHIP) builds on the base created by Medicaid. It targets near-poor children, those with family incomes between 100 and 200 percent of the federal poverty level (FPL), who are unlikely to have coverage through a parent's job but whose family income puts them above the eligibility limits for most states' Medicaid programs. Enacted on a bipartisan basis as part of the Balanced Budget Act of 1997, the law arose from an unusual political compromise brokered primarily by Senators Edward M. Kennedy and Orrin Hatch, whose political philosophies are quite different but who share the view that health insurance coverage for children is an important national goal. The compromise was made possible by three factors: bipartisan agreement that incremental reform was the only viable option in health insurance coverage, the political appeal of doing something for children, and last-minute upward revisions in projected federal revenues that created room for the program within the framework of a balanced federal budget (Weil 1999).

SCHIP follows the Medicaid pattern of shared federal-state financing and administration, but the relationship is structured differently. Under Title XXI of the Social Security Act, SCHIP is authorized for 10 years and provides a total of almost $40 billion in federal matching grants to the states. Unlike Medicaid, the total amount each state may receive in a given year is capped. States receive a higher federal match for their SCHIP expenditures than for Medicaid, ranging from a low of 65 percent to a high of 84 percent of total program dollars, depending on the state. Medicaid match rates range from 50 to 77 percent.

Title XXI affords states considerable flexibility in designing their child health programs. States may set income eligibility standards at 200 percent of the FPL or even higher, and they may increase coverage through expansions of Medicaid, the creation of a separate child health program, or a combination of both. While states that choose to expand Medicaid are required to abide by that program's rules, states that opt for separate programs can adopt more limited benefit packages than those required for Medicaid (as long as they meet certain minimum standards), impose significantly higher cost sharing than allowed by Medicaid, and adopt various measures to prevent SCHIP from crowding out private health insurance. Particularly important for the states, separate child health programs do not have to entitle any children to benefits, and enrollment can be capped at any point the state wishes. States are not only allowed, but actually encouraged, to publicize the availability of new coverage and to simplify enrollment procedures (Centers for Medicare and Medicaid Services [CMS] 2001).[2]

Can the early experiences of SCHIP tell us what balance of national and state authority yields the best outcomes in health care? Scientifically, the best way to find out would be to conduct an experiment comparing the effectiveness of SCHIP with the effectiveness of alternative designs (such as a mandatory expansion of Medicaid to the same population) at improving critical outcomes, such as children's health insurance coverage, access to and use of services, and health status. The program design that generated the best results would have shown itself to be the best approach.

Because a scientific experiment is not possible, this chapter offers a qualitative assessment of SCHIP implementation. Comparing the experiences of SCHIP and Medicaid, its closest counterpart, one can identify areas of tension between the states and the federal government—tensions that can impede effective program design, implementation, and administration. If SCHIP has faced fewer of these tensions than Medicaid, or has overcome them more readily, that experience suggests a form of success. In contrast, if SCHIP has created new tensions or has failed to address those that have arisen, that would suggest a type of failure.

Similarly, a qualitative examination of SCHIP can reveal whether the potential benefits or costs of the federal structure are being realized. State flexibility creates the possibility that states will adopt different approaches and learn from each other, thereby improving overall program design more quickly than is possible with a unified national approach. Conversely, excessive state flexibility can impede achievement of national goals. The degree to which SCHIP has demonstrated these strengths or weaknesses of federalism is one factor in evaluating the program, even if it does not offer definitive evidence of whether SCHIP is the best approach to improving children's health insurance coverage.

This chapter discusses states' early experiences in implementing SCHIP and explores seven areas of possible or actual tension between the states and the federal government: program start-up, integration with Medicaid, benefit and cost-sharing design, program financing, entitlement to services, administrative rules, and interstate competition. Discussion focuses on how effectively SCHIP seems to have addressed challenges in each area. The chapter then describes the features of SCHIP that have helped it achieve the success it has and the implications of those features for other health care programs. Finally, it addresses the question of whether SCHIP provides a useful model for additional expansions of health insurance coverage.

SCHIP and Federalism

Program Start-Up

Within six months of SCHIP's enactment in August 1997, 18 states had submitted plans for a program to the Health Care Financing Administration (now the Centers for Medicare and Medicaid Services, CMS), and four plans had been approved. By the first anniversary of the law, 48 states had submitted plans and 41 had received approval. Within slightly more than two years, every state and the District of Columbia had plans in place, and only three awaited final federal approval (Hill 2000). Not since Medicaid expanded coverage to pregnant women and infants in the mid- to late 1980s had the United States seen such a rapid adoption of optional coverage authority.

Several factors fueled this rapid response, according to national evaluations of SCHIP implementation: strong bipartisan support for children's health insurance expansions, the availability of enhanced federal matching funds, and strong economies in the states at the time (Hill 2000). In addition, the fact that two-thirds of the states chose to create separate child health programs, either alone or in combination with smaller Medicaid expansions, reveals how appealing state officials found the added flexibility granted under Title XXI. Case studies have revealed that policymakers in the majority of states liked the fact that SCHIP could be crafted as a non-entitlement program, that benefits could be limited, and that cost sharing could be imposed on participating families. Together, these options allowed states to design programs that were "more like private insurance" and less like traditional Medicaid (Hill, Hawkes, and Harrington 2003).

Medicaid, created in 1965 as an optional, adjunct benefit program for recipients of cash assistance under the Aid to Families with Dependent Children and the Aid to the Aged, Blind, and Disabled programs, got off the blocks quickly, although not at the same pace as SCHIP. Twenty-six states implemented Medicaid in 1966, and another 11 did so in 1967. Several states with conservative political traditions, such as Alaska, Alabama, and Mississippi, were slower to adopt the program, but nearly all states implemented Medicaid within four years. It was not until 1982 that the last state, Arizona, implemented the program—and then only after receiving a comprehensive waiver from the federal government that permitted it to adopt a unique program design (Congressional Research Service 1993).

The states' rapid embrace of SCHIP is also reflected in the income eligibility standards they adopted—over three-quarters of the states set upper limits at twice the FPL or higher. As table 9-1 shows, 25 states and the District of Columbia adopted expansions at 200 percent of the FPL, and 14 states opted to cover children in families with even higher incomes. The remaining 11 states set eligibility at incomes less than 200 percent of the poverty level (Dubay, Hill, and Kenney 2002).

States have achieved significant enrollment. As of June 2002, 3.6 million low-income children were enrolled in SCHIP, an increase of roughly 30 percent over December 2000 (Smith and Rousseau 2002). SCHIP has been credited with driving net decreases in the number of uninsured

Table 9-1. *State Children's Health Insurance Program (SCHIP) Income Eligibility Standards for Children, 2002*

Below 200% of the FPL (11 states)	Colorado (185%), Idaho (150%), Illinois (185%), Montana (150%), Nebraska (185%), North Dakota (140%), Oklahoma (185%), Oregon (170%), South Carolina (150%), Wisconsin (185%), Wyoming (133%)
At 200% of the FPL (25 states and D.C.)	Alabama, Alaska, Arizona, Arkansas, Delaware, District of Columbia, Florida, Hawaii, Indiana, Iowa, Kansas, Kentucky, Louisiana, Maine, Massachusetts, Michigan, Mississippi, Nevada, North Carolina, Ohio, South Dakota, Tennessee, Texas, Utah, Virginia, West Virginia
Above 200% of the FPL (14 states)	California (250%), Connecticut (300%), Georgia (235%), Maryland (300%), Minnesota (285%), Missouri (300%), New Hampshire (300%), New Mexico (235%), New Jersey (350%), New York (250%), Pennsylvania (235%), Rhode Island (250%), Vermont (300%), Washington (250%)

Sources: SCHIP plan information available at http://www.cms.hhs.gov/schip; *Kaiser Family Foundation State Health Facts Online,* "Eligibility Levels for Children under SCHIP as a Percent of FPL, 2002," http://www.statehealthfacts.kff.org.

Notes: FPL = federal poverty level. Tennessee lowers its eligibility to 100 percent of the FPL for 18-year-olds. Minnesota's program covers children under age 2 from 280 to 285 percent of the FPL.

children (Holahan and Pohl 2002). Moreover, there have been substantial declines in the number of uninsured near-poor children (Dubay and Kenney 2003a). Still, millions of children who are eligible for SCHIP and Medicaid remain uninsured (Dubay, Kenney, and Haley 2002). A complex set of factors helps explain why, including insufficient knowledge of available coverage, administrative hassles associated with enrollment, and parents not wanting public insurance for their children or feeling such coverage is not needed (Kenney and Haley 2001; Kenney, Haley, and Dubay 2001).

As SCHIP matured, spending increases tracked enrollment growth. In 1998, SCHIP's first year, states spent just $121 million, or 3 percent of that year's federal allotment (table 9-2). In 2002, states are expected to spend $3.4 billion, which exceeds the $3.1 billion in SCHIP funds appropriated for that year.[3]

Integration with Medicaid

A common critique of new federal programs is that they are layered on top of existing programs, creating separate funding streams rather than integrated systems that work together to achieve broader objectives. SCHIP runs that risk, because eligibility for the program starts where Medicaid ends, with children in the same family sometimes eligible for different programs.

Table 9-2. *SCHIP Expenditures and Enrollment, 1998–2002*

Year	Federal Expenditures ($ millions)	Enrollment[a]
1998	121.2[b]	897,106
1999	901.8	1,806,920
2000	1,866.5	2,682,018
2001	2,627.2	3,462,442
2002	3,387.9[c]	—

Sources: Expenditure data: Centers for Medicare and Medicaid Services (CMS) data, Urban Institute tabulation of CMS data. Enrollment data: Smith (2001); Smith and Rousseau (2002).

a. Enrollment data represent average monthly enrollment for the quarter ending December of the year indicated.

b. 1998 expenditures from Kaiser Commission on Medicaid and the Uninsured (2001).

c. 2002 expenditures are projected from first quarter expenditures.

A fundamental feature of Title XXI is that it gives states a choice of how to expand children's health coverage. For the roughly one-third of states that elected to expand coverage through Medicaid, SCHIP and Medicaid were integrated by definition. But for the two-thirds of states that created separate programs, numerous challenges have emerged surrounding the coordination of these two sometimes very different programs.

ELIGIBILITY AND ENROLLMENT

To work well for families, the eligibility policies and enrollment procedures of SCHIP and Medicaid should be aligned to achieve something like seamless coverage. In a seamless system, children would be able to move easily (or automatically) between SCHIP and Medicaid enrollment as their eligibility was affected by changes in family income and circumstances. However, because the two programs are so different in their underlying statutory structure, and because many states adopted separate programs explicitly to be different from Medicaid, seamlessness has not been easily achieved. Studies have found that families are often confused or negatively affected by the misaligned rules of SCHIP and Medicaid (Wooldridge et al. 2003).

One critical aspect of simplifying eligibility has been to standardize it for children of different ages. Federal minimum Medicaid standards set different income eligibility standards for children depending upon their age, and states' choices of optional Medicaid expansions have echoed this pattern. One of the first steps most states took in their SCHIP programs was to create a uniform eligibility standard, regardless of a child's age (Ullman, Hill, and Almeida 1999). In states with SCHIP programs that are separate from Medicaid, this may still result in two children in the same family having different sources of coverage, but at least it avoids the previous situation of having some children on Medicaid and others uninsured.

States have also made enrollment simplification a priority. Using a host of streamlining strategies that were first tested and proven effective when states expanded Medicaid coverage of low-income pregnant women and infants, the vast majority of states have designed short, simple application forms for SCHIP that can be used jointly to determine eligibility for SCHIP and Medicaid. States have dropped assets tests for the application process, reduced or even eliminated the need to submit documentation of items noted on the application, and permitted parents to submit applications by mail (Cohen Ross and Cox 2000; Cohen Ross and Hill 2003).

Perhaps the most innovative development has been the emergence of community-based application assistance programs, through which community-based organizations receive either grants or reimbursement to help parents fill out applications. Such assistance programs have been credited with fueling enrollment growth (Wooldridge et al. 2003). Moreover, many of the innovations in enrollment have spilled over to Medicaid, making it easier for families to qualify for that program as well.

Unfortunately, while both SCHIP and Medicaid have been simplified significantly, the specific policies used by the two programs are often different, with Medicaid rules typically being less simple. As a result, program coordination suffers, and coverage can be lost or interrupted as families are forced to understand and negotiate two different programs.

Lack of coordination between separate SCHIP programs and Medicaid seems to affect families most during the federally required screen-and-enroll process. At that time, states must determine whether SCHIP applicants are eligible for Medicaid; if they are, the state must enroll them. This requirement is designed both to ensure that children entitled to the broader Medicaid benefit package receive it and to avoid the possibility that states inappropriately receive enhanced SCHIP matching funds for Medicaid children. States initially reacted negatively to the screen-and-enroll requirement, reporting that some families preferred to have their children enrolled in SCHIP, even if they were eligible for Medicaid, because they did not view SCHIP as welfare (Schwalberg et al. 1999).

The federal concerns that led to adoption of the screen-and-enroll rule were not unfounded, however. In New York, prior to the enactment of SCHIP, the state-funded Child Health Plus program was free to enroll any income-eligible child because there was no statutory prohibition against enrolling Medicaid-eligible children. After the enactment of Title XXI and the influx of federal funds, the New York State Controller estimated that as many as 41 percent of Child Health Plus enrollees might actually have been eligible for Medicaid in 1998 (McCall 1998).

States realized fairly quickly that the best way to achieve rational and efficient screen-and-enroll processes was to align SCHIP and Medicaid rules. They achieved this primarily by making state Medicaid programs simpler rather than by making SCHIP programs more complicated. Alignment between the two programs has made it easier for families to enroll in the correct program and to make the transition between the two when their income or other family circumstances change. Today, while state Medicaid programs are still more complicated than their SCHIP counterparts, they are edging closer to one another, and both offer much simpler enrollment processes than Medicaid programs of the recent past (Cohen Ross and Cox 2002).

Despite these encouraging trends, not all has been smooth with regard to SCHIP enrollment. After about a year, states began having trouble retaining children. It turns out that states had been so focused on simplifying initial enrollment, they had given little thought to the processes in place for renewing coverage. Some states have experienced losses as high as 50 percent; many policymakers and analysts believe the high rate can be explained largely by administrative barriers and confusion surrounding the requirements of SCHIP renewal (Hill and Lutzky 2003).

OUTREACH
One potential benefit of more state flexibility is a greater sense of program ownership by state and local administrators. SCHIP stands in stark contrast to Medicaid in this regard, particularly when it comes to states' efforts to reach eligible families and enroll their children. Indeed, evaluations reveal that states made outreach and enrollment simplification their leading priorities during the early years of SCHIP implementation and invested unprecedented amounts of creativity and resources in these areas.

Typically, separate SCHIP programs were given catchy, attractive names, such as *Healthy Families* in California, *Child Health Plus* in New York, and *Peachcare for Kids* in Georgia. Employing a two-pronged approach, most states used the mass media to raise public awareness of SCHIP and its availability, coupled with community-based efforts aimed at reaching families considered hard to reach. Marketing campaigns are characterized by colorful, attractive advertisements and print materials that present positive, colorful images of healthy mothers, infants, and children and use upbeat slogans like "Growing Up Healthy" and "A Healthier Tomorrow Starts Today" (Perry et al. 2000).

Community-based efforts enlisted the support of trusted local groups and organizations, often closely tied to ethnic communities, to promote SCHIP, educate families about the value and importance of health insurance for their children, and persuade reluctant working parents that SCHIP and Medicaid are no longer equated with the welfare programs they may have encountered in the past. For immigrant families, these workers played a critical role in convincing parents that enrolling their children in SCHIP and Medicaid would not harm their efforts to obtain citizenship for themselves or their families (Wooldridge et al. 2003).

Unfortunately, SCHIP marketing campaigns often do not promote Medicaid, even though states almost universally use joint application forms for the two programs. As a result, SCHIP is often portrayed as a preferred program that is like private insurance, whereas Medicaid retains its image as a government welfare program. These dynamics can result in confusion, and sometimes anger, when parents come forward to apply for SCHIP, only to be told that their children are being enrolled in Medicaid (Wooldridge et al. 2003).

Delivery Systems

In states where SCHIP and Medicaid programs share the same (or at least similar) provider networks, children are more likely to receive continuous care from the same health care provider, regardless of which program is paying the bills. If the opposite is true, continuity of care and child-caregiver relationships are likely to be disrupted when a child must be transferred from one program to the other because of changes in family income or circumstances. Such issues may be especially important for mixed coverage families, which have one or more children covered by each program and must therefore negotiate two systems of care.

Fortunately, from an integration of services perspective at least, most states set out to build their SCHIP delivery systems on those of Medicaid. However, in states that created separate systems of care, families have reported experiencing problems when their children must switch from one program to the other (Wooldridge et al. 2003).

Benefits and Cost Sharing

Two areas of state flexibility in SCHIP caused substantial concern among some children's advocates (Mann 1997). States that elected to adopt separate child health programs were required to cover certain benefits, but coverage was far from comprehensive. Moreover, these states could impose cost-sharing requirements amounting to as much as 5 percent of a family's income, a very burdensome amount for families with little disposable income. In contrast, states that chose to adopt Medicaid expansions were required to extend SCHIP enrollees the same benefits they would have received under Medicaid and to follow Medicaid's cost-sharing rules, which essentially prohibit cost sharing for children. In fact, it was these provisions, perhaps more than any others, that led some child and family advocates to recommend that states pursue Medicaid expansions under SCHIP (Center for Health Policy Research 1997).

As it happened, the states adopted rather generous benefits and limited cost sharing when designing their separate SCHIP programs. Benefit packages cover a broad range of preventive, primary, and acute care services, and most go beyond minimum requirements to cover important services for children, including hearing, vision, and dental care (table 9-3) (Hill and Snow 2003). Fully one-third of the states with separate programs chose to cover the full Medicaid package of benefits for SCHIP enrollees (Riley and Pernice 2001), and at least six others designed policies to ensure that equivalent coverage would be extended to children with special health care needs (Hill, Lutzky, and Schwalberg 2001). Separate programs most commonly omit services such as case management, which is often needed by children with chronic illnesses; such omissions could adversely affect the neediest children (Rosenbaum et al. 2001). However, among a broad range of persons interviewed for national evaluations of SCHIP, including child advocates, the consensus was that SCHIP benefits are very generous and are meeting the needs of the vast majority of enrolled children, including those with special health care needs (Hill and Snow 2003; Wooldridge et al. 2003).

A similar story unfolded with regard to cost sharing. More than three-quarters of the states with separate programs impose some combination of monthly premiums, annual enrollment fees, or copayments on selected services (Riley and Pernice 2001). Of the 35 states with separate programs, 31 require some kind of cost sharing, 25 require monthly premiums or annual enrollment fees, or both, and 21 impose copayments. Most of these states do not impose such fees upon the poorest of families—only eight states require premiums for families with incomes less than 150 percent of the FPL, at an average monthly amount of less than $7 for a family with one child. Eighteen states require premiums for families with incomes more than 150 percent and less than 200 percent of the FPL, at an average monthly amount of $12.50 for a family with one child. Copayments are most often required for physician visits, prescription drugs, and emergency room visits; payments generally run between $2 and $5 for physician visits, $1 and $5 per prescription for generic drugs, and $5 and $25 for emergency room visits.

Case study informants and participants in focus groups have consistently expressed the belief that premiums and copayments are "affordable"

Table 9-3. SCHIP Program Coverage of Selected Optional Benefits and Services

	Prenatal Care	Family Planning Service	Inpatient Mental Health	Outpatient Mental Health	Inpatient Substance Abuse	Outpatient Substance Abuse	DME, Medical Supplies
Alabama							
Alaska	▓	▓	▓	▓	▓	▓	▓
Arizona							
Arkansas	▓	▓	▓	▓	▓	▓	▓
California							
Colorado							
Connecticut							
Delaware							
District of Columbia	▓	▓	▓	▓	▓	▓	▓
Florida							
Georgia							
Hawaii	▓	▓	▓	▓	▓	▓	▓
Idaho							
Illinois							
Indiana							
Iowa							
Kansas							
Kentucky							
Louisiana	▓	▓	▓	▓	▓	▓	▓
Maine							
Maryland							
Massachusetts							
Michigan							
Minnesota	▓	▓	▓	▓	▓	▓	▓
Mississippi							
Missouri							
Montana							
Nebraska	▓	▓	▓	▓	▓	▓	▓
Nevada							
New Hampshire							
New Jersey							
New Mexico	▓	▓	▓	▓	▓	▓	▓
New York							
North Carolina	■						
North Dakota							
Ohio	▓	▓	▓	▓	▓	▓	▓
Oklahoma	▓	▓	▓	▓	▓	▓	▓
Oregon							
Pennsylvania							
Rhode Island	▓	▓	▓	▓	▓	▓	▓
South Carolina							
South Dakota							
Tennessee	▓	▓	▓	▓	▓	▓	▓
Texas					■		
Utah							
Vermont							
Virginia							
Washington							
West Virginia							
Wisconsin	▓	▓	▓	▓	▓	▓	▓
Wyoming							

■ Not covered □ Covered ▓ Covered under Medicaid expansion

Source: Hill and Snow (2003).

Notes: DME = durable medical equipment; PT = physical therapy; ST = speech therapy; OT = occupational therapy.

Home Health	Nursing Facility	Personal Care	PT/ST/OT	Dental	Hearing and Vision	Case Management	Medical Transportation	Translation

and "nominal." Many believe there may actually be some positive effects of nominal cost sharing—it helps distinguish SCHIP from welfare, makes families feel good about contributing to the cost of their care, and encourages appropriate use of services (Bellamy et al. 2002; Riley et al. 2002; Wooldridge et al. 2003). Furthermore, at current levels, it is highly unlikely that even families with the neediest children will approach the 5 percent cap on cost sharing set by the federal government (Markus, Rosenbaum, and Roby 1998). Among 14 states with premiums that were closely studied as part of the Urban Institute's SCHIP evaluation, 11 states set premiums at less than 1 percent of family income for a family of four, and 1 state set premiums above 4 percent of family income—but this rate was for families with incomes greater than 225 percent of the FPL (Hill, Stockdale, and Kapustka 2003).

While many politicians, administrators, and families express positive attitudes toward modest premiums and cost sharing, these provisions may pose a barrier to enrollment and service use that can only be detected through quantitative analyses. Research has found that premiums adversely affect enrollment, albeit typically when they are set at significantly higher percentages of income, and that copayments can suppress utilization (Anderson, Brook, and Williams 1991; Markus et al. 1998). Two studies of state programs that preceded SCHIP found that the introduction of premiums into fully subsidized programs led to significant disenrollment (Bluestone and Rosenthal 2000; Shenkman et al. 1996). Both studies also found that large proportions of the children whose families dropped out were subsequently reenrolled; however, evidence indicates that some of those children may have had greater health care needs, which suggests that premiums result in some adverse selection. More research is warranted on the effects of modest premiums and cost sharing on enrollment and utilization.

An important potential benefit of state flexibility is the possibility that states will adopt different policies and learn from each other. This occurred in Colorado. Hoping to promote family responsibility and avoid the stigma of welfare, Colorado adopted the highest premiums of any SCHIP program in the country. As many families fell behind in their payments and enrollment fell short of state targets, Colorado officials looked to other states and determined that their policies were outside the mainstream. State officials ultimately forgave all delinquent payments, dropped the monthly premium, and adopted a simpler, less expensive annual enrollment fee.

Program Financing

Designing SCHIP as a capped matching grant, the federal government created a fundamentally different fiscal and political dynamic than exists in an entitlement program like Medicaid. Simply put, with a capped grant, states are playing a zero-sum game against each other to obtain a share of the funding. In contrast, under an entitlement program, states can expand or contract their programs without any implications for the funding other states will receive.[4] As a result, certain aspects of SCHIP's funding have created tension.

The first challenge is how to direct funds to where the need is greatest without penalizing states that have already taken steps on their own to solve the underlying problem. SCHIP was overlaid on highly varied state choices regarding income eligibility standards for children under Medicaid and on a patchwork of other sources of coverage for children. Thus, at the time of SCHIP's enactment, uninsurance among children varied from more than 6 percent in Vermont to almost 26 percent in Arizona (U.S. Census Bureau 2002).[5]

The SCHIP statute created a formula for allocating the annual federal appropriation based on two aspects of need. One is the number of low-income uninsured children in the state, a reflection of present need. The other is the total number of low-income children in the state, a reflection of underlying need that is not affected by state policy regarding health insurance coverage. The formula shifts over time, starting with full weighting of present need and shifting to 50-50 weighting of present and underlying need.[6] Thus, in the early years of the program, funding is directed toward states with the largest problem, while in later years, funding shifts somewhat toward states with less favorable underlying economic characteristics.

The formula immediately came under criticism. It allocates less money to states with fewer uninsured children, and it prevents states from using SCHIP funds to pay for children whom states had already made eligible for Medicaid. These two provisions penalize states that had taken steps to insure children prior to SCHIP's enactment. Whether a state does or does not have many low-income uninsured children depends largely upon the participation rate of children eligible for Medicaid—and that has nothing to do with whether a state needs SCHIP funds. The controversy was exacerbated by the data source used to allocate funds: the Current Population Survey (CPS). The CPS has been criticized for the structure of its health insurance questions (which has subsequently been changed) and for its small sample sizes in smaller states (which have subsequently been increased). Some states have conducted their own surveys, and they generally find fewer people without health insurance than the CPS does (State Health Access Data Assistance Center 2001). While higher CPS figures might increase a state's SCHIP allocation, states were troubled because the figures created political pressure to enroll more children in SCHIP programs than some believed were eligible.

Controversy over the state allocation formula is not unique to SCHIP, nor did it arise solely because the program's budget is capped. Medicaid funding is not capped, but the federal matching rate varies by state and is tied to a formula that takes into consideration each state's per capita income. A number of proposals have been made for a formula based upon the percentage of the population in poverty (U.S. General Accounting Office [GAO] 1995a, 1995b, 1996, 1999).

The second challenge to the funding formula arose when a large portion of the SCHIP appropriation went unspent in the first few years as states were getting their programs up and running. While states adopted SCHIP rapidly, they were criticized for not achieving higher rates of enrollment more quickly. Various factors most likely contributed to this, including the administrative delays that can accompany a new program and the fact that some states' initial expansions were quite small. The primary feature of some early SCHIP programs was to accelerate already scheduled coverage of adolescents. Moreover, states had a strong incentive to adopt a program—even a minimal one—to secure their share of federal funding.

Low initial rates of enrollment probably received disproportionate scrutiny because of SCHIP's funding design. Congress allocated an average of $4 billion per year over 10 years, but it funded SCHIP to the tune of $4.2 billion in its first year. States were allowed three years to spend any given year's allocation, but their spending in the early years fell significantly short of available funding, leading to many negative, attention-grabbing news stories. Robert Pear wrote in the *New York Times* in May 1999 that "states are using less than 20 percent of the federal money that Congress made available . . . to subsidize health insurance for low-income families." A year and a half later he wrote, on the front page, "forty states will soon lose hundreds of millions of dollars of federal money that was supposed to provide health insurance to children in low-income families" (Pear 1999, 2002). Such stories could not have been written about an entitlement program, which gives states an open-ended claim on the federal treasury and imposes no cap against which to measure how much federal money is "lost."

Few people had anticipated that such a large amount of money would go unspent and therefore be available for redistribution. New York, which already had a program for children in place when SCHIP was created, quickly created the largest SCHIP program in the nation and was poised to obtain a very large amount of federal funds from the reallocation pool. Even so, it appeared that $500 million would be returned to the federal treasury in federal fiscal year (FY) 2001 (Guyer 2000).

Political debates surrounding the disposition of unspent funds are characteristic of a capped grant program. Most states treat the allocations made to them as "their" money, even if they do not have programs mature enough or large enough to need the entire amount. From the typical state's perspective, the obvious response to the accumulation of unspent funds was to give the states longer than three years to spend them. Poised against the typical states were a few states with larger programs built in part on the expectation that they would receive reallocated funds. These states felt that they were taking the lead in insuring children and should be allowed to use the funds that other states were not spending. The compromise that was ultimately reached reallocated some funds to meet the most pressing needs of states that had spent beyond their allocations and gave the other states two additional years to draw down their funds.

The SCHIP allocation formula seems to have achieved at least one of its intended goals—it brought about an early narrowing of the differences across states in low-income children's eligibility for health insurance coverage (Ullman, Hill, and Almeida 1999). Offsetting this early convergence was the role played by the reallocation provision. With the total SCHIP allocation set at just under $4.3 billion per year for the first four years of the program, and only $5.8 billion spent during that period, a substantial amount of money was available for reallocation in the early years of the program. Allowing the states with the most expansive SCHIP programs to draw upon the additional funds resulted in more children receiving health insurance, but at the cost of increasing inequity across the states.

Entitlement to Services

Enactment of SCHIP was almost blocked by a heated congressional debate over whether the program should entitle children to coverage. Under Medicaid, any child who meets a given state's eligibility criteria has the right to receive coverage, without enrollment caps or waiting lists. Governors were among the most vocal opponents of making Title XXI an individual entitlement, because they were loath to adopt a program that would demand fiscal resources without regard to the state's ability to pay. A compromise was eventually reached whereby states were given the option of either expanding Medicaid under the new authority or creating a separate state program. With the former choice came the requirement that states continue to cover all eligible children, even if federal SCHIP monies ran out, but also the promise of additional federal funds at the normal Medicaid matching rate for those extra children. With a separate program, states could discontinue coverage when funds ran out, impose enrollment caps when shortfalls threatened, or both.

The compromise simply shifted the debate over entitlements from the federal government to the states. In some states, as in Congress, the issue nearly blocked passage of any program. Some state legislators fully supported expanding Medicaid programs because to do so would be relatively easy, because the state had experience in administering the program, and because the benefit package was rich. Other legislators fervently opposed Medicaid expansion because they did not want to expand entitlement programs, they viewed Medicaid as unmanageable, and they believed that some families avoided the program because of its onerous, welfare-based eligibility system. Many legislators favored modeling the new program on private insurance and relying on public-private partnerships to build its infrastructure. The intense debates often led to compromise: expanding Medicaid to streamline eligibility across age groups for the lowest-income groups and creating a separate program modeled after private insurance for higher-income groups (Hill 2000).

One cannot know what the states' response would have been if SCHIP had been passed as an entitlement program. Given the history of Medicaid and the choices states actually made, it is reasonable to conclude that an entitlement program would not have been adopted by all the states, nor would it have been adopted as quickly as SCHIP was. Denying states the option of designing SCHIP as a Medicaid expansion almost certainly would have slowed enrollment in the program, yielding a greater impetus for the federal government to cut the program's budget. It also would have required every state to adopt a new administrative structure, which probably would have impeded implementation in some states. In this instance, state flexibility seems to have served the nation well.

Not setting SCHIP up as an individual entitlement may pose two problems in time. First, funding is likely to fall short by the middle of the decade. The so-called "SCHIP dip," in which the federal allotment drops from $4.3 billion per year to $3.2 billion for FY 2002 through FY 2004 arrives at precisely the time when state programs have matured and enrollment is continuing to rise. Combined with the scheduled reversion of nearly $3 billion in unspent federal dollars to the U.S. Treasury by the end of FY 2003, this dip led the Office of Management and Budget to estimate that some 900,000 children may lose their SCHIP eligibility between 2003 and 2006 (Office of Management and Budget 2002: 297). Meanwhile, the weakening economy has yielded a reduction in employer-sponsored insurance (U.S. Census Bureau 2002), potentially making more children eligible for SCHIP. All three factors make the federal spending cap far more relevant than it was when the program began.

States may respond to lower funds and higher eligibility by capping enrollment and creating waiting lists. Thus far, there is little evidence that this is occurring. The first state to impose an enrollment cap under SCHIP—North Carolina—lifted the cap after less than a year, when the state legislature approved additional general revenue support for the program. Even in the face of declining strength in the national economy as a whole and shrinking state budgets, the number of cuts to nonentitlement programs has arguably been small. Two states have frozen enrollment (Montana and Utah), two states have proposed lowering income eligibility (Oklahoma and New Mexico), and a handful of other states have curtailed outreach efforts or reversed certain enrollment simplification policies as a means of containing enrollment growth (Ornstein 2002). Still, long-term state fiscal problems could lead to increased use of these strategies.

A second concern is that, without an entitlement, individuals cannot enforce their right to obtain services under SCHIP. A defining feature of Medicaid is the individual's right to go to federal court and obtain an order requiring the state to provide all services guaranteed by the program. Under SCHIP, the federal courts can only be called upon to enforce related constitutional and statutory rights, such as those of due process and equal protection and those embodied in the Americans with Disabilities Act. States can create an individual entitlement in their SCHIP programs, but most have not (Rosenbaum and Smith 2001). To date, there is no evidence that the absence of a federal or state legal entitlement to eligibility or benefits has presented difficulties for eligible families, but such problems might emerge after the program has been in existence for a longer time.

Administrative Rules

Whereas federal and state relations surrounding the Medicaid program have been contentious for some time (National Governors Association 2002), relations surrounding SCHIP have been largely cooperative. The CMS, which oversees Title XXI, has arguably assumed the role of facilitator in SCHIP implementation, as evidenced by its placing a priority on reviewing and approving SCHIP plans in an expeditious manner; providing states with a template for their required annual reports; creating a clearinghouse to identify best practices in outreach; helping to sponsor a national campaign to promote SCHIP and Medicaid enrollment; compiling and presenting aggregate SCHIP enrollment on its web site; and sending out more than 50 letters to states to clarify federal policy and provide guidance on topics as varied as coverage of immigrant children, cost sharing, school-based and other outreach strategies, enrollment simplification strategies, the Vaccines for Children program, and demonstration waivers under SCHIP.

Interviews with state officials, conducted as part of national evaluations of SCHIP, reveal very few areas in which states think federal oversight and rules are hampering their ability to administer effective programs. Two notable exceptions are the stringent rules surrounding states' ability to subsidize employer-sponsored insurance using SCHIP funds (Wooldridge et al. 2003) and some states' complaint about federal requirements that they institute policies preventing SCHIP from crowding out private insurance.

Interstate Competition

The most visible manifestation of interstate competition is a race to the bottom, in which states compete to cut benefits. Whether such a race materializes or not, economic theory suggests that states will spend less than is optimal because they worry that taxpayers with higher incomes will leave the state and needy populations will move in from other jurisdictions (see Chapter 2; Brueckner 1998). An examination of states' behavior since their initial adoption of SCHIP provides no evidence of a race to the bottom.

Spurred in part by criticism of their low enrollment and failure to spend allocated funds, states have continued to expand their support of SCHIP. For a number of states, expansions have focused on extending coverage to children in families with higher incomes. For example, California, Georgia, Mississippi, New York, and Virginia have received approval of SCHIP plan amendments to raise income eligibility for children. To date, seven states have received federal approval to use Title XXI monies to cover low-income parents of SCHIP enrollees (Arizona, California, Minnesota, New Jersey, New Mexico, Rhode Island, and Wisconsin), and Colorado has received approval to cover pregnant women under SCHIP (Howell et al. 2002). Policymakers report that coverage of parents has led to even greater enrollment of children, and there is some evidence that coverage of parents improves enrolled children's use of services as well (Davidoff et al. forthcoming; Dubay and Kenney 2003b; Ku and Broaddus 2000). No states have lowered their income eligibility standards for SCHIP.

What SCHIP Teaches about Federalism

While SCHIP replicates the shared federal-state design of Medicaid, it balances the relationship differently. Should this balance be replicated in other areas of health policy? This section examines the aspects of SCHIP that have made it successful, considers the caveats that remain, and discusses whether SCHIP's positive features can be replicated.

Successful Characteristics of SCHIP Design

An important reason for the states' embracing SCHIP is its higher federal matching rate. Indeed, for the states that expanded Medicaid as their SCHIP plan, the only new aspect was the higher match.[7] Yet five additional features make SCHIP appealing to states and the federal government alike: its clearly stated goal, manageable financing system, administrative flexibility, choice regarding entitlements, and the Medicaid base on which it builds.

The goal of insuring children is politically popular and entails few of the ideological tensions surrounding work incentives that plague welfare programs. The goal is shared by both levels of government, so they can work in concert to achieve it. The goal is concrete. Its simplicity makes SCHIP's performance relatively easy to measure, with ever-increasing numbers of enrollees providing the basis for press releases touting the program's success.

The financing structure of SCHIP, while the subject of some controversy, makes the federal and state governments comfortable about the extent of their fiscal exposure. The capped federal appropriation limits federal outlays and reduces states' incentives for abusing the system. States must contend with funding caps, but they have experience managing other programs with caps, and they have the tools they need to contain costs.

Programmatic flexibility encourages states to participate actively in SCHIP. Flexibility is difficult to quantify, but comparisons with Medicaid demonstrate that SCHIP is more flexible. For example, Medicaid's mandatory benefit package is set out in the federal statute and regulations, while SCHIP requires states to meet standards based upon local market practices. Imposing cost sharing on children is proscribed under Medicaid without a waiver, but SCHIP permits such cost sharing within federal standards. An important difference between the two programs is legal oversight: Federal courts interpret Medicaid rules and oversee states' administration of their programs, while state policy choices under SCHIP will be interpreted by state courts.

Giving states the choice of whether or not to treat SCHIP as an individual entitlement has also been central to the program's success. The matter of entitlements evokes such strong political sentiment that it must be addressed directly for a program to succeed. In some states, entitlements are anathema because of their first-priority call on fiscal resources and their associations with welfare. For those states, the ability to design a program that is unencumbered by the practical and political burdens of entitlement is essential. In other states, the ability to draw down potentially uncapped federal funds to meet a policy objective is a strong motivation for expanding entitlement programs.

SCHIP builds upon the solid base of the Medicaid program. While children receiving benefits under SCHIP are in low-income families, they are not the poorest of the poor. Children with severe disabilities are already covered by Medicaid, ensuring that they will not be subject to enrollment caps, limits on benefits, or cost-sharing provisions. In essence, Medicaid serves as a safety net under SCHIP. This makes experimentation under SCHIP, with the implicit possibility of missteps and failures, more palatable.

Caveats for the Future

While SCHIP seems to have maneuvered effectively through some of the challenges inherent in the federal-state relationship, the program may face harder challenges ahead. Two risks warrant attention.

First, SCHIP may accumulate bureaucratic rules and statutory categories and restrictions over time. Responses to problems—perceived inequities across populations, concerns about fraud, newly identified deserving groups—accrete, making programs increasingly complex. Administrative enthusiasm and attention may fade with time as other priorities arise. While federal-state relations regarding SCHIP are good today, they may be a reflection of the program's youth rather than the enduring success of an innovative model.

Second, capped funding may threaten the long-term stability of the program. An important advantage of entitlement programs is that they expand and contract in response to the needs of the population and the costs of providing services. A program like SCHIP, with a defined block of funding, runs the risk of allocating too much or too little funding to meet underlying needs.

A number of possible problems have arisen already. The early accumulation of unspent funds prompted an unsuccessful congressional initiative to redirect some of the money (Guyer 2000). Limited spending by the states led to the reversion of more than $1 billion in allocated funds at the end of FY 2002 (Pear 2002). Neither of these events is fatal, but they do suggest the possibility of recurrent efforts to cut federal support if states are not viewed as needing the money.

One consequence of some states' not spending their entire allocation is that the funds are reallocated to other states. Experience with Medicaid shows that states with higher incomes tend to develop larger programs with broader eligibility and larger draws of federal dollars, despite the fact that their federal matching rates are lower than those of other states (see Chapter 4). Over time, SCHIP may exhibit a similar pattern. Nothing is inherently wrong with this pattern, but it could generate political problems for the program. If SCHIP is perceived as providing greater benefits to some states than others—particularly if that differential is not based on the underlying needs of the states—it may lose support in Congress.

An alternative, when excess funds exist, is to expand the program. The Clinton administration opened the door to SCHIP waivers that allowed states to cover parents as well as children. The Bush administration developed the Health Insurance Flexibility and Accountability Demonstration Initiative, which allows states to use unspent SCHIP funds for broader insurance coverage. A recent U.S. General Accounting Office report (GAO 2002) was highly critical of the Department of Health and Human Services' decision to grant Arizona a waiver permitting that state to use SCHIP funds to cover adults without children. If SCHIP funds can be spent on other populations, the political consensus that created the program—insuring near-poor children—could unravel.

In its early years, SCHIP faced the challenges associated with having more money appropriated than the states could spend. This situation will most likely change in the future. The Center on Budget and Policy Priorities (Park, Ku, and Broaddus 2002) estimates that 20 states will face funding constraints that will require them to cut their programs by 2007. In the short run, these constraints can be overcome with a different formula for reallocating the unspent funds of other states, but in the long run, the cap on SCHIP will constrain the size of state programs.

Funding shortages may not provoke a crisis. One scenario is that the existence of children on waiting lists for coverage creates political pressure to expand funding, thereby alleviating the problem. States, such as Washington, that have experience running their own nonentitlement programs for health insurance periodically find themselves with waiting lists when funding runs short, yet their programs remain popular. Still, the nation is unaccustomed to keeping children with apparent health care needs on waiting lists because funding has fallen short. It is hard to know what response the political process will yield.

Ultimately, the capped grant structure of SCHIP creates tensions, both among states and between states and the federal government, that are fundamentally different from the tensions created by Medicaid. It is impossible to know how they will be resolved, but it is unrealistic to think that these tensions will not arise or that they may not periodically pose challenges to the long-term stability of the program.

Extending the SCHIP Model to Other Programs

SCHIP benefits from some features that cannot be replicated in other areas of health policy. Children have a favored political status. Public policies to benefit them are not as subject to concerns about fostering dependency as policies that benefit adults. In addition, extending health insurance to more children is inexpensive. Children with complex medical conditions are covered by Medicaid, and infants—the most expensive group of children to cover—are covered by Medicaid to higher income levels than other children.

The political dynamics set into motion by welfare reform, enacted one year earlier than SCHIP, also benefited the program. As welfare caseloads fell, public policy focused on helping families new to the labor force retain their jobs. Providing the children in those families with health insurance was viewed as part of that task. Thus, an expansion of public health insurance coverage that in the early 1990s would have been viewed as an expansion of welfare could be portrayed in the late 1990s as an integral part of a broader strategy to move families from welfare to work. If this political shift is permanent, other programs may benefit from it as well; if it is temporary, political support for SCHIP may ultimately be viewed as an anomaly.

Strong fiscal conditions helped states adopt expansive SCHIP programs. But these conditions have deteriorated dramatically, as discussed in Chapter 3. States are finding it more difficult to fund their portion of the existing SCHIP program, and presumably they would face similar challenges if a new program modeled on SCHIP were made available.

Three distinct design features should be considered when entertaining the possibility of modeling other health programs on SCHIP: the enhanced matching rate, the pairing of capped federal funding with the state option of not operating the program as an entitlement, and the other kinds of programmatic flexibility states were given.

The higher matching rate for SCHIP would be fairly easy to replicate if the federal government chose to spend more money on health programs. A higher match gives a program favored status in state budget debates. States know that cutting their SCHIP programs yields only limited improvement in their general fund, because much of the cut simply returns funds to the federal government. With SCHIP, the nation may have found a balance point at which all states are willing to put up their own funds to meet health care needs. Therefore, it is fairly easy to imagine other programs borrowing this feature and benefiting from the state response that would probably ensue.

Extending the capped funding feature to new areas would surely be more controversial. Capped funding implies the possibility that some people with a defined need will go without services if budgets are tight or if enrollment or costs exceed projections. Many social service programs, such as child care and housing assistance, do not operate as entitlements. Even in health care, waiver programs, such as Medicaid's home and community-based waivers, have enrollment caps that can lead to waiting lists (although the ability to cap enrollment may be threatened by the *Olmstead* decision). Still, core health care services may be viewed differently, especially because untreated conditions can worsen, necessitating more spending in the long run and causing greater human hardship.

The third feature of SCHIP—substantial state programmatic flexibility—is consistent with a general trend toward allowing states to reflect their own political priorities and market circumstances in the programs they run. However, it is difficult to look at flexibility outside the context of the capped appropriation. Certain kinds of flexibility, when provided in conjunction with an open-ended entitlement, can be an invitation to the kind of refinancing and fiscal games that have plagued the Medicaid program. Complete flexibility in designing benefits could open the door to states' refinancing major portions of their current public health and safety net spending. Flexibility in setting premiums or cost sharing would be harder to manipulate in this manner.

Conclusions

The SCHIP model cannot be extended very far into other areas of health policy. For the neediest populations—the frail elderly and people with disabilities—the capped grant raises the possibility that funds will run out, leaving people with nowhere to turn. Efforts to scale back coverage of poor children from the current comprehensive Medicaid package to the somewhat more limited SCHIP benefits would be met with understandable resistance. Shifting any currently eligible Medicaid population to SCHIP would involve taking away its entitlement, which is the legal expression of the federal government's promise to cover the health care needs of the population. This shift could not be justified solely on the grounds of improving federal-state relations.

Similarly, SCHIP is not an appropriate model for the ambitious goal of universal health insurance coverage. The federal government would be understandably reluctant to commit the necessary funds without more assurances that all states would participate and that citizens would receive something reasonably consistent across the states. States would reasonably resist bearing responsibility for achieving a broad goal when the federal financial commitment is capped at a level that might or might not enable them to reach it.

Thus, the structure of SCHIP is probably best suited to marginal expansions, such as the one for which it was designed. Presumably, it could have similar success with additional groups, such as the parents of eligible children and other low-income adults who are relatively inexpensive to insure. Moreover, the model might be used to expand access to home and community-based services, as proposed in Chapter 8. That expansion is appealing because it shares SCHIP's incremental ambitions.

Nonetheless, there are lessons to be learned from the program. It has demonstrated a rebalancing of powers that holds promise for achieving the goals of both the federal government and the states. At a minimum, this can be accomplished if the federal government puts up a large share of the funding, establishes a clear objective that is shared by the states, and then leaves substantial flexibility to the states in how they administer the program.

When fundamental program objectives and large sums of money are at stake, tension between the federal government and the states may be inevitable, but good relations are nonetheless possible. When those relations are generally cooperative, it is possible to stimulate creativity, overcome obstacles, and build systems that meet the needs of the population being served.

NOTES

1. The term appears in Grodzins (1966).

2. For more detailed discussion of states' options under the State Children's Health Insurance Program (SCHIP) and states' use of program flexibility, see Rosenbaum et al. (1998) and Dubay, Hill, and Kenney (2002).

3. Federal funding for the program is U-shaped, with the amounts highest in the early and late years, and lowest in the middle. The first year of the so-called "SCHIP dip," when funding falls, is 2002.

4. In the long run, each state's behavior affects the other states because it affects the overall costs of the program; overall costs, in turn, affect the federal government's willingness to fund the program. However, none of these factors are in play in the short run.

5. Urban Institute tabulations of Current Population Survey data.

6. The formula contains other features as well: a cost-of-living adjustment and floors and ceilings on what each state may receive and how much the amount may change from year to year.

7. All children made eligible under SCHIP could have been made eligible under previously existing coverage options in Medicaid.

REFERENCES

Anderson, Geoffrey, Robert Brook, and Albert Williams. 1991. "A Comparison of Cost Sharing Versus Free Care in Children: Effect on Demand for Office-Based Medical Care." *Medical Care* 29(9): 890–98.

Bellamy, Hilary, Renee Schwalberg, Dorothy Borzsak, Jennifer Dunbar, Christopher Botsko, Jamie Hart, Michael Perry, and Adrianne Dulio. 2002. *Findings from the State Children's Health Insurance Program Focus Group Study.* Washington, D.C.: Health Systems Research.

Bluestone, Maura, and Jaren Rosenthal. 2000. *Child Health Plus: The Impact of Recent Policy Changes on Enrollment and Utilization Behavior.* New York: United Hospital Fund.

Brueckner, Jan K. 1998. *Welfare Reform and Interstate Welfare Competition: Theory and Evidence.* Washington, D.C: The Urban Institute. *Assessing the New Federalism* Occasional Paper No. 21.

Center for Health Policy Research. 1997. "Implementing Title XXI: States Face Choices." Washington, D.C.: George Washington University Center for Health Policy Research.

Centers for Medicare and Medicaid Services (CMS). 2001. *Continuing the Progress: Enrolling and Retaining Low-Income Families and Children in Health Coverage.* Washington, D.C.: U.S. Department of Health and Human Services.

Cohen Ross, Donna, and Laura Cox. 2000. *Making It Simple: Medicaid for Children and CHIP Income Eligibility Guidelines and Enrollment Procedures.* Publication No. 2166. Washington, D.C.: The Kaiser Commission on Medicaid and the Uninsured.

———. 2002. *Enrolling Children and Families in Health Coverage: The Promise of Doing More.* Washington, D.C.: The Kaiser Commission on Medicaid and the Uninsured.

Cohen Ross, Donna, and Ian Hill. 2003. "Enrolling Eligible Kids and Keeping Them Enrolled." *The Future of Children* 13 (1): 81–97.

Committee on Federalism and National Purpose. 1985. *To Form a More Perfect Union.* Washington, D.C.: National Conference on Social Welfare.

Congressional Research Service. 1993. *Medicaid Source Book: Background Data and Analysis.* Washington, D.C.: U.S. Government Printing Office.

Davidoff, Amy, Lisa Dubay, Genevieve Kenney, and Alshadye Yemane. Forthcoming. "The Effect of Parents' Insurance Coverage on Access to Care for Children." *Inquiry.*

Dubay, Lisa, and Genevieve Kenney. 2003a. *Coverage Improvements Found among Low-Income Children Targeted by SCHIP.* Washington, D.C.: The Urban Institute.

———. 2003b. "Expanding Public Health Insurance Coverage to Parents: Effects on Children's Coverage under Medicaid." *Health Services Research* (forthcoming).

Dubay, Lisa, Ian Hill, and Genevieve Kenney. 2002. "Five Things Everyone Should Know about SCHIP." Washington, D.C.: The Urban Institute. *Assessing the New Federalism* Policy Brief A-55.

Dubay, Lisa, Genevieve Kenney, and Jennifer Haley. 2002. "Children's Participation in Medicaid and SCHIP Early in the SCHIP Era." Washington, D.C.: The Urban Institute. *Assessing the New Federalism* Policy Brief B-40.

Grodzins, Morton. 1966. "Marble-Cake Federalism." In *The American System: A New View of Government in the United States,* edited by Daniel J. Elazar. Chicago: Rand McNally.

Guyer, Jocelyn. 2000. *Senate Appropriations Committee Proposal Poses Threat to SCHIP.* Washington, D.C.: Center for Budget and Policy Priorities.

Hill, Ian. 2000. "Charting New Courses for Children's Health Insurance." *Policy and Practice of Public Human Services* 58(4): 30–38.

Hill, Ian, and Amy Westpfahl Lutzky. 2003. *Is There a Hole in the Bucket? Understanding SCHIP Retention.* Washington, D.C.: The Urban Institute.

Hill, Ian, and Jennifer Snow. 2003. *Are Children Covered for the Benefits They Need? An Assessment of Service Coverage under SCHIP.* Washington, D.C.: The Urban Institute.

Hill, Ian, Corinna Hawkes, and Mary Harrington. 2003. *Congressionally Mandated Evaluation of SCHIP: Final Cross-Cutting Report on Findings from Case Studies of Ten States.* Washington, D.C.: U.S. Department of Health and Human Services.

Hill, Ian, Amy Westpfahl Lutzky, and Renee Schwalberg. 2001. *Are We Responding to Their Needs? States' Early Experiences Serving Children with Special Health Care Needs under SCHIP.* Washington, D.C.: The Urban Institute. *Assessing the New Federalism* Occasional Paper No. 48.

Hill, Ian, Holly Stockdale, and Heidi Kapustka. 2003. *SCHIP Cost Sharing—What Do Case Studies Tell Us about Policies, Their Implementation, and Perceived Effects?* Washington, D.C.: The Urban Institute.

Holahan, John, and Mary Beth Pohl. 2002. "Changes in Insurance Coverage: 1994–2000 and Beyond." *Health Affairs* Web Exclusive at http://www.healthaffairs.org /WebExclusives/Holahan_Web_Excl_040302.htm. (Accessed April 29, 2003.)

Howell, Embry, Ruth Almeida, Lisa Dubay, and Genevieve Kenney. 2002. "Early Experiences Covering Parents under SCHIP." Washington, D.C.: The Urban Institute. *Assessing the New Federalism* Policy Brief A-51.

Kaiser Commission on Medicaid and the Uninsured. 2001. *Trends in CHIP Expenditures: State-by-State Data.* Washington, D.C.: The Kaiser Commission on Medicaid and the Uninsured.

Kenney, Genevieve, and Jennifer Haley. 2001. "Why Aren't More Uninsured Children Enrolled in Medicaid or SCHIP?" Washington, D.C.: The Urban Institute. *Assessing the New Federalism* Policy Brief B-35.

Kenney, Genevieve, Jennifer Haley, and Lisa Dubay. 2001. "How Familiar Are Low-Income Parents with Medicaid and SCHIP?" Washington, D.C.: The Urban Institute. *Assessing the New Federalism* Policy Brief B-34.

Ku, Leighton, and Matthew Broaddus. 2000. *The Importance of Family-Based Insurance Expansions: New Research Findings about State Health Reforms.* Washington, D.C.: Center on Budget and Policy Priorities.

Mann, Cindy. 1997. *Why Not Medicaid? Using Child Health Funds to Expand Coverage through the Medicaid Program.* Washington, D.C.: Center for Budget and Policy Priorities.

Markus, Anne, Sara Rosenbaum, and Dylan Roby. 1998. *CHIP, Health Insurance Premiums and Cost Sharing: Lessons from the Literature.* Washington, D.C.: George Washington University.

McCall, H. C. 1998. "McCall Calls for Expanded Health Coverage for New York's Uninsured Children; Urges Governor, Legislature to End Delays and Act to Improve Access." Albany: New York State Controller's Office.

National Governors Association. 2002. *Policy Positions.* Policy HR-32. Health Reform Policy. Washington, D.C.: National Governors Association.

Office of Management and Budget. 2002. *Analytical Perspectives, Budget of the United States Government, Fiscal Year 2001.* Washington, D.C.: Office of Management and Budget.

Ornstein, Charles. 2002. "States Cut Back Coverage for Poor." *Los Angeles Times,* February 25, p. A1.

Park, Edwin, Leighton Ku, and Matthew Broaddus. 2002. *OMB Estimates Indicate that 900,000 Children Will Lose Health Insurance Due to Reductions in Federal SCHIP Funding.* Washington, D.C.: Center on Budget and Policy Priorities.

Pear, Robert. 1999. "Many States Slow to Use Children's Insurance Fund." *New York Times,* May 9, p. A1.

————. 2002. "States Forfeit Unspent U.S. Money for Child Health." *New York Times,* October 14, p. A17.

Perry, Michael, Vernon K. Smith, Catherine N. Smith, and Christina Chang. 2000. *Marketing Medicaid and CHIP: A Study of State Advertising Campaigns.* Washington, D.C.: The Kaiser Commission on Medicaid and the Uninsured.

Riley, Trish, and Cynthia Pernice. 2001. *Charting SCHIP.* Portland, Maine: National Academy for State Health Policy.

Riley, Trish, Cynthia Pernice, Michael Perry, and Susan Kannel. 2002. *Why Eligible Children Lose or Leave SCHIP.* Portland, Maine: National Academy for State Health Policy.

Rosenbaum, Sara, and Barbara Smith. 2001. "State SCHIP Design and the Right to Coverage." Policy Brief No. 1. Washington, D.C.: George Washington University Center for Health Services Research and Policy.

Rosenbaum, Sara, Anne Markus, Colleen Sonosky, and Lee Repasch. 2001. "State Benefit Design Choices under SCHIP—Implications for Pediatric Health Care." Policy Brief No. 2. Washington, D.C.: George Washington University Center for Health Services Research and Policy.

Rosenbaum, Sara, Kay Johnson, Colleen Sonosky, Anne Markus, and Chris DeGraw. 1998. "The Children's Hour: The State Children's Health Insurance Program." *Health Affairs* 17(1): 75–89.

Schwalberg, Renee, Ian Hill, Hilary Bellamy, and Judith Gallagher. 1999. *Making Child Health Coverage a Reality: Lessons Learned from Case Studies on Medicaid and CHIP Outreach and Enrollment Strategies.* Washington, D.C.: The Kaiser Commission on Medicaid and the Uninsured.

Shenkman, Elizabeth, Donna Hope Wegener, Jane Pendergast, and Traci Hartzel. 1996. *Premium Subsidies and "Adverse Retention" in a Children's Managed Care Program.* Gainesville, Fla.: Institute for Child Health Policy.

Smith, Vernon K. 2001. *SCHIP Program Enrollment: December 2000.* Washington, D.C.: The Kaiser Commission on Medicaid and the Uninsured.

Smith, Vernon K., and David M. Rousseau. 2002. *SCHIP Program Enrollment: December 2001 Update.* Washington, D.C.: The Kaiser Commission on Medicaid and the Uninsured.

State Health Access Data Assistance Center. 2001. "State Health Insurance Coverage Estimates: Why State-Survey Estimates Differ from CPS." Issue No. 3. Minneapolis: University of Minnesota School of Public Health.

Ullman, Frank, Ian Hill, and Ruth Almeida. 1999. "CHIP: A Look at Emerging State Programs." Washington D.C.: The Urban Institute. *Assessing the New Federalism* Policy Brief A-35.

U.S. Census Bureau. 2002. *Health Insurance Coverage: 2001.* Washington, D.C.: U.S. Department of Commerce.

U.S. General Accounting Office (GAO). 1995a. *Medicaid: Matching Formula's Performance and Potential Modifications.* HEHS-95-226. Washington, D.C.: U.S. General Accounting Office.

———. 1995b. *Medicaid: Restructuring Approaches Leave Many Questions.* HEHS-95-103. Washington, D.C.: U.S. General Accounting Office.

———. 1996. *Medicaid Formula Transition.* HEHS-96-169R. Washington, D.C.: U.S. General Accounting Office.

———. 1999. *Medicaid Formula: Effects of Proposed Formula on Federal Shares of State Spending.* HEHS-99-29R. Washington, D.C.: U.S. General Accounting Office.

———. 2002. *Medicaid and SCHIP: Recent HHS Approvals of Demonstration Waiver Projects Raise Concerns.* GAO-02-817. Washington, D.C.: U.S. General Accounting Office.

Weil, Alan. 1999. "The New Child Health Insurance Program: A Carefully Crafted Compromise." Paper presented at Henry J. Kaiser Family Foundation Conference, *Options for Expanding Health Insurance Coverage: What Difference Do Different Approaches Make?* Washington, D.C., February 17.

Wooldridge, Judith, Ian Hill, Mary Harrington, Genevieve Kenney, Corinna Hawkes, Jennifer Haley. 2003. *Interim Evaluation Report: Congressionally Mandated Evaluation of the State Children's Health Insurance Program.* Washington, D.C.: Mathematica Policy Research, Inc., and The Urban Institute.

10

Making Medicaid a National Program

Medicare as a Model

Marilyn Moon

M edicare and Medicaid were created in 1965 by the same legislation, but they have taken distinctly different paths over time. While both have played crucial roles in expanding health insurance coverage in the United States, the Medicare program has achieved greater public acceptance and satisfaction. Medicare is a national program with uniform benefits, making it easy to understand. In contrast, Medicaid is a joint federal-state program targeted at people with low incomes and assets. It is complicated, varying by state across a wide range of dimensions. This chapter considers whether a program like Medicare might meet the needs of low-income Americans better than the current federal-state partnership.

Most discussion concerning changes to the Medicaid program focuses on how much flexibility should be given to states, how federal matching contributions could be adjusted, and, occasionally, whether some pieces of Medicaid should be pulled out and made the responsibility of the federal government. Much less frequently discussed is the option of turning Medicaid, or sizable shares of it, over to the federal government. The most obvious barrier is the federal government's lack of enthusiasm for taking on more responsibilities, particularly in this time of economic troubles. Nonetheless, states are in even greater fiscal distress. A federal effort could aid states and reduce the serious inequities that exist in access to care for vulnerable populations.

Is there something about treating low-income people that needs to be handled at the state level? Or has it simply been done this way because Medicaid replaced and expanded targeted programs that also followed a federal-state model? The demographic categories for Medicaid eligibility were traditionally linked to the income assistance programs controlled, at least initially, at the state level. But the links between state income assistance programs changed over the years, with the advent of Supplemental Security Income (SSI) and the delinking of categorical eligibility from Aid to Families with Dependent Children (AFDC). Did these changes make the structure of Medicaid an anachronism? Is a clean break needed, with the federal government taking full responsibility for this program?

This chapter examines the implications of moving Medicaid from a joint federal-state responsibility to a purely national program, such as Medicare. The new model would be a federal program that standardizes benefits, eligibility, and payment systems. States would be allowed to supplement or wrap around the basic program (probably with the current federal matching rates), and those that offer generous benefits and eligibility now might continue to do so. The goals would be to achieve a more uniform program across the states and to expand coverage to more of the low-income population. In this sense, the new model would resemble SSI, which establishes a national floor of cash benefits for the disabled and elderly but allows states to add benefits to some or all of the eligible groups.

The chapter begins with a discussion of why it may make sense to turn Medicaid into a national program for all or part of the services it provides. Next is an examination of the advantages offered by retaining control at the state level, followed by a consideration of what a federal program might look like. The chapter concludes with some discussion of the political and practical issues surrounding such a policy change.

Making Medicaid a National Program

The lack of health insurance for a substantial portion of Americans is a serious national problem. Uninsurance rates vary across the country, but the consequences are felt on a national scale. For example, children who receive poor medical care are likely to have problems as they become workers, and there is no guarantee that they will remain in the same state where they grew up. Similarly, older Americans who retire often relocate to areas far from where they originally lived and worked, sometimes leaving family behind. When they need long-term care, they may remain in place or return to be close to family members. This mobility raises issues about standardization of benefits and eligibility. The high costs of caring for individuals, lower worker productivity from continuing health care problems, and even concerns about public health issues such as HIV treatment and prevention know no state boundaries. Thus far, the federal response has been to offer generous matching payments to states. But, while the federal contributions to Medicaid have helped reduce the number of uninsured persons, substantial numbers remain—and they are disproportionately high in some states.

The history of Medicaid has been one of tremendous diversity in the treatment of those it serves. This is more than just a case of rich states versus poor states. Attitudes toward people with low incomes vary across the country. Even within the Medicaid program, there is considerable variation in how groups are treated (for example, children versus the disabled) and in how care is provided. Because uninsurance is a national problem, a strong case can be made for establishing national standards of coverage, eligibility, and delivery of care.

The federal government has a greater ability to raise taxes, particularly during economic downturns, and it can produce economies of scale in evaluating delivery systems, overseeing quality, and refining payments. Finally, the combined federal-state structure generates complexities that most likely raise the costs of administering and overseeing the Medicaid program.

Equity

States differ dramatically in the Medicaid benefits they offer. As explained in Chapter 4, rates of employer-sponsored insurance, which also vary substantially, are a very important factor in determining the number of uninsured persons in a state. How many low-income individuals remain without insurance depends to a significant degree on the Medicaid program and, increasingly, on the State Children's Health Insurance Program (SCHIP). States thus begin with different sizes of uninsured populations and make different efforts to close the gap between the insured and the uninsured. For these reasons, uninsurance rates vary greatly. The resulting problems with access to care and health status are an important cause for concern (Hadley 2002).

Over the years, the federal government has used differential matching rates to encourage states that devote proportionately fewer resources to Medicaid to raise their standards. For example, Mississippi receives a matching rate of 77 percent from the federal government. Just $1 of state spending brings in $3 of federal money. Yet enormous disparities remain, with Mississippi and other low-income states offering much less generous benefits than wealthier states such as New York and Massachusetts. Some observers have suggested that the higher matching rates available from SCHIP and the greater flexibility that program allows states will make it popular even in areas where Medicaid is inadequate. The higher matching rates smooth, but do not eliminate, variations across states, suggesting that if equity is the key concern, a federal program with national standards would make more sense.

Determining eligibility for a means-tested program usually requires government oversight, if not control. The federal government establishes minimum bounds for Medicaid, but to expand coverage without man-dating change, it has to give states incentives for equalizing their eligibility standards. Instead, it could establish those rules and apply them uniformly. Further, application processes—tools that can be used by states to encour-age or discourage participation—could also be standardized.

Another consequence of creating a federal program to ensure that low-income individuals have access to health care would be to shift resources from richer to poorer states, assuming that the national minimum would be considerably higher than what is now offered in many states. With no additional resources—in fact, with a likely decline in demands on the treasuries of low-income states—eligibility and the delivery of care could be improved, because standards would rise to meet the new national minimum. The other side of the coin—potential losses to states like Massachusetts that have long used open-ended federal matching rates to provide a generous program—is discussed below.

Financing

The federal government has a stronger financial base from which to pro-vide benefits. As the entity first in line to levy taxes, the federal government relies on personal and corporate income taxes and payroll taxes, all of which have broad revenue bases. Federal income taxes are progressive, thus distributing the burdens of aiding low-income individuals more equitably. The states' ability to tax these same sources is substantially restricted by the existence of federal taxes. Moreover, interstate competition makes states reluctant to raise taxes for fear of losing business or population. Therefore, state income taxes, for example, are substantially lower than federal income taxes. States often rely on excise taxes, which are more regressive than most federal taxes.

The problems that states face in financing Medicaid are not likely to decline in the future. The aging of the baby boom generation suggests that demands for long-term care services and benefits to supplement Medicare will expand. Moreover, if employer-sponsored insurance declines, the burden of caring for children and their families will most likely increase. Finally, health care cost growth shows few signs of slowing down, at least in the near term. Thus, demands for health care protections are likely to grow more rapidly than the revenue base of many state governments (see Chapter 3).

In periods of economic downturn or simply slow growth, federal spending tends not to fall off as sharply as state and local government spending. The federal government can, and often does, use deficit spending as a means of bolstering the economy. Most states may not use deficit spending. They must balance their budgets, which leads them to cut back on programs. Because demand for health care assistance for persons with low incomes is likely to rise precisely when the economy is weak, a strong argument can be made that the federal government is in a far better position than the states to meet that demand. The ability of the federal government to step in with spending during downturns is referred to as countercyclical spending. In fact, in 2003, a number of proposals were made for the federal government to adjust state matching rates or make other changes so as to send dollars to the states to help with Medicaid and other programs for low-income persons.

Any level of government that contributes a substantial amount of resources to an activity is likely to demand accountability, if not direct control. The track record of states in using the Medicaid program as a conduit for other expenditures—thus increasing their flow of revenues and allowing them to undertake other activities, as described in Chapter 5—has undermined many federal policymakers' enthusiasm for funding the Medicaid program more generously. The upper payment limit schemes and other efforts by states to maximize Medicaid payments without a commensurate increase in care or state expenditures have frustrated federal policymakers, leading some to conclude that the states can no longer be trusted to do their share.

Complexity of Administration and Care Delivery

The federal government has established a broad range of regulations and requirements to achieve its goals of controlling the Medicaid program. The states, in turn, complain bitterly about the lack of flexibility this gives them to undertake creative initiatives. In practice, both sides have considerable ability to affect how care is delivered and to whom. If the program were moved to the federal government, complexity would decline because only one unit of government would be involved in decisionmaking.[1] Moreover, consistency in treatment of enrollees should improve. Finally, Medicare's achievements in terms of low administrative costs and innovations in developing prospective payment systems indicate that the federal government can be a successful overseer of health care (Moon 2000).

Another important advantage that a federal program could presumably offer would be better coordination for those elderly persons and disabled persons who are currently eligible for both Medicare and Medicaid. Known as dual eligibles, these individuals are a very important subgroup of both programs, because they are financially vulnerable and often very sick. In 1997, for instance, dual eligibles accounted for about 17 percent of the Medicare population and about 28 percent of Medicare expenditures, and they represented about 19 percent of Medicaid beneficiaries and 35 percent of expenditures (Clark and Hulbert 1998). The states and the federal government have been wrangling for years over who should control financing and services for this important group.

In the meantime, individuals are left to contend with two separate programs, each of which vies to have the other foot the bill for as many services as possible. That is one reason why more institutionalized beneficiaries are hospitalized each year than would be the case if the best care were being delivered. Medicaid-paid nursing homes sometimes believe they can save costs by shipping sick patients to Medicare-financed hospitals. Medicaid often provides incentives for such activities by paying less than is required to give patients appropriate care in the nursing home (Meiners 1996). It should be noted, however, that if some services like long-term care are left to the states, coordination problems would remain.

There is some discussion of new federal efforts to reduce the number of uninsured persons in the United States. One approach would be to use tax credits. Another would be to expand coverage under programs such as SCHIP or Medicaid. In either case, the bulk of the funding would come from the federal government. If the federal government does move in this direction, it may be a good idea to have most publicly supported health care under the control of just one level of government.

Economies of scale in evaluating programs, refining payment structures, and conducting evaluations of the effectiveness of care all support federal oversight. Many state governments have few such resources on which to draw, and even if they did, they would end up duplicating efforts. Medicaid has not established a track record of standardizing administrative statistics or other data that would allow the federal government to collect information from states and then process it. Quality and timeliness of data remain problems. In contrast, Medicare data are standardized, enabling a wide range of researchers, both in and out of government, to use them easily. Such resources are important not only for evaluating activities but also for counterbalancing the lobbying of powerful interest groups pushing their own agendas. (It is not clear, however, that the federal government has a substantially better record than the states of resisting the influence of the health care industry, as discussed below.) So again, a federal approach could offer advantages to the Medicaid program.

Keeping Medicaid at the State Level

The case for moving Medicaid to the national level as a uniform program is not clear-cut. For a number of reasons, Medicaid might be kept at the state level or at least under state supervision. Alternatively, some pieces of Medicaid might appropriately be kept at the state level and some moved to the federal level.

Health Care Is Local

Health care varies substantially across the United States. Some parts of the country have much higher rates of hospitalization than others. Certain procedures are performed more frequently in some regions than others. The role of specialists versus primary care physicians also differs. These differences can be found regardless of the health insurance source, whether Medicaid, Medicare, or employer-sponsored insurance. While a number of studies have documented such variations, there is no consensus on why differences remain over time or what levels of care are most desirable or appropriate. In that sense, health care is local and may respond better to control at a level lower than the federal government. On the other hand, there is a legitimate question about whether local variation is defensible, particularly when there is evidence indicating what treatments and procedures are most appropriate.

If local areas continue to vary in the care they deliver, a decision could be made to keep responsibility for low-income health programs in state hands—thus allowing participants to receive the same type of care as other people in the area—rather than establishing national standards that would apply only to public programs. On the other hand, Medicare allows considerable variation in care delivery and use of services. Beneficiaries' freedom to go to doctors and hospitals in the traditional fee-for-service part of the program allows them to participate in care in much the same way as the nonelderly do in different areas of the country.

Medicare has not done as well as Medicaid in establishing managed-care options for its beneficiaries. Among the problems that the Medicare+ Choice option has faced is the difficulty of establishing appropriate payment levels for plans in various areas of the country. Before 1997, payments were too high, thus attracting a large number of health maintenance organizations (HMOs). In response to the restrictions on payment growth mandated by the Balanced Budget Act of 1997, health care plans have begun to pull out of Medicare or restrict the extra benefits they offer. The availability of Medicare+Choice is therefore spotty, and plans vary in terms of what additional benefits they offer (Gold 2001).

One of the expectations for Medicare managed care was that it could help move the system toward a national norm of care through active management by health plans. Instead, the plans now participating in Medicare are seeking to return to a payment system that reflects local differences in health care delivery.

Medicaid has also faced crises with managed care, but it has usually been able to negotiate new payment levels and arrangements to retain managed care as a major delivery structure. This reflects both the willingness of states to accept Medicaid-only managed care plans and the fact that children and young adults—who make up the bulk of Medicaid managed care participants—have fewer and less complex health care needs than Medicare beneficiaries.

Innovation and Experimentation

Should any particular aspects of Medicaid be retained at the local level? In what ways have states taken advantage of the ability to experiment and develop their own approaches? To what extent have other states learned about and adopted new approaches? These questions relate to a classic reason for allowing differences by states—the claim that states can be laboratories for change. In theory, innovation should take place more quickly on the state level, because it is difficult to allow a large number of different approaches to coexist in a national program. In addition, a lower level of government can try new approaches without affecting the overall health care delivery system. (If the argument of health care as local is correct, then experimentation by states may have a big impact on the state's health care system.)

In practice, the results of states as laboratories for innovation are mixed. Many states do not try new ways of providing or delivering care. Further, innovation in expanding coverage has been limited. This may result from lack of resources or lack of expertise in overseeing demonstrations or studying other states' activities. Or it may result from fear of being so innovative that people from other states will move in to take advantage of the improvements.

States have been very aggressive in moving enrollees into Medicaid managed care plans. Early experiments were undertaken without much research that states could use to learn from each other's mistakes, but even later, they seem to have gone largely their own ways. In many respects, states have done as well as or better than the commercial sector in establishing managed care. They have also adapted their primary care case management model to ensure reasonable availability and delivery of care in rural areas, certainly in contrast to the Medicare program. But some of the innovation was too aggressive, causing a number of problems for states and the people they serve (see Chapter 7 for a discussion). States also have some experience with competitive bidding for providing services—an area in which Medicare has twice been unable to mount a successful demonstration (Nichols and Reischauer 2000).

Long-term care offers important examples when considering whether innovation has been effective. Because of their regulatory role and the much smaller role of Medicare and private insurance, the states can control long-term care services to a considerable degree. Important innovations have been made in developing home and community-based services— optional benefits that often require Medicaid waivers from the federal government (see Chapter 8 for a discussion). The size of these programs varies dramatically, however. Thus, while states may have been innovative in this area, they do not necessarily look to each other for models. Concern is sometimes expressed that generous states could become magnets for potential beneficiaries from other states, resulting in a race to the bottom, but there is little evidence to justify this concern.

The case for innovation is less convincing when successful new approaches in one area are not adopted elsewhere. Oregon, for example, has been very successful in using facilities other than nursing homes to provide long-term care. Yet despite the considerable attention paid to Oregon's efforts, other states have been slow to follow. Further, Chapter 8 points out problems with quality that have plagued states, with little progress in improving delivery of services.

Medicare has been responsible for a number of innovations in payment policy, and the program has a good track record in management relative to its modest administrative budget. With a broader mandate for providing coverage to vulnerable populations and some additional flexibility to allow state demonstrations (which might lead to implementation elsewhere), a federal program may do better with innovation than most states are able to do.

Size Itself as a Problem

Although gaining market share, and therefore bargaining power, is often touted as a distinct advantage for purchasers of care, large size may not always be an advantage for public programs. For example, small providers of health care services, such as local home health agencies, may have difficulty meeting national requirements for participation or reporting. This situation may bias federal purchasers of services toward chains and for-profit organizations that have the resources to deal with federal regulators. In addition, many health care organizations operate only locally or regionally, making it likely that states will be more responsive to their needs. But this obviously cuts two ways: Which level of government is better able to resist inappropriate interference with policymaking?

An interesting example of this is government's role in offering a prescription drug benefit. The Department of Veterans Affairs engages in tough negotiations with drug companies and achieves very favorable prices. State Medicaid programs have recently begun to negotiate aggressively with drug companies. Yet the debate over a Medicare prescription drug benefit has focused on using prescription benefit managers as negotiators rather than relying on administered prices by the government. Because Medicare beneficiaries consume more than one-third of all prescription drugs, many policymakers seem to fear the clout such a powerful public purchaser could wield. Drug companies have convinced many policymakers that price controls under Medicare would harm research and development programs for new pharmaceuticals. States may be able to make inroads in coverage expansions (as some have with prescription drugs) in areas that get too much scrutiny at the national level.

On the other hand, if the national government were willing to negotiate aggressively, it should be able to get even greater discounts than states. The recent announcement that nine states are planning to negotiate jointly with drug companies for lower prices underscores the possible advantages of a national drug benefit.

The Potential Inadequacy of a National Minimum

Perhaps the most important reason to be skeptical of a national approach to Medicaid is that while it would raise minimum standards in a number of states, it might actually cause a decline in eligibility and benefits for beneficiaries in states that have been leaders in providing high-quality, generous benefits. It is very unlikely, for example, that low-income persons in states like Massachusetts would be guaranteed the same eligibility and benefits by the federal government that they now receive.

While an obvious response is that states could be allowed to establish wraparound benefits, perhaps with federal matching dollars attached, would this result in a system as good as what the more generous states now offer? Supplementation of benefits or higher income eligibility might be easily accomplished, but a state's goal of offering better delivery and coordination of care would probably be hard to achieve through a wraparound benefit. For example, disease management and coordination of care, which have been initiated in some states, would be more difficult to provide as a supplement to a basic federal program. Thus, moving to a national program would entail trading the innovative activities in perhaps a dozen states for greater national equity and consistency of care.

What a Federal Program Might Look Like

Although many ways of structuring a federal low-income health program are possible, this chapter focuses on only a few that illustrate some of the issues raised above, specifically eligibility, benefits, provider payments, and administration. But first, it is important to consider some over-arching questions.

Basic Design Decisions

Any strategy for creating a federal Medicaid program must consider a few key questions that will affect its design. Perhaps most important are basic eligibility and benefits levels and how the federal program should be orga-nized. A closely related question is how much state supplementation should be encouraged and how to go about encouraging it. The federal program should be comprehensive enough to meet the desires of a sub-stantial number of states; otherwise, there is no justification for reconfig-uring the existing Medicaid program. Furthermore, it is important to con-sider whether the states that begin with supplemental programs would maintain them or eventually press for greater federal responsibility. SSI presents an interesting example of a program in which state supplemen-tation has declined over the years. A federal match of supplemental bene-fits (not provided under SSI) should provide incentives for keeping states active.

Another key question is financing—that is, what level of spending will be possible and what does it imply about a national floor of coverage and benefits? In 2002, the federal government spent $146 billion on Medicaid, and the states spent $110 billion.[2] The federal contribution would have to rise substantially unless only a bare-bones program were offered or unless some pieces were left to the states. While the overall costs to society might not change very much with increased federal financing, these overall budget issues might nonetheless constrain the federal government in what it would be willing to undertake. (This issue is discussed in more detail with the practical concerns raised below.)

Thus, a final key question is how many states would experience an improvement in coverage for their low-income populations and how many would see a decline? Moreover, if the federal government is not likely to take on substantial new funding, some of the advantages of cre-ating a national system will be undercut by states' continuing responsi-bility for providing mini-Medicaid benefits. The greater the number of states that gain, the less important the issue of supplementation becomes.

Eligibility

An important rationale for a federal program would be the establishment of a minimum standard determining who is eligible for benefits, probably with similar income cutoff rules for all populations, or at least within broad groups, such as children. All groups now covered by Medicaid should be part of any federal proposal. The core package might set the eligibility cutoff at 200 percent of the federal poverty level (FPL), with no asset test, at least for children and pregnant women. Thirty-nine states currently set coverage for some or all children (including those on SCHIP) at twice the FPL or higher, but many fewer states set eligibility that high for parents or other groups. Just seven states make parents eligible at 200 percent of the FPL or above (see Chapter 6).

Creating a federal program would offer the opportunity to expand eligibility to all low-income persons. Some progress was made in this direction when eligibility was delinked from receipt of AFDC for children and their parents, but individuals must still fall into one of the Medicaid eligibility categories to be covered. Consequently, whole groups of the low-income population, such as individuals and couples without children, remain ineligible. Extending eligibility at the federal level could offer coverage to everyone below a certain cutoff point—say, the FPL—thereby relieving burdens on many safety net institutions and simplifying the program. Such an extension would be expensive, however, and may be difficult if the federal government also takes on greater financing responsibilities for children and parents. Thus, making additional groups eligible could be treated as an option for the federal program or left to the states to provide (with support from federal matching rates). Some states have programs of their own to help such individuals, although they tend to be limited.

A uniform eligibility standard should be established for the medically needy, currently an optional group. Eligibility usually requires that individuals spend down to less than 60 percent of the FPL, and some states have no medically needy program at all. The national standard might be set at the FPL, for example. Together, these eligibility criteria would make the federal program more generous for some groups than most current programs are.[3]

One issue is whether federal and local responsibilities should be divided across eligibility groups or benefits. Areas for which the federal government is responsible would be more standardized. Thus, it makes more sense on equity grounds to shift everyone who is currently covered under Medicaid to the federal government for at least some of their benefits. Then the division between federal and state responsibilities could be limited to benefits.

Benefits

Most states provide a broader range of benefits under Medicaid than the federal government requires. At a minimum, then, the benefits offered by a federal Medicaid program need to be more inclusive than current mandatory standards. A basic benefit should certainly include prescription drugs and at least some diagnostic, screening, and preventive services. Other items that states may offer under Medicaid, such as hospice and primary care case management, might be included or reserved for state supplementation. Unless the federal government picks up all costs, some way of leaving states with the responsibility for some services must be devised. It will be difficult to choose which benefits will be offered under the federal plan and which will remain with the states.

Two areas now covered by Medicaid that are very important but that may be easier to separate from the rest of the benefit package are long-term care and dental benefits. Because these benefits can be separated from most acute care, they may present a reasonable way to have the states continue to contribute some of the costs of Medicaid. Currently, part of long-term care is mandatory, while all dental benefits are optional for all eligibility groups other than children. Nonetheless, most states provide benefits in these areas. In the case of long-term care, local attitudes and even geography can affect coverage. Under this swap, states that wish to receive federal matching funds could be required to offer both benefits at a certain level or above. Current federal matching rates could be used.

In 2002, long-term care accounted for almost 38 percent of total Medicaid spending on services, so what happens to this benefit is a major consideration.[4] If long-term care is separated from the federal benefit package, the savings could allow a more generous basic package for acute care without massive new federal funding. A more generous basic package would reduce or eliminate incentives to provide wraparound acute care benefits. It would also create substantial political challenges, because states devote very different shares of their Medicaid dollars to long-term care. Thus, Nevada and California, which devote only about one-quarter of their

Medicaid dollars to long-term care, would be better-off with this deal than North Dakota and Minnesota, which devote about 60 percent of their Medicaid dollars to long-term care.

Payments to Providers and Reliance on Managed Care

States have often been criticized for offering a comprehensive benefit package to a large number of eligible persons but then being unable to deliver the benefits because their payments to care providers are so low that the providers are unwilling to take on Medicaid patients. Thus, payment policy is a crucial piece of any federalization proposal. After some negative publicity regarding payments for obstetricians and gynecologists, many states did review their payment schedules and improve them (see, for example, Fox, Weiner, and Phua 1992). But a recent analysis of payments for dental care suggests that low payments for those services create access problems (Damron 2002). Others have found a general decline in provider willingness to participate in Medicaid (Cunningham 2002).

In economic downturns, it is not unusual for states to freeze or even lower payments in an attempt to hold down Medicaid costs. Similarly, efforts to place Medicaid participants in managed care plans have sometimes suffered from unrealistic expectations concerning the level of payments needed to entice private managed care organizations to take these persons.

State diversity in payment policies has undoubtedly affected access to care for Medicaid beneficiaries. Improvements in those policies could therefore lead to greater access in some states. Uniformity of payment systems could ease administrative costs for both the government and for providers that serve multiple states. Medicare's payment systems could be adopted for fee-for-service benefits, thereby reducing the number of public systems that providers would have to deal with, as well as raising payments. More attention would have to be paid to services that children and younger adults use, but Medicare's systems are in place and work reasonably well.

As a federal program, Medicaid would face many of the issues raised in regard to Medicare. Medicare's payment levels are generally higher than Medicaid's, but Medicare has been criticized for its efforts to reduce payment variations across the country. For example, the original goal of the Medicare hospital prospective payment system was to standardize payments after adjusting for local conditions. Over the years, special exceptions and adjustments have been added to correct for what were seen as unreasonably low payment levels in certain areas and to achieve other goals, such as helping to support sole community hospitals. In the case of adjustments for hospitals that serve a disproportionate share of Medicaid and uninsured people (DSH payments), it should be possible to devise a more rational system if the impacts from Medicare and Medicaid can be combined and overseen by one authority. But political groups are likely to form coalitions to maintain the exceptions they have achieved.

Administration

Administration includes eligibility determination, quality oversight, payment setting, and bill processing. Some or all of these functions could be centralized at the federal level, and insurance carriers and intermediaries could carry out much of the claims-processing activity, as they do for Medicare and Medicaid. Medicare's carriers and intermediaries usually cover multistate areas, and there has been some discussion of consolidating them further to standardize coverage determinations.

Alternatively, states could determine eligibility and carry out other administrative functions, as they often do with SSI. Managed care arrangements, for example, might be difficult to control at the national level. Medicare has not been very successful at it, in large part because of disagreement about how much state variation to allow (Boccuti and Moon 2002). States could negotiate with plans to provide managed care services in local areas, an arrangement that could give states enough flexibility to do more than just offer wraparound benefits, thus affecting the delivery of acute care. However, the states would have to meet more stringent oversight and reporting standards than they currently do under Medicaid to ensure that beneficiaries' quality of and access to care remain high.

One advantage of moving Medicaid to the federal level would be the ability to coordinate acute care services for dual eligibles.[5] Currently, states must not only provide full Medicaid benefits to Medicare beneficiaries who qualify, they must also manage the Medicare Savings Programs (the new catchall term for the Qualified Medicare Beneficiary and Specified Low-Income Medicare Beneficiary Programs), which contribute to premiums (and sometimes cost-sharing liabilities) for persons with incomes as high as 135 percent of the FPL (Liu, Long, and Aargon 1998).

In addition, if low-income disabled persons now on Medicaid become a responsibility of the federal government, the two-year waiting period for such benefits under Medicare would make little sense. In fact, it might be better to move all acute care responsibilities for the aged and qualifying disabled persons into the Medicare program, rather than retaining two separate programs for these groups. Thus, the new federal program would exclude the aged and disabled persons, and Medicare would have an income-related component.[6] If federalization of Medicaid were done in increments, dual eligibles could be shifted first, because the move would not be particularly disruptive and would, in fact, simplify receipt of benefits for them.

To put this in context, shifting the full costs of the elderly, blind, and disabled to the federal government would have reduced state burdens by $25.4 billion in 2002 (against a base of $110 billion). A complicating factor is that not all blind and disabled Medicaid beneficiaries are eligible for Medicare. Some of them are in the two-year waiting period, but others do not and will not qualify for Medicare disability. However, it would be unwieldy to shift only some of the disabled to the federal program.[7]

What Should Be Included in a Federal Program?

A broad range of decisions regarding eligibility, payment levels, and benefits guaranteed at the federal level will affect how much costs to the federal government would rise, as well as what savings would accrue to the states. What financial responsibilities should be shifted to the federal government? Perhaps more important, what effect will the move have on costs for federal and state governments? The answer depends upon the goals of federalization of Medicaid.

If the primary goal is to maximize the number of low-income people with insurance coverage, the program must contain mandates for states to redirect the funds they save from the adoption of the federal program into coverage that goes beyond the federal base. If the primary goal is to promote equity across states while expanding overall levels of coverage, the program could rely upon incentives for states to extend coverage beyond the federal base. If the primary goal is to provide fiscal relief to all states, the federal government could assume responsibility for the cost of a defined population currently covered by Medicaid or simply increase the federal match rate. If the primary goal is to promote equity across states without increasing overall levels of coverage, the federal government could reduce its financial support of some states and redirect those funds to increase support in others.

As mentioned above, four major variables will be in play when deciding on a federal program: eligibility, payment levels, and benefits. Eligibility is likely to be expanded in a number of states, raising federal costs. Greater standardization and increases in average payment levels are also likely, raising aggregate spending above current Medicaid standards. If the federal government does not assume complete responsibility for the program, the most likely area for division of funding is the benefit package. If funding of benefits is not divided, it may be more difficult to improve eligibility and payment levels.[8]

Examining a few possible combinations of responsibility for benefits and availability of federal matching rates will illustrate how greatly the financial balance between the federal government and the states could change—by orders of magnitude in some cases. Similar proposals to divide up the responsibility for various services—called swap proposals—have been offered in the past.[9] Further expansions of eligibility, either within Medicaid categories or for all low-income persons, are more difficult to estimate and are not attempted here.

Even the simple examples given below need several caveats. Shifting responsibility for acute care to the federal government would probably result in both greater participation, especially if federal standards are above those in many states, and higher provider payments than those shown here. Thus, the examples do not capture the costs involved in equalizing eligibility and payment rates under a federal program. If those costs were included, benefits would be higher in some of the "losing" states, and it could be argued that society there would be better-off, but the impact on state governments would remain in the same range.

The impact on each state of even simple changes will vary because the combination of services provided and the relative size of specific populations differ. Table 10-1 shows a state-by-state breakdown of the shares of spending going to each category of service (probably the best way to divide up the program) estimated for 2002. Difficulties with the data make it hard to separate out all the types of services, so optional acute care services are shown together in the table, even though in practice these might be further subdivided. Note, in particular, the variation in the share of these benefits going to long-term care and to DSH payments.[10] The long-term care shares range from about 24 percent in Tennessee and Georgia to almost 62 percent in North Dakota. Thus, states like Tennessee would gain much more than states like North Dakota if a swap proposal moved responsibility for acute care to the federal govern-

Table 10-1. Distribution of Medicaid Expenditures by Type of Service, 2002 Estimates

| State | Acute Care (%) | | | | Long-Term Care (%) | DSH Payments (%) |
	Mandatory Services[a]	Payments to Medicare	Prescription Drugs	Optional Services[b]		
U.S. Total	36.8	22.9	8.2	8.5	37.5	6.6
Alabama	30.3	3.2	9.59	10.2	34.9	11.8
Alaska	45.9	1.4	7.21	14.7	28.6	2.2
Arizona[c]	N/A	N/A	N/A	N/A	N/A	N/A
Arkansas	34.6	3.0	9.4	13.1	38.8	1.1
California	44.5	3.6	8.0	9.1	27.4	7.3
Colorado	40.1	1.2	5.4	9.1	36.1	8.0
Connecticut	21.9	3.6	6.4	5.1	54.7	8.3
Delaware	39.0	1.5	9.5	15.2	34.1	0.6
District of Columbia	46.0	1.7	4.8	13.8	28.4	5.3
Florida	39.4	5.2	12.0	8.3	31.5	3.6
Georgia	50.8	2.1	10.8	4.9	23.8	7.4
Hawaii	47.1	4.0	8.2	8.7	32.1	0.0
Idaho	35.1	1.5	10.5	13.2	38.4	1.3
Illinois	48.1	1.4	7.9	6.5	31.9	4.3
Indiana	29.7	1.3	10.1	5.7	36.7	16.4
Iowa	32.0	4.7	10.0	6.5	46.1	0.8
Kansas	22.2	1.6	8.0	11.0	54.6	2.6
Kentucky	40.4	2.4	12.7	10.1	29.2	5.2
Louisiana	28.0	2.0	9.7	2.9	38.7	18.7

(continued)

Table 10-1. Continued

State	Acute Care (%)				Long-Term Care (%)	DSH Payments (%)
	Mandatory Services[a]	Payments to Medicare	Prescription Drugs	Optional Services[b]		
Maine	27.1	3.2	9.8	20.2	36.3	3.4
Maryland	41.2	1.9	5.3	14.2	35.7	1.7
Massachusetts	34.3	2.4	8.2	7.7	41.1	6.3
Michigan	44.4	2.2	5.8	8.8	33.3	5.6
Minnesota	30.3	1.6	4.8	8.4	53.5	1.5
Mississippi	42.5	3.3	14.3	4.7	28.6	6.6
Missouri	36.0	2.3	10.3	5.7	36.7	9.0
Montana	35.9	2.0	10.3	8.8	42.9	0.0
Nebraska	31.4	3.7	10.3	6.3	48.3	0.1
Nevada	44.6	2.4	5.8	10.8	26.3	10.2
New Hampshire	19.6	0.6	8.0	14.0	41.0	16.9
New Jersey	24.9	1.6	6.6	6.4	45.8	14.6
New Mexico	53.7	1.6	2.8	12.0	29.3	0.6
New York	31.0	0.8	6.9	10.3	44.2	6.9
North Carolina	39.6	2.7	11.1	6.1	34.1	6.4
North Dakota	23.6	0.9	7.6	6.2	61.5	0.2
Ohio	31.0	1.2	9.3	4.9	46.6	7.0
Oklahoma	38.8	2.5	5.6	10.7	41.3	1.0
Oregon	37.5	1.2	6.4	10.1	43.7	1.0
Pennsylvania	33.1	1.8	4.6	6.8	48.3	5.4

Rhode Island	33.4	1.2	5.9	17.9	35.5	6.1
South Carolina	36.2	2.3	9.9	10.4	30.0	11.1
South Dakota	31.0	2.3	8.0	8.7	49.9	0.2
Tennessee	53.5	2.4	9.3	11.1	23.7	0.0
Texas	38.7	3.4	8.2	6.9	32.8	10.0
Utah	40.8	1.9	9.9	15.7	31.3	0.4
Vermont	33.6	1.5	12.0	15.9	33.0	4.0
Virginia	35.9	2.7	9.9	6.5	38.0	7.0
Washington	37.2	1.5	7.4	12.4	34.5	6.9
West Virginia	34.9	2.6	11.7	9.2	36.3	5.4
Wisconsin	26.9	3.9	8.7	9.3	50.9	0.3
Wyoming	33.1	1.9	9.2	4.6	51.2	0.0

Source: Urban Institute 2002.

Notes: DSH = disproportionate share hospital; N/A = not applicable.

a. Mandatory acute care services include inpatient and outpatient hospital services; Federally Qualified Health Center (FQHC) and rural health clinic services; physician services; laboratory and radiology services; early and periodic screening, diagnostic, and treatment (EPSDT) services; family planning (including sterilizations); nurse midwife; and nurse practitioner services. This analysis assumes that 80 percent of expenditures of prepaid health care services (e.g., health maintenance organization, HIO, and Prepaid Health Plan programs) are for mandatory acute care services. This analysis also assumes that 100 percent of expenditures for children for dental services, other practitioners, health clinics, and prescribed drugs is mandatory due to EPSDT requirements, and that 50 percent of expenditures for unspecified services ("other care") for children is also mandatory due to EPSDT requirements.

b. Optional acute care services include other practitioners' services (e.g., podiatrists, optometrists, chiropractors); private duty nursing; clinic services (except FQHC and rural clinic services); dental services; physical therapy; occupational therapy; speech, hearing, and language disorder services; dentures, prosthetic devices, and eyeglasses; rehabilitative services; Christian Science practitioners; hospice services; targeted and primary care case management; emergency hospital services; and other services as allowed by state Medicaid plans.

c. Data for Arizona are not included because spending for the Arizona Long-Term Care System (ALTCS, the state's prepaid long-term care program) could not be separated from spending for the Arizona Health Care Cost-Containment System (AHCCS, the state's prepaid acute care program).

ment and left long-term care to the states. Variations in DSH payments are also quite large. If the federal government eliminated its contribution to these payments—which often involve creative accounting—Louisiana, Indiana, and New Hampshire would be hurt more than other states.

Now look at what happens to federal and state spending under four proposals that simply shift responsibility for current spending (table 10-2). (As noted earlier, a federal program like the one described here would also raise provider payments and expand eligibility in some states. Thus, overall spending would be higher than for Medicaid as currently organized.)[11] The numbers in this case are more pertinent to the relief available to the states, but they are nonetheless instructive about overall burdens.

Table 10-2 indicates at the national level how big the shifts in spending would be if various combinations of services were just swapped—that is, if some benefits were the full responsibility of the states and some the full responsibility of the federal government. In every case, the federal government would be responsible for mandatory acute care services, payments to Medicare, and prescription drugs. The states would always be responsible for long-term care.

Two options are given for a full swap, depending on whether the federal government or the states are responsible for DSH payments. Because long-term care represents a large share of Medicaid spending, both of the full swap options leave substantial responsibility for these services with the states. In the first option, which gives states the responsibility for DSH payments, the swap proposal raises the states' burdens above where they currently stand. If the federal government were also taking on more of the uninsured, this might be a reasonable approach, although it would not achieve the goal of reducing state burdens. In the second full swap option, only long-term care is left to the states. The overall impact of that swap would be an 11 percent rise in the federal burden and a 14 percent decline in state burdens. This swap would provide modest relief to states.

The partial swap options in table 10-2 also assume that the federal government takes on all responsibility for mandatory services, payments to Medicare, and prescription drugs. But in a partial swap, the federal government continues to pay its matching rate for all remaining benefits. As a consequence, the states would be considerably better-off, because they are relieved of some responsibility and must only maintain their current level of effort for others.

In the first partial swap, costs of optional services, DSH payments, and long-term care are shared by the states and the federal government, with

Table 10-2. *Changes in State Spending for Full and Partial Swap Options*

| | | Spending by Option ($ billions)[a] | | | |
| | | Full Swap with State Responsible for | | Partial Swap, with State Spending Based on Federal Match, for | |
Medicaid Benefit	Estimated 2002 Spending ($ billions)	DSH and Long-Term Care	Long-Term Care Only	Optional Services, DSH, and Long-Term Care	Long-Term Care and DSH
Mandatory services, payments to Medicare, prescription drugs					
Federal	64.5	113.5	113.5	113.5	113.5
State	49.0	0	0	0	0
Optional services					
Federal	11.6	20.6	20.6	11.6	20.6
State	9.0	0	0	9.0	0
Long-term care					
Federal	50.6	0	0	50.6	50.6
State	39.5	90.1	90.1	39.5	39.5
DSH payments					
Federal	9.0	0	15.9	9.0	9.0
State	6.9	15.9	0	6.9	6.9
Total state spending	104.4	106.0	90.1	55.4	46.4

(continued)

Table 10-2. *Continued*

| | | Spending by Option ($ billions)[a] | | | |
| | | Full Swap with State Responsible for | | Partial Swap, with State Spending Based on Federal Match, for | |
Medicaid Benefit	Estimated 2002 Spending ($ billions)	DSH and Long-Term Care	Long-Term Care Only	Optional Services, DSH, and Long-Term Care	Long-Term Care and DSH
Net state change over current spending	—	+2%	−14%	−47%	−56%
Total federal spending	135.7	134.1	150.0	184.7	193.7
Net federal change over current spending	—	−1%	+11%	+36%	+43%

Note: DSH = disproportionate share hospital.

a. Unless otherwise indicated, the federal government is responsible for spending.

the current Medicaid matching rates in effect. In the second, the federal government takes over most of the costs of Medicaid, leaving states with only a share of long-term care costs and DSH payments. In this second partial swap, state spending would fall by 56 percent, on average, and federal spending would rise by 43 percent. This scenario is likely to be the least feasible because its costs are added to other potential increases in federal spending, as noted earlier.

The four examples shown here demonstrate that, by varying who pays for optional acute care services, DSH payments, and long-term care, the impacts on states change from $1.6 billion in added costs above what they currently spend to a savings of $58 billion.

State-by-state estimates of the first example—the full swap that leaves only long-term care benefits and DSH payments to the states—are shown in table 10-3. This swap adds very little to the overall state burden (see table 10-2), but on a state-by-state basis burdens would vary substantially. Spending would increase in 33 states, rising by more than 50 percent in Alabama (58 percent), Louisiana (93 percent), Montana (58 percent), North Dakota (105 percent), and West Virginia (69 percent). The states experiencing the greatest relief would be Tennessee and Delaware (both by more than 30 percent).

State-by-state estimates of the third example—the partial swap in which costs of long-term care, DSH payments, and optional services continue to be provided jointly by the states and the federal government—are shown in table 10-4. The aggregate reduction in state spending would be 47 percent (table 10-2), but again the reductions vary by state. The District of Columbia would experience a 23 percent drop in spending and New Hampshire 28 percent, but Georgia's spending would fall by 64 percent and Tennessee's by 65 percent.[12] These changes reflect both the impact of different federal matching rates and the impact of varying long-term care and DSH spending as a share of total expenditures.

As discussed above, these examples should be viewed as merely illustrative, because in actuality, individuals would most likely change their behavior in response to policy changes, and standardization at the federal level would probably increase the federal contribution substantially. The goals of relief to the states and expansion of coverage to individuals are likely to conflict. Further, while state spending would probably be designed to fall under any serious swap proposal, the problem of declining resources in times of economic downturn would still affect services left to the states.

Table 10-3. Results of Full Swap, 2002 Estimates

State	New Federal Services ($ millions)				New State Services ($ millions)		Change in Funding ($ millions)		Change in Funding (%)	
	Mandatory Acute Care[a]	Payments to Medicare	Prescribed Drugs	Optional Acute Care[b]	Long-Term Care	DSH Payments	Federal	State	Federal	State
U.S. Total	$88,418.7	$5,489.3	$19,602.8	$20,514.2	$90,156.7	$15,922.1	–$1,687.6	$1,687.6	–1%	2%
Alabama	972.9	103.2	307.7	326.0	1,118.8	378.8	–549.9	549.9	–24	58
Alaska	300.1	8.8	47.1	95.8	187.1	14.3	77.1	–77.1	21	–28
Arizona[c]	N/A	N/A	N/A	N/A	N/A	N/A	N/A	N/A	N/A	N/A
Arkansas	713.0	61.4	194.2	269.6	799.2	23.5	–258.8	258.8	–17	46
California	12,098.8	990.6	2,181.1	2,470.0	7,451.1	1,987.7	3,770.3	–3,770.3	27	–29
Colorado	962.6	30.0	130.7	218.2	867.3	192.2	141.0	–141.0	12	–12
Connecticut	819.4	135.6	240.9	191.1	2,050.9	309.3	–486.6	486.6	–26	26
Delaware	260.5	10.0	63.6	101.3	227.5	4.3	101.8	–101.8	31	–31
District of Columbia	502.8	18.2	52.6	150.8	310.5	57.5	–40.3	40.3	–5	12
Florida	3,838.6	502.2	1,168.7	804.7	3,069.9	350.0	821.3	–821.3	15	–19
Georgia	2,953.9	124.2	629.6	285.3	1,384.4	431.8	565.6	–565.6	17	–24
Hawaii	336.0	28.3	58.6	61.7	228.8	—	82.7	–82.7	21	–27
Idaho	277.7	12.2	83.4	104.3	304.1	10.4	–85.0	85.0	–15	37
Illinois	4,367.3	125.7	713.7	586.3	2,896.5	393.5	1,251.5	–1,251.5	28	–28
Indiana	1,335.1	58.6	454.7	258.0	1,647.8	735.7	–679.1	679.1	–24	40
Iowa	618.0	91.4	192.3	124.7	890.7	14.7	–187.9	187.9	–15	26
Kansas	415.0	30.3	149.6	205.5	1,020.6	48.5	–325.1	325.1	–29	44

Kentucky	1,533.4	91.2	483.3	382.9	1,108.9	197.5	−164.9	164.9	−6	14
Louisiana	1,353.7	96.0	466.7	141.7	1,867.8	901.1	−1,335.2	1,335.2	−39	93
Maine	410.1	48.4	148.7	304.7	548.6	50.8	−94.3	94.3	−9	19
Maryland	1,529.4	70.3	195.5	527.6	1,328.1	64.6	465.1	−465.1	25	−25
Massachusetts	2,567.0	180.1	613.1	579.7	3,082.3	470.6	193.5	−193.5	5	−5
Michigan	3,563.5	174.0	469.0	706.3	2,672.3	449.7	384.4	−384.4	8	−11
Minnesota	1,319.9	68.5	209.4	364.9	2,329.8	65.8	−216.4	216.4	−10	10
Mississippi	1,190.8	91.9	401.4	132.2	802.3	184.6	−316.6	316.6	−15	47
Missouri	1,881.4	119.6	537.1	297.5	1,913.7	470.1	−351.3	351.3	−11	17
Montana	205.2	11.6	58.7	50.4	244.7	0.3	−89.8	89.8	−22	58
Nebraska	425.1	49.8	139.5	85.5	654.8	1.3	−107.6	107.6	−13	20
Nevada	343.0	18.2	44.8	82.9	202.3	78.6	104.0	−104.0	27	−27
New Hampshire	189.9	6.2	77.1	135.2	396.7	163.6	−76.0	76.0	−16	16
New Jersey	1,980.3	126.6	527.2	509.9	3,640.0	1,158.6	−827.2	827.2	−21	21
New Mexico	861.3	25.1	45.5	193.0	470.0	9.5	−46.9	46.9	−4	11
New York	10,904.4	266.2	2,420.2	3,632.3	15,531.9	2,424.5	−366.6	366.6	−2	2
North Carolina	2,760.0	191.2	770.7	426.0	2,375.0	448.8	−136.9	136.9	−3	5
North Dakota	109.2	4.3	35.0	28.7	284.8	1.1	−146.4	146.4	−45	105
Ohio	2,925.9	112.5	874.8	461.2	4,396.7	657.5	−1,167.7	1,167.7	−21	30
Oklahoma	893.1	56.8	129.9	247.0	950.6	23.8	−294.0	294.0	−18	43
Oregon	1,120.0	36.5	192.0	302.9	1,306.2	30.6	−117.7	117.7	−7	10
Pennsylvania	4,014.0	222.3	558.8	824.0	5,846.9	649.3	−1,001.9	1,001.9	−15	18
Rhode Island	456.0	15.7	80.6	244.8	484.5	83.7	81.0	−81.0	11	−12
South Carolina	1,248.7	79.8	340.6	357.7	1,035.5	384.2	−363.0	363.0	−15	34
South Dakota	163.5	11.9	42.0	45.9	263.6	1.1	−84.8	84.8	−24	47
Tennessee	3,298.9	150.0	573.2	681.6	1,460.0	—	781.1	−781.1	20	−35
Texas	4,968.5	432.4	1,048.7	887.5	4,213.8	1,279.2	−382.8	382.8	−5	7

(continued)

Table 10-3. *Continued*

State	New Federal Services ($ millions)				New State Services ($ millions)		Change in Funding ($ millions)		Change in Funding (%)	
	Mandatory Acute Care[a]	Payments to Medicare	Prescribed Drugs	Optional Acute Care[b]	Long-Term Care	DSH Payments	Federal	State	Federal	State
Utah	388.4	17.6	94.3	149.7	298.1	3.9	−16.3	16.3	−2	6
Vermont	227.4	10.2	81.6	107.8	223.4	27.4	−0.5	0.5	0	0
Virginia	1,237.6	93.5	340.4	224.2	1,309.5	241.4	122.4	−122.4	7	−7
Washington	1,824.5	75.8	364.4	608.1	1,690.0	339.8	403.4	−403.4	16	−17
West Virginia	608.9	45.5	204.0	160.2	633.5	94.7	−296.2	296.2	−23	69
Wisconsin	1,052.7	153.6	340.3	364.1	1,994.1	12.2	−383.5	383.5	−17	24
Wyoming	91.2	5.3	25.5	12.7	141.1	<0.1	−36.2	36.2	−21	35

Source: Urban Institute 2002.

Notes: DSH = disproportionate share hospital; N/A = not applicable.

a. Mandatory acute care services include inpatient and outpatient hospital services; Federally Qualified Health Center (FQHC) and rural health clinic services; physician services; laboratory and radiology services; early and periodic screening, diagnostic, and treatment (EPSDT) services; family planning (including sterilizations); nurse midwife; and nurse practitioner services. This analysis assumes that 80 percent of expenditures of prepaid health care services (e.g., health maintenance organization, HIO, and Prepaid Health Plan programs) are for mandatory acute care services. This analysis also assumes that 100 percent of expenditures for children for dental services, other practitioners, health clinics, and prescribed drugs is mandatory due to EPSDT requirements, and that 50 percent of expenditures for unspecified services ("other care") for children is also mandatory due to EPSDT requirements.

b. Optional acute care services include other practitioners' services (e.g., podiatrists, optometrists, chiropractors); private duty nursing; clinic services (except FQHC and rural clinic services); dental services; physical therapy; occupational therapy; speech, hearing, and language disorder services; dentures, prosthetic devices, and eyeglasses; rehabilitative services; Christian Science practitioners; hospice services; targeted and primary care case management; emergency hospital services; and other services as allowed by state Medicaid plans.

c. Data for Arizona are not included because spending for the Arizona Long-Term Care System (ALTCS, the state's prepaid long-term care program) could not be separated from spending for the Arizona Health Care Cost-Containment System (AHCCS, the state's prepaid acute care program).

Table 10-4. Results of Partial Swap, 2002 Estimates

| | Federal Services ($ millions) | | | Shared Services ($ millions) | | | | | | Change in Funding ($ millions) | | Change in Funding (%) | |
| | Mandatory Acute Care[a] | Prescribed Drugs | Payments to Medicare | Optional Acute Care[b] | | Long-Term Care | | DSH Payments | | | | | |
State	Federal	Federal	Federal	Federal	State	Federal	State	Federal	State	Federal	State	Federal	State
U.S. Total	$88,418.7	$19,602.8	$5,489.3	$11,560.1	$8,954.1	$50,639.4	$39,517.3	$8,993.0	$6,929.1	$48,990.7	–$48,990.7	36%	–47%
Alabama	972.9	307.7	103.2	229.7	96.3	788.2	330.6	266.9	111.9	408.9	–408.9	18	–43
Alaska	300.1	47.1	8.8	55.0	40.8	107.3	79.7	8.2	6.1	151.7	–151.7	40	–55
Arizona[c]	N/A	N/A	N/A	N/A	N/A	N/A	N/A	N/A	N/A	N/A	N/A	N/A	N/A
Arkansas	713.0	194.2	61.4	195.8	73.8	580.5	218.7	17.1	6.4	265.0	–265.0	18	–47
California	12,098.8	2,181.1	990.6	1,269.6	1,200.4	3,829.9	3,621.3	1,021.7	966.0	7,421.5	–7,421.5	53	–56
Colorado	962.6	130.7	30.0	109.1	109.1	433.7	433.7	96.1	96.1	561.6	–561.6	47	–47
Connecticut	819.4	240.9	135.6	95.6	95.6	1,025.5	1,025.5	154.6	154.6	597.9	–597.9	32	–32
Delaware	260.5	63.6	10.0	50.7	50.7	113.8	113.8	2.1	2.1	167.1	–167.1	50	–50
District of Columbia	502.8	52.6	18.2	105.5	45.2	217.3	93.1	40.3	17.3	172.1	–172.1	23	–23
Florida	3,838.6	1,168.7	502.2	454.1	350.6	1,732.4	1,337.6	197.5	152.5	2,400.5	–2,400.5	44	–57
Georgia	2,953.9	629.6	124.2	168.3	117.0	816.8	567.6	254.8	177.0	1,520.2	–1,520.2	44	–64
Hawaii	336.0	58.6	28.3	34.8	26.9	128.9	99.9	—	—	184.7	–184.7	46	–59
Idaho	277.7	83.4	12.2	74.1	30.2	216.0	88.1	7.4	3.0	108.2	–108.2	19	–47
Illinois	4,367.3	713.7	125.7	293.2	293.2	1,448.2	1,448.2	196.8	196.8	2,603.3	–2,603.3	57	–57

(continued)

Table 10-4. Continued

State	Federal Services ($ millions)			Shared Services ($ millions)						Change in Funding ($ millions)		Change in Funding (%)	
	Mandatory		Payments to Medicare	Optional Acute Care[b]		Long-Term Care		DSH Payments					
	Acute Care[a]	Prescribed Drugs											
	Federal	Federal	Federal	Federal	State	Federal	State	Federal	State	Federal	State	Federal	State
Indiana	1,335.1	454.7	58.6	160.1	97.9	1,022.3	625.5	456.4	279.3	701.6	−701.6	25	−41
Iowa	618.0	192.3	91.4	78.4	46.3	559.9	330.8	9.3	5.5	334.9	−334.9	28	−47
Kansas	415.0	149.6	30.3	123.7	81.8	614.4	406.2	29.2	19.3	236.7	−236.7	21	−32
Kentucky	1,533.4	483.3	91.2	267.8	115.1	775.6	333.3	138.1	59.4	633.7	−633.7	24	−56
Louisiana	1,353.7	466.7	96.0	99.6	42.1	1,313.0	554.7	633.5	267.6	569.2	−569.2	17	−40
Maine	410.1	148.7	48.4	202.9	101.8	365.3	183.4	33.8	17.0	202.9	−202.9	20	−40
Maryland	1,529.4	195.5	70.3	263.8	263.8	664.1	664.1	32.3	32.3	897.6	−897.6	48	−48
Massachusetts	2,567.0	613.1	180.1	289.9	289.9	1,541.1	1,541.1	235.3	235.3	1,680.1	−1,680.1	45	−45
Michigan	3,563.5	469.0	174.0	398.1	308.2	1,506.1	1,166.2	253.5	196.3	1,835.7	−1,835.7	41	−52
Minnesota	1,319.9	209.4	68.5	182.4	182.4	1,164.9	1,164.9	32.9	32.9	798.9	−798.9	37	−37
Mississippi	1,190.8	401.4	91.9	100.6	31.6	610.4	191.8	140.5	44.1	402.7	−402.7	19	−60
Missouri	1,881.4	537.1	119.6	181.7	115.9	1,168.5	745.2	287.0	183.1	988.3	−988.3	31	−49
Montana	205.2	58.7	11.6	36.7	13.7	178.2	66.5	0.2	0.1	74.9	−74.9	18	−48
Nebraska	425.1	139.5	49.8	50.9	34.6	389.9	264.8	0.8	0.5	248.5	−248.5	31	−45

Nevada	343.0	44.8	18.2	41.4	41.4	101.2	101.2	39.3	39.3	203.0	-203.0	53	-53
New Hampshire	189.9	77.1	6.2	67.6	67.6	198.4	198.4	81.8	81.8	136.6	-136.6	28	-28
New Jersey	1,980.3	527.2	126.6	255.0	255.0	1,820.0	1,820.0	579.3	579.3	1,317.1	-1,317.1	33	-33
New Mexico	861.3	45.5	25.1	141.0	52.0	343.3	126.7	6.9	2.6	251.3	-251.3	21	-58
New York	10,904.4	2,420.2	266.2	1,816.1	1,816.1	7,766.0	7,766.0	1,212.3	1,212.3	6,795.4	-6,795.4	39	-39
North Carolina	2,760.0	770.7	191.2	261.8	164.2	1,459.7	915.3	275.8	173.0	1,434.4	-1,434.4	33	-53
North Dakota	109.2	35.0	4.3	20.1	8.7	199.0	85.8	0.8	0.3	44.7	-44.7	14	-32
Ohio	2,925.9	874.8	112.5	271.1	190.1	2,584.4	1,812.3	386.5	271.0	1,613.0	-1,613.0	29	-42
Oklahoma	893.1	129.9	56.8	173.9	73.0	669.5	281.1	16.8	7.1	319.3	-319.3	20	-47
Oregon	1,120.0	192.0	36.5	179.3	123.6	773.3	532.9	18.1	12.5	550.1	-550.1	31	-45
Pennsylvania	4,014.0	558.8	222.3	450.3	373.7	3,195.3	2,651.6	354.8	294.4	2,174.6	-2,174.6	33	-40
Rhode Island	456.0	80.6	15.7	128.4	116.4	254.1	230.4	43.9	39.8	262.6	-262.6	37	-40
South Carolina	1,248.7	340.6	79.8	248.1	109.7	718.0	317.5	266.4	117.8	511.8	-511.8	21	-48
South Dakota	163.5	42.0	11.9	30.2	15.6	173.8	89.8	0.7	0.4	74.1	-74.1	21	-41
Tennessee	3,298.9	573.2	150.0	433.8	247.8	929.1	530.8	—	—	1,462.4	-1,462.4	37	-65
Texas	4,968.5	1,048.7	432.4	534.0	353.5	2,535.4	1,678.4	769.7	509.5	2,568.9	-2,568.9	33	-50
Utah	388.4	94.3	17.6	104.8	44.9	208.6	89.4	2.7	1.2	150.1	-150.1	23	-53
Vermont	227.4	81.6	10.2	67.9	39.8	140.9	82.5	17.3	10.1	117.9	-117.9	28	-47
Virginia	1,237.6	340.4	93.5	115.3	108.8	673.8	635.8	124.2	117.2	811.5	-811.5	46	-48

(continued)

Table 10-4. Continued

| | Federal Services ($ millions) | | | | | Shared Services ($ millions) | | | | | | | | |
| | Mandatory Acute Care[a] | Prescribed Drugs | Payments to Medicare | Optional Acute Care[b] | | Long-Term Care | | DSH Payments | | Change in Funding ($ millions) | | Change in Funding (%) | |
State	Federal	Federal	Federal	Federal	State	Federal	State	Federal	State	Federal	State	Federal	State
Washington	1,824.5	364.4	75.8	306.3	301.8	851.2	838.7	171.1	168.6	1,124.0	−1,124.0	46	−46
West Virginia	608.9	204.0	45.5	120.6	39.6	476.8	156.7	71.3	23.4	212.3	−212.3	16	−49
Wisconsin	1,052.7	340.3	153.6	213.3	150.9	1,167.9	826.1	7.2	5.1	640.8	−640.8	28	−39
Wyoming	91.2	25.5	5.3	7.8	4.8	87.4	53.6	<0.1	<0.1	46.4	−46.4	27	−44

Source: Urban Institute 2002

Notes: DSH = disproportionate share hospital; N/A = not applicable.

a. Mandatory acute care services include inpatient and outpatient hospital services; Federally Qualified Health Center (FQHC) and rural health clinic services; physician services; laboratory and radiology services; early and periodic screening, diagnostic, and treatment (EPSDT) services; family planning (including sterilizations); nurse midwife; and nurse practitioner services. This analysis assumes that 80 percent of expenditures of prepaid health care services (e.g., health maintenance organization, HIO, and Prepaid Health Plan programs) are for mandatory acute care services. This analysis also assumes that 100 percent of expenditures for children for dental services, other practitioners, health clinics, and prescribed drugs is mandatory due to EPSDT requirements, and that 50 percent of expenditures for unspecified services ("other care") for children is also mandatory due to EPSDT requirements.

b. Optional acute care services include other practitioners' services (e.g., podiatrists, optometrists, chiropractors); private duty nursing; clinic services (except FQHC and rural clinic services); dental services; physical therapy; occupational therapy; speech, hearing, and language disorder services; dentures, prosthetic devices, and eyeglasses; rehabilitative services; Christian Science practitioners; hospice services; targeted and primary care case management; emergency hospital services; and other services as allowed by state Medicaid plans.

c. Data for Arizona are not included because spending for the Arizona Long-Term Care System (ALTCS, the state's prepaid long-term care program) could not be separated from spending for the Arizona Health Care Cost-Containment System (AHCCS, the state's prepaid acute care program).

Political Caveats

In addition to the many details that would need to be worked out in a full proposal for federalizing Medicaid, numerous practical and political questions stand in the way. The most important would be the willingness of Congress to shoulder a responsibility that the states now bear. It would be difficult to drum up political support for raising federal taxes to provide benefits that already exist. Moreover, there are few ways for members of Congress to take credit for lowering state taxes.

Provider groups are likely to oppose a federalized program for fear of the power it would give the federal government. Medicare and Medicaid together accounted for more than 36 percent of national expenditures on health care in 1998. Even if some responsibilities were left to the states, such as their traditional share of long-term care and optional acute care benefits, the federal government's share of national health expenditures would rise to nearly one-third. In the past, Congress has shown a strong interest in micromanaging the Medicare program, allowing little flexibility to the administrators. The political stakes would be even higher if the federal government also had greater control over the Medicaid program. Offsetting this fear is the likelihood that the federal government would set rates higher than states do, as is currently the case when one compares Medicare with Medicaid.

Perhaps most important, ensuring that all states benefit from a shifting of responsibilities, and that the benefits are fairly distributed, will be difficult. This concern has often proven to be a deal breaker when other changes in federal versus state responsibility for Medicaid have taken place. In the examples shown above (tables 10-3 and 10-4), the federal government would have to assume a substantially greater financial burden in order to ensure that no state became a loser in a swap involving benefits.

Conclusion

Ultimately, decisions about how to change Medicaid must focus on the goals for improving the program. Proponents of states' rights celebrate the diversity that greater state flexibility makes possible. But it is exactly this diversity of eligibility, coverage, and access to care that alarms others and leads to calls for better, nationally established standards. Improvement in one-third to one-half of all states on those standards is perhaps the strongest rationale for creating a fully federal Medicaid program.

The advantages of the federal government in achieving the type of redistribution necessary to raise standards, particularly in low-income states, are considerable. Administrative simplicity and leverage on providers also offer advantages at the federal level. Progressive taxation, a larger pool from which to draw resources for redistribution, and the ability to maintain spending during periods of economic decline all make a federal program better for financing this care.

Some state flexibility would most likely remain. States would probably continue to finance long-term care, for instance, so that the full cost of shifting Medicaid financing to the federal government would be mitigated. Continued state efforts in health care can be encouraged in a number of ways. For example, states with a track record of good stewardship might, if they wish, be given greater responsibility and a share of any efficiencies they create to help support supplemental benefits or eligibility.

In a political environment where concerns about new federal responsibilities and the return of deficit spending are paramount, it seems unlikely that federalization of Medicaid will get a serious hearing. Some shifting of responsibilities to the federal government might be part of Medicare reforms—affecting drugs or the Medicare Savings Programs, for example. But if state budget pressures worsen, in part because of the burden of financing health care, and if inequities in coverage and insurance worsen, there may well come a time when federalization is more likely.

NOTES

1. It might be more feasible to limit full federalization of administration to the dual eligibles and leave enrollment and eligibility determination for children and younger families to states, because they already have the infrastructure in place. Greater federal oversight might be needed to ensure equity, however.

2. Considerable creative financing is included in that $110 billion figure. See Chapter 5.

3. Chapter 6 cites 13 states as innovators in eligibility; many of them limit eligibility for parents but go higher than 200 percent of the federal poverty level for children.

4. As indicated in unpublished Urban Institute analyses of benefits only.

5. But because this leaves long-term care to the states, the amount of coordination would be less than ideal (see Feder and Lambrew 1996).

6. Such an approach would be controversial, however, as some supporters of Medicare have long fought to keep any income relating or means testing out of that

program. For example, this is in part why the Medicare Savings Programs are in Medicaid.

7. While it is difficult to determine the exact share of the disabled population that is eligible for both programs, it is probably at least 40 percent.

8. Moreover, there has long been criticism of the high levels of federal support for older people through Medicare and Medicaid, compared with what is done for younger families. Splitting up the population could lead to more problems of this type.

9. For example, a swap proposal was included in President Ronald Reagan's 1983 budget (Executive Office of the President 1983). In addition, Senator Nancy Kassebaum introduced such a bill (S. 140) in 1995.

10. This table focuses only on services and leaves out some other parts of Medicaid spending, in particular, administrative costs and disproportionate share hospital (DSH) payments.

11. One possible offset to higher federal spending could be to eliminate the DSH program, which totaled about $15 billion in 1998.

12. Arizona's contributions would fall even further, but in many ways Arizona represents a special case and, thus, its spending is not included in these tables.

REFERENCES

Boccuti, Cristina, and Marilyn Moon. 2002. "Location, Location, Location: Geographic Spending Issues and Medicare Policy." Health Policy Brief No. 2. Washington, D.C.: The Urban Institute.

Clark, William D., and Melissa M. Hulbert. 1998. "Research Issues: Dually Eligible Medicare and Medicaid Beneficiaries, Challenges and Opportunities." *Health Care Financing Review* 20(2): 1–10.

Cunningham, Peter J. 2002. "Mounting Pressures: Physicians Serving Medicaid Patients and the Uninsured, 1997–2001." Tracking Report No. 6. Washington, D.C.: Center for Studying Health System Change.

Damron, David. 2002. "Poor Kids' Dental Care Nothing to Smile About." *Orlando Sentinel.* November 10, p. B1.

Executive Office of the President. 1983. *Major Themes and Additional Budget Details: Fiscal Year 1983.* Washington, D.C.: U.S. Government Printing Office.

Feder, Judy, and Jean Lambrew. 1996. "Why Medicare Matters to People Who Need Long-Term Care." *Health Care Financing Review* 18(2): 99–112.

Fox, Michael H., Jonathan P. Weiner, and Kai Phua. 1992. "Effect of Medicaid Payment Levels on Access to Obstetrical Care." *Health Affairs* 11(4): 150–61.

Gold, Marsha. 2001. "Medicare+Choice: An Interim Report Card." *Health Affairs* 20(4): 120–38.

Hadley, Jack. 2002. *Sicker and Poorer: The Consequences of Being Uninsured.* Menlo Park, Calif.: The Henry J. Kaiser Family Foundation.

Liu, Korbin, Sharon K. Long, and Cynthia Aargon. 1998. "Does Health Status Explain Higher Medicare Costs of Medicaid Enrollees?" *Health Care Financing Review* 20(2): 39–54.

Meiners, Mark R. 1996. "The Financing and Organization of Long-Term Care." In *The Future of Long-Term Care: Social and Policy Issues*, edited by Robert H. Binstock, Leighton E. Cluff, and Otto Von Mering (191–214). Baltimore: Johns Hopkins University Press.

Moon, Marilyn. 2000. "Medicare Matters: Building on a Record of Accomplishments." *Health Care Financing Review* 22(1): 9–22.

Nichols, Len, and Robert Reischauer. 2000. "Who Really Wants Price Competition in Medicare Managed Care?" *Health Affairs* 19(5): 30–43.

Norton, Stephen A., and Stephen Zuckerman. 2000. "Trends in Medicaid Physician Fees, 1993–1998." *Health Affairs* 19(4): 222–32.

11

Alternative Models of Federalism

Health Insurance Regulation and Patient Protection Laws

Randall R. Bovbjerg

N ew federalism has meant devolution of power to states to run low-income health insurance programs (see Chapters 7 and 9), but regulation of health insurance has followed a different path. Federal policy has occasionally preempted traditional state authority over insurance, has increased standardization of regulatory policy across states, and has gone much further toward enforcing desired policy results on a national basis than toward using financial support to encourage disparate states to advance federal goals. All pending federal proposals for national patient protection legislation of managed care plans would set minimum national standards as well. These insurance issues are important in their own right, given that the majority of Americans have health insurance and that most of it is now managed care. They are also important for illustrating a different approach to federalism as it applies to health care.

Some evolutionary perspective is needed to appreciate the extent of the most recent changes in the balance of state and federal authority. Accordingly, this chapter traces developments in health insurance from the traditional federal deference to state autonomy through the current debates on national minimum standards for patient protection. Other federal activity also greatly affects the insurance industry, but this chapter focuses on health insurance.[1]

Evolving Authority in Insurance Regulation

Federal-state roles in health insurance regulation have evolved through three eras. First, federal policy deferred completely to state authority over insurance until the 1970s. The mid-1970s through the early 1990s saw major federal intervention, including the federal Employee Retirement Income Security Act of 1974 (ERISA).[2] ERISA wholly preempted state regulation of employee benefit plans in favor of federal oversight, although initially very limited federal oversight. The current era began in the mid-1990s. The Health Insurance Portability and Accountability Act of 1996 (HIPAA)[3] created a new federal regime of obligations, both for states and for private providers of coverage, mainly in the interest of promoting portability of coverage for enrollees leaving a job and its health plan. More recent federal action and pending patient protection proposals build on the HIPAA model.

Traditional Preeminence of State Authority

For a century after the beginning of organized state regulation of insurance in the mid-1800s, exclusive state authority was unquestioned. There was no federal role, as the U.S. Supreme Court held in 1869 that insurance was not commerce, much less interstate commerce subject to federal control.[4] Similarly, states exercised exclusive authority over most matters related to everyday general welfare, including public health and health care quality. State officials nonetheless recognized the value of coordinating oversight of multistate insurers and formed the National Association of Insurance Commissioners (NAIC) in 1871. The NAIC initially developed uniform financial reporting standards and later began promulgating model acts and regulations for states to adapt to their own situations. States also began to regulate medical education and to license medical practitioners.

Early state insurance regulation focused mostly on financial safeguards. One focus was maintaining the solvency of operating insurers—by ensuring that their rates were adequate to pay future claims and that they had sufficient capital to cover losses from underestimated premiums. Another focus was to protect policyholders after insurer insolvency, mainly through regulators' authority to take over failing firms and to require that the entire insurance industry participate in guaranty funds to pay claims against a failed insurer. States also taxed insurance premiums as a source of general state revenue. Concerns over insurers' overcharging and other consumer issues were minimal. Indeed, insurers were encouraged to set rates high enough to build substantial reserves, working in concert with competing firms to pool claims data for rate-setting purposes.

Regulatory practices begun for earlier lines of insurance were extended to health insurance once it was invented by Blue Cross and Blue Shield plans in the early 1930s. The Blues plans, however, received special regulatory status, including lower requirements for capitalization than the "commercial" insurers that began to compete with them (Bovbjerg, Griffin, and Carroll 1993). The rationale was that the Blues plans had advantages unavailable to commercial carriers because they were owned by medical provider associations and had contracts with participating hospitals and doctors.

The *Southeast Underwriters* decision by the U.S. Supreme Court in 1944 abruptly redrew the constitutional boundary between state and federal authority over insurance.[5] The Court overruled its 1869 precedent and allowed a federal antitrust challenge against insurers' sharing of rating data, notwithstanding state policy authorizing such collaboration. Congress quickly responded with the McCarran-Ferguson Act of 1945.[6] This landmark legislation ceded the newfound federal oversight authority back to the states, meaning that federal law would not apply to insurers where states adequately regulated insurance. In practice, the only significant federal oversight was antitrust litigation, not ongoing administrative regulation.

After 1945, states increasingly exercised their regulatory authority over health insurance rates and benefits. Demand for regulation increased as health insurance enrollment and prices rose in the 1960s and the new consumer movement argued for public action. By the early 1970s, mandated benefits had become a major thrust of state law—that is, health plans were required to cover certain types of care (such as pregnancy and mental health services) or medical practitioners (for example, chiropractors and physician assistants) (Gabel and Jensen 1989).

Federal Preemption of State Authority

The next era began with the Health Maintenance Organization (HMO) Act of 1973[7] and ERISA of 1974. These landmark federal statutes markedly restricted what had been absolute state power over insurance and for the first time called for federal regulation of some aspects of health coverage for the general population. HMOs were the first form of managed care, embraced by President Richard M. Nixon in 1970 because of growing concerns over rising health spending and incomplete insurance coverage. HMOs embodied the kind of prepaid medical practice that many states had made illegal by regulation or judicial doctrine, so federal action was needed. After compromises with Congress, the HMO Act overturned the state bans. The act also created new rules for federal certification of HMOs, allowed certified HMOs to force large employers to offer them as a coverage option, and struck down (preempted) all state laws inconsistent with the new HMO regime.

States remained free to impose additional requirements as long as they were not inconsistent with federal rules. Almost all states passed their own HMO statutes. Because HMOs combined financing of medical care (previously the province of insurers) with provision of care (previously the domain of physicians, hospitals, and other providers), state HMO regulations went well beyond conventional insurance oversight. In addition to insurance commissioners, state departments of health often played a role, particularly in assessing the adequacy of licensees' participating provider networks and the credentials of those providers.

The HMO Act and the certification process initially helped legitimize HMOs, but the influence of federal rules for winning certification waned as buyers' and sellers' preferences in managed care evolved far from the original federal specifications. Managed care organizations (MCOs) now include not only HMOs but also preferred provider organizations (PPOs) and point-of-service plans.[8] Perhaps the HMO Act's most enduring contribution was to encourage new state regulation, which has grown to include regulation through patient protection or patients' bills of rights, as considered below.

The second major increase of federal authority came with ERISA. ERISA broadly preempted state laws that "relate to any employee benefit plan," with some exceptions, such as those of state and local governments and of churches. ERISA focused primarily on retirement income; it extensively reformed employee pension benefits, establishing federal rules that superceded the patchwork of state oversight. Employee health benefits were included in the same preemption, but no substantive federal rules were created on the nature or extent of those benefits. Instead, the act emphasized largely procedural requirements: that enrollees be informed about their health benefit plan, that plan trustees carefully manage plan assets, and that disputes be resolved in federal court.

The substantive policy rationale for ERISA was that benefit design should be left to the labor market and employer-employee negotiations.[9] The federalism policy rationale was that firms increasingly operated across state borders and should be allowed to operate a nationally uniform benefit plan, free from state requirements, which vary across the country.

ERISA's preemption is extremely broad, applying to "any and all" state laws that "relate to" employee benefit plans. Thus, it supercedes state administrative regulation and judicial rulings, as well as legislation. ERISA left one major exception for states: They could continue their traditional regulation of insurers, although not of employee benefits.[10] States could not require that any firm insure its employees nor that any employee benefit plan contain particular provisions.

ERISA had little impact on health coverage in the 1970s because almost all employers bought fully insured, state-regulated coverage, under which an outside insurer agrees to pay for future health services in exchange for a fixed current premium. So state regulation continued to influence how health plans worked. However, large employers were increasingly self-insuring their health benefits—that is, paying for covered health care services as they arose, not transferring the risk of future claims to an insurer. Insurance companies were typically hired to administer the plans and pay claims, but they did so as contractors for a fee, not as insurers for a premium. Self-insured firms avoided not only state regulation of their benefits but also taxes on premiums. The spread of self-insurance greatly reduced the reach of state authority without substituting any federal rules, and the resulting regulatory vacuum eventually prompted debate over what regulations are needed, at what level of government. By the late 1990s, about half of all health insurance coverage was estimated to be self-insured and hence beyond direct state regulation, so ERISA became far more influential than when it was first enacted. The boundary between what constitutes ERISA preempted regulation of "benefits" and allowed regulation of "insurance" also became more important, as discussed below.

Federal authority grew on two additional fronts. First, Congress created new federal rules for Medicare supplement insurance—private coverage that beneficiaries often buy to fill in the gaps in coverage under the federal program. Two federal Medigap laws were enacted as Congress in 1980 built upon prior state rules and then in 1990 standardized allowable benefit packages.[11] Second, the Consolidated Omnibus Budget Reconciliation Act of 1985 (COBRA) required that large employers (more than

25 workers) allow employees leaving their jobs to pay premiums to continue their group coverage for 18 months or more. COBRA thus made national an obligation that some states had previously created for some types of coverage.[12]

ERISA's biggest early impact was to remove states' option of requiring employers to provide coverage for workers. Hawaii was the first and only state to enact a workplace mandate, in 1974, a few months before ERISA.[13] The state achieved the highest rate of coverage in the nation. In the early 1980s, other states took note of Hawaii's example, when uninsurance rates began to rise nationally—for the first time ever. Hawaii became concerned that ERISA might preempt its rules, so it sought and received federal approval to retain its coverage mandate through an amendment to ERISA in 1983.[14] (Other amendments allowed states to regulate purportedly self-insured workplace benefits plans run for multiple-employer trusts. The marketing of such trusts to groups of small employers had generated frequent complaints of abuses to state regulators.)

Ultimately, however, no other state followed Hawaii's example. Massachusetts came closest, enacting in 1988 a payroll tax on employers that did not provide health coverage; the tax was designed to fund state coverage, but the law was never implemented and was repealed in 1991.[15] Concerns about effects on job formation and cross-border competition also discouraged states from enacting mandates, but broad judicial interpretations of ERISA made it conventional wisdom that only the federal government could legally mandate coverage.

Workers and their dependents constitute 80 percent of the uninsured, and low-wage jobs are least likely to come with health benefits (Garrett, Nichols, and Greenman 2001). This situation poses special concerns for states trying to encourage shifts from welfare to work. States can and do continue Medicaid coverage for low-income workers who have left welfare, and they are free to create state programs for low-income workers or to subsidize private coverage, as a few states have done. But under ERISA, states cannot mandate employers to provide coverage, as they routinely do for workers' compensation, for example. In sum, ERISA effected the biggest single shift in federalism until the mid-1990s, reducing state authority while federal authority largely deferred to private action.

A New Era? Federal Coverage Standards with State Enforcement

HIPAA 1996 extended the Medigap insurance model—federal minimum standards enforced by the states—to the general population (Nichols and

Blumberg 1998). Previously, the key federal statutes had been preemptive, cutting back state authority. In contrast, HIPAA sought to make states do more, in keeping with national rules. Its passage inaugurated another era, as subsequent federal activity has been modeled on HIPAA.

Substantively, HIPAA addressed two problems: insurance portability for employees who changed or lost their jobs and access to coverage for individuals with adverse health histories. It built upon the reforms of individual and small-group insurance markets that many states enacted from 1989 to 1996. Among the reforms' stronger provisions were requirements that insurers guarantee the issuance of coverage without unduly long exclusions of preexisting conditions—that is, insurers had to accept all applicants on an equal basis and could not exclude coverage of known health problems for an unreasonable time. Provisions differed greatly by state, however, and states did not reform large-group insurance, which was thought to have fewer access problems.[16]

HIPAA adapted some of those state provisions to help people maintain coverage. For example, it set national rules requiring employers, insurers, and states to guarantee people leaving their jobs access to similar new coverage without discrimination based on health status or long-term exclusion of preexisting conditions. Federal enforcement responsibility is split. The Centers for Medicare and Medicaid Services (CMS) oversee regulation of insurers, which is largely delegated to states. The Department of Labor oversees self-insured employee benefit plans, because the department administers ERISA, which exempted the plans from state regulation. (Other HIPAA provisions, meant to simplify claims and protect patients' privacy in regard to record keeping and record sharing, constitute a pure federal takeover, with no state role. Privacy rules were imposed on state Medicaid programs, for example, just as they were on other health plans and medical providers.)[17]

From a federalism perspective, HIPAA broke new ground in two main ways. It was the first law to set national minimum standards for all health coverage, including HMOs and conventional insurance, regardless of the size of the group plan involved, regardless of insured or self-insured status, and regardless of whether the insureds were Medicare beneficiaries. Second, the new federal rules were designed to be implemented and overseen by states, through changes to state statutes if necessary. States were allowed to impose more stringent requirements, and they could use one of several ways to make certain insurance was available to individuals.

Technically, the law merely permitted states to choose to implement the federal regime. However, HIPAA provided that the federal government would act if the states did not. In practice, therefore, states almost unanimously chose to comply in order to preserve their control and to harmonize HIPAA with their other regulatory provisions; moreover, federal enforcers have not shown themselves eager to intervene (CMS 2002; U.S. General Accounting Office [GAO] 2000). State compliance often entailed passing significant legislation: *Assessing the New Federalism* (ANF) case studies of 13 representative states from 1996 to 1997 found that only two—New Jersey and Washington—were initially in full compliance with HIPAA insurance reform requirements; New York was very close (Nichols and Blumberg 1998).

Federal authority in HIPAA is analogous to that in Medicaid, but in some ways it is more sweeping. A state can avoid Medicaid rules by choosing not to offer Medicaid coverage. However, a state cannot avoid HIPAA rules by opting not to implement HIPAA—it will simply get federal implementation instead. Moreover, although Medicaid and HIPAA both have national minimum standards and state implementation, they differ in federal-state relations. Medicaid uses a financial carrot (federal matching funds for state spending), but HIPAA uses a regulatory stick (direct federal regulation in absence of state compliance) with no funding. Finally, HIPAA standards apply to all forms of insurance and are truly national, although state implementation does vary, whereas Medicaid applies only to a subset of the low-income population and allows states to set vastly different levels of eligibility and coverage.

Despite HIPAA's importance as a model of federalism, its insurance reforms have had little practical effect. Like most of its state forerunners, HIPAA addressed access to coverage, not affordability of coverage. Nor were any federal funds committed to subsidize purchase of HIPAA-regulated coverage.[18]

Congress subsequently amended HIPAA to add further substantive requirements on a national basis, again mainly implemented through the states, except for self-insured plans (CMS 2002). The Newborns' and Mothers' Health Protection Act of 1996[19] set minimum lengths of covered hospitalization after childbirth, responding to complaints that hospitals were discharging mothers and infants too soon under managed care. The Mental Health Parity Act of 1996[20] was passed after a long campaign by mental health professionals and clients for improved benefits. The act barred large-group health plans (more than 50 workers) from setting dollar limits on mental health benefits lower than the limits on medical and surgical benefits—although plans may impose higher cost sharing or lower limits on the number of visits for mental health care. The Women's Health and Cancer Rights Act required large-group health plans that cover mastectomies to cover breast reconstruction and related patient services as well. These requirements can be seen as the first federal patient protection initiatives, which were done piecemeal rather than as an omnibus act.

Growing State Oversight of Managed Care

The federal government's role in insurance regulation continues to evolve, mainly with regard to managed care. Managed care reached a critical mass in the early 1990s. Employee health benefit plans increasingly turned to HMOs, PPOs, and other forms of managed care to cope with rising health costs and recession-squeezed revenues. As of 1988, 71 percent of the workplace insurance offered by large employers consisted of traditional fee-for-service indemnity coverage with open-ended access to care and reimbursement; only 29 percent of enrollees were in managed care. The figures had reversed by 1998, when managed care predominated by 86 percent to 14 percent.[21] State Medicaid programs also shifted to managed care for most beneficiaries other than the elderly and the disabled (see Chapter 7).

Managed care achieved desired economies by imposing new restrictions, both on medical providers and on enrollees. Providers had to agree to discount their fees in order to be accepted into managed care networks, and enrollees faced limits on their choice of providers and new requirements for cost sharing and preauthorization of services, often even in emergency rooms. However, managed care also provoked a substantial backlash, as providers and patients experienced its constraints but not its savings (Peterson 1999). The backlash prompted lobbying for protective legislation along with lawsuits against managed care by patients and providers. The demand for public oversight of private managed care began at the state level but quickly became a federal issue as well. Collaterally, pressure built for employers to drop restrictions on access to providers and services, and many private plans responded as well (Bernstein 2000).

Anti-Selective Contracting Provisions

The first wave of state action addressed the exclusion of some physicians, hospitals, and other providers from managed care networks, under PPOs and similar forms of managed care that evolved from the early HMO models (Leone 1994). Contracting only with selected providers enabled the newer plans to negotiate favorable terms with participants, but it hurt nonparticipants. It also prevented patients from choosing among all licensed practitioners at the point of service, a prerogative to which enrollees were accustomed under indemnity coverage. In response, many states enacted laws requiring plans to accept any willing provider or to give patients freedom of choice among providers. Such provisions had sometimes been required early in the history of health insurance and were one way that state policy had barred HMOs prior to the HMO Act (Weller 1984). Organized medicine lobbied heavily for statutes to bar selective contracting in the early 1990s, while managed care and large employer lobbies were opposed.

By the end of 1996, almost 30 states had passed some form of law requiring acceptance of any willing provider and giving patients freedom of choice.[22] Pioneers tended to be states in which MCOs existed but did not yet dominate the market. The laws did not stop all selective contracting, however. Most laws applied only to pharmacies or other ancillary providers; fewer covered doctors or hospitals. Some statutes required only that enrollees be offered the option to buy a point-of-service feature for their managed care plan. Employers and health plans also had some political success in resisting further controls, calling it "provider protection," and they had some judicial success in challenging laws already passed as contrary to ERISA, at least until the U.S. Supreme Court upheld the states' powers to impose restrictions in 2003.[23] The peak year for restrictions on selective contracting was 1994. Enactment of laws dwindled thereafter,[24] perhaps because fewer plans relied on excluding providers, but interest may revive in the wake of U.S. Supreme Court approval.

The Shift to Patient Protection

In the mid-1970s, the legislative debate moved on to provisions that more directly addressed enrollees' concerns about managed care's new restrictions. Proponents of managed care term such laws as anti–managed care legislation, but patient protection is the dominant term. Some refer to a patients' bill of rights, which is what President Bill Clinton asked a presidential commission to develop in 1997 (President's Advisory Commission on Consumer Protection and Quality in the Health Care Industry 1997).

A thorough review of state and federal proposals and legislation (Marsteller and Bovbjerg 1999) identified four key sources of concern that motivated reforms:

- plans' limited provider networks,
- restrictions on the scope of benefits,
- utilization management at the point of service, and
- financial incentives to providers and patients to encourage cost cutting.

States took the lead, enacting standards of practice or oversight processes for MCOs that addressed each of these four concerns, such as

- standards on the adequacy of participating provider networks,
- requirements of more open access to emergency care and clinical trials,
- minimum lengths of hospital stays for childbirth and the right to appeal denial of benefits or sue for damages in case of resulting injury, and
- restrictions on financial incentives for practitioners to deny care.

In the first phase of patient protection, from 1996 to 1998, state legislatures saw nearly 600 bills proposing one or more provisions. Some provisions passed in every state (Stauffer 1998). Case studies of health policy in 13 representative states found that patient protection was typically a significant policy concern, but it was usually a much lower priority than Medicaid policy, including promotion of Medicaid managed care (Holahan, Wiener, and Lutzky 2002). An exception was Texas, where legislative leaders and Governor George W. Bush took high-profile, conflicting stances. A veto blocked the first bill passed, although the governor implemented many provisions by regulation. Stronger legislation was passed in 1997, including the nation's first right-to-sue provision (Wiener et al. 1997).

Through mid-1999, more than two dozen types of provisions were enacted in at least two states (table 11-1). Some of these provisions passed in substantially more states than others.[25] Of the 28 provisions tracked, 2 were nearly universal. One required MCOs to have internal processes for enrollees to appeal denials of payment (review by an independent, external authority was rarer), and the other banned so-called gag clauses in

Table 11-1. *Patient Protection Provisions and Extent of Their Enactment, by Year*

Patient Protection Provisions Adopted by States (by category of issue addressed)	Number of States with Each (popularity) 1999	2001
Network Formation		
Network access standards		
Out-of-network access if network is inadequate	20	24
Freedom-of-choice option	—	24
Point-of-service option	17	18
Continuity of care	21	34
Provider selection/termination		
Written notice of contract termination/nonselection	24	29
Provider appeals process	14	18
Disclosure of selection criteria	17	28
Any willing provider	24	21
Benefits Coverage and Limitations		
Emergency room access	43	41
Access to clinical trials	3	11
Disclosure	27	30
Breast cancer hospital stays	18	17
Utilization Management		
Acceptable definition of medical necessity	3	14
Ban on gag clauses	47	48
Access within network:		
Specialists as primary care providers/direct access	10	15
Direct access to obstetrician-gynecologists	31	26
Standing referrals	13	29
Health plan liability:		
Enrollee right to sue plan for damages	2	7
Prohibition of hold harmless clauses	18	25
Coverage decision notice/timeframes	3	15
Internal appeals process	50	49
Independent external review	22	40
Access to medical records and confidentiality	12	38
Prohibition of genetic discrimination	27	13
Procedures to obtain nonformulary drugs	8	23
Requirements for utilization review	19	33

Table 11-1. *Continued*

Patient Protection Provisions Adopted by States (by category of issue addressed)	Number of States with Each (popularity)	
	1999	2001
Mandated quality assurance/improvements	11	22
Health Maintenance Organization medical directors	—	28
Financial Incentives		
Prohibition on financial incentives to deny care	24	31
Other Provisions		
Managed care report cards	—	25
Consumer assistance program	3	12
Total number of provisions tracked in each year	28	31
Popularity median (number of states with provision of 50th percentile extent)	18	25

Source: Author's compilation from secondary sources; see Marsteller and Bovbjerg (1999) for methods.

Note: State counts are subject to some imprecision, owing to disparate sources.

any plan's contracts with providers (believed to inhibit practitioners from fully informing patients about treatment options).[26] Some provisions were passed in only a handful of states, including acceptable definitions of "medical necessity," a term used to approve or deny payment for care, and statutory authority to sue for personal injury damages. The median provision in terms of "popularity" was enacted in 18 states, and the top seven provisions in about half of the states.[27]

It appears that states sometimes subjected Medicaid managed care plans to the same general patient protection rules as commercial plans and sometimes created separate rules for Medicaid. How many took each approach is unclear. In any case, the Balanced Budget Act of 1997 and its implementing regulations created somewhat less extensive federal provisions for Medicaid MCOs (Rosenbaum and Sonosky 2001).

Legislation has continued to spread, and by mid-2001, the median provision had been enacted in 25 states (of 31 tracked; see figure 11-1). Among states, the most active (Texas) had 26 of the 31 provisions, and the least (Mississippi) had 6; the median state had 16 provisions. Patient protection has had much more legislative success than the any-willing-

Figure 11-1. *Extent of Patient Protections Enacted, 2001*

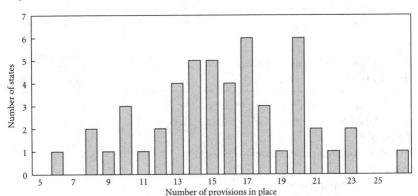

Source: Author's compilation from secondary sources; see Marsteller and Bovbjerg (1999) for methods.

provider and freedom-of-choice laws, possibly because patient protection's lobbying coalitions were stronger. Patients and trial lawyers joined together with medical providers to seek restraints on managed care. Recently, prompt pay statutes have become more frequent. These laws require health plans to pay physician claims within a fixed period unless some problem with a submission is documented.

Follow-up state case studies in 2001 confirmed that many of the 13 states surveyed had enacted additional reforms, often seeking to make their approach more comprehensive. California was the leading example. It not only enacted new reforms in late 1999, including an unusual right to sue, it also created an entirely new administrative agency to write implementing regulations and conduct ongoing oversight (Lutzky and Zuckerman 2002). The California Department of Managed Health Care is the only department of its kind in the country. Massachusetts undertook a lesser reorganization, creating new entities in its departments of health and insurance (Bovbjerg and Ullman 2002). Wisconsin copied other states' significant provisions, but it followed the general national legislative trend rather than respond to specific in-state problems (Bruen and Wiener 2002).

Variations in the number of provisions enacted are easily counted, but variations in the stringency of requirements as written or as implemented also exist. Appeals processes are one provision that has been described in some detail, suggesting considerable differences in operations from state to state (Dallek and Pollitz 2000; Pollitz, Dallek, and Tapay 1998). Better understanding of actual enforcement would be helpful to understand the state-federal balance of interventions on managed care. Expectations about differences in state and federal judicial cultures have already influenced the federal debate over lawsuits against MCOs.

ERISA's Division of State and Federal Responsibility

ERISA affects both how health plan rules are set in advance and how disputes are resolved after the fact.

Patient Protection through Conventional Administrative Regulation

Almost all patient protection provisions call for traditional administrative oversight. State insurance commissioners and departments of health are to promulgate general rules in advance to encourage compliance by MCOs. They then enforce compliance through conventional tools such as administrative review of submitted documentation or plan procedures. Regulatory tools include fines, directives or injunctions, and potentially even withdrawal of licenses to operate in the state. A relatively new administrative tool is independent external appeal of individual benefit denials by MCOs. Independent review is normally delegated to a medically expert private entity, but state agencies decide which entities hear the appeals and oversee the process.

Because of ERISA preemption, states cannot regulate all MCOs, but they have authority over the plans that cover most Americans (table 11-2). States have complete regulatory authority over health insurance sold as individual policies and over state and local employee plans. Sharing power with federal authorities, states may regulate MCOs in Medicaid and Medicare, federal employees' coverage, and private plans sold to employer groups on a fully insured basis, which mainly means small employers. (Non–managed care insurance regulation can also apply, but patient protection applies almost exclusively to managed care.) State regulation can thus reach MCOs covering most enrollees. Perhaps 76 to 92 million people are in fully insured, private workplace plans. States may regulate their health insurers, although not the underlying workplace benefits plan.[28]

Table 11-2. *Employee Retirement Income Security Act (ERISA) Division of Patient-Protection Regulatory Authority*

| | Authority | | |
Type of Health Plan	State	Federal	Comments
Individual private coverage	X		States can regulate because coverage is fully insured and ERISA does not apply.
Medicaid managed care	X	X	States and federal government can regulate Medicaid contractors. States can also regulate because contracted plans are fully insured.
Medicare managed care	X	X	States and federal government can both regulate plans that are Medicaid contractors. States can also regulate because plans are fully insured.
State and local government employees, insured or self-insured	X		States can regulate plans as state contractors and as insurers. No federal regulation because ERISA excepts such plans— and church plans.
Federal Employees Health Benefits Plan	X	X	States can regulate because all plans are insured. Federal government can regulate plans as federal contractors (with Office of Personnel Management).
Private employee benefit plan, insured (small groups, some large ones)	X	X	States can regulate only via rules on insurance practice. Federal government can regulate via ERISA rules on employee benefits plans.
Private employee benefit plan, self-insured (large groups)		X	States cannot regulate at all. Federal government can regulate via ERISA rules on employee benefit plans.

Source: Adapted from President's Advisory Commission on Consumer Protection and Quality in the Health Care Industry (1998).

Some 56 million workers and dependents are in self-insured workplace plans, according to patient protection proponents (Frist 2002). This is the core group subject only to federal rules administered by the Department of Labor. Requirements were traditionally sparse, as noted above, but new standards for employee plans were added in the late 1990s, including more disclosure rules and requirements for internal appeals processes. Department of Labor rules fall well short of typical state patient protections.

Because states can regulate insurance practices but not workplace benefit plans under ERISA, whether courts hold that a particular state rule regulates insurance or instead regulates employee benefits becomes important. Traditionally, what constitutes insurance regulation was interpreted narrowly by courts, which often disallowed regulation of network formation or utilization review, for example. More recently, courts have taken a broader view, either by holding that traditional state authority to tax or regulate medical quality was not meant to be pre-empted by ERISA or by expanding the definition of insurance.[29] A June 2002 U.S. Supreme Court decision upheld an Illinois statute mandating independent external review of disputed benefits denials as protected insurance regulation rather than proscribed regulation of employee benefits.[30] In April 2003, a unanimous U.S. Supreme Court upheld state authority to regulate insurers' selective contracting.[31]

Patient Protection through Managed Care Lawsuits

Since the mid-1990s, judicial determinations about managed care practices have emerged as a key issue (Morgan 2002). The ability to file lawsuits against health plans is now considered part of patient protection, but lawsuits are quite different from legislative provisions in how standards are created and enforced. Lawsuits create oversight by trial judges and juries rather than by administrators, through individual cases decided after the fact rather than general rules set in advance. Judicial standards emerge slowly, as appeals court precedents accumulate in each jurisdiction, and they need not relate to regulatory rules.[32] Judicial enforcement relies on claimants and their lawyers to select cases to litigate, and personal injury law naturally requires claimants to show that they were injured, not just wrongfully treated. Judicial power to impose fines in the form of punitive damages is unlimited, whereas administrators can impose only measured fines set by statute. Lawsuit penalties are paid to claimants and their lawyers, whereas administrative fines are paid to states.

Trial judges oversee each lawsuit, but there is no centralized judicial oversight or record keeping to enable health care regulatory agencies to track the judicial process and its results. Relationships between conventional regulation and lawsuits are formed on an ad hoc basis. A celebrated case may prompt administrators to intervene as well. Results of a landmark lawsuit may prompt one or more states to promulgate new regulations. Conversely, regulators can encourage administrative complainants to sue, or litigants can refer to regulatory standards as a way of showing wrongful behavior.

Ordinarily, judges continuously create new standards of conduct on which to decide personal injury cases without any need of legislative authority. The only reason personal injury lawsuits have become a statutory issue is because traditional interpretations of ERISA preemption bar most such suits from being tried in state court. State lawsuits can be brought against non-ERISA plans, but private benefit plans under ERISA have traditionally been protected because state court proceedings do not constitute insurance regulation (table 11-3). ERISA provides that a claimant dissatisfied with employee health benefits can sue in federal court but can collect as monetary damages only the value of the benefits denied—the standard judicial remedy for a breach of contract.[33]

The rules of personal injury law allow far higher recovery, however. In state personal injury litigation for damage caused by wrongful denial of health benefits, claimants may normally sue for the cost of all remedial health care, past and future, all wages lost, as well as pain and suffering and other nonpecuniary losses the claimant has suffered. Many states cap nonpecuniary awards against medical providers, and some cap such awards for other defendants, including health plans. If a health plan's denial is egregious, punitive damages may also be awarded, and these are not capped. Thus, if a health plan enrollee has suffered an injury serious enough for a contingent-fee lawyer to take the case, both claimant and lawyer would greatly prefer being able to bring state personal injury lawsuits rather than federal ERISA claims.

A few states, starting with Texas and Missouri, have enacted state right-to-sue provisions to create a new basis for personal injury claims and to influence courts' interpretations of ERISA.[34] Advocates have independently persuaded courts to reinterpret ERISA in some instances, finding a plan liable in its capacity as a health care provider or as a supervisor of providers, reasoning that ERISA meant to preempt state oversight of benefits, not of medical quality (Mariner 2001; Rooney 1998).

Table 11-3. *Traditional Employee Retirement Income Security Act (ERISA) Doctrine on Managed Care Litigation*

Type of Health Plan	Authority		Comments
	State	Federal	
Individual private coverage	X		In most states, enrollees can sue health plans in state courts either under contract law to claim denied benefits or under tort law for personal injury, to claim compensation for monetary and intangible losses as well as punitive damages.
Medicaid managed care	X	X	Enrollees cannot sue the federal government but can sue state Medicaid programs and health plans in state courts under either contract law or tort law for personal injury; can also sue state Medicaid programs in federal court to enforce Medicaid statute.
Medicare managed care	X		Claimants cannot sue the federal government but can sue health plans in state courts under either contract law or tort law.
State and local government employees, insured or self-insured	X		In most states, individuals can sue health plans in state courts under contract law for benefits or under tort for personal injury (no ERISA preemption).
Federal Employees Health Benefits Plan	X	X	Enrollees can sue either Office of Personnel Management in federal court or a health plan in state or federal court. Remedies are limited to provision of the service denied, an injunction to order the plan to act, and clarification of future benefits.
Private employee benefit plan, insured (small groups, some large ones)		X	Enrollees can sue plans in federal court, where remedies are limited to provision of the covered service or the cost of that service, an injunction ordering the plan to act, and clarification of future benefits. Traditional rule is that enrollees cannot sue health plans in state courts, but more courts are holding that plans may be sued for personal injury, usually for provider negligence that can be attributed to the plan.
Private employee benefit plan, self-insured (large groups)		X	States cannot regulate at all. Federal government can regulate via rules on employee benefits plans. Lawsuits are the same as for insured employee benefit plans (yes for contract in federal court, sometimes for injury in state court).

Source: Adapted from President's Advisory Commission on Consumer Protection and Quality in the Health Care Industry (1998).

Proponents also seek ERISA modifications in Congress to allow easier access to state courts. Very recent U.S. Supreme Court decisions enhancing state regulatory power over managed care plans under ERISA encourage doctrinal change with regard to liability preemption as well (Bennett 2003).

Proposed Federal Patient Protection Acts

Despite extensive state reforms, there is substantial support for new federal rules as well. One school of thought is that, given the evolution of managed care, self-insured ERISA-only plans should be regulated under uniform federal rules. President Bill Clinton asked the Department of Labor to implement the President's Advisory Commission bill of rights; however, the agency mainly addressed benefit claims procedures and appeals, as there was some concern about the limits of existing ERISA authority (Department of Labor, Pension and Welfare Benefits Administration 2000).

Proponents of patient protection bills offer two sweeping alternative rationales for federal action. One is that ERISA prevents states from regulating as much as they would like, so it needs to be changed. This requires reducing federal authority (the preemption). The other is that varying state action does not go far enough to protect basic rights in health coverage. This calls for increasing federal intervention to set national standards or at least minimum standards—which need to be applied both for insurance regulation (state) and for regulation of self-insurance (federal). Few advocates seem to support full federalization, that is, uniformity of standards nationwide.

Many federal proposals have been made, starting with Representative Charlie Norwood's proposal for the Patient Access to Responsible Care Act, introduced in the mid-1990s. The House passed one version in 1998, but it was never taken up in the Senate. The federalism debate was sharpest in 1999 (106th Congress, first session). In many contending bills, Democrats, including President Bill Clinton, generally supported national minimum standards for MCOs, while Senate Republicans and the House Republican leadership took a states-rights posture of deference to state regulations and only limited new federal regulation of self-insurance.[35]

With regard to lawsuits, Democrats wanted to rely on state courts, while the Republican leadership wanted to keep litigation federal.

After much legislative jockeying, the Senate passed a narrowly drawn Republican bill led by Senator Trent Lott in July 1999, while the House passed a more sweeping bipartisan bill led by Representatives John Dingell and Charlie Norwood in October. The competing bills languished in conference after the House leadership appointed only opponents of the House bill to serve on the conference committee. Senate supporters failed to revive the House bill the following spring after attaching it to a defense spending bill, and activity waned as political energies turned to the 2000 election campaigns.[36]

George W. Bush's presidential campaign touted patient protection on the Texas model, although as governor he had resisted many of its provisions. Under the Bush administration and the new Congress in 2001, the previously salient political differences on federalism—state versus federal authority—almost disappeared.[37] The Republican congressional leadership dropped its insistence on regulating only self-insured ERISA plans and its refusal to intervene in state regulation; consensus grew on basic federal protections of such things as access to emergency rooms and obstetricians; and the ongoing dispute centered almost entirely upon lawsuits. Broad proposals favored giving state courts jurisdiction and setting no limits on state awards, although some limits would be set on federal awards. The narrow bill supported by the administration sought to keep all benefits litigation in federal court and to limit nonpecuniary awards to $500,000. Democrats and many rank-and-file Republicans, including Representative Norwood, held that only unfettered litigation in state court could give teeth to patient protection, while President Bush urged appeals rights as superior to litigation and said he would veto any bill that did not impose significant caps on court awards.

In late June 2001, the Senate passed the broad Kennedy-McCain-Edwards bill after Senator Jim Jeffords dropped his Republican affiliation and Democrats assumed control of that chamber. The Bush administration lobbied for narrower rights to sue and in early August announced a compromise with Representative Norwood to support limitations on state courts and caps on awards. The resulting $1.5 million cap on pain and suffering is much higher than the $250,000 to $1 million caps set by about half the states. However, there was a $1.5 million cap on punitive awards, which states do not cap. The House quickly passed a bill largely adhering to this compromise, on a nearly party-line vote, and the two chambers' bills were referred to a conference committee. The terrorist attacks of September 11, 2001, diverted attention from the bills, however, and only sporadic negotiations on patient protection have since occurred, not sustained progress toward enactment.[38]

How Federal Patient Protection Would Affect States

The impact of any new federal patient protection statute would vary by state, depending on the extent of existing state regulation and the proportion of the insured population covered by managed care. States with high managed care penetration and few existing regulations would be greatly affected by any new federal rules, whereas states with low penetration and more existing regulations would see little change. Figure 11-2 illustrates these variations.

The range of state variation shows in an assessment of the 13 *Assessing the New Federalism* states in mid-1999 (Marsteller and Bovbjerg 1999). Since that time, the impact of any new federal law has probably been

Figure 11-2. *Likely Impact of Federal Enactment*

A Function of Extent of State Regulation and Managed Care Organization (MCO) Penetration

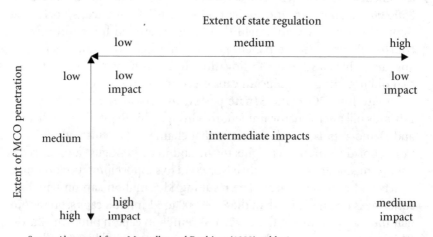

Source: Abstracted from Marsteller and Bovbjerg (1999), table 6.

reduced, for a number of reasons. HMOs, the form of managed care that restricts patient options most at the time of care, are no longer growing. All forms of managed care seem to have reduced restrictions on patients and financial incentives for providers and to have increased choice for consumers. Managed care regulation has increased as well, which means that fewer states fall below likely national minimum standards.

Nevertheless, the significant federal legislative proposals would increase MCO regulation and enrollee rights considerably. All states would see big changes for their self-insured enrollees in managed care. New federal authorization to sue for personal injury in state court would be a significant change everywhere, whether or not damage awards are capped. Accordingly, lawsuit provisions have drawn very sharp objections not only from MCOs but also from large employers, who greatly fear being targeted for some alleged MCO wrongdoing, despite legislative drafters' attempts to shelter them.[39]

Even unenacted federal patient protection has probably helped shift managed care practice, along with the employee backlash during the tight labor market of the late 1990s (Draper et al. 2002; Gabel et al. 2002; Robinson 2001). In response, as noted above, many managed care plans reduced restrictions. They also deemphasized financial incentives, increased reliance on quality-oriented guidelines, and accepted more consumer-oriented processes for dispute resolution. The American Association of Health Plans, the national trade association of MCOs, promulgated a code of conduct that has added patient protections over time, partly in an effort to stave off additional federal legislation (American Association of Health Plans, undated; Ignagni 1999).

Concluding Discussion: Implications for Federalism

The shift in state-federal responsibilities in insurance regulation holds several lessons for health care federalism but less insight into policy for increasing health insurance coverage.

State Innovation and Diffusion of Methods across Governments

Innovation in insurance regulatory policy has occurred largely at the state level. Historically, this was true because the states were in charge. But states have continued to lead in managed care regulation, even though managed care really began with a federal law, the HMO Act of 1974, and even though a presidential commission developed a patient bill of rights in 1997.

Innovation has diffused across states, generating similar statutes in most of them. A kind of race to the top in managed care legislation has occurred, in that many states continue to add new provisions, following the lead of others. This is consistent with the idea of states as laboratories of democracy, but cross-state learning so far appears mainly to have taken the form of copying other states' provisions, often those promoted nationally by medical and consumer interest groups. Less cross-state learning seems to have occurred about best practices in design and implementation. Over time, through the NAIC or other mechanisms, such learning could occur.[40] For now, individual states are still learning about their own success, as shown by California's starting over with a new managed care department—a development not much imitated elsewhere.

Even with considerable copying of one another's provisions, states' regulatory regimes vary considerably. Enforcement may vary even more, but that has received little study. State variation in protections has been a key argument for higher federal standards—just as much lower Medicaid income eligibility ceilings in some states generate proposals for higher federal minimum standards.

Federal lawmakers have often followed the lead of pioneering states, often explicitly seeking lessons from the field (Sebelius 1999). Virtually every enacted or proposed federal provision copies a preexisting state provision (Marsteller and Bovbjerg 1999, table 6). Such copying and extension are not new. COBRA requirements built on state ones. Federal Medigap legislation first required all states to use NAIC model state rules, then observed the result for a number of years, and finally set more binding federal standards, which were themselves based on some states' efforts to standardize competing Medigap plans. HIPAA adapted some provisions from state individual and small-group insurance market reforms to apply to all coverage, and the HIPAA amendments, such as minimum maternity, were also copied from some states' reforms.

Willingness of Federal Policymakers to Supersede State Authority

Federal policymakers may look to state policy for regulatory models, but they have shown themselves quite willing to override states when they perceive a national interest. The federal government has moved from delegating all of its insurance regulatory authority to the states in 1945 (McCarran-Ferguson Act) to preempting state authority in the 1970s (HMO Act and ERISA), setting targeted national rules in the 1980s (Medigap and COBRA continuation coverage), and creating a broader, more organized framework in the 1990s for federal standards with state implementation and enforcement (HIPAA). Pending bills for federal patient protection use the HIPAA framework.

Federal enactments have seldom sought to create national uniformity, although the second Medigap reform of 1990 came close. Some interstate commerce calls for federally imposed uniformity—for example, air traffic control—but insurance regulation and patient protection have not been seen this way. For insurance regulation, one could argue for repeal of McCarran-Ferguson to deregulate insurance in favor of nationally consistent consumer protection and policing of competition through the antitrust laws. Or one could support uniform regulation to level the playing field, with consistent rules for all competitors. Increasingly, some insurers are showing a willingness to consider uniform federal regulation as an alternative to compliance with numerous state regimes. A uniform deregulatory strategy has often been proposed based on enhanced competition, but the political demand for regulation has been strong at both state and federal levels. So far, federal policymakers have wanted, at most, a fallback role for federal insurance regulation, as under HIPAA; and for most of the time since ERISA, federal policy has not sought much regulation of employee benefit plans by the Department of Labor.

As to patient rights, one might argue for national rights as an attribute of national citizenship and thus call for equality of rights across states and across health plans as a matter of equity. The President's Advisory Commission seemed to view rights as national, although subject to differing modes of implementation, and the breadth of the consumer backlash against managed care suggests that the population may agree. But the national rights view has not prevailed politically or legislatively. ERISA reflected the concern that variation in state rules would impair interstate operations of employee benefit plans, but it left the nature and extent of health coverage up to each plan. Thus, ERISA allowed each plan to operate uniformly across states but did not require any uniformity across plans. Without the ERISA preemption, states would have autonomy over insurance and benefits, which would probably achieve more uniformity across different forms of coverage within each state, yet would eliminate uniformity for each benefits plan across states. Only uniform federal rules could create the same patient rights, or other regulations, across states and plans simultaneously.

In practice, insurance and managed care fall into the constitutional realm of overlapping federal-state authority, not governed exclusively by either level of government. Within this realm of shared authority, the federal role has grown over time. HIPAA and federal patient protection proposals rely on federal minimum standard setting and state implementation, at least for insured coverage. Because standards are minimums rather than preemptive, cross-state variation is reduced rather than eliminated. For large, self-insured groups, direct federal regulation applies, thus maintaining national uniformity.

How does this Medigap-HIPAA-patient protection model of regulation fit within the history and theory of federalism (see Chapter 2)? In a way, HIPAA-style minimum standards expect the states to act as agents of the federal government. But states are expected to go beyond the federal directive and above the federal minimums. Even in implementing the minimums, states have far more discretion than most agents are given by their principals. Nor does the federal government delegate all similar activities to the quasi-agent states; instead, it keeps the self-insured benefit plans separate from similar ones that buy insured coverage.

The HIPAA model superficially follows the theory that federal-state responsibilities should be sorted out on the basis of the nature of an activity and the respective capabilities of state and federal oversight. One might argue, as the President's Advisory Commission seemed to imply, that the general nature and extent of consumer rights in health care call for national standards, but that the states can best address enforcement issues, such as adequacy of managed care networks or resolution of fact-specific complaints.[41]

The analogy breaks down, however, because in practice states also set rights and the federal government also enforces requirements, like those on plans covered under ERISA. A functional analysis of roles suggests that some aspects of insurance and managed care operate nationally, even internationally—for example, the generation of capital, some pooling of risk and reinsurance, and the investment of reserves—much as other financial markets do. For such reasons, some observers find state-by-state regulation illogical and inefficient.[42]

Other aspects of health insurance are closely tied to local medical markets—including doctor-patient relationships and decisionmaking on care, which are what most patient protections seek to protect. The managed care practices being protected against can be either local (such as the creation of metropolitan area networks of primary care doctors) or regional and national (such as the selection of medical centers of excellence for specialized inpatient care, development of hospital utilization standards, or operation of telephone preauthorization centers).[43] To date, regulatory debates have not involved such sorting out.

States have largely acquiesced in the emergence of national rules, so long as they control implementation and day-to-day regulatory operations. Despite some complaints about unfunded mandates, almost all states quickly accepted responsibility for enforcing federal standards under HIPAA and passed conforming state legislation when needed (CMS 2002). Acceptance may have been improved because the budgetary demands of regulating insurance are not large, certainly not compared with Medicaid mandates, and because the new federal requirements closely resembled prior state enactments.[44]

Increasing Patient Protections and Increasing Coverage

The regulatory developments discussed in this chapter have done little to expand health care coverage. Some state insurance reforms and the federal HIPAA statute sought to improve access to coverage, but neither has done much to keep premiums affordable or subsidize the purchase of premiums (GAO 1998; Sloan, Conover, and Hall 1999). State patient protection laws have improved insured managed care enrollees' access to some medical services, but the rights conferred apply only to those already covered. Ample evidence shows that people without health insurance coverage have much less access to care (Hadley 2002), and patient protections "often are meaningless to Americans who cannot obtain health care when they need it," in the words of the President's Advisory Commission (1998). A federal patient protection act would have the greatest impact on the legal rights of persons enrolled in large self-insured plans, already the population with the best coverage. It would bring about little change in coverage of low-income people, most of whom lack coverage or have state patient protection within Medicaid managed care or privately insured individual and small-group plans.

New Federal Standards for State Insurance Regulation as a Precedent for State Coverage Expansion

The history of insurance regulation and the evolution of managed care regulation show a great increase in federal activism. Does this suggest an evolution in attitudes that would support a larger federal role in promoting health coverage through states?

On one hand, it may be argued that the growth in federal insurance regulation has little relevance to the federal role in promoting state coverage expansion. Full federal patient protection has not been enacted. The HMO Act and ERISA are the strongest federal interventions in private coverage, but these acts imposed few new federal requirements, instead preempting state regulation and promoting deregulation and market-based evolution of health coverage. The federal Medigap statutes and HIPAA intervened most to improve access to coverage, but neither involved any financial support or much changed levels of coverage.

Finally, consensus for federal patient protection lags behind consensus for visibly attacking managed care. Legislative positions have reflected attitudes about managed care more than beliefs about federal versus state roles. Managed care opponents favored stronger national regulation but also stronger state judicial authority. Proponents, in stark contrast, have often favored state regulation (perceived to be less potent) but completely federal managed care lawsuits (perceived to be less potent). Attitudes about litigation also dominate philosophies of federalism; final compromise was blocked by disagreements on lawsuits, not states' rights.

On the other hand, growing federal regulation shows more willingness to assert federal authority when policymakers perceive a national interest. Legislators have not committed many federal funds, but they have been willing to compel state and private spending, especially for HIPAA compliance. On patient protection, starting with Representative Norwood's original bill, it is notable that proposals have drawn active support from both liberals and conservatives, Democrats and Republicans. Despite early differences over federal patient protection that were couched in terms of federalism, rough consensus has grown on major regulatory provisions, and states' rights arguments have almost vanished from the debates. As of mid-2002, even the bills of House Republicans who formerly refused to intervene in state policymaking included federal minimum standards for states.

Federal coverage policy might emulate regulatory policy in becoming more activist. Given the need for financing, however, considerable political effort is needed to support federal activism to increase coverage.

NOTES

1. For example, federal tax law influences reserving and accounting practices, as well as the design of health benefits; federal programs such as flood insurance compete with or supplant private coverage (which was believed to be unfairly limited); and federal rules on the structure of the financial services industry (changed in the Gramm-Leach-Bliley Act of 1999) affect state regulation of insurance, banking, and securities.

2. PL 93-406, 29 U.S. Code §§ 1001 and following. A basic source on health insurance law and federal enactments is Furrow et al. (2000); Chapter 8 (423–65) covers ERISA.

3. PL 104-191, 29 U.S. Code §§ 1181-1182. HIPAA is also known as the Kennedy-Kassebaum Act, after its principal Senate sponsors.

4. New Hampshire in 1851 created the first regulatory body, a board of insurance commissioners. Other states quickly followed. *Paul v. Virginia*, 231 U.S. 495 (1869) found that insurance is not "interstate commerce" reserved for federal control and upheld the right of Virginia to force Samuel Paul to obtain a state license and pay a security deposit. See also Vaughan and Vaughan (1999), Chapter 6 (92–120) on "Regulation of the Insurance Industry."

5. *U.S. v. South-Eastern Underwriters Association*, 322 U.S. 533 (1944) (antitrust case against multiple competing insurers' joint rate making through a rating bureau).

6. PL 15, 15 U.S. Code §§ 1011-1015.

7. PL 93-222, 42 U.S. Code § 300e; Mitka (1998).

8. Preferred provider organizations (PPOs) selectively contract with medical providers to offer services at a discount, and patients must pay more to visit nonpreferred providers (Gabel et al. 1986). Point-of-service plans allow health maintenance organization (HMO) subscribers at the time of care the option to use providers outside the HMO group or network, on a PPO-like basis. See Aventis Pharmaceuticals (2000). The original federal HMO requirements were also modified in keeping with market developments—for example, with regard to community rating of premiums, which employers often felt allowed HMOs to charge them higher prices than merited for the younger, healthier population that often elected HMO coverage when given the choice (HMO Act Amendments of 1988, PL 100-517, codified in various portions of 42 U.S. Code § 300e).

9. Conventional wisdom suggests that congressional decisionmakers were focused on pensions rather than health benefits; they did not expect ERISA to last long in health coverage, as national health insurance was expected (Fox 1989). A close reading of the record, however, shows that preemption of state health insurance regulation was intended by the conference committee that wrote the final legislation (Nichols and Blumberg 1998). It is notable that health benefits less clearly needed new rules than pensions. Health benefits are renegotiated year to year and promise benefits only for that term, rather than over a lifetime of potentially different employment. The ERISA preemption for employment benefit plans somewhat paralleled the earlier state practice of regulating nongroup insurance more closely than group plans, on the theory that large groups can look after themselves.

10. Key cases are *New York State Conference of Blue Cross and Blue Shield Plans v. Travelers Insurance Company*, 514 U.S. 645 (1995) (state may surcharge health plan sold to employer group); *Rush Prudential HMO v. Moran*, 536 U.S. 355 (2002) (states may regulate benefits/dispute resolution of HMOs); and *Kentucky Association of Health Plans v. Miller*, No. 00-1471, April 2, 2003 (http://laws.findlaw.com/us/00-1471.html).

11. The Baucus Amendment of 1980 offered federal certification for Medigap policies meeting National Association of Insurance Commissioners (NAIC) standards administered by states. Medigap reform provisions in the Omnibus Budget Reconciliation Act of 1990 strictly defined 10 types of policies that could be sold; states must enforce the federal rules or no Medigap policy may be sold, and insurers selling non-state-approved policies face strong federal fines (Fox, Rice, and Alecxih 1995). See also the Centers for Medicare and Medicaid Services (CMS) Medigap Web page at http://cms.hhs.gov/medigap/frnnaic.pdf.

12. PL 99-272, codified at 29 U.S. Code §§ 1161-1168. The basic continuation period is 18 months, but under various circumstances it may be extended.

13. Hawaii's Prepaid Health Care Act of 1974; see Miike (1993).

14. Codified at 29 U.S.C. § 1144(b)(5); see Miike (1993).

15. *An Act to Make Health Security Available to All Citizens of the Commonwealth and to Improve Hospital Financing*, Chapter 23 of the Acts of 1988. Technically, the law did not mandate insurance, only tax on uninsured companies; it was a play-or-pay mandate. See Holahan et al. (1997). On states' options under ERISA, see Butler (2000).

16. Evaluations of the effectiveness of these state rules show mixed results (Marsteller et al. 1998; Morrisey and Jensen 1996; Sloan, Conover, and Hall 1999).

17. See, for example, CMS (2002) and the Department of Health and Human Services (DHHS), Office for Civil Rights-HIPAA, "Medical Privacy—National Standards to Protect the Privacy of Personal Health Information" (http://www.hhs.gov/ocr/hipaa).

18. The privacy and other aspects of HIPAA have had large effects, however, necessitating major efforts by states, medical providers, and health plans to alter their information and record-keeping systems.

19. PL 104-204, 29 U.S. Code § 1185(a); 42 U.S. Code § 300gg.

20. Ibid.

21. See Gabel et al. (2000) for data on employer groups of 200 or more employees.

22. This discussion is based on Marsteller et al. (1997). Numbers reflect compilation from several tracking services and news accounts.

23. *Kentucky Association of Health Plans v. Miller*, No. 00-1471, April 2, 2003 (http://laws.findlaw.com/us/00-1471.html).

24. One recent tally showed even fewer provisions in force than tabulated in early years from multiple sources (Morgan 2001).

25. For full details, see Marsteller and Bovbjerg (1999). Some provisions may be established by regulation under preexisting statutory authority, but significant ones appear to come through legislation.

26. Anti-gag clause provisions were a top priority of medical societies. A U.S. General Accounting Office review of managed care contracts could find no actual examples of such clauses (GAO 1997).

27. For a full list of provisions and extent of state enactment as of mid-1999, see Marsteller and Bovbjerg (1999), table 3.

28. It is important to keep in mind that an employee benefit plan differs from a health plan—which is one reason that ERISA doctrine seems so complex and nonintuitive. In ordinary usage, a health plan can mean any form of coverage, private or public, whether insured or not. Health plans include indemnity insurers, MCOs (including HMOs and PPOs), self-funded employer-sponsored plans, Taft-Hartley trusts, church plans, association plans, state and local government employee programs, and Medicare and Medicaid. A benefit plan, however, refers to a workplace undertaking to provide health or other fringe benefits, which might or might not use an outside insurer or health plan. Benefit plans are also called ERISA plans.

29. A turning point was the U.S. Supreme Court decision *New York State Conference of Blue Cross and Blue Shield Plans v. Travelers Insurance Company,* 514 U.S. 645 (1995). See Furrow et al. (2000).

30. *Rush Prudential H.M.O. Inc. v. Moran,* 536 U.S. 355, 2002 (http://supct.law .cornell.edu/supct/html/00-1021.ZS.html); see Greenhouse (2002).

31. *Kentucky Association of Health Plans v. Miller,* No. 00-1471, April 2, 2003 (http://laws.findlaw.com/us/00-1471.html).

32. An injured party normally shows that a defendant health plan behaved wrongfully in reference to judicially created principles of tort law. However, tort law allows proof of wrongdoing based on failure to follow duties created by statute as well, including patient protection statutes.

33. Not dissimilarly, where a state Medicaid program is the target of a federal court lawsuit for improper refusal of a Medicaid benefit, only injunctive relief is possible—an order to pay the benefit or otherwise modify administrative practice—not monetary damages. See the extended discussion in Blumstein and Sloan (2000). One well-publicized lower federal court decision, *Westside Mothers v. Haveman,* held that no lawsuits could be brought by beneficiaries against states, as states were only voluntary contractors with the federal government to run Medicaid (Pear 2001b). This theory was overturned on appeal, and the U.S. Supreme Court let that decision stand (US LEXIS 8694, No. 02-277 [U.S. Dec. 2, 2002] http://supct.law.cornell.edu/supct/html/120202.ZOR.html).

34. Fourteen states had enacted some form of liability for managed care plans as of August 2002; about 30 legislatures had considered such bills without passing them (National Conference of State Legislatures, Managed Care Insurer Liability, updated August 7, 2002; http://www.ncsl.org/programs/health/liable.htm).

35. One recurring Republican proposal would have preempted state law (not for patient protection rules but for the limited purpose of promoting deregulatory Republi-

can ideas) for association health plans and health marts that the bills would free from state regulation. These are similar to multiple-employer groupings now regulated by states under an ERISA amendment. The bills would deregulate them so that small groups could band together to buy insurance of their own design on a quasi-group basis. See, for example, U.S. House of Representatives, Small Business Committee (1999).

36. On these early developments, see Marsteller and Bovbjerg (1999) (multiple contending bills); *American Health Line* (1999) (Senate passage of Senator Lott's S. 1344 on July 15); Hohler (1999) (House passage of H.R. 2723 of Representatives Dingle and Norwood on October 7); *American Health Line* (2000) (House patient protection bill loses as rider to Senate spending bill).

37. One side-by-side news analysis of provisions in the House and Senate bills noted that they "are almost identical in the protection they offer people with insurance ... the bills differ in the way patients would be allowed to enforce their rights" (Lee 2001).

38. On developments in 2001 and 2002, see Goldstein (2001) (Bush position); Welch (2001); *American Health Line* (2001) (passage of S.1052, June 29); Pear (2001a) (Bush-Norwood compromise); Goldstein and Eilperin (2001) (House passage of H.R. 2563 of Rep. Ganske); Pear (2002) (continuing negotiations); Ornstein (2002) (history of failed federal proposals).

39. Schnader et al. (1999); American Benefits Council (2002) (association representing employer-sponsored benefit programs, has hyperlinks to numerous documents opposing expansion of liability).

40. By 1999, the NAIC had promulgated model acts with a number of patient protection provisions, particularly the most common ones (Sebelius 1999).

41. The federal government, however, oversees dispute resolution for all of Medicare, including managed care, using national models and some private contractors for appeals from managed care determinations.

42. See Bishop (2002). ("Why is insurance regulated not federally but at the state level, mostly by elected insurance commissioners? Nobody really thinks this makes sense.") The insurance industry has long supported state rather than federal regulation, but in the late 1990s some large companies for the first time began to lobby for a federal regime (Harrington 2002).

43. There are philosophical and practical rationales for deferring to state authority in medicine, as discussed in Chapter 2, but it is hard to argue that standards for technical effectiveness or quality of medical care appropriately vary by state.

44. HIPAA's main budgetary impact on states comes not from having to regulate private insurance but from its Medicaid programs having to comply with federal electronic data and privacy rules, which requires substantial effort for them, along with all other health care actors.

REFERENCES

American Association of Health Plans. "Code of Conduct" (undated, continuously updated). http://www.aahp.org/Content/NavigationMenu/About_AAHP/What_ We_Stand_For/Code_of_Conduct/Code_of_Conduct.htm.

American Benefits Council. 2002. "Health: Patients' Bill of Rights." http://www.american benefitscouncil.org/issues/health/billofrights.htm. (Accessed October 22, 2002.)

American Health Line. 1999. "Politics & Policy—Patients' Rights: GOP Scores, Dems Plot Future Course." *American Health Line,* July 16.

———. 2000. "Politics & Policy—Patients' Rights: Senate Narrowly Rejects Measure." *American Health Line,* June 9.

———. 2001. "Patients' Rights: Senate Approves Kennedy-McCain-Edwards." *American Health Line,* July 2.

Aventis Pharmaceuticals. 2000. "HMO Point-of-Service Plans, Managed Care Digest Series." http://www.managedcaredigest.com/edigests/hm2000/hm2000c01s06g01 .html. (Accessed April 16, 2003.)

Bennett, Johanna. 2003. "Ruling on Kentucky Law May Boost HMOs' Litigation Risks." *Wall Street Journal,* April 2.

Bernstein, Sharon. 2000. "Under Pressure, Health Plans Pledge Reforms." *Los Angeles Times,* July 19.

Bishop, Matthew. 2002. "Survey: International Finance; The Regulator Who Isn't There: Does a Global Financial System Need a Global Regulator?" *The Economist,* May 16. http://www.economist.com/surveys/displayStory.cfm?story_id=1119911.

Blumstein, James F., and Frank A. Sloan. 2000. "Health Care Reform Through Medicaid Managed Care: Tennessee (TennCare) as a Case Study and a Paradigm." *Vanderbilt Law Review* 53(1): 125–270.

Bovbjerg, Randall R., and Frank C. Ullman. 2002. "Health Insurance and Health Access: Reengineering Local Safety Nets." *Journal of Legal Medicine* 22(2): 247–62.

Bovbjerg, Randall R., Charles C. Griffin, and Caitlin E. Carroll. 1993. "U.S. Health Care Coverage and Costs: Historical Development and Choices for the 1990s." *Journal of Law, Medicine and Ethics* 21(2): 141–62.

Bruen, Brian K., and Joshua M. Wiener. 2002. *Recent Changes in Health Policy for Low-Income People in Wisconsin.* Washington, D.C.: The Urban Institute. *Assessing the New Federalism* State Update No. 25.

Butler, Patricia A. 2000. *ERISA and State Health Care Access Initiatives: Opportunities and Obstacles.* New York: Commonwealth Fund, pub. no. 411, October. http://www .cmwf.org/programs/insurance/butler_erisa_411.pdf.

Centers for Medicare and Medicaid Services (CMS). 2002. "HIPAA Insurance Reform: Direct Enforcement." http://cms.hhs.gov/hipaa/hipaa1/content/enforcement.asp. (Accessed August 29, 2002.)

Committee on the Consequences of Uninsurance, Institute of Medicine. 2002. *Care Without Coverage: Too Little, Too Late.* Washington, D.C.: National Academy Press.

Dallek, Geraldine, and Karen Pollitz. 2000. *External Review of Health Plan Decisions: An Update.* Washington, D.C.: The Henry J. Kaiser Family Foundation.

Department of Labor, Pension and Welfare Benefits Administration. 2000. "Employee Retirement Income Security Act of 1974; Rules and Regulations for Administration and Enforcement; Claims Procedure; Final Rule." *Federal Register* 65(225): 70245–271, 29 CFR Part 2560.

Draper, Debra A., Robert E. Hurley, Cara C. Lesser, and Bradley C. Strunk. 2002. "The Changing Face of Managed Care." *Health Affairs* 21(1): 11–23.

Fox, Daniel M. 1989. "Health Policy and ERISA: Interest Groups and Semipreemption." *Journal of Health Politics, Policy and Law* 14(2): 239–60.

Fox, Peter D., Thomas Rice, and Lisa Alecxih. 1995. "Medigap Regulation: Lessons for Health Care Reform." *Journal of Health Politics, Policy and Law* 20(1): 31–48.

Frist, Bill. 2002. "Patients' Bill of Rights: Summary of the Frist-Breaux-Jeffords Bipartisan Patients' Bill of Rights Act of 2001." http://frist.senate.gov/2002/health/patients rights.cfm. (Accessed October 22, 2002.)

Furrow, Barry R., Thomas L. Greaney, Sandra H. Johnson, Timothy Stoltzfus Jost, and Robert L. Schwartz. 2000. *Health Law,* 2d ed. St. Paul, Minn.: Westlaw.

Gabel, Jon, and Gail Jensen. 1989. "The Price of State Mandated Benefits." *Inquiry* 26(4): 419–31.

Gabel, Jon, Dan Ermann, Thomas Rice, and Gregory de Lissovoy. 1986. "The Emergence and Future of PPOs." *Journal of Health Politics, Policy and Law* 11(2): 305–22.

Gabel, Jon, Paul B. Ginsburg, Heidi H. Whitmore, and Jeremy D. Pickreign. 2000. "Withering on the Vine: The Decline of Indemnity Health Insurance." *Health Affairs* 19(5): 152–57.

Gabel, Jon, Larry Levitt, Erin Holve, Jeremy Pickreign, Heidi Whitmore, Kelley Dhont, Samantha Hawkins, and Diane Rowland. 2002. "Job-Based Health Benefits in 2002: Some Important Trends." *Health Affairs* 21(5): 143–51.

Garrett, Bowen, Len M. Nichols, and Emily K. Greenman. 2001. "Workers without Health Insurance: Who Are They and How Can Policy Reach Them?" Washington, D.C.: The Urban Institute/Kellogg Foundation. http://www.urban.org/pdfs /workershealthins.pdf. (Accessed October 21, 2002.)

Goldstein, Amy. 2001. "Bush Backs New Patients' Rights Bill: Bill Offers Restricted Ability to Sue, and Other Safeguards." *Washington Post*, May 15.

Goldstein, Amy, and Juliet Eilperin. 2001. "House Passes Patients' Rights: Bush-Norwood Deal Prevails, Setting Up Battle in Conference." *Washington Post*, August 3.

Greenhouse, Linda. 2002. "Court, 5-4, Upholds Authority of States to Protect Patients." *New York Times*, June 21. http://www.nytimes.com/2002/06/21/national /21HEAL.html. (Accessed October 22, 2002.)

Gruber, Jonathan. 1994. "State-Mandated Benefits and Employer-Provided Health Insurance." *Journal of Public Economics* 55: 433–64.

Hadley, Jack. 2002. *Sicker and Poorer: The Consequences of Being Uninsured.* Washington, D.C.: The Henry J. Kaiser Family Foundation.

Harrington, Scott E. 2002. "Repairing Insurance Markets." *Regulation* 25(2): 58–63.

Hohler, Bob. 1999. "House OK's Protections for Patients: Sweeping Plan Lets Consumers Sue HMOs after Improper Care." *Boston Globe*, October 8.

Holahan, John, Joshua M. Wiener, and Amy Westpfahl Lutzky. 2002. "Health Policy for Low-Income People: States' Responses to New Challenges." *Health Affairs* 21(4): W187–W218. http://www.healthaffairs.org/WebExclusives/2104Holahan2.pdf. (Accessed October 22, 2002.)

Holahan, John, Randall Bovbjerg, Alison Evans, Joshua Wiener, and Susan Flanagan. 1997. *Health Policy for Low-Income People in Massachusetts.* Washington, D.C.: The Urban Institute. *Assessing the New Federalism State Reports.*

Ignagni, Karen M. 1999. *Statement on Role of Government in Regulating Health Insurance Plans, Before the United States Senate Health, Education, Labor and Pensions*

Committee. Washington, D.C.: American Association of Health Plans, March 11, 1999. http://www.aahp.org/DocTemplate.cfm?Section=Comprehensive&template=/ContentManagement/ContentDisplay.cfm&ContentID=974. (Accessed April 16, 2003.)

Lee, Christopher. 2001. "House OKs Patients' Rights Bill." *Dallas Morning News*, August 3.

Leone, Peter R. 1994. "New Developments in 'Any Willing Provider' Laws." *Healthcare Financial Management* 48(5): 32, 34–5.

Lutzky, Amy Westpfahl, and Stephen Zuckerman. 2002. *Recent Changes in Health Policy for Low-Income People in California.* Washington, D.C.: The Urban Institute. *Assessing the New Federalism* State Update No. 14.

Mariner, Wendy K. 2001. "Slouching toward Managed Care Liability: Reflections on Doctrinal Boundaries, Paradigm Shifts, and Incremental Reform." *Journal of Law, Medicine and Ethics* 29(3–4): 253–77.

Marsteller, Jill A., and Randall R. Bovbjerg. 1999. *Federalism and Patient Protection: Changing Roles for State and Federal Government.* Washington, D.C.: The Urban Institute. *Assessing the New Federalism* Occasional Paper No. 28.

Marsteller, Jill A., Randall R. Bovbjerg, Len M. Nichols, and Diana K. Verrilli. 1997. "The Resurgence of Selective Contracting Restrictions." *Journal of Health Politics, Policy and Law* 22(5): 1133–89.

Marsteller, Jill A., Len Nichols, Adam Badawi, Bethany Kessler, Shruti Rajan, and Stephen Zuckerman. 1998. *Variations in the Uninsured: State and County Level Analyses.* Washington, D.C.: The Urban Institute. http://www.urban.org/UploadedPDF/variatfull.pdf. (Accessed April 16, 2003.)

Miike, Lawrence. 1993. *Health Insurance: The Hawaii Experience.* Washington, D.C.: U.S. Congress, Office of Technology Assessment, Background Paper, OTA-BP-H-108, June; NTIS order #PB93-203743. http://www.wws.princeton.edu/cgi-bin/byteserv.prl/~ota/disk1/1993/9327/9327.pdf.

Mitka, Mike. 1998. "A Quarter Century of Health Maintenance." *Journal of the American Medical Association* 280: 2059–60.

Morgan, Rachel. 2001. "Any Willing Provider." *Issue Brief.* Washington, D.C.: Health Policy Tracking Service, National Conference of State Legislatures.

———. 2002. "Insurer Liability." *Issue Brief.* Washington, D.C.: Health Policy Tracking Service, National Conference of State Legislatures.

Morrisey, Michael A., and Gail A. Jensen. 1996. "State Small-Group Insurance Reform." In *Health Policy, Federalism, and the American States*, edited by Robert F. Rich and William D. White (71–95). Washington, D.C.: Urban Institute Press.

Nichols, Len M., and Linda J. Blumberg. 1998. "A Different Kind of 'New Federalism'? The Health Insurance Portability and Accountability Act of 1996." *Health Affairs* 17(3): 25–42.

Ornstein, Charles. 2002. "Little Hope Is Seen in Reviving Bills on Patients' Rights." *Los Angeles Times*, January 10.

Pear, Robert. 2001a. "Deal Is Reached on a Bill to Set Patients' Rights." *New York Times*, August 2.

———. 2001b. "Ruling in Michigan Bars Suits Against State Over Medicaid." *New York Times*, May 13.

———. 2002. "Kennedy and Bush Negotiate on Patients' Rights, Alarming Their Allies." *New York Times*, January 23.

Peterson, Mark, ed. 1999. "The Managed Care Backlash." *Journal of Health Politics, Policy and Law* 24(5): 876–1218.

Pollitz, Karen, Geraldine Dallek, and Nicole Tapay. 1998. *External Review of Health Plan Decisions: An Overview of Key Program Features in the States and Medicare.* (Prepared for the Kaiser Family Foundation by the Institute for Health Care Research and Policy, Georgetown University). Washington, D.C.: The Henry J. Kaiser Family Foundation.

President's Advisory Commission on Consumer Protection and Quality in the Health Care Industry. 1997. *Consumer Bill of Rights and Responsibilities*, issued as a *Report to the President of the United States* in November, published as appendix A of the Commission's final report, *Quality First: Better Health Care for All Americans*, March 12, 1998. http://www.hcqualitycommission.gov/final/append_a.html.

———. 1998. *Quality First: Better Health Care for All Americans. Report to the President*, March 12. http://www.hcqualitycommission.gov/final.

Robinson, Jaime C. 2001. "The End of Managed Care." *Journal of the American Medical Association* 285(20): 2622–28.

Rooney, Curtis D. 1998. "The States, Congress, or the Courts: Who Will Be First to Reform ERISA Remedies?" *Annals of Health Law* 7: 73–106.

Rosenbaum, Sara, and Colleen Sonosky. 2001. *An Analysis of the Bush Administration's Proposed Medicaid Managed Care Regulations.* Washington, D.C.: Center for Health Services Research and Policy, George Washington University Medical Center. http://www.gwhealthpolicy.org/downloads/nprm_analysis.pdf.

Schnader, Harrison, Segal, and Lewis, LLP. 1999. *HR 2723, The Dingell-Norwood Bill: A Direct Liability Threat to Employers Through the Impairment of ERISA Preemption.* Washington, D.C.: The Business Roundtable, August 31. http://www.brtable.org/pdf/333.pdf. (Accessed October 22, 2002.)

Sebelius, Kathleen. 1999. *Testimony of the Special Committee on Health Insurance of the National Association of Insurance Commissioners before the Committee on Health, Education, Labor and Pensions of the United States Senate on "Key Patients' Protections: Lessons from the Field,"* March 11. http://www.naic.org.

Sloan, Frank A., Christopher J. Conover, and Mark A. Hall. 1999. "State Strategies to Reduce the Growing Numbers of People without Health Insurance." *Regulation* 22(3): 24–32.

Stauffer, Molly. 1998. "Comprehensive Consumer Rights Bills." *Issue Brief.* Washington, D.C.: Health Policy Tracking Service, National Conference of State Legislatures.

U.S. General Accounting Office (GAO). 1997. *Managed Care: Explicit Gag Clauses Not Found in HMO Contracts, but Physician Concerns Remain.* Letter Report, GAO/HEHS-97-175. Washington, D.C.: U.S. General Accounting Office.

———. 1998. *Health Insurance Standards: New Federal Law Creates Challenges for Consumers, Insurers, Regulators.* Letter Report, 02/25/98, GAO/HEHS-98-67. Washington, D.C.: U.S. General Accounting Office.

———. 2000. *Implementation of HIPAA: Progress Slow in Enforcing Federal Standards in Nonconforming States.* Report No. HEHS-00-85. Washington, D.C.: U.S. General Accounting Office.

U.S. House of Representatives, Small Business Committee. 1999. *Hearing on Association Health Plans: Giving Small Business the Benefits They Need.* 106th Congress, Hearing 106-19, June 10.

Vaughan, Emmett J., and Therese Vaughan. 1999. "Regulation of the Insurance Industry." In *Fundamentals of Risk and Insurance*, 8th ed. (92–120). New York: Wiley.

Welch, William M. 2001. "Jeffords Officially Becomes an Independent." *USA Today*, June 5, p. A1.

Weller, Charles. 1984. " 'Free Choice' as a Restraint of Trade in American Health Care Delivery and Insurance." *Iowa Law Review* 69: 1351–92.

Wiener, Joshua M., Alison Evans, Crystal Kuntz, and Margaret Sulvetta. 1997. *Health Policy for Low-Income People in Texas.* Washington, D.C.: The Urban Institute. *Assessing the New Federalism* State Reports.

12

Improving the Federal System of Health Care Coverage

Alan Weil
John Holahan
Joshua M. Wiener

Most Americans place greater trust in state and local governments than they do in the more distant federal government (National Public Radio, Henry J. Kaiser Family Foundation, and Harvard University 2000), but when confronted with a national crisis or a persistent problem, they expect the federal government to provide a solution. Health policy reflects this ambivalence, with responsibility for different domains of health care spread across different levels of government. This allocation of responsibility does not reflect an orderly, consistent approach derived naturally from principles of federalism. Rather, it reflects American pragmatism—a combination of historical practices, political power, and present-day values. Thus, the United States has a federal Medicare program, state responsibility for licensing health care professionals and regulating the insurance market, and local departments of public health.

There is nothing natural or immutable about the current arrangement. Insurance regulation, for example, was once purely a state matter, but the federal government intervened to encourage the creation of health maintenance organizations (HMOs) and to ensure portability of coverage across plans, and it is considering providing patient protections against certain insurance company practices. Public health has strong roots in the community, but the role of the federal government increased gradually as the country's population became more mobile, and it has grown sharply amidst new concerns about bioterrorism (Institute of Medicine 1988).

399

In the area of health insurance coverage for low-income populations—the major focus of this book—the same ambivalence is revealed. No national consensus has emerged on whether or how all low-income Americans should be provided with health insurance coverage. Yet Americans demonstrate sufficient concern about the issue that they are unwilling to leave this matter entirely in the hands of states and local governments, as the compromise that created the Medicaid program in 1965 shows. That compromise created a substantial financing role for the federal government but left critical issues of eligibility and breadth of coverage to the states.

Enacted 32 years later, the State Children's Health Insurance Program (SCHIP) reflects the identical tension built into Medicaid. To health policy analysts, the differences between Medicaid and SCHIP are major: Medicaid is an individual entitlement, SCHIP is not; Medicaid has open-ended funding, SCHIP funding is capped. But to students of American federalism, what is striking is how similar the programs are, given the time that elapsed between their enactment. Both programs rely upon shared financing and administration between the federal government and the states. Both have a base of rules set by the federal government with substantial state discretion over coverage, benefits, and payment rates.

For the foreseeable future, Americans can expect to continue having a truly federal system—one in which responsibility is shared between the national and state governments—as it relates to health insurance coverage. That is, the political process is unlikely to yield a policy that gives all responsibility to the federal government. It is equally unlikely that the federal government will turn all responsibility for health insurance coverage over to the states and local governments. That being the case, what strengths and weaknesses of the existing federal system are revealed in current health policy? What do alternative models of health care teach us about the balance of federal and state authority? And, ultimately, what changes in the current federal system might improve health care coverage?

Strengths of the Current Federal System

The current system of shared federal-state responsibility provides a base of coverage for the nation's most vulnerable populations and supports safety net providers that care for the substantial share of the population who are uninsured. The system has also demonstrated the flexibility necessary to take on new challenges as they arise and has led to some positive sharing of ideas across states.

A Base of Coverage

Medicaid is the cornerstone of the American system for providing health coverage to those in need. SCHIP extends that coverage to children with family incomes higher than the eligibility limits for Medicaid (and, in a handful of states, to their parents). Both programs are optional for the states, but every state has chosen to implement them.

In combination, Medicaid, SCHIP, and a few state-funded programs have gone some distance in addressing the needs of those who do not have private health insurance. Despite the gaps that exist, it is fair to say that the current federal-state system of health insurance provides a base of comprehensive acute and long-term care coverage to the neediest populations. The federal mandates regarding populations and services covered ensure that this base will remain in place. In addition, decisions in most states to go beyond the federal minimums have yielded far more coverage than that required under federal law.

Supporting the Safety Net

The nation relies upon safety net providers—hospitals, clinics, and individual practitioners—to deliver care to the approximately 40 million Americans who have no health insurance. It is well documented that uninsured Americans have less access to care than those with coverage and that their health suffers because of it (Institute of Medicine 2001, 2002a). Yet, it is striking how many uninsured Americans obtain health care services when they need them. For example, 77 percent of parents of uninsured children with family incomes below 200 percent of the federal poverty level (FPL) report that their children have a usual source of care other than a hospital emergency room (Haley and Fragale 2001). An even larger share (89 percent) of these parents report that they are confident they can get their children care if they need it (Kenney, Dubay, and Haley 2000). Fewer than 17 percent report that their children have any unmet health care needs (Haley and Fragale 2001). Adults do not fare as well as children on these measures, but the data demonstrate that there is a functioning safety net that meets many of the needs of the uninsured.

Financial support for the safety net comes in many forms. Many providers use their revenues from paying patients to cover the costs of those who cannot pay. The federal government provides direct grants to certain clinics. Nonprofit hospitals and clinics receive donations from people in the community. Medicaid's disproportionate share hospital (DSH) program allows states to set higher payment levels for, or to make direct supplementary payments to, hospitals that serve a disproportionate share of uninsured and Medicaid patients.

Certain Medicaid rules have been designed to ensure a continued revenue stream for safety net providers as the program has come to rely increasingly upon managed care. Federal law requires that Federally Qualified Health Centers be paid on the basis of their costs, even if the centers are part of a Medicaid managed care system. This provision helps those centers cover some of the costs of providing care to the uninsured. In addition, many states, after becoming aware of the negative consequences Medicaid managed care could have on safety net providers if they were excluded from the provider networks, included provisions in their managed care contracting rules that require health plans to include these providers in their networks (Hurley and Wallin 1998).

The health care safety net in America is under substantial pressure, and warning signs that it is fraying should not be ignored (Lewin and Altman 2000). Still, a major accomplishment of the existing system is that it has enabled many providers to extend care to the uninsured.

Meeting Emerging Needs

The existing federal system has shown substantial ability to handle new issues as they arise. It has covered new populations as important gaps in coverage have been identified, and it has adapted to and sometimes initiated shifts in the health care delivery system.

Medicaid eligibility has expanded substantially since the program began. In response to evidence showing the importance of prenatal care, the program mandated an expansion of coverage to pregnant women. Medicaid has also expanded children's coverage dramatically, consistent with the view that preventive and therapeutic services for children promote healthy development. Medicaid has become the largest payer of services for people with acquired immunodeficiency syndrome (AIDS). Medicaid programs are very gradually extending eligibility to people with disabilities who have some earnings; thus, Medicaid can be a source of comprehensive health care benefits that are not generally available through employer-sponsored health insurance.

Medicaid has evolved with changes in the health care delivery system. The largest of these was the widespread adoption of managed care in the 1990s. Medicaid has also initiated changes in health care delivery, especially in the area of long-term care, where it is the dominant purchaser of services. Medicaid has gradually increased spending on home and community-based services, emerging from its original bias toward institutional care. A handful of states are now experimenting with consumer-directed approaches to care, which give individuals with disabilities and their families far more control over their choice of caregivers.

States as Laboratories of Democracy

Many examples of state experimentation are documented in this book. Some states have experimented with comprehensive waiver programs, state-funded programs, and other initiatives to expand health insurance coverage. While some of these efforts have been fairly standard coverage expansions, others, such as TennCare or Oregon's experimentation with setting priorities for health care spending, have been unique approaches that, while too risky to adopt all at once on a national scale, may teach important lessons when implemented by a single state.

A good example of states learning from each other can be found in outreach and enrollment in SCHIP. The states were criticized shortly after SCHIP was enacted for not having achieved sufficient enrollment. Some states then took the lead in building enrollment, adopting a variety of approaches to publicize the program, reach out to families that were potentially eligible, and simplify enrollment processes. Other states followed, wanting to achieve the same success. Other examples of experimentation include the dissemination of managed care in Medicaid, the adoption of patient protection legislation, and the redesign of states' long-term care systems.

Weaknesses of the Current Federal System

While it has strengths, the current allocation of responsibilities between the federal government and the states also limits the ability of the nation to meet the needs of low-income families. Despite a major state and federal investment in coverage, a large number of Americans remain without health insurance. The current system is also inequitable—a needy family's eligibility for public coverage depends on where that family lives. Variations in coverage are dramatic and difficult to justify. In addition, the current allocation of fiscal responsibility places a large share of the burden on state governments, which are not in a position to cope with short-term economic fluctuations or to absorb steadily growing costs in the long term.

The existing federal system has other problems as well. Friction between states and the federal government regarding financing has led to distrust in areas such as the DSH program and the use of upper payment limit arrangements. This distrust has tested the ability of the two levels of government to cooperate, slowing progress toward meeting the needs of the uninsured. Some experiments and innovations have spread among the states, but given the range of approaches that the states have taken toward various issues, the nation seems to be learning much less from experimentation than one would desire.

The Unsolved Problem of the Uninsured

The fundamental criticism of the current federal system is that, despite its accomplishments, it leaves more than 40 million people without health insurance. Some may consider this criticism unfair—after all, Medicaid and SCHIP were never designed to provide universal health insurance coverage. Yet the test of the federal system is not just whether the programs it has yielded have met their goals but also whether shared responsibility effectively identifies solutions to broader social problems. In this respect, the record is mixed.

Enrollment in Medicaid has increased from 4 million in 1966 to an estimated 47 million in 2002.[1] In the absence of Medicaid, the number of Americans without health insurance would surely be much larger than it is today. Yet the current system, patched together over many decades, ultimately leaves many very needy people without the insurance coverage they need. One-quarter of poor children remain uninsured—21.3 percent of those with incomes below twice the poverty level.[2] The figures are far worse for adults whose eligibility for public coverage is quite limited. Nearly half of all poor adults and 38 percent of adults with incomes between the poverty level and twice the FPL are uninsured.

Unfortunately, the programs designed to give low-income people access to health care are not administered or implemented in a way that reaches many of them (Dubay, Kenney, and Haley 2002). Most uninsured children—and all poor children except for many immigrants—are eligible for public coverage. In addition, while the package of covered benefits in Medicaid is comprehensive, coverage does not always translate into access to quality services. Reports of barriers to access among Medicaid enrollees are common. Concerns about the quality of care in nursing homes, often paid for by Medicaid, are substantial (Institute of Medicine 2001, 2002a; Wunderlich and Kohler 2001). Thus, while the federal government provides a floor of eligibility and benefits, some Medicaid enrollees go without needed services in practice.

Inequities

Insurance coverage varies tremendously around the country. Rates of uninsurance for children vary by a ratio of more than 3 to 1, with just over 8 percent uninsured in Minnesota and more than 25 percent uninsured in Texas. Although the absolute percentages are higher, the ratio is similar for adults.

As with so many matters of social policy, the question of how much variation across states and populations is appropriate is a matter of values. If one considers health insurance to be what economists call a normal good, one would expect and accept that those with more resources spend more on it. Indeed, in wealthier states, employers are more likely to offer coverage to their employees, and public spending on health programs is higher. It is arguably inefficient and unfair to force those with fewer resources to spend more on health insurance than they desire, leaving them with less to spend on food, housing, and other needs.

Yet, when polled, the American people consistently and overwhelmingly reject the notion that health care should be treated like any other economic good, where variable access flows naturally from differences in the ability to pay (Henry J. Kaiser Family Foundation and NewsHour with Jim Lehrer 2003). People reject treating health care solely as a commodity for a range of practical and moral reasons. From a practical standpoint, providing health care to those without the means to pay improves their ability to be productive members of society; reduces the incidence of public health crises that arise from untreated conditions; and reduces cost shifting, a source of inefficiency in the health care system. From a moral perspective, providing health care to the needy indicates a fundamental respect for the worth of each human being and for individual autonomy.

The structure of American health programs reflects the goal of reducing disparities across states. In Medicaid, low-income states receive more generous federal matching payments. SCHIP also has a variable formula, basing the allocation of funds across states in part on state poverty rates and the numbers of uninsured children. Despite these policies, variation across states is substantial. It is even greater across local areas and among different subgroups of the population. This degree of variation is a weakness in the current system that should be rectified.

State Fiscal Burden

The current allocation of responsibility between states and the federal government places a substantial fiscal burden on states. Over the long run, health care costs have grown more rapidly than general inflation or the gross domestic product. Demographic trends—the aging of the population and the growing role chronic illness and disability play in the health care system—particularly burden the Medicaid program. Thus, the system's current financing structure places a steadily growing burden on state budgets, a burden that outstrips state revenues.

The heavy fiscal burden of health care on states poses two major problems. First, health care ends up in direct competition with education, transportation, and public safety, the other dominant components of state budgets. Competition for resources places political and fiscal constraints on how much states can devote to health needs. Second, states' budgets and revenues rise and fall with the same economic cycle that affects enrollment in and the costs of the Medicaid program. States are least able to afford the costs of Medicaid at precisely the time when demands on the program are greatest.

The federal government is not immune to either of these problems, but Medicaid represents a smaller portion of the federal budget (about 7 percent) than of state budgets, making growth easier to absorb. In addition, the federal government can run a deficit, unlike the states, and it has a broader tax base across which to spread the funding burden. Moreover, SCHIP has demonstrated that states will respond with coverage expansions when given a higher federal matching rate. All of these factors suggest that a larger federal fiscal role would be appropriate.

Fiscal Distrust

The perpetual efforts of states to shift a larger portion of the cost of Medicaid onto the federal government through various accounting schemes have generated substantial distrust between the federal government and the states. Some states have used fiscal maneuvers to substantially raise the share of their health costs borne by the federal government.

The states counter with two arguments. First, they say, everything they have done is legal and part of a state plan that has been approved by the federal government. Although true, this argument in no way responds to concerns that the underlying Medicaid financing structure has lost its integrity. Second, states argue that their initiatives were developed largely in response to new federal mandates to cover additional populations, federal court rulings requiring higher payments to hospitals and nursing homes, and other federal practices that have limited the ability of states to implement program efficiencies, such as managed care and prescription drug formularies.

With distrust flowing in both directions, it is difficult to convince either side that coverage expansions should build upon the current federal-state structure. Fiscal distrust is one of the reasons some people endorse proposals to convert Medicaid into a block grant or establish per capita caps on spending. Regardless of the merits of these options, they demonstrate that the current fiscal structure of Medicaid has proven itself to be a barrier to additional expansions of health care coverage.

Limited Benefits from Experimentation

When states are given flexibility in setting their own policies, their choices are likely to vary because they have different goals, they have unique circumstances that argue for particular approaches, and they are uncertain what will work, so they try different strategies (Weil 2002). The metaphor of states serving as laboratories of democracy reflects the third reason. While this book documents a number of successful experiments, the list is disappointingly short, given the degree of policy variation across states.

Why is there not more evidence of dissemination of results from state experimentation? One possible reason is that most innovations fail. States look at the results from innovators and reject new approaches as ineffective or unlikely to work in their state. But this answer seems unlikely. More likely, experiments are seldom evaluated and thus other states do not learn from them, or other states are unable to implement innovations even when they are proven effective.

Very modest innovations have been made in long-term care delivery systems. It is notable that few states have adopted these innovations, despite their well-documented success in a handful of leadership states. It is difficult to believe that other states do not share the goal of providing home and community-based services in a manner that more closely meets the needs of the population. Therefore, the primary barriers to further adoption seem to be bureaucratic inertia, lobbying power by dominant providers, and limited leadership within states to effect these changes. These barriers indicate that, while experimentation may yield valuable information, the current system has difficulty translating the results of experiments into practice.

Another example of experimentation is managed care in Medicaid. This idea was adopted so rapidly for political and cost containment reasons that states had little time to learn from each other, thereby limiting opportunities for benefiting from experimentation. Still, learning did occur over time. The story of managed care in Medicaid—with its good and bad points—may represent the best case for the value of state experimentation.

Another barrier to the dissemination of innovation is cost. Only about one-quarter of the states can be characterized as leaders in extending coverage of the uninsured. These leaders include states that developed a new approach and those that adopted an approach pioneered by another state. The failure of more states to adopt these approaches probably reflects the fact that other states did not have as their primary goal reducing the number of people without health insurance. Those states may have set a higher priority on keeping taxes low, limiting the government's involvement in the health care market, or spending limited resources on education and other areas.

Innovations designed to expand health insurance coverage generally require spending money and redistributing resources—tasks that are difficult for states to do. In the name of allowing states to innovate, the federal system allows them to vary their policy choices based on their political and policy priorities. This is a valid reason for interstate variation, particularly in a nation as economically and socially diverse as ours, but it is also an impediment to achieving national goals.

Where Should Federalism in Health Care Go?

Medicaid's structure can be characterized as a modest national floor of coverage and benefits, structured state flexibility to go beyond that floor, shared financial responsibility, and shared responsibility for the delivery system. This structure has yielded substantial accomplishments, but it leaves much of the job undone. Is it possible to learn from our experience with the Medicaid model, bring in aspects of other models, and design a better health care system?

What Can We Learn from Other Models?

This book presents a number of alternative models of health care, each of which allocates responsibilities between the states and the federal government somewhat differently. What can we learn from these models?

SCHIP builds upon the foundation laid by Medicaid. It benefits from a higher federal matching rate, which encourages aggressive state participation in the program, and it offers states substantial flexibility in program design, which appears to have been central to their embrace of it. An important but controversial aspect of flexibility is the option of designing the program either as an entitlement or not, a feature that seems to have boosted the program's political popularity among state government officials. Yet SCHIP's capped funding may have negative consequences for the long-term stability of the program and its ability to meet the underlying insurance needs it is designed to address. Still, SCHIP is a model of high national funding combined with substantial state flexibility in program design that has generated some early admirers.

Medicare's national structure brings with it uniformity, and therefore equity, in eligibility and benefits. Its centralized administration allows for the efficient use of resources and the quick adoption of new approaches, such as prospective payment. A federal program that offers Medicare-like uniformity of coverage for low-income Americans while preserving a state role in offering more expansive wraparound coverage is attractive. Medicare is a model of the efficiency and uniformity, but also the rigidity, of a national program.

Patient protection is an example of competitive federalism, with states taking the lead in developing the features of patient protection legislation and the federal government wanting to jump into the fray but unable thus far to reach consensus on key features of the proposed legislation. State leadership in the early years of patient protection legislation provided a good opportunity for experimentation, although the political pressures for patient protection were often so strong that states could not wait until they learned from each other before adopting their own statutes. Interestingly, the primary area of dispute remaining at the national level—provisions for legal liability—is precisely the area in which state experimentation is barred by the Employee Retirement Income Security Act of 1974. Patient protection shows what states can accomplish on their own, how federal preemption can impede state action, and how building consensus at the national level can be more difficult than it is at the state level.

Building a Better System

A health care system that improves coverage and access should build upon the strengths and minimize the weaknesses identified above. Two approaches illustrate better federal models of health care coverage.

BUILD FROM THE BASE

One option is to rely on the existing federal-state allocation of responsibilities, while expanding and simplifying the base of coverage and giving states stronger incentives to extend it. The federal government would redefine the base of Medicaid and SCHIP coverage by simplifying and raising eligibility criteria. Income eligibility could be set at 200 percent of the FPL for children and pregnant women and at the poverty level for all other adults. These standards would replace the multiple existing eligibility categories.

The federal entitlement to benefits would remain in place, as would the federal definition of a comprehensive set of benefits for people who meet the eligibility criteria. States would be subject to federal standards regarding payment to providers. Minimum payment levels would be established to ensure that enrollees have access to services, while maximum payment levels would protect the fiscal integrity of the program.

The current mélange of Medicaid optional eligibility groups as well as optional services and SCHIP would be replaced by a simplified set of options that states could adopt to extend coverage beyond the federally defined core. States would have substantial flexibility in how they structured the options—they could impose copayments, premiums, limits on benefits, and limits on the number of enrollees, all within federal guidelines designed to protect low-income beneficiaries. The states could extend coverage as far up the income scale as they wish, and they could add services. They could expand eligibility to targeted groups, permitting people with high medical costs or those in need of long-term care to buy into Medicaid coverage. Federal matching funds would be available for all spending associated with these options.

The federal government would take over all financial responsibility associated with limitations in Medicare's acute care benefits package. That would include prescription drug costs and the full cost of premiums and cost-sharing for Medicaid enrollees who are also enrolled in Medicare. Medicare would also assume the costs states now bear for the Medicare Savings Programs (Qualified Medicare Beneficiaries, Specified Low-Income Medicare Beneficiaries, and Qualified Individuals).[3]

States would receive the same federal matching rate for the core program and for all optional populations and services. This rate would be set about 15 percent higher than the existing rate under Medicaid, but below the 30 percent enhancement in the current SCHIP. A less than 30 percent enhancement is appropriate because it applies to the entire program, not just to the additional enrollees in SCHIP. One benefit of setting the same matching rate for all populations and services is that it improves fiscal integrity by eliminating incentives for states to enroll people in one program as opposed to another.

A new waiver process would be created to allow states to experiment with programs that go beyond the federally defined options. Experiments would be allowed in delivery systems, financing systems, and benefit design. The experiments would not be expected to be cost-neutral—in fact, federal funds would be available on a competitive basis to test new approaches. Waivers would be for a limited time and would be permitted only for proposals that include rigorous evaluation of results.

The Medicaid home and community-based services waiver system would be replaced by a flexible program modeled on SCHIP, with the same enhanced matching rate and substantial state flexibility in service design. Such a program reflects the need for new investment to encourage the move away from institutionalization.

The DSH program would be eliminated. While the program has been an important source of funds for safety net providers, it has come at the cost of program integrity. Fiscal integrity in a matching grant program can only be ensured if the program has a defined population, set of benefits, and payment structure. DSH has provided an opportunity for fiscal games because it operates outside such a structure. The federal government should reassess all remaining uncompensated care and perhaps develop a new grant program to meet those needs.

A NEW FEDERAL PROGRAM

A second option is to identify a substantial portion of the health care safety net for low-income people and shift responsibility for it to the federal government. The federal government could assume full responsibility for covering the acute care costs of the same groups described above: children and pregnant women with incomes up to twice the FPL, and all other adults with incomes up to the FPL.

The federal government would finance and run this program in a nationally uniform manner, as it does Medicare. The new program would operate as an entitlement to individuals, with a federally defined, comprehensive package of benefits and a national system for paying providers.

States could still cover populations beyond the federally defined minimum and could use the fiscal relief they obtain from the new federal program to do so. Presumably, many states would accept the base of federally provided acute care coverage for their low-income populations as sufficient and go no further. However, some states—particularly those whose current programs extend to people with higher incomes—would continue to operate programs on top of the federal base. States also might wish to provide their low-income populations with benefits that are not covered by the new federal program.

As in the first option, the federal government would assume full financial responsibility for acute care services in the Medicare benefits package for people enrolled in both Medicare and Medicaid. All state costs associated with the Medicaid Savings Programs would be assumed by the federal government as well. The existing shared responsibility for long-term care services would remain in place. The new program for home and community-based services described above would also be included in this option. The DSH program would be eliminated, and possibly reconstituted, as in the first plan.

COMPARING THE APPROACHES

Both of the approaches described above create a sturdy federal floor of coverage for low-income populations with the possibility of expansion. The first proposal gives states fiscal relief and provides generous matching funds for expansions that states can design with the sort of flexibility they now have in SCHIP. The second proposal gives states even more fiscal relief and leaves expansions entirely in the hands of the states, with no federal rules (and no federal matching funds). Under either proposal, the federal government could take additional steps if progress in reducing the number of uninsured is inadequate. The federal government could layer tax credits on top of this base of coverage, it could provide additional funding to states in the form of block or matching grants, or it could raise the eligibility standards for the basic program to a higher income level. It is impossible to know in advance whether these approaches would decrease or increase the variations in coverage across states, but coverage nationally should increase.

The approaches differ in how much variation across states would exist in how care is delivered to the low-income population. The first option essentially retains the existing state-administered system, although states would be subject to federal oversight regarding provider payment rates as a means of improving access to care. On matters such as patient education, provider relations, use of managed care, and general accessibility of the enrollment system, states would continue to vary substantially. The second approach puts the federal government in control of the delivery system, bringing about greater uniformity around the country. Along with federal control and responsibility would likely come greater political pressure on the federal government to finance the program at a level appropriate to the needs of the population. A federal commitment to administration would allow for more rapid dissemination of innovations such as risk-adjusted payments. Federal funding would overcome the tendency of states to invest less in programs serving poor people than their citizens prefer because of concerns about interstate competition.

The fiscal implications for states differ also. In the first option, states that already provide coverage approaching the levels of the new federally defined core would receive some fiscal relief because of the higher matching rate. They would also obtain substantial fiscal relief with respect to the population eligible for both Medicaid and Medicare. States with more limited coverage would have to assume the costs of building their coverage to the new core. These costs would be offset by the higher matching rate for the population they already cover and fiscal relief for the dual eligible population. While low-coverage states would receive less overall fiscal relief, the people in those states would experience the largest increases in coverage. In the second option, states providing high coverage would receive substantial fiscal relief, as the federal government would assume the cost of covering many people for whom the state currently pays.

States with low coverage would obtain less fiscal relief because they are spending less, but their citizens would experience a very large increase in coverage.

The dynamics with respect to provider payment rates are more complex. The first option retains state control over these rates, within federal guidelines. States with very low rates would incur costs in bringing them up to the federal standards. In the second option, the federal government sets the method of payment. The federal government would probably find it difficult to set rates below existing Medicare rates, which are higher than Medicaid rates in most states (Norton 1999). Therefore, providers in low-payment states would see a substantial gain.

The first approach retains the cyclical effects of Medicaid on state budgets. The second smoothes out cycles in states' Medicaid budgets by eliminating state responsibility for the eligibility group that grows during economic downturns when state budgets are under pressure.

Do Other Structures Offer Better Models?

Other models that exist already or that have been proposed warrant consideration. Tax credits could be provided to individuals to pay for health insurance coverage. While tax credits are a common strategy for promoting federal objectives, there is very little experience in coordinating a federal tax credit with varying state programs. The leading health insurance tax credit proposals are entirely national—they leave little or no role to the states and they permit no state-level variation in their design or administration. Indeed, they are designed in large part to bypass state and local governments and put decisions in the hands of individuals. A full exploration of the merits of tax credits as an approach to covering the uninsured is beyond the scope of this book. However, it seems likely that a new federal tax credit would complicate rather than simplify federal-state relations regarding insurance coverage. Unless carefully crafted, the possible benefits of federal tax credits could easily be offset by reduced state spending on health care for their low-income populations.

Medicaid could be converted into one or more block grants. In this model, the federal government would cap its fiscal commitment to the program while holding states to certain broad standards of coverage. This approach is likely to exacerbate some of the weaknesses in the federal system described above. For example, leaving states with the entire cost of any program expansions will almost certainly increase disparities across states in levels of coverage, thereby increasing inequity. Fixing the federal grant to states in nominal terms leaves states even more exposed to economic cycles and possible shocks to the health care system (such as outbreaks of disease) than they are today, when such costs are shared with the federal government. Block grants lower the base of coverage and increase variability across states.

States can be encouraged to expand coverage via waivers. This approach was used by states like Tennessee, and it is embodied in the Bush administration's Health Insurance Flexibility and Accountability initiative. Waivers seek to balance the federal government's desire to give states increased flexibility with its desire to hold states accountable for the funds they receive. Under current Office of Management and Budget rules, waivers must be budget-neutral, which necessarily limits their ability to expand insurance coverage. In addition, the administrative discretion implied in the waiver process has created some concerns about the allocation of policy authority between the legislative and executive branches of the federal government (U.S. General Accounting Office 2002). As currently structured, waivers are unlikely vehicles for meeting the needs of the uninsured on a national basis. A more promising alternative would be to establish large, state-based demonstrations of universal insurance coverage in which additional coverage is funded by the federal government, as recommended by the Institute of Medicine (Institute of Medicine 2002b).

The most common means of expanding coverage in the last two decades has been the federal government's gradual inclusion of more mandatory and optional eligibility groups. Fiscal conditions in the states and the states' success in asserting that the federal government should issue no more unfunded mandates make such options seem unlikely today.[4] Yet, without fundamental Medicaid reforms, this is the most likely path of expansions in the future. While each incremental mandate may cover a new population, history suggests that such increments will never yield anything that approaches universal coverage.

Conclusion

The current balance of federal and state responsibilities for health insurance coverage has achieved a great deal. Ultimately, however, it has failed to insure 40 million Americans. The existing system makes only incremental changes in coverage, with successive steps offering only modest advances over prior ones. No state, and certainly not the nation as a whole, has developed and implemented a comprehensive approach to the problem of uninsurance. The states are now largely playing defense against an eroding employer base of coverage and a fiscal future in which expenditures are likely to exceed revenues. There is no reason to believe the current federal structure will ever yield a system of universal coverage or even a system that comes close.

Decades of experience show that major progress in covering the uninsured will require a substantial new investment of funds by the federal government. Heavy reliance upon state financing is the primary reason for dramatic interstate variations in coverage and, ultimately, for the large gaps in coverage that remain. While states have substantial financial capacity, that capacity is more limited than the federal government's; it falls with economic downturns, at precisely the same time as needs increase; and its funding sources are less progressive than the federal government's, making states less able to redistribute funds to services for low-income families.

Yet the state role in financing serves important purposes. It is politically impossible to separate financing and administration. Therefore, if state-guided administration is valuable, it cannot be expected to exist in the context of entirely federal financing. "He who pays the piper calls the tune" is an appropriate aphorism when it comes to health care financing. State financing ensures that the state policymaking apparatus is engaged. Highly leveraged state funding, as in SCHIP, also gives states a sense of ownership that encourages good performance. Finally, it reduces the share of the fiscal burden that must be borne by the federal government, making expansions more likely.

The challenge for federalism is to devise a financing role for the states that continues to engage them in administrative innovation while minimizing the inequities that arise when they must bear a large fiscal burden. The two approaches described above take different paths to achieving this balance. The first retains a large role for states, while the second diminishes that role. Both seek to maximize the base of coverage and incentives for expanding beyond it, while encouraging innovation and the benefits of experimentation. Neither approach eliminates interstate variation or the inequities it implies. However, because both start from a higher base of coverage, the inequities are more defensible than those in the current system.

The nation should take advantage of its diversity by encouraging true experimentation and learning across states. The greatest potential benefit of interstate variation—the creation of laboratories of democracy—can only be realized if state policies are documented, examined, and evaluated. Too many opportunities for learning are squandered in the current environment, where state flexibility is valued for its own sake rather than for the benefits it can generate with respect to public policy.

Proposals that require a substantial amount of new federal funding may be unrealistic in the fiscal climate of 2003, when large federal budget deficits have returned. However, without additional federal funds, the states are unlikely to sustain their current levels of coverage, let alone increase them. Changing the balance of federalism involves risk. Yet such a rebalancing may be necessary to achieve the goal of substantially reducing the number of Americans without health insurance coverage. The approaches proposed here offer two paths that hold greater promise for the future.

NOTES

1. These figures are for the number of people enrolled at some point during the year, which is larger than the number enrolled in an average month.

2. Author's calculations from the 2002 Current Population Survey.

3. This shift in financial responsibility would likely yield some improvements in coordinating between Medicare and Medicaid for the "dual eligible" population. Additional coordination is warranted—a topic beyond the scope of this chapter.

4. Technically, a Medicaid expansion is not an unfunded mandate, since state participation in the Medicaid program is optional. However, since the consequences of withdrawing from the program are substantial, mandatory expansions of the Medicaid program have consequences for states that are essentially indistinguishable from mandates. A Medicaid expansion is also not "unfunded," since the federal government pays more than half of the cost. Still, expansions do impose new fiscal burdens on states.

REFERENCES

Dubay, Lisa, Genevieve Kenney, and Jennifer Haley. 2002. "Children's Participation in Medicaid and SCHIP: Early in the SCHIP Era." Washington, D.C.: The Urban Institute. *Assessing the New Federalism* Policy Brief B-40.

Haley, Jennifer M., and Matthew Fragale. 2001. *Health Insurance, Access, and Use: Tabulations from the 1999 National Survey of America's Families.* Washington, D.C.: The Urban Institute.

Henry J. Kaiser Family Foundation and NewsHour with Jim Lehrer. 2003. "Kaiser HealthPoll Report." http://www.kff.org/healthpollreport/templates/detail.php?page=6&feature=feature3. (Accessed March 27, 2003.)

Hurley, Robert E., and Susan Wallin. 1998. *Adopting and Adapting Managed Care for Medicaid Beneficiaries: An Imperfect Translation.* Washington, D.C.: The Urban Institute. *Assessing the New Federalism* Occasional Paper No. 7.

Institute of Medicine. 1988. *The Future of Public Health.* Washington, D.C.: National Academy Press.

———. 2001. *Coverage Matters: Insurance and Health Care.* Washington, D.C.: National Academy Press.

———. 2002a. *Care Without Coverage: Too Little, Too Late.* Washington, D.C.: National Academy Press.

———. 2002b. *Fostering Rapid Advances in Health Care: Learning from System Demonstrations.* Washington, D.C.: National Academy Press.

Kenney, Genevieve, Lisa Dubay, and Jennifer Haley. 2000. "Health Insurance, Access, and Health Status of Children." *Snapshots of America's Families II: A View of the Nation and 13 States from the National Survey of America's Families.* Washington, D.C.: The Urban Institute.

Lewin, Marion Ein, and Stuart Altman, eds. 2000. *America's Health Care Safety Net: Intact but Endangered.* Washington, D.C.: National Academy Press.

National Public Radio, Henry J. Kaiser Family Foundation, and Harvard University. 2000. "Attitudes Toward Government." http://www.kff.org/content/2000/3036/toplines.pdf. (Accessed February 20, 2003.)

Norton, Stephen A. 1999. *Recent Trends in Medicaid Physician Fees, 1993–1998.* Washington, D.C.: The Urban Institute. *Assessing the New Federalism* Discussion Paper 99-12.

U.S. General Accounting Office. 2002. *Medicaid and SCHIP: Recent HHS Approvals of Demonstration Waiver Projects Raise Concerns.* GAO-02-817. Washington, D.C.: U.S. General Accounting Office.

Weil, Alan. 2002. "Program Redesign by States in the Wake of Welfare Reform: Making Sense of the Effects of Devolution." In *For Better and For Worse: Welfare Reform and the Well-Being of Children and Families,* edited by Greg J. Duncan and P. Lindsay Chase-Lansdale (63–80). New York: Russell Sage Foundation Press.

Wunderlich, Gooloo S., and Peter O. Kohler, eds. 2001. *Improving the Quality of Long-Term Care.* Washington, D.C.: National Academy Press.

About the Editors

John Holahan is director of the Health Policy Research Center at the Urban Institute. His recent work has focused on the Medicaid program, as well as state health policy in general and issues of federalism and health. His research includes analyses of the recent growth in Medicaid expenditures, variations across states in Medicaid expenditures, the implications of block grants and expenditure caps, and the effects of changes in matching formulas on states. He has also published research on the growth in the number of uninsured over the past decade, and on the effects of expanding health insurance coverage on the number of uninsured and the resulting cost to federal and state governments.

Alan Weil is director of the Urban Institute's *Assessing the New Federalism* project. His research focuses on health policy, welfare policy, and federalism. He is the coeditor, with Kenneth Finegold, of *Welfare Reform: The Next Act* (Urban Institute Press, 2002). He was formerly the executive director of the Colorado Department of Health Care Policy and Financing.

Joshua M. Wiener contributed to this volume when he was a principal research associate at the Urban Institute. He is now senior program director of Aging, Disability, and Long-Term Care Programs at RTI International. He is the author or editor of eight books and more than 100 articles on long-term care, Medicaid, health reform, health care rationing, and maternal and child health. He has also conducted policy analysis and research for the Brookings Institution, the Health Care Financing Administration, the Massachusetts Department of Public Health, the Congressional Budget Office, the New York State Moreland Act Commission on Nursing Homes and Residential Facilities, and the New York City Department of Health.

About the
Contributors

Randall R. Bovbjerg is a principal research associate at the Urban Institute. He has almost 30 years of experience in the areas of public and private insurance; medical injury, liability, and patient safety; state and local health policy; safety net issues; and state regulation. The author of four books and more than 90 other publications, he currently conducts research on malpractice issues and reinsurance in Medicaid managed care. A member of the D.C. Health Care Reform Commission, he has acted as a journal editor and peer reviewer, and has served on the faculties of Duke University, Johns Hopkins University, and the University of Maryland–Baltimore County. He came to the Institute from the Massachusetts Insurance Department.

Donald J. Boyd is the director of the Fiscal Studies Program at the Rockefeller Institute of Government, the public policy research arm of the State University of New York that provides practical independent research about state and local government finances in the 50 states. He has more than 20 years of experience in analyzing state and local government fiscal issues in academia, in private consulting, and in the executive and legislative branches of state government.

Teresa A. Coughlin is a principal research associate at the Urban Institute's Health Policy Center, where her research focuses on Medicaid and other health care programs for low-income populations. She is the co-author of a book on Medicaid and has written widely on health care. Most recently, her work has centered on a major evaluation of Medicaid waiver programs, a study of state variation in Medicaid beneficiaries' access and use, and a survey of Medicaid disproportionate share hospital (DSH) and upper payment limit (UPL) programs.

Ian Hill is a senior research associate with the Urban Institute's Health Policy Center, where he directs the qualitative components of the Institute's State Children's Health Insurance Program (SCHIP) evaluations and has developed a series of crosscutting papers on states' implementation experiences under SCHIP. For more than 17 years, he has directed federal and state evaluation and technical assistance contracts related to Medicaid, maternal and child health, children with special health care needs, and managed care. He has served as associate director of Health Systems Research, Inc., as a senior policy analyst for the National Governors Association, and as a presidential management intern for the Health Care Financing Administration.

Michael Housman contributed to this volume as an intern at the Urban Institute and is presently a research analyst at The Lewin Group, a health care consulting firm. His current work focuses on state variations in the use of Medicaid to fund evidence-based behavioral health services and state implementation of federal requirements to screen nursing home residents for mental illness.

Robert E. Hurley is a faculty member in the Department of Health Administration at the Virginia Commonwealth University, where he teaches graduate courses in managed care and organization theory. He has been conducting research in managed care and other health services issues for nearly 20 years, with a particular focus on managed care in public sector programs. He serves on the editorial boards of *Health Affairs, Medical Care Research & Review, Milbank Quarterly,* and *Managed Care Quarterly.*

Marilyn Moon wrote her chapter for this volume while a senior fellow at the Urban Institute, and is currently a vice president at the American Institutes for Research. She has written extensively on issues primarily focused on Medicare and aging issues, although she has also worked on health reform issues in general. She has also served as a public trustee of the Social Security and Medicare trust funds and written a column on health coverage issues for the *Washington Post.*

Mary Beth Pohl was formerly a research assistant in the Urban Institute's Health Policy Center. She conducted many studies of insurance coverage, including modeling public health expansion programs using the Census Bureau's Current Population Survey. She currently serves as a health policy analyst for the state of Maryland.

Jane Tilly is a senior research associate at the Urban Institute and has more than 15 years' experience in public policy research and analysis. Her primary research interests are related to health and supportive services for people with disabilities. Before joining the Urban Institute five years ago, Jane Tilly was associate director for public policy research at AARP's Public Policy Institute, where her work focused on long-term care and public benefits programs.

Stephen Zuckerman is a principal research associate in the Health Policy Center of the Urban Institute. His current research interests are Medicaid managed care, the State Children's Health Insurance Program and crowd out of private coverage, racial and ethnic disparities in health care, the duration of uninsurance, and the health care safety net. He directs the health care component of the National Survey of America's Families—a survey of 42,000 households being conducted as part of the Institute's *Assessing the New Federalism* study. He has also worked on research related to Medicare physician payment, hospital rate setting, medical malpractice, health care price indices, and health system reform.

Index